Golf Clubs of the MGA

Golf Clubs of the MGA

A Centennial History of Golf in the New York Metropolitan Area

COMPILED BY THE METROPOLITAN GOLF ASSOCIATION
WITH DR. WILLIAM L. QUIRIN

PUBLISHED BY GOLF MAGAZINE PROPERTIES

Frontmatter Photography

Endpapers: A reunion of former caddies
at Fairview Country Club Elmsford, NY. circa.1926

Half Title: Walter Travis

Title: 16th hole at National Golf Links,
Long Island

CONTENTS

13th hole at The Stanwich Club, Greenwich, Connecticut

CREDITS

Project Directors: Jay Mottola, Brad Felenstein

Author: Dr. William L. Quirin

Editorial Committee: Cornelius Deloca,
Jeanne McCooey, Howie Munk, George Peper
C.A. "Tony" Wimpfheimer

Editor: Jim Frank

Copy Editors: Alena Bubniak, Sandra Tomassetti

Designer: Larry Hasak

Production: Kit Taylor, Kelli Daley

Distributed to the Book Trade by:
Triumph Books, Chicago, IL
(312) 939-3330

Library of Congress Catalog Card Number :97-071292
ISBN: 0-89204-590-6

Text copyright © 1997 Dr. William L. Quirin
and the Metropolitan Golf Associaton

Published in 1997 for the Metropolitan Golf
Association, Elmsford, NY (914) 347-4653 by
Golf Magazine Properties. No parts or contents of
this book may be reproduced without the written
permission of the publishers.

I am very pleased to join in the Metropolitan Golf Association's centennial celebration with the publication of this handsome book—and I must say, I'm particularly delighted to take part because, at 100 years, the MGA is only five years older than I am!

Although I've lived on Marco Island in Florida for the past 30 years, my roots are firmly in the metropolitan area. It's where I was born and raised, where I was introduced to golf, and where I won two of my seven major championships.

I was eight years old, in the first grade at the Harrison Public School in Harrison, New York, when I got my first taste of golf. Along with one of my school chums, I hopped on the old trolley marked "Larchmont" and rode up to the now defunct Larchmont Country Club. I had never seen such green, green grass or sand as white as in those things they called bunkers.

It didn't take me long to learn the caddie's duties, which in those days included teeing the ball up on a pinch of sand and water. Back then, the pay was 20 cents per bag, and if you did a good job you got a 25-cent tip. That was the most money I had ever seen.

I was in the process of caddying when I hit a golf ball for the first time. One of my regular loops at Larchmont, Mr. Sutherland, hit his ball over the top of a hill. Since I was forecaddying, and no one could see me on the other side of that hill, I raced out to the fairway, dropped a ball, and hit a quick shot with Sutherland's jigger. It jumped off my club, sailed to the green, and stopped about seven feet form the hole. Sutherland caught me as I ran to get the ball, and I almost lost my job. But from that moment, I had the bug.

My first try at competitive golf was a caddie tournament. I skipped school that day, shot about 110, and finished dead last. That was at Apawamis, where I did most of my caddying, although I also had some loops at Nassau, Garden City, Greenwich, Sleepy Hollow, and St. Andrew's.

One of my fellow caddies at Apawamis was Ed Sullivan, who went on to have quite a career, first as a syndicated columnist and then as host of America's most widely watched television show. Ed was a little guy, like me, but he could run like a rabbit, and that was a big asset for an Apawamis caddie. You see, all the caddies knew that the fellas with the new bags were the best tippers, and when the bags came up from the locker room we'd all dash for them—the caddie who got there first got his pick.

I remember one day when Ed outran me and got a big new bag that turned out to belong to the Police Commissioner of New York City. I got a smaller, less fancy bag with the initials GR on it. My man turned out to be a pretty good player—he was also a great guy who would later become one of my dearest friends. His name was Grantland Rice, one of the giants of American sports writing. Good tipper, too.

One day Sullivan and I were toting the bags down the last hole at Apawamis, when the banker I was caddying for said, "Did you know that a caddie just won the U.S. Open?" I couldn't believe it. He was of course referring to Francis Ouimet's victory [1913] over Harry Vardon and Ted Ray at The Country Club in Boston. When I heard the whole story, it inspired me to work hard on my game.

Not long after that, my family moved to Bridgeport, Connecticut, where I started playing at a public course called Beardsley Park. It was at this time that I made a name for myself as a golfer—literally. One morning, the Bridgeport paper carried the headline, "Eugenio Saraceni Scores Hole-in-One." When I saw it in print, my name struck

Gene Sarazen

me as better suited to a violonist than a golfer. So I decided to change it. There was no one named Sarazen in the Bridgeport phone book, so I became Gene Sarazen.

The game came easily to me, but I think even I was a bit surprised when in 1922, at the age of 20, I won both the U.S. Open and the PGA Championship. But in any case, when in 1923 the PGA moved to Pelham Country Club, just 20 minutes from my hometown, I was the defending champion.

I was also played out. In the year following my burst from obscurity to fame, I'd done my best to capitalize, traveling all over the country to play in lucrative exhibition matches. As a result, may game had deteriorated. But being back home inspired me.

Somehow I got past Jim Barnes in the quarterfinals and then Bobby Cruickshank in the semis to face the great Walter Hagen for the title. And we had quite a match—after 36 holes we were all tied. We halved the 37th too, and then at the 38th hole I gave Sir Walter a dose of his own medicine: From deep trouble, I pulled off a miracle shot.

Walter had driven perfectly, but I had yanked my tee shot toward the greenkeeper's house, which was out of bounds. To my eternal good fortune, however, the ball stayed in by about a yard. Walter took one look at the lie and said, "That ball hit the house and the greenkeeper threw it back." When I protested he would have none of it. "Just look at the ball," he said, pointing to the "WILSON" in red letters. "He threw it back from the kitchen—it's got spaghetti sauce all over it."

I was angry, and the result was one of the finest pressure shots of my career, a lengthy draw that rolled to within a foot of the cup. The Haig put his approach in a bunker, and although he then nearly holed out, he had to settle for a 4, and I won my second straight PGA title.

In 1932, the Met Area turf again was my friend when the U.S. Open came to Fresh Meadow on Long Island where I'd been the pro a few years before.

My game had been good in that summer of '32. A few weeks earlier I had won the British Open at Princes in England. This was also the year that I invented the sand wedge, it was an ability to get up and down around those tightly bunkered greens that helped me shoot 66 in the last round and play the last 28 holes in just 100 strokes. It gave me a three-stroke victory over Bobby Cruickshank and Phil Perkins.

But to tell the truth, I have great memories from all sorts of events in the Met Area. There was the Met Open, which in those days was tantamount to a major championship and every bit as hard to win. Heck, I played in the Met as often as I did the U.S. Open, but I have only one Met title (1925) compared to two in the National Open.

Beyond the competitions, there are the great courses. I'll never forget Baltusrol, where I played with Tony Manero in the final round of his upset victory of 1936, or Ridgewood, where we won the 1935 Ryder Cup, or Westchester, which Hagen, Barnes, Jock Hutchison, and I opened in 1923.

You know, in my nearly 90 years of playing this game, I've been lucky to see a lot of the world, and there is nowhere—anywhere—with a larger collection of superb places to play than the New York metropolitan area.

This book is a fitting tribute of that unrivaled richness of golf courses, and I'm awfully proud to be a part of it.

Gene Sarazen
Marco Island, Florida
January, 1997

The Metropolitan
Golf Association:
The First 100 Years

*1936 Met Open at Quaker Ridge where
Byron Nelson launched his legendary career.*

THE METROPOLITAN GOLF ASSOCIATION

"Birth of the Association"

ON MARCH 31, 1897, just a few hours before April Fools Day, a group of what many would have considered eccentric middle-aged sportsmen gathered to discuss the governance of a sport with which most Americans were unfamiliar. Two weeks later, on April 14th, many of the same men reconvened and the Metropolitan Golf Association was born.

The site for both meetings was Delmonico's, a famous restaurant located in lower Manhattan. Those attending the meetings were well-to-do gentlemen representing 26 golf clubs from New York City and the vicinity. Their first get-together was called at the suggestion of the Green Committee of the St. Andrew's Golf Club in Yonkers, which consisted of James Brown, R.L. Cuthbert, Arthur Livermore, W.D. Baldwin, and M.C. McEwen.

Delegations from 23 clubs (Shinnecock Hills and Englewood were represented in spirit, if not physical presence) joined the St. Andrew's contingent at Delmonico's. Their stated purpose was to form an organization interested in the *"promotion of the interests of golf locally, and the arrangement of dates for open tournaments among the members, in consultation with the United States Golf Association."* They proposed to call their new organization the "Metropolitan League of Golf Clubs."

The result of that first meeting was the creation of a committee to formulate the exact role of the new organization. The committee consisted of five men: Daniel Chauncey (Dyker Meadow), Oliver W. Bird (Meadow Brook), Grenville Kane (Tuxedo), Richard H. Williams (Morris County), and T. Hope Simpson (Staten Island Cricket). The committee presented its results at Delmonico's two weeks later. A draft of the constitution and a set of bylaws were adopted by the 19 men, representing 18 clubs, in attendance at the second meeting. The other clubs sent their best wishes, each indicating a willingness to join the new organization.

The Metropolitan Golf Association was officially formed that evening, with membership limited to member clubs of the USGA located within 55 miles of New York City, but including the whole of Long Island. (At that time, the entire USGA roster included just slightly more than 100 clubs.) The MGA's ter-

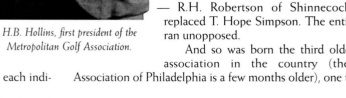

H.B. Hollins, first president of the Metropolitan Golf Association.

ritory reached as far as Morris County to the west, Shinnecock Hills to the east, Lakewood to the south, Tuxedo to the north, and to Greenwich in Connecticut. The limit was set at 55, rather than 50, miles at the suggestion of Julian Curtiss of the Fairfield County Golf Club, so his club (today's Greenwich Country Club) might gain admittance.

Two other proposals were discussed, and rejected, at those two meetings. The first called for orchestrating a series of interclub team matches and was defeated when Daniel Chauncey argued it would create a class of semi-professional players, which he vehemently opposed. The second called for the exchange of country club courtesies among member clubs; Oliver Bird successfully argued that it would destroy the notion that a club was a special sanctuary for its members.

H.B. Hollins of Westbrook, who chaired the two meetings, was elected the first president of the new organization along with J.C. Ten Eyck of St. Andrew's as vice-president, R. Bage Kerr of the Golf Club of Lakewood as treasurer, and John du Fais of Baltusrol as secretary. Five directors were also elected, the same five men chosen at the first meeting with one exception — R.H. Robertson of Shinnecock Hills replaced T. Hope Simpson. The entire slate ran unopposed.

And so was born the third oldest golf association in the country (the Golf Association of Philadelphia is a few months older), one that has

Right: Delmonico's restaurant in Manhattan was the site of the signing of the MGA's original charter on April 14th, 1897. The 26 original clubs created the MGA to "promote the best interests and the true spirit of the game of golf." One-hundred years later we are still committed to those principles.

PRESIDENTS OF THE
METROPOLITAN GOLF ASSOCIATION

YEAR	PRESIDENT	CLUB
1897-99	H.B. Hollins	Westbrook
1900	R.H. Robertson	Shinnecock Hills
1901-02	Percy Chubb	Nassau
1903-04	Horace Russell	Garden City Golf
1905-06	Daniel Chauncey	Dyker Meadow
1907-08	Wm. Fellowes Morgan	Baltusrol
1909-10	Adrian H. Larkin	Yountakah
1911-13	Frederick S. Wheeler	Apawamis
1914-15	Darwin P. Kingsley	Apawamis, Maidstone
1916-17	J. B. Coles-Tappan	Nassau
1918-20	Cornelius J. Sullivan	Garden City Golf
1921	E. Mortimer Barnes	Piping Rock
1922-24	Findlay S. Douglas	Nassau, Apawamis
1925-26	H.Y. Barrow	Baltusrol
1927	George A. Nichol Jr.	Wykagyl, Apawamis
1928-29	Walter A. Shafer	Westchester Hills
1930	John A. Ladds	Cherry Valley, Canoe Brook, Morris County
1931-33	Stacey Bender	Shackamaxon
1934-35	Stuart C. McLeod	Apawamis, Ardsley
1936	Jess W. Sweetser	Siwanoy, Maidstone
1937-38	Edmund H. Driggs Jr.	Sleepy Hollow
1939	Henry S. Sturgis	Rockaway Hunt
1940	Max. B. Kaesche	Ridgewood
1941	Walker L. Trammell	Deepdale
1942	Mark J. Stuart	Winged Foot
1943-45	Isaac B. Grainger	Montclair
1946-47	Percival B. Furber	Wee Burn
1948-49	Shepard Barnes	Baltusrol
1950-51	Earl A. Ross	Winged Foot
1952-53	James M. Robbins	Garden City Golf/ Bedford
1954	Stephen Berrien	Upper Montclair
1955	William P. Turnesa	Knollwood
1956-57	Frederick A. Marsh	Garden City CC
1958-59	Jack H. Wallace	Upper Montclair
1960-61	Clarence "Gus" Benedict	Winged Foot
1962-63	Bertrand L. Kohlmann	Inwood
1964-65	William Y. Dear Jr.	Morris County
1966-67	Vincent C. Ross	Westchester
1968-69	Joseph Schlanger	Woodmere
1970-71	Kenneth T. Gordon	Montclair
1972-73	Thomas G. Burke	Apawamis
1974-75	George E. Sands	North Shore
1976-77	Allen B. DuMont	Upper Montclair
1978-79	Ira L. Mendell	Quaker Ridge
1980-82	Joseph A. Donahue	Cherry Valley
1983-84	W. Sydnor Settle	Somerset Hills
1985-86	James Stotter	Sunningdale
1987-88	Arthur P. Weber	Old Westbury
1989-90	John F. Kelsey Jr.	Montclair
1991-92	James M. Cotter	Greenwich
1993-94	John C. Baldwin	Meadow Brook
1995-96	James D. Patton	Arcola
1997	Martin J. Connelly	Sedgewood

worked closely and harmoniously with the USGA for a full century (see sidebar on page 17).

At that second meeting, the following 26 clubs (listed with their representatives) were admitted as charter members of the MGA:

Ardsley Casino ....Thomas W. Stiles
Baltusrol GC ....John du Fais
Bedford G & TC ....T.T.P. Luquer
Dyker Meadow GC ....Daniel Chauncey, W.A. Putnam
Englewood CC ....F.A. Coppell
Essex County CC ..................T.H. Powers-Farr, John Watson
Fairfield County GC (Greenwich) ........................F.W. Savage, Julian Curtiss, Frank Sanger
Hillside T & GC (Plainfield) ...............H.W. Beebe, F.W. Walz
Knollwood CC...................L.E. Van Etten, P. Gilbert Thebaud
Golf Club of Lakewood ....James Miley, C.C. Curtis, R. Bage Kerr
Meadow Brook Hunt ....Oliver W. Bird
Golf Club of Montclair ....Arthur Schroeder, W. Reed
Morris County GC ............................R.H. Thomas, E. Nichols
New Brunswick CC ....Major C.A. Kenney, J.P. Street
Oakland CC ....Lawrence E. Embree, H. McKeever
Paterson Club (North Jersey) ....Henry Hewat, Malcolm Gordon
Queens County CC (Nassau) ......L.C. Murdoch, W.C. Adams
Richmond County GC. ....James Park, A.E. Patterson
Richmond Hill CC ....Arthur Smith, Frank Paddock
Rockaway Hunting Club ....Porter, Frothingham
St. Andrew's GC ....Green Committee, J.C. Ten Eyck
Seabright Club (Rumson)...............F. Potts, Albert Symington, F.W. Simonton
Shinnecock Hills GC ....R.H. Robertson
Staten Island Cricket Club..............................T. Hope Simpson
Tuxedo Club...................................Grenville Kane, E.C. Kent
Westbrook CC ................................H.B. Hollins, J.M. Knapp

Eight of the founding clubs no longer exist (see "Lost Courses", on page 296) and five others continue to exist, albeit under different names. Paterson became the North Jersey Country Club in 1897, two years before Queens County changed its name to Nassau Country Club. Hillside Tennis became known as the Plainfield Country Club in 1904, and Fairfield County became Greenwich Country Club in 1909, one year after Seabright had been subsumed by the newly-formed Rumson Country Club. In all, 18 of the founding clubs are in existence today.

From those first meetings at Delmonico's 100 years ago has grown one of the world's leading golf organizations, encompassing more than 400 member clubs and serving more than 120,000 golfers. While the size and the scope of its service programs have grown, the MGA remains true to its founding purpose, as stated in Article II of its original Constitution: *"To promote in all ways the best interests and the true spirit of the game of golf."* ❑

Daniel Chauncey,
MGA President from 1905-06.

Clubs of the Metropolitan Golf Association

LONG ISLAND
Atlantic
Barry National
Bellport
Bergen Point
Beth Hills
Bethpage
Bethpage Pro
Duffers
Birdies & Bogeys
Brentwood
Bretton Woods
Bridgehampton
Bridgeview
Broadway
Brookville
Calverton Links
Cedarbrook
Cherry Creek
Cherry Valley
Cold Spring
Colonial Springs
Crab Meadow
Creek
Deepdale
Eisenhower Park
Emerald GA
Fishers Island
Fox Hill
Fresh Meadow
Garden City Country
Garden City Golf
Gardiner's Bay
Glen Cove
Glen Head
Glen Oaks
Glenwood
Green Fields
Hamlet
Hamlet Wind Watch
Hampton Hills
Harbor Green
Hauppauge
Hay Harbor
Heatherwood
Hempstead
Holbrook
Huntington
Huntington Crescent
Indian Hills
Indian Island
Inis Fada
Inwood
Island Hills
Island's End
Kings Park
Lake Success
Lawrence
Lido
Links at Lido
Maidstone
Meadow Brook
Men's Club at Lido
Meroke
Merrick Park
Middle Bay

Middle Island
Midway
Mill River
Montauk Downs
Muttontown
Nassau
Nassau Players
National Golf Links
Nissequogue
North Fork
North Hempstead
North Hills
North Shore
Noyac
Old Westbury
Oyster Bay
Peninsula
Pine Hills
Pine Hollow
Piping Rock
Plandome
Ponds
Port Jefferson
Quogue
Riverhead Swingers
Rock Hill
Rockaway Hunting
Rockville Links
Rolling Oaks
Round Swamp
Royal & Honorable
Sag Harbor
Salisbury
Sands Point
Seaford Volunteer
Seawane
Shamrock
Shelter Island
Shinnecock Hills
Shore View
Smithtown Landing
South Fork
Southampton
Southward Ho
Spring Lake
St. George's
Sunken Meadow
Swan Lake
Tam O'Shanter
Timber Point
Towers
Village C. at Sands Pt.
West Sayville
Westhampton
Wheatley Hills
Woodcrest
Woodmere

STATEN ISLAND &
NEW YORK CITY
AGC/Clearview
AGC/Dyker Beach
AGC/LaTourette
AGC/Pelham Bay
     Split Rock
AGC/Silver Lake

AGC/South Shore
AGC/Van Cortlandt
Bedford of Brooklyn
Bronx River
Bklyn. Marine Dunes
Brookridge
Cavan
Clearview
Coral Reefer
Douglaston
Emerald GS
Emerald Isle
Esquire
Forest
Governors Island
Highrise
Irish American
Islander
Kissena Park
Lakeside

Mac's Golf Society
Met Restaurant
Mosholu
New York City
NY Irish
Pfizer
Randalls Island
Richmond County
St. Philip Neri
Sandtrappers Sr.
Shotmakers
South Shore Men's
Silver Lake
Silvette
Staten Island Seniors
United Nations

NEW JERSEY
Alpine
Apple Ridge
Arcola
Ash Brook
Baltusrol

Bamm Hollow
Battleground
Beacon Hill
Beaver Brook
Bedens Brook
Belfast
Bergen Community
Bowling Green
Brooklake
Canoe Brook
Cedar Hill
Cherry Valley
Colonia
Copper Hill
Cranford
Cream Ridge
Crestmont
Crystal Springs
Deal
Due Process

East Orange
Echo Lake
Edgewood
Emerson
Essex County
Essex Fells
Fairmount
Fiddler's Elbow
Forest Hill
Forsgate
Fox Hollow
Galloping Hill
Glen Ridge
Greenacres
Green Brook
Hackensack
Harbor Pines
Harkers Hollow
Haworth
High Mountain
Hollywood
Knickerbocker
Lake Mohawk

Madison
Manasquan River
Maplewood
Mendham
Metedeconk National
Metuchen
Moggy Brook
Monmouth Golfing
Montammy
Montclair
Morris County
Morris County GA
Mountain Ridge
Navesink
Newton
Nomad
North Jersey
Northwood
Oak Hill
Oak Ridge

Old Tappan
Panther Valley
Pascack Brook
Pebble Creek
Plainfield
Plainfield West
Preakness Hills
Ramsey
Raritan Valley
Ridgewood
Rivervale
Rock Spring
Rockaway River
Rolling Greens
Roselle
Roxiticus
Rumson
Shackamaxon
Shore Oaks
Somerset Hills
Southern Jersey
Spring Brook
Springdale

Spring Lake
Stanton Ridge
Suburban
Tri-County
Twin Brooks
Upper Montclair
Weequahic
White Beeches
Woodlake

CONNECTICUT
Amber View
Aspetuck Valley
Birchwood
Brooklawn
Bruce Men's
Burning Tree
Connecticut
CC of Darien
CC of Fairfield

CC of New Canaan
Fairview
Greenwich
Hibernian
Innis Arden
Milbrook
Mill River
Oak Hills Men
Patterson
Redding
Richter Park
Ridgewood
Rockrimmon
Rolling Hills
Round Hill
Shorehaven
Silvermine
Silver Spring
Stanwich
Sterling Farms
Tamarack
Wee Burn
Woodway

HUDSON VALLEY
Beekman
Concord
Dogwood Knolls
Dutcher
Dutchess
Garrison
Granit
Grossinger
Harlem Valley
Highlands
James Baird
Kutshers
Mahopac
McCann Memorial
Mid-Hudson Valley
Millbrook
Mohonk
New Paltz
Putnam
Quaker Hill
Sedgewood
Segalla
Southern Dutchess
Sullivan County
Swan Lake
Taconic Valley
Tarry Brae
Thomas Carvel
Twaalfskill
Vails Grove
Villa Roma
Wiltwyck

WESTCHESTER
Apawamis
Ardsley
Bedford
Blind Brook
Bonnie Briar
Brae Burn
Briar Hall
Canyon
CC at Pleasantville
CC of Purchase
Celtic
Century
Crown City
Donnybrook
Doral Arrowwood
Dunwoodie
East Hill
Elmwood
Fenway
Flamingo Gaze
Gaelic
Hampshire
Heritage Hills
Hudson National
Innisfail
Knollwood
Lake Isle
Leewood
Maple Leafs
Maple Moor

Metropolis
Mohansic
Mohansic Hills
Mount Kisco
Old Oaks
Pehquenakonck
Pelham
Pound Ridge
Quaker Ridge
Ridgeway
Rye
Salem
Sanctuary
Saxony
Scarsdale
Siwanoy
Sleepy Hollow
Sprain Lake Men
Sprain Valley
St. Andrew's
Sunningdale
Waccabuc
Westchester
Westchester Hills
Whippoorwill
Willow Ridge
Winged Foot
Woodlawn
Wykagyl
Yonkers Amateur

ROCKLAND
Blue Hill
Broadacres
Dellwood
Haverstraw
Minisceongo
New York
Rockland
Rockland Valley
Spook Rock

ORANGE
Central Valley
Hickory Hill
Monroe
Orange County
Osiris
Otterkill
Port Jervis
Powelton
Scotts Corners
Stony Ford
Storm King
Tuxedo
Wallkill
Warwick Valley

HONORARY
West Point
Suneagles at
    Fort Monmouth

Governers Island

SERVICES OF THE MGA

"To The Game, Golfers and Its Member Clubs"

The non-profit Metropolitan Golf Association is a service organization in the truest sense of the word, dedicated to serving its member clubs and golfers. When the MGA's charter was signed on April 14, 1897, its original goals were simple: "to promote in all ways the best interests and the true spirit of the game of golf and to organize tournaments." Its mission has grown during the past 100 years, but service to golf remains the association's cornerstone.

TOURNAMENT AND RULES

Right from the start, one of the MGA's primary tasks was to conduct regional championships. A Tournament Committee was quickly established to conduct and oversee local events and coordinate a schedule of invitationals and USGA championships. The MGA's major events, the Met Amateur and Met Open, quickly established themselves as championships of national consequence, and the association's tournament program was on its way.

Through the years, several factors helped create a nationally respected tournament program. For one, the tri-state region is blessed with the world's greatest collection of courses, virtually all of which have graciously hosted MGA events. The area also has been doubly blessed with a roster of outstanding players through the years. The MGA has supplemented its major events with tournaments that give a wide variety of golfers the opportunity to compete under championship conditions. Whether you are a senior, junior, or public-links player, looking to compete for the Met Open's Walker Trammell Trophy or a net prize in the Father & Son tournament, the MGA has an event for you.

Dr. Richard Silver

Training our officials.

A key event in the expansion of the tournament program was the launching of the Men's Net Team Championship in 1977. Often referred to as "the U.S. Open for the average player," the Net Team was the brainchild of then-MGA President Allen DuMont. Designed for the mid-handicapped player, it annually attracts one of the largest fields in golf. A women's version was established in 1985 and also proved immediately popular. Both events are sponsored by MetLife.

MGA tournaments are well-known for the manner in which they are conducted. Much of the work is done by more than 150 volunteers, who are well-versed in the Rules of Golf. Indoor seminars, on-course training, and an annual Rules Quiz keep the "blue coats" well prepared. Over the past 30 years, the Tournament and Rules Committee has been led by a succession of dedicated chairmen: Edward Hilbert, Dr. Richard Silver, Dr. Harold Lenobel, and Joseph Cantwell have served in this role with distinction, insisting on the highest standards for all MGA events.

Dr. Silver — a "national treasure" in the words of former USGA president William J. Williams Jr. — was one of the MGA's most influential leaders. A foremost authority on the Rules, he was instrumental in bringing the public-links golfer into the MGA. Groups of players who formed organized clubs without owning a facility were welcomed into the association in 1956; at Dr. Silver's urging, these publinks players were extended full tournament privileges in 1963.

The MGA recently began bringing its Rules expertise to the larger golf community, conducting seminars for club officials, local golf associations, local PGA Sections, high school coaches, and numerous professional and civic organizations, as well as member clubs. A Rules column is a popular feature of *The Met Golfer*, the association's magazine, while the staff handles thousands of phone calls every year from golfers, club officials, and golf professionals with Rules questions.

The MGA staff also plays a key role in running tournaments. Peter Bisconti, tournament director from 1975 to '79 and an excellent player, fine-tuned the management of events, adding a "field team" of part-time staff members to help conduct championships and qualifying rounds. One of the team's "graduates," Gene Westmoreland, has served as staff Tournament Director and Assistant Executive Director since 1980. On Westmoreland's watch, the number of players and tournament days involved in MGA events have more than doubled, while the MGA's reputation in the field of tournament administration has been enhanced.

From the beginning, the MGA has assisted the USGA by conducting local and sectional qualifying rounds for national championships. Today, the MGA oversees more USGA qualifying rounds than any association in the country. At the MGA's 1995 Annual Meeting, USGA Executive Director David Fay recognized this work, saying, "we could not conduct our national championships without the regional and state associations, and there is no one we rely on more heavily, and no one that does a better job for us, than the Metropolitan Golf Association."

HANDICAPPING AND COURSE RATING

The MGA's Handicap Committee was established in 1899, and the first Handicap Tournament took place that same year. Arthur Taylor of Oakland Golf Club, a 17-handicapper, won the event with a pair of net 82s — obviously sandbagging had yet to be invented. In those days, handicapping was just starting to take hold in the United States and was clearly more art than science. As the system evolved, the MGA played a major part in its development.

Leighton Calkins, a turn-of-the-century MGA Executive Committee member from Plainfield Country Club, is widely credited with developing the first national handicap system. First used by the MGA in 1905, it was tested for several years before being adopted, in modified form, by the USGA in 1911. The system for handicapping and course rating has been redefined and improved over the years, yet it still serves a purpose unique in sport — allowing players of different abilities to compete fairly and equitably with one another.

Today, the MGA assigns USGA Course and Slope Ratings to more than 300 golf courses in the Met Area and calculates USGA Handicap Indexes for more than 100,000 golfers.

A timeline of the development of handicapping services — from Leighton Calkins to modern networked computer systems — illuminates the MGA's leadership role.

1905 Calkins is the first to base handicapping on modified par scores, the forerunner of course ratings, with each course assigned a par score based on the expected score of the U.S. Amateur Champion. His system also incorporates the British concept of basing a golfer's handicap only on his best scores in "formal competition." Early systems used the three best scores of the year.

1911 USGA adopts a modified form of Calkins' system for use nationwide.

1920s MGA assigns handicaps to individuals, but only the better players. In 1927, the limit is eight so only 608 players have official MGA handicaps.

1928 Then-MGA president Walter Schafer says "give the duffer a break—handicaps for all." Handicaps are offered directly to all area golfers for $1.

1930 Led by Bobby Jones, golf's popularity explodes and 5,500 golfers have MGA handicaps. That will be the high for many years due to the Depression and World War II.

1934 The responsibility for obtaining an MGA handicap is

Clarence "Gus" Benedict   Joseph A. Donahue

Year	Winner
1973	Clarence "Gus" Benedict
1974	Joseph C. Dey
1975	Jerry Courville Sr.
1976	William P. Turnesa
1977	Fred Corcoran
1978	Al Laney
1979	Cynthia Alexandre [Foshay]
1980	Harry Cooper
1981	Robert Trent Jones Sr.
1982	Dr. Richard S. Silver
1983	P.J. Boatwright Jr.
1984	Isaac B. Grainger
1985	George E. Sands
1986	James R. Hand
1987	Dana Mozley
1988	Arthur E. Lynch
1989	John F. McGillicuddy
1990	Arthur "Red" Hoffman
1991	Ann Beard
1992	Ira L. Mendell
1993	Joseph A. Donahue
1994	Guido Cribari
1995	Arthur Weber
1996	C.A. "Tony" Wimpfheimer

shifted from individual golfers to the club secretary.

1947 Willie Turnesa is given a handicap of "plus one" in honor of winning the British Amateur. Four players — Ray Billows, Richard Chapman, Frank Strafaci, and Robert Sweeney—are "scratch."

1949 USGA introduces the "Basic Handicap System," including casual rounds for the first time. The system uses a player's lowest 10 of his last 50 scores.

1950s The concept of "course rating" replaces "par score" in evaluating course difficulty. USGA begins studying how obstacles might be evaluated more objectively.

1953 USGA adds the "Current Handicap System", basing handicaps on the lowest 10 of the last 15 scores, making handicaps far more volatile. Most, but not all, MGA clubs use the new system.

1964 MGA handicap service is the nation's first to be computerized.

1969 MGA Handicap Chairman Herman Freydberg from Metropolis and Executive Director James McLoughlin refine the MGA handicap service. It becomes a model for other golf associations.

1971 MGA's first Course Rating Committee is formed with Alanson B. Davis of Canoe Brook as Chairman. Accurate course measurements become an essential part of the rating process and the MGA launches a program to measure all area courses.

1980 MGA is the first golf association to offer clubs "in-house" handicapping, utilizing personal computers.

1981 In an action that would have a far-reaching impact, the MGA and USGA create a new handicap computation service. The MGA service is the basis for the original Golf Handicap & Information Network (GHIN) Service. MGA is the first association to use GHIN, offered to others in 1982.

1982 USGA research shows a "portability" problem in handicapping. Testing starts on a new calculation method called "slope."

1983 USGA "obstacle evaluation technique" for rating courses, a requirement for the introduction of Slope Handicapping, is ready for implementation. The MGA Course Rating Committee, led by Jerold Benavie of Westchester Country Club, is greatly expanded to prepare for the re-rating process.

1983 to 1985 MGA is among the first golf associations preparing for the "slope system." More than 200 Met Area courses are re-rated.

1986 After an extensive educational program, slope handicapping is implemented at all MGA member clubs. The procedures and educational materials developed by the MGA to introduce the new system are used by associations around the country.

1994 The Handicap and Course Rating Committees are combined, with William McTurk from Sleepy Hollow as chairman. The MGA handicap service now reaches more than 100,000 golfers. GHIN serves 60 golf associations and more than 1.5 million golfers.

1996 Virtually every member of the MGA's 400-plus member clubs have official USGA Handicap Indexes and handicapping is the Association's most visible and widely used service.

EXPANDING THE ASSOCIATION'S MISSION

For its first quarter-century, the MGA focused on conducting tournaments and evaluating the handicaps of those who played in them. With the Roaring '20s came an

explosion in the popularity of the game. As its member clubs grew in number, the association broadened its role.

Service Bureau... to Green Section... to Green Committee
In 1925, the MGA Service Bureau was formed to provide additional services to "greenskeepers," as they were known, and Green Chairmen. Under the direction of Harry Kidd, the Service Bureau, renamed the Green Section in 1928, worked closely with the USGA to disseminate information on course operations. The section brought Green Committees together to discuss mutual concerns, provide cooperative buying services, and maintain experimental turf gardens at four local courses including Kidd's home club, Wheatley Hills.

The Green Section's role changed during the Depression and World War II when course maintenance was severely curtailed. When the USGA moved to New Jersey and developed its own Turf Advisory Service, the MGA Green Section became less active. It was revived in 1983 as the MGA Green Committee, led by future MGA President Arthur Weber, a leader in turf research and an expert in the relationship between golf courses and the environment. The committee was re-launched with three purposes: improve the working relationship between area superintendents and Green Chairmen; act as a clearinghouse for information on all phases of course maintenance; and support turfgrass research.

The Tri-State Turf Research Foundation grew out of the Green Committee. Organized in 1989, with the cooperation of the area's golf course superintendents associations, this group helps identify and fund research projects dealing with issues faced by local superintendents. In this environmentally sensitive age their work in fighting turf disease and developing disease- and drought-resistant grasses is ever more important.

Club Operations, Education, Communications and Client Groups
In the years after World War II, as the MGA increased the scope of its activities, its operations changed as well. For many years, a small staff worked out of a modest office on Rector Street in Manhattan. In 1950, the offices moved in with the USGA at the first "Golf House," at 40 East 38th Street, remaining there for 16 years, sharing facilities

James E. McLoughlin

and staff. For a long time, the only full-time staffer was office manager Winifred Macfie, who served for 35 years before retiring in 1964. The position of Executive Secretary was added in 1955, with several people holding the title for brief stints.

Handicapping and Course Rating, two of the MGA's most widely used services.

THE MGA AND USGA: PERFECT PARTNERS

Findlay Douglas

For all of its 100 years, the Metropolitan Golf Association has enjoyed a special relationship with the United States Golf Association.

At the turn of the century, the Met Area was the hub of golf activity in the United States, so it is no wonder the two organizations shared many leaders and champions. And with both groups located in New York City, a spirit of cooperation was natural. As the two associations grew and their primary concerns evolved, one goal has remained constant—to serve the game of golf and uphold its traditions. That common thread has sustained this special relationship for a century.

Good leadership was essential to the success of both organizations, and in that area the MGA and USGA have had much in common. Twenty USGA presidents hailed from the Met Area:

R.H. Robertson ....Shinnecock Hills....1901-1902
Ransom Thomas ....Morris County 1905-1906
Daniel Chauncey ....Garden City Golf ..1907-1908
Robert Watson ....National 1913-1914
Frederick Wheeler ....Apawamis 1918-1919
George Walker ....National 1920
Howard Whitney ....Nassau..............................1921
Wynant Vanderpool ......Morris County 1924-1925
Findlay Douglas ....Apawamis 1929-1930
Herbert Ramsay ....National 1931-1932
Prescott Bush ....Round Hill 1935
John Jackson ....Deepdale 1936-1937
Archibald Reid ....St. Andrew's............1938-1939
Morton Bogue ....Deepdale 1944-1945
Charles Littlefield ....Montclair................1946-1947
Isaac Grainger.................. Montclair 1954-1955
Clarence "Gus" Benedict ..Winged Foot 1964-1965
William Ward Foshay ....Round Hill 1966-1967
James Hand ....Sleepy Hollow 1984-1985
William J. Williams, Jr. ....Siwanoy.................1986-1987

Six of these men also served as president of the MGA: R.H. Robertson (1900); Daniel Chauncey (1905 to 1906); Frederick

Wheeler (1911 to 1913); Findlay Douglas (1922 to 1924); Isaac B. Grainger (1943 to 1945); and Clarence Benedict (1960 to 1961).

Our common ties go much deeper into the ranks. As a hotbed of avid golfers, the Met Area has produced many talented individuals who love the game and have devoted their time and expertise to making it better. Some have made lasting contributions to the game, including Joseph Dey, a former MGA Executive Committee member who was Executive Director of the USGA, Captain of the Royal and Ancient Golf Club of St. Andrews, and the first Commissioner of the PGA TOUR. Dr. Richard Silver, MGA Tournament & Rules Chairman for many years, served the USGA as a consulting member of the Rules of Golf Committee. Arthur Weber, a former MGA president, serves on the USGA Green Section Committee and created the first Environmental Code of Conduct for golf courses. C.A. "Tony" Wimpfheimer, who helped create *The Met Golfer* magazine, was an influential member of the USGA Communications Committee.

We have also shared staff members — David Fay, Executive Director of the USGA since 1989, began his golf career as Communications Director of the MGA (1976 to 1978) — and we have shared Manhattan office space.

But our relationship is based on more than geography. We have called on each other to explore new ideas, develop new programs, and conduct tournaments. When the MGA developed a practical handicap system in 1905, it was quickly adopted by the USGA for use nationwide. Many years later, in the 1970's and '80s, it would be MGA Executive Directors James McLoughlin and Jay Mottola who would help the USGA launch GHIN, their very successful handicap computation service.

When the MGA Foundation was formed in 1992, the USGA lent guidance, financial support, and aid in developing programs for education and junior golf.

David Fay

And, of course, the MGA still runs golf events — 15 of our own championships and qualifying rounds for seven USGA national championships each year.

The USGA is only three years older than the MGA. The associations have grown up together, relying on each other through good times and bad. This unique relationship has made both organizations stronger and more effective in assuring the good of the game.

In 1965, the Association hired James McLoughlin as its first Executive Director and in 1966 moved into its own offices at 60 East 42nd Street. During McLoughlin's 16-year tenure, the association's size and the quality of its services to member clubs increased dramatically. The Club Operations Committee expanded its role as a clearinghouse for information on club management and provided clubs with educational programs and survey information. The Group Insurance Advisory Committee was formed and in cooperation with the John Treiber Agency offered clubs insurance programs for their employees. A new Public Information Committee produced periodic newsletters, while the Real Estate Tax Committee was

formed to fight the rising tax burden faced by clubs. The professional staff also expanded to include a Tournament Director and Communications Manager. (During the 1970s, the communications position was held by George Peper, now Editor-In-Chief of *GOLF Magazine*, and by David Fay, now Executive Director of the USGA.)

While growing, the MGA also took on the administration of the United States Seniors, Westchester and Long Island Seniors, and the Father & Son golf associations. More recently, the Metropolitan Golf Writers, Metropolitan Club Managers, Metropolitan Golf Course Superintendents, and the Eastern Seniors associations have become client groups.

MGA officers elected at the 1996 Annual Meeting:
President Martin J. Connelly (seated), from the left, Paul R. Dillon (Secretary),
Joseph C. Cantwell (Vice President), and Cornelius E. DeLoca (Treasurer).

COMING OF AGE

A number of significant changes took place at the MGA during the early 1980s. Under the leadership of presidents Ira Mendell and Joseph Donahue, the office staff was completely revamped. In March of 1980, Jay Mottola was hired as Deputy Executive Director. Later that same year Executive Director James McLoughlin left and was replaced by Gerald T. Mahoney and former field team member Gene Westmoreland was hired as Tournament Director. Mottola moved into the Executive Director's position in 1982 when Mahoney became the Director of Golf Programs. In March of 1981, the office relocated to Mamaroneck in Westchester County, the first time the MGA was headquartered outside New York City.

The association has experienced rapid growth and expansion of its services. Between 1980 and 1996, membership nearly doubled to more than 400 clubs, with the biggest gains in the public sector and the Hudson Valley. There also have been dramatic increases in the number of golfers participating in MGA events and the number of clubs using the Handicap Service.

The MGA benefited from a healthy economy and the increasing popularity of golf. However, of the many new initiatives launched during this time, four had the greatest impact on the association's relationship with both member clubs and individual golfers.

The Met Golfer

Despite its range of services, the MGA struggled to establish an identity in the mind of the club member. That changed in the summer of 1983 with the first issue of *The Met Golfer*. Suddenly the association had a means of communicating with every club member, bringing them updated news and infor-

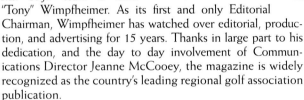

mation about Met Area golf. First published by Martin Davis and The Sports Marketing Group, those duties were assumed by Golf Magazine Properties in 1990 when SMG was purchased by Times Mirror Magazines. The magazine has recorded steady growth in circulation, frequency, and stature. In 1997, *The Met Golfer* will be sent to the homes of nearly 100,000 club members, six times a year.

A key member of *The Met Golfer* team is C.A. "Tony" Wimpfheimer. As its first and only Editorial Chairman, Wimpfheimer has watched over editorial, production, and advertising for 15 years. Thanks in large part to his dedication, and the day to day involvement of Communications Director Jeanne McCooey, the magazine is widely recognized as the country's leading regional golf association publication.

Property and Casualty Insurance

A few months after *The Met Golfer's* premiere, the MGA inaugurated a very different program. Working with Richard Fowler and John Dana from FAI Insurance Counseling, the association, led by President Sydnor Settle and the Insurance Committee, headed by John F. Kelsey Jr., created a property and casualty insurance program that offered member clubs extraordinary coverage at competitive rates. Using the collective buying power of MGA member clubs was not new, nor were insurance programs. But this plan surpassed all that had come before. It grew rapidly, saving clubs more than a million dollars in premiums in the first three years alone. In 1996, 171 member clubs participated,

GOLFWORKS, the MGA Foundation's student intern program.

making it the largest and most successful golf association-sponsored insurance program in the country. The program has been expanded and is offered through golf associations around the country. Building on the success of the property and casualty program, the MGA has recently added additional insurance and employee-benefits products.

"A Foundation for The Future"

The MGA has long supported programs for junior golf, caddies, and education. To ensure the continued success of these initiatives, the MGA Foundation was created in 1992 with the mission of "building a foundation for the future of golf." James Cotter, MGA president at the time, said the Foundation would allow the MGA "to reinforce our commitment to several service programs that are important to us, and to the future of the game… The Foundation will insure that these and similar programs receive the attention and funding they deserve."

Cotter is the personification not only of the Foundation but of many of the MGA's accomplishments over the last quarter-century. He has given countless hours to the MGA, first as Legal Counsel in 1972, through his presidency, and as Centennial Chairman in 1997. His devotion and leadership to the MGA have had a profound influence on the association.

James Cotter, one of the MGA's most influential leaders.

The Foundation was established as a 501-C(3) charitable organization, meaning contributions are tax-deductible. Local golfers responded generously, donating nearly $1 million in its first five years. Under the Foundation banner, the MGA's existing junior events, caddie programs, and schedule of educational programs were all expanded.

A new program, added in 1993, has become the cornerstone of the Foundation's junior golf activities. GOLFWORKS places underprivileged high-school-age students in summer jobs at MGA member clubs, exposing them to career opportunities, successful role models, and the game of golf. Under the watchful eye of Jeanne McCooey, the program has grown steadily, placing more than 50 students in 1996. GOLFWORKS has been enthusiastically supported by clubs and minority groups and has the potential to help hundreds of young people each year.

Golf Central

In 1994 the MGA created a foundation of another kind, this one with bricks and mortar. A two-story, 8,200-square-foot headquarters was built on three acres of land purchased from Knollwood Country Club in Elmsford, New York. The central location in Westchester County is ideally suited to making the staff more accessible to member clubs, while owning the building and the land allows control of long-term operating costs.

With the Met Area's concentration of

Staff members Gene Westmoreland, Jeanne McCooey and Jay Mottola

clubs and golf activity, it is not surprising that there are a number of golf organizations serving the game. The new building has allowed several of these groups to come together under one roof for the first time. The Women's Metropolitan Golf Association, the Metropolitan Section of the PGA, the Metropolitan Golf Course Superintendents Association, and the Westchester Golf Association all moved into the MGA headquarters building within a short time of its official opening in October of 1994. In addition, the MGA was already serving the Metropolitan Club Managers and Golf Writers Associations as well as four senior golf groups. Dubbed "Golf Central," the name has stuck and, more importantly, the facility has helped all of these groups work cooperatively to serve the local golf community more effectively than ever before. The MGA Foundation also plans to develop a library and reference center at Golf Central.

The brochure outlining the activities of the MGA Foundation sums up its mission with one simple sentence: "Building a foundation for the future of golf." In many ways this is what the Metropolitan Golf Association has been doing for 100 years. The association and the thousands of people who have helped over the years have done their job well and the MGA is now prepared for its second century of service to golf.   ○

MGA's headquarters "Golf Central" opened in 1994.

THE MGA CHAMPIONSHIPS
"The Best In The World"

WHEN THE ASSOCIATION was formed in 1897, one of its fundamental purposes was to conduct tournaments for its members. Today that remains one of the its most important functions. MGA events have been distinguished by their historic import, their storied winners, the quality of the venues, and the manner in which they are conducted. Each year during the 1970s and '80s, longtime MGA Tournament Chairman Dr. Richard Silver, would reinforce this mission by opening the meeting of the Tournament and Rules Committee with the reminder to the body that their job was "to conduct the best tournaments in the world."

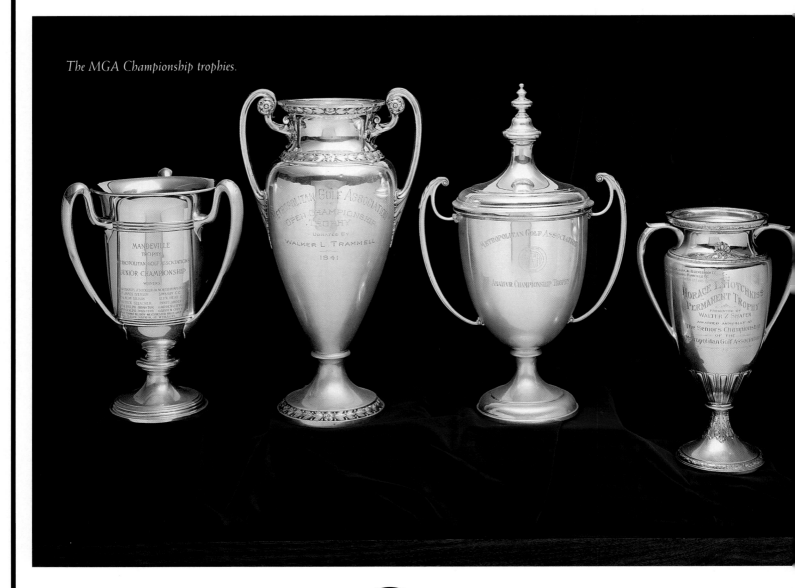

The MGA Championship trophies.

THE METROPOLITAN AMATEUR

Dick Siderowf won five Met Amateurs.

In 1898, the MGA's governors voted to establish a championship amateur tournament, an interclub four-ball competition, and a handicap event. The first tournament of historic importance was the Metropolitan Amateur Championship, inaugurated the following year. The "Met Am," which is rivaled for longevity in this country only by the U.S. Amateur, was contested for the first time at the Garden City Golf Club. The championship plate was donated by H.B. Hollins, with the condition that it be retired after three victories by representatives of the same club, a feat accomplished for the Nassau Country Club by Findlay Douglas (two wins) and Jerry Travers. The subsequent trophy was the gift of then-MGA president, Daniel Chauncey.

The Met Amateur immediately set a lofty precedence for quality. Its first two winners, Herbert Harriman (1899) and Walter Travis (1900), also were that year's U.S. Amateur champions. Two early rivalries—first between Travis and Douglas, then Travis and Travers—established the tournament as an event of national consequence.

The Met Amateur has always been played at match play, with only slight changes to the format over the years. It remains the Met Area's most important amateur event, a demanding, sometimes grueling test of championship golf with the victor surviving multiple days of 36-hole competition. From Travis and Turnesa to Gardner, Siderowf, and Zahringer, the list of winners is testament to its ability to identify the region's best amateur.

THE METROPOLITAN OPEN

The Metropolitan Open is the third oldest Open championship in this country, following the U.S. and Western Opens. It was staged for the first time in 1905, thanks to the generosity of the Fox Hills Golf Club on Staten Island, which played the dual role of host and sponsor. A similar situation prevailed the following year, when the Hollywood Golf Club wore both hats. After a year's hiatus, the MGA raised its dues in 1908 to

finance the event itself.

Until World War II, the Met Open was considered one of the "major tournaments" on the professional circuit, in part because it offered one of the richest purses. During its glory years, the Met Open attracted virtually every top player and its winner was almost guaranteed a spot on the Ryder Cup team.

The first winner, Alex Smith, also proved to be the most frequent, with four victories between 1905 and 1913. His brother, Macdonald Smith, added three more (in 1914, '26, and '31), with his victory at Scarsdale in 1914 establishing a new world's record (278) for a 72-hole event.

Despite its strong fields and national prominence, the Met Open was a financial burden, causing the MGA to discontinue the event in 1941. The association suspended all formal "open" competitions until 1949, holding only various pro-am tournaments. The lack of success and support for these events led the MGA Executive and Tournament Committees to jointly recommend that the Met Open be reinstated and contested concurrently as a three-day tournament that included a one-day pro-am. The trophy, still awarded today, was donated by former MGA president Walker L. Trammell.

The Met Open quickly re-established itself as the Met Area's premier event. Jackie Burke Jr. won the first reinstated Open in 1949 at Metropolis by six shots over Gene Sarazen. The purse and entries have increased steadily, reaching $100,000 in 1997 and attracting nearly 800 of the area's top pros and amateurs. Since 1969, a club team pro-am has preceded the Met Open and has raised mor than a quarter of a million dollars for the Caddie Scholarship Funds of the Long Island, New Jersey, and Westchester Golf Associations.

back to win in 1935.

For a number of years, the Junior Committee "was" A. Fred Williamson. A volunteer, he obtained the sites, arranged for the housing of contestants by members of host clubs, and insisted on the highest level of sportsmanship. The junior program broadened in 1969 with the addition of a Boys Championship for those under 16 and a Pro-Junior Tournament preceding the Junior Championship, which gave contestants an opportunity to be paired with a local professional and play the host course before the actual competition.

In 1964, Williamson was instrumental in starting an annual international junior competition, called the Williamson Cup Matches in honor of Fred's father, a founder of Winged Foot Golf Club. Teams of four juniors representing golf associations from throughout the Northeast and Canada compete each year. The matches rotate among the associations each August, giving top junior players a wonderful competitive and educational experience.

With the start of the MGA Foundation in 1992, the Junior Committee, under the leadership of chairman Cornelius De-Loca, has expanded its role into new areas while still maintaining the highest standards for the Junior and Boys Championships and the Williamson Cup Matches.

A. Fred Williamson with 1980-81 MGA Boys Champion Don Edwards.

MGA JUNIOR CHAMPIONSHIP

The MGA's involvement with junior golf dates back to its first president, H.B. Hollins, who believed that golf provided the ideal form of recreation and exercise for young men, especially school boys. Leighton Calkins, a member of the MGA's Executive Committee, implemented Hollins' plans in 1912 by founding the MGA Junior Championship, the oldest such tournament in the country. The Met Junior was held for its first three years at Plainfield Country Club, where Calkins was a member.

Among the many prominent names on the MGA Junior trophy, two stand out: Philip V.G. Carter and Billy Edwards. Carter won the tournament from 1913 to 1915 while successfully competing in open competitions, but disappeared quickly thereafter. Edwards won an incredible five consecutive championships, 1946-1950, at a time when the age limit was 21 (it was reduced to 17 in 1956).

In the 1933 tournament, three Strafaci brothers — Frank, Ralph, and Tom —reached the semifinals. Ralph won the title, while his brothers lost in the semi-finals. Frank came

Philip Carter, three-time winner of the MGA Junior.

Ike Tournament Founder Dana Mozley.

THE IKE

The Ike Tournament was founded in 1953 by *Daily News* sportswriter Dana Mozley and nurtured through the years by Mozley and former MGA President George Sands. Although always immensely popular, the event suffered during the late 1970s and early '80s after the *Daily News* dropped its sponsorship. In 1986, the MGA (with the financial support of MetLife) purchased the rights to the Ike. With the MGA's involvement, the event regained its stature and quickly became the area's premier stroke-play amateur event. The Ike today attracts more entries than any other MGA championship for individuals.

Despite a long list of outstanding champions — including Goodwin, Gardner, Turnesa, Burns, Zahringer, and Thomas —the Ike always will be synonymous with the name Courville. The late Jerry Courville Sr. dominated the event in the 1960s, winning a record six titles between 1961 and 1970 while son Jerry Jr. grabbed the baton with back-to-back victories in 1990 and '91. The duo also combined to win three Ike Team Championships for Shorehaven Golf Club.

TEAM AND INTERNATIONAL COMPETITIONS

Although the organization of team matches was voted down at its organizational meeting in 1897, it was not long before the MGA became actively engaged in such endeavors. The matches soon broadened from interclub events to an ongoing series between teams from New York and Philadelphia that started in 1900.

Robert W. Lesley, a member of the Merion Cricket Club outside Philadelphia, decided that a competition for men similar to the Griscom Cup for women would help promote the game and allow for the exchange of ideas and information. The result was the Lesley Cup Matches, which evolved into a four-sided competition among teams representing New York, Massachusetts, Pennsylvania, and Quebec. Formal rules governing the competition were drawn up on July 15, 1905, and signed by Daniel Chauncey, then-president of the MGA. The first matches were played that year at the Garden City Golf Club and won by the Metropolitan team.

In the years preceding World War II, the Lesley Cup attracted the leading amateurs from the four districts. The rules were changed in the late 1940s, limiting the number of low-handicap players each team could enlist. More recently, the matches have featured "officials" representing each jurisdiction with little formal involvement by the local associations.

From 1982 to '87, the region's leading professionals and amateurs competed against one another in the Jennings Cup, which honored the late William Jennings, former president of the New York Rangers and the driving force behind the Westchester Classic in its first decade. The inaugural Jennings Cup was held at Quaker Ridge Golf Club, the only year the amateurs bested the Met PGA professionals.

The MGA entered the "transatlantic" arena in 1990 with the founding of the French/American Challenge for FRED's Cup. Named after its sponsor, the international jeweler FRED Joaillier, it pits teams of men and women representing the MGA/WMGA against the Ligue de Paris. The first competition was held at Chantilly Golf Club outside Paris. Since then, it has alternated annually between France and the Met Area, having been played over some of the Met Area's and Paris' most outstanding courses. A spot on this prestigious team is one of the most sought after positions by Met Area competitors. The competition has been dominated by the Ligue de Paris.

Later in the fall of that same year (1990), a team from the Golfing Union of Ireland came to compete against the MGA in the first Metedeconk International Challenge Cup. The con-

The 1996 Carey Cup teams.

THE MGA AND METLIFE

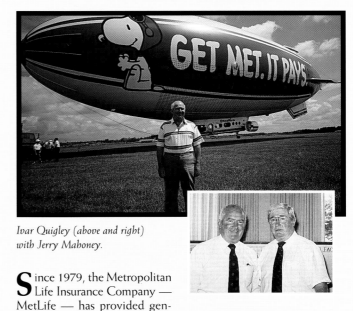

Ivar Quigley (above and right) with Jerry Mahoney.

Since 1979, the Metropolitan Life Insurance Company — MetLife — has provided generous sponsorship support to the MGA. This relationship has evolved into one of the longest and strongest corporate relationships in golf, with MetLife sponsoring 10 annual MGA championships and enabling the association to expand its tournament program and reach out to players at many levels while maintaining the highest standards. Thanks in large part to the personal involvement of Ivar Quigley and Bob Pizzute, MetLife's directors of sports promotions during that time, and the efforts of the MGA's Director of Golf Programs Jerry Mahoney, the relationship has developed into a true partnership that has greatly benefited both organizations.

cept is credited to Metedeconk founders Richard and Herbert Sambol and perennial club champion and international golfer Finbarr Kiely. The MGA won their first encounter with the GUI, but were not so fortunate when invited to Waterville, Ireland in 1992. The competition resumed in 1996 after former New York Governor Hugh L. Carey donated a silver claret trophy to the effort and spearheaded the revival of the matches. Renamed the Carey Cup, the first installment was held at the spectacular new Hudson National Golf Club, where the MGA won by the narrowest of margins.

AND MORE

The MGA also conducts a full range of tournaments for golfers of all ages and skill levels, including the Senior, Public Links, Father & Son, Mixed Pinehurst, Net Team for Men and Women, and Intercollegiate championships. The Senior and Father & Son events became so popular that, during the 1990s, separate Net Tournaments were added for these events. In 1997, the MGA will conduct its first Senior Open, at The Tuxedo Club, and also expand the Net Team Championships during the Centennial Year.

Each year, MGA Championships attract more than 6,000 local golfers. And no matter what the event or who the players are, the MGA lives up to its commitment, "to conduct the best tournaments in the world." ❍

THE GREAT PLAYERS
"From Anderson to Zahringer"

THE EARLY YEARS

During its infancy, the Met Area was clearly the focal point of American golfdom and mirrored the national scene. All of the leading early players, both amateur and professional, played here and were linked directly to local clubs.

Indeed, by 1900, all previous U.S. Amateur champions hailed from Met Area clubs, most of them migrating to the Garden City Golf Club, including Charles Blair Macdonald and his son-in-law, H.J. Whigham, who between them won the first three official national championships. The first two Met Amateur champions, Herbert M. Harriman of Meadow Brook (1899) and Walter J. Travis of Garden City (1900) won the U.S. Amateur that same year, and both engaged in stirring battles with the long-hitting Scot, Findlay Douglas from the Greenwich Country Club (then called Fairfiield County), the 1898 national champion. But soon the focus shone on two men, whose rivalry may have been the keenest of the century: Walter Travis and Jerry Travers.

Walter Travis was born in 1862, in Victoria, Australia. The cigar-chomping Travis took up golf relatively late in life. He said he "first knelt at the shrine of the Godess of Golf" at the age of 34 at the Oakland Golf Club in Bayside, New York (he'd emigrated to the United States in his childhood). Travis' accomplishments include U.S. Amateur titles in 1900, '01, and '03, Met Amateur titles in 1900, '02, '09 and '15, and a then-astonishing victory in the 1904 British Amateur, which made him the first foreigner to win that hallowed championship. So shocking was his triumph, in fact, that the center-shafted Schenectady putter he used was soon banned by Britain's ruling body, the Royal & Ancient Golf Club of St. Andrews! Nevertheless, Travis is considered by many to have been the greatest putter of all time.

Travis' rule was challenged by Travers, a native of Long Island, who was born May 19, 1887, in Oyster Bay, and learned the game there on the lawns of his father's estate, then later under the tutelage of Alex Smith at Nassau Country Club. Travers' career lasted from 1903 to 1920, not counting the time he took off between 1910 and 1911 to hone his skills as a playboy! During the latter half of his competitive career, Travers moved to New Jersey and played out of the Montclair Golf Club, then the Upper Montclair Country Club. Like Travis, Travers was a superb putter and to overcome an often-balky driver, he frequently used a driving iron from the tee —

Gene Sarazen

to win U.S. Amateurs in 1907, '08, '12, and '13, and Met Amateurs in 1906, '07, '11, '12, and '13. Travers capped his brilliant career off with a victory in the 1915 U.S. Open at Baltusrol's "Old Course," making him the only Met Area amateur ever to capture the U.S. Open. Travers also emerged the victor on five of the seven occasions he confronted Travis in major amateur competition (U.S. or Met Amateur).

The professional ranks also featured a great rivalry during the century's first decade between Willie Anderson and Alex Smith. Anderson, with his four U.S. Open titles (1901-1905), clearly had the upper hand, but Smith, often Anderson's key victim in the U.S. Open, turned the tide in the very first Met Open (1905), defeating his arch rival in an 18-hole playoff.

Smith, head professional at Nassau Country Club, later at Wykagyl and Westchester Country Clubs, went on to win four Met Opens (1905, '09, '10, '13), more than any other man — and a pair of U.S. Opens as well, in 1906 and 1910. He also was the mentor of such amateur legends as Travers and Glenna Collett Vare.

Beatrix Hoyt was America's first female golf phenom, playing out of Shinnecock Hills Golf Club. A granddaughter of Salmon Chase, Secretary of the Treasury under Abraham Lincoln and later Chief Justice of the Supreme Court, Hoyt won three consecutive Women's Amateurs, from 1896 to 1898, while still a teenager. Hoyt was one of the five founders of the WMGA in 1899, but retired from competitive golf at age 20 immediately after losing in the semifinals of the 1900 Women's Amateur at Shinnecock and never played in a WMGA competition.

Genevieve Hecker Stout was the first woman to write about golf. Stout contributed a series of articles to *"Golf"* magazine (no relation to today's monthly) in 1902, and then wrote an instructional book titled, "Golf For Women." On the course, Hecker won the 1901 and 1902 U.S. Women's Amateurs, and four WMGA Match-Play titles. She played out of Apawamis and Wee Burn before marrying Charles Stout of the Richmond County Country Club.

A gathering of some of the Met Area's greatest players (clockwise from top left): Jim Albus, Dick Siderowf, Walter Travis, Maureen Orcutt, Alex Smith with Willie Anderson and George Zahringer (center photo).

Genevieve Hecker Stout

Jerry Travers

WORLD WAR I AND THE ROARING 20s

During the years that surrounded World War I, bridging the gap between the first decade of the century and the Roaring 20s, a relatively unsung hero dominated, that being Oswald Kirkby of the Englewood Golf Club. During a six-year period, during which the tournament was twice canceled because of the war effort, he won three Met Amateurs (1914, 1916, 1919) defeating Travis for the title in 1914, and was runner-up in the event twice (1911, '12) to Jerry Travers.

In roared the 20s and so did the "Siwanoy Slugger" Jess Sweetser. Some believe that Sweetser was the equal of Bobby Jones during the first half of the 1920s. His credits include the 1922 U.S. Amateur, the 1926 British Amateur (he was the first American-born winner) and Met Amateurs in 1922 and '25. Jones himself later called his 8 & 7 defeat at the hands of Sweetser in the 1922 U.S. Amateur at The Country Club in Brookline the "tidiest licking" he'd ever suffered in major amateur competition.

The 1920s was a halcyon era for women's golf, especially for women representing Met Area clubs. Glenna Collett Vare was a six-time U.S. Women's Amateur champion between 1922 and 1935, and did play locally from 1927 to '31 as an honorary member of the Greenwich Country Club.

Long-driving Lillian Hyde Feitner, a member of the now-defunct South Shore Field Club in West Islip, won six WMGA titles — 1910, '11, '14, '15, '16 and '20 — and lost in the final of the U.S. Women's Amateur at Baltusrol in 1911.

Marion Hollins, an all-round athlete who was highly proficient at tennis and polo as well as golf, was the daughter of H. B. Hollins, first president of the MGA. She played at her father's Westbrook Club in Islip and at the Piping Rock Club. Hollins won the 1921 U.S. Women's Amateur at Hollywood Golf Club, as well as three WMGA titles, and was named

captain of the first American Curtis Cup team in 1933. She also was the driving force behind the organization of the Women's National Golf & Tennis Club in Glen Head, and later was instrumental in bringing Alister Mackenzie on board to design the Cypress Point and Pasatiempo layouts in northern California. She also spent a good deal of time marching the streets of Manhattan for worthy causes.

Alexa Stirling Fraser, a childhood friend of Bobby Jones' at the East Lake Country Club in Atlanta, was one of a foursome of teenagers, Jones included, who toured the East Coast during World War I for the benefit of the Red Cross. She would win three Women's Amateurs, 1916, '19, and '20, and then two WMGA championships while representing the North Hempstead Country Club, which "outbid" several other local clubs in bestowing upon Fraser an honorary membership when she lived in New York briefly to pursue a business career.

Among the professionals, "Long Jim" Barnes was Walter Hagen's greatest rival for a number of years. He won the first two PGA Championships (1916 and 1919; with the 1917 and 1918 championships canceled because of World War I), a U.S. Open (1921), and a British Open (1925), but never a Met Open. Barnes represented a number of Met Area clubs, starting with Pelham in 1921, also including Rockwood Hall, Huntington Crescent, Essex County, and North Hempstead.

Gene Sarazen, perhaps the best professional ever to emerge from the Met Area, was born in Harrison, NY, in 1902. Sarazen was nurtured as a caddie at the Apawamis Club and apprenticed as a professional at Brooklawn Country Club in Fairfield, CT, Sarazen was the first golfer to win all four modern majors, capturing the U.S. Open in 1922 and '32, the PGA in 1922, '23, and '33, the Masters in 1935 and the British Open in 1925. No other Met Area professional boasts a portfolio that

Johnny Farrell

"Long Jim" Barnes

includes seven majors. And, other than Sarazen, only three other golfers in the history of the game have won all four modern majors — Ben Hogan, Jack Nicklaus and Gary Player.

"The Squire," as Sarazen was called, represented three Met Area clubs early in his career: the Briarcliff Lodge in Briarcliff, NY, where he is said to have received the highest salary paid to a golf professional at that time; the Fresh Meadow Country Club and Lakeville Club on Long Island.

Johnny Farrell, the longtime professional at Quaker Ridge and Baltusrol Golf Clubs, gained immortality in 1928 by winning the U.S. Open in a playoff against none other than Bobby Jones. A year earlier, he won the Met Open. His other career credits also include the Westchester and New Jersey Opens and a remarkable 10 wins (seven consecutive) during the 1927 campaign.

DEPRESSION AND WAR YEARS

A number of outstanding amateurs represented the Met Area during the Depression and war years, including George Voigt, a top international competitor who almost snipped Bobby Jones' Grand Slam in the bud, leading the immortal Georgian by two holes with five to play in the second round of the British Amateur before faltering; George Dunlap of Pomonok, winner of the 1933 U.S. Amateur; and Robert Sweeney of Meadow Brook, 1937 British Amateur kingpin.

Dick Chapman won the amateur championships of five countries (United States, United Kingdom, Canada, France and Italy) and three states (New York, Connecticut and Massachusetts), but never the Met Amateur. The socialite represented both Greenwich and Winged Foot.

Willie Turnesa, "Wee Willie The Wedge" of Knollwood Country Club, was the youngest of seven legendary golfing

brothers, and the only one to retain his amateur status. Turnesa won the Met Amateur only once, in 1937, but he was not a regular competitor in the event. He also won the U.S. Amateur in 1938 and '48 and the British Amateur in 1947, and played on three Walker Cup teams.

Each of Willie's six brothers enjoyed outstanding careers as playing and teaching professionals. Their record in the PGA Championship alone is impressive, Jim captured the 1952 PGA, Mike was runner-up to Ben Hogan in 1948 and Joe second to Walter Hagen in 1927.

Frank Strafaci, the more accomplished of four golfing brothers (all amateurs), played in roughly the same years as Willie Turnesa, and belonged to several clubs, both public and private. Strafaci captured the Met Amateur a record seven times, in 1938, '39, '45, '46, '47, '50 and '54. His 1938 victory was attained at the direct expense of Turnesa, whom he edged 3 & 1 in the final. Unlike Turnesa, however, Strafaci never made his mark in national or international competition. His best effort in our national amateur championship came in 1949, when he advanced to the quarterfinals, only to be eliminated by Turnesa. These two matches represent the only times the pair met in major competition.

Regarded by many as the best woman player that Long Island ever produced, Helen "Billie" Hicks won the 1931 U.S. Women's Amateur representing Lido Golf Club as well as the 1931 and 1933 WMGA, and was a member of the first American Curtis Cup team. She was the first of the great women amateurs to turn professional, doing so in 1935.

Maureen Orcutt captured 10 WMGA titles over an amazing span of 43 years, 1926-1968. Although never able to win top national honors, Orcutt was runner-up in the 1927 U.S. Women's Amateur at Cherry Valley Club and again in 1936 at the Canoe Brook Country Club. A *New York Times* reporter

Craig Wood   *Willie Turnesa*

who also contributed regularly to *Golf Illustrated*, she played most of her career from the White Beeches Country Club.

Orcutt, who was born in 1907, was a champion from the moment she first wielded a mashie. When her mother, the serious golfer in the family, returned home with the White Beeches club championship, 11-year-old Maureen, who had never played a round of golf, told her she could beat her. A match was arranged immediately, and the indignant mother bet her bag of golf clubs on the outcome, claiming that if she was beaten she would give up the game. Well, young Maureen played her first round in 120 strokes, and edged her mother 1up. The golf bag passed to the new champion, and Mrs. Orcutt kept her word about quitting the game. The daughter learned quickly thereafter, playing in her first U.S. Women's Amateur in 1923, at age 16. She won her first WMGA title as a teenager, and was still winning when she passed her 60th birthday.

Orcutt won 64 women's championships during her career (and lost several others because of her fondness for staying out late dancing), including the Women's Eastern seven times, the New Jersey Women's Amateur 10 times, and the first U.S. Women's Senior Championship, in 1962. She also played on four Curtis Cup teams, including the first, in 1933. Orcutt eventually moved to Durham, NC, where she won her club's championship in 1990 at the tender age of 85!

There were a number of outstanding assistant professionals in the area during this period. One was Ben Hogan, assistant at Century from 1938 to '40 and runner-up in the 1940 Met Open; another, Jimmy Demaret, 1941 Connecticut Open winner while an assistant at Wee Burn; also, Byron Nelson, winner of the 1936 Met Open at Quaker Ridge while an assistant at New Jersey's Ridgewood Country Club. Nelson considered his victory at Quaker Ridge the key to launching his remarkable career.

While golf professional at Metropolis from 1931 to '43, Paul "Little Poison" Runyan captured the 1934 and 1938 PGA championships, the 1934 Met Open, three Met PGAs and six Westchester Opens. He later became a nationally recognized teacher specializing in the short game.

Craig Wood's 264 in the 1940 Met Open at Forest Hill established a new standard for the event. He defeated runner-up Ben Hogan by 11 shots. Wood, then professional at Winged Foot Golf Club, added both the Masters and U.S. Open in 1941, then capped off this magnificent run in 1942 by taking the Met PGA Championship. He also won four New Jersey PGAs and a New Jersey Open while head professional at Hollywood and Crestmont.

POST-WAR ERA

The immediate post-war years were dominated by professionals. Among them was Claude Harmon, the legendary Winged Foot professional, who won the 1948 Masters and completed a rare double in 1951, winning that season's Met Open and Met PGA. He also won six Westchester Open titles.

Another Yonkers native, Doug Ford, sandwiched a victory in the 1956 Met Open between triumphs in the 1955 PGA Championship and the 1957 Masters. Ford served as head professional at four Met Area clubs: Putnam Golf Club; Concord Hotel; Vernon Hills (today's Lake Isle) Country Club, and Spook Rock Golf Course, and during his career also captured four Met PGA crowns.

Wes Ellis was a dominant force in the Met Area in the early 1960s. This four time winner on the PGA Tour (1958 Canadian Open) won three Met Opens, in 1957, '61 and '63; two New Jersey Opens, in 1962 and '63, and four consecutive New Jersey PGAs, from 1961 through 1964. He won eight of

Frank Strafaci

Jerry Courville Sr.

the titles within a four-year span while professional at Mountain Ridge. In 1963 he captured a "Jersey Slam," winning the Met Open at Plainfield, New Jersey Open, and New Jersey PGA. Al Mengert, Echo Lake professional who dominated the Jersey scene before Ellis, accomplished the same feat in 1960.

Al Brosch (the first man to shoot 60 on the PGA Tour) won a record 10 Long Island Opens and a record six Met PGA titles from 1938 to 1959. Likewise, Babe Lichardus won four New Jersey Opens and five New Jersey PGAs during his career. Neither was able to win the Met Open.

The first great amateur to come along in the post-war years was Chet Sanok of Upper Montclair, who remains the only amateur to have won both the Met Open and New Jersey Open (the latter twice). Sanok never won the Met Amateur, but did win the 1975 Ike and five New Jersey Amateurs.

Another great amateur competitor of that era was Bob Gardner of Montclair Golf Club. Gardner authored the greatest streak in Met Amateur history, winning six times between 1958 and 1964. His sole loss came in the 1959 final, to Paul Kelly of Sleepy Hollow Country Club. Gardner's best performance nationally was a runner-up finish to Deane Beman in the 1960 U.S. Amateur. Ironically, he never won the club championship at Montclair — the lightning fast and undulating greens there left him tense before he reached the club gates!

Sharing the local spotlight in women's golf with Maureen Orcutt during the 1950s and 1960s was Carolyn Cudone, winner of five WMGA Match Play Championships (1955, '61, '63-65), and later an amazing five consecutive U.S. Senior Women's Amateur Championships (1968-1972). Cudone also won no fewer than 17 New Jersey Women's Amateur titles, played on the 1956 Curtis Cup team, and was named Curtis Cup captain in 1970. She, like Gardner, was a member of the Montclair Golf Club.

MOVING INTO THE MODERN ERA

As the '60s turned into the '70s, Jimmy Wright dominated the Met Area professional scene. Another moderately successful Tour player, he won the 1969 Met Open, four Met PGAs and a like number of Long Island Opens while representing Inwood and Fenway. He was named Met PGA Player of the Year seven times between 1969 and 1980. His best performance nationally was a fourth-place finish in the 1969 PGA Championship behind Raymond Floyd. He is also remembered for firing a course-record 62 over Westchester Country Club's West Course during the 1976 Westchester Classic.

Next came Jim Albus. Winner of the 1970 and 1984 Met Opens, a pair of Met PGAs and a similar number of Long Island Opens, Albus gained national recognition in 1991 with his first Senior Tour victory over a field that included Jack Nicklaus, Lee Trevino, and Gary Player in the Senior Players Championship at the TPC of Michigan. This win would launch the long-time Piping Rock professional on a Senior Tour career that now includes five wins and more than $3 million in earnings.

Two other Met Area professionals have joined Albus in gaining successful "second careers" on the Senior Tour. Former New Jersey Open winner Jack Kiefer, who has become one of the senior circuit's most consistent players in the early '90s and long-time Pine Hollow professional, cigar-chomping Larry Laoretti, who won the 1992 U.S. Senior Open.

David Glenz is yet another Met Area professional who, like Ellis and Wright, was moderately successful on Tour, but was a dominent figure on the local scene. He won the 1978 and 1986 Met Opens, four New Jersey Opens and two New Jersey PGAs while establishing himself as one of the region's most sought-after instructors at Morris County Golf Club and Crystal Springs Golf Club. In 1986 alone, Glenz won

John Baldwin

David Glenz

four Met-Area "majors" — the Met Open, New Jersey Open, New Jersey PGA, and Nissan Classic. He has been named New Jersey PGA Player of the Year six times, and many believe is destined to make his mark on the Senior circuit when he comes of age in 1999. Glenz's fellow New Jersey professionals Mike Burke Jr. of Mountain Ridge and Knickerbocker's Ed Whitman have also put together outstanding careers.

Among the amateurs to dominate during this era was Jerry Courville Sr., who played out of Shorehaven Golf Club. Jerry Sr. won the Ike Championship a record six times between 1961 and 1970, as well as the Met Amateur in 1973 and 1979 and the Met Open in 1967, the last of these being a four-stroke thrashing of the best Met Area professionals at Winged Foot's West Course. The affable nutmegger's best performance on a national level came in 1974 when he reached the quarterfinals of the U.S. Amateur. Courville also won an MGA Senior, four Ike team events, and in all, captured more MGA titles than any other golfer in history. He was also one of the first recipients of the MGA's Distinguished Service Award.

With five Met Amateur victories (1968, '69, '70, '74, '89) over a 22-year period, and two British Amateur titles (1973 and 1976), Dick Siderowf is perhaps the most internationally accomplished Met Area representative in the last quarter-century. Among his many achievements, Siderowf played on three Walker Cup teams, won the Canadian Amateur, five Conneticut Amateurs, and the Connecticut Open, has competed in numerous U.S. Senior Opens and Amateurs and won the 1996 MGA Senior. He was also the recipient of the first MGA Player of the Year award, in 1976.

As we move into the 80s one name clearly stands above the rest: George J. Zahringer III. Zahringer, who played a limited schedule, captured five Met Amateur titles (1982 and 1984-1987) and a record eight Player of the Year awards between

1979 and 1992. In 1985 he became the only player ever to capture the Met Open and Met Amateur in the same season, and has also had four top-three finishes in the Met Open and finished low amateur eight times. A multiple winner of virtually every Met Area event, including a record five Hochster Memorials, Old Oaks professional Bobby Heins referred to him as the best Met Area player — pro or amateur — after Heins edged Zahringer in a playoff at the Black course at Bethpage to cature his second consecutive Met Open title.

Another top player during this period was Jim McGovern of Hackensack, now playing the PGA Tour, who became the fourth player to win both the Met Open and Amateur when he birdied his way into the Open title at Winged Foot in 1987 and racked up a par-shattering win in the 1988 Met Amateur at Plainfield to hold both titles simultaneously.

Two more names who can not be overlooked and whose talents have stood the test of time are John Baldwin of Meadow Brook and Bob Housen of Manasquan River. A former MGA president and two-time MGA Player of the Year (1990 and 1991), Baldwin established the record for the longest span between Met Amateur victories, winning in 1967 and 1990, and has accumulated dozens of state and local titles. Baldwin's best performance outside the Met Area was a runner-up/medalist effort in the 1984 French Amateur.

Likewise Housen's career has spanned four decades and includes six New Jersey State Amateurs, the 1976 Ike and numerous area titles. Housen also has established himself as one of the nation's top senior amateurs with two low-amateur finishes in the U.S. Senior Open and an appearance in the semi-finals of the U.S. Senior Amateur.

On the distaff side we have Karen Noble, the most accomplished female golfer to represent the Met Area in recent years. Karen is a second generation champion of the New Jersey Amateur (and student of David Glenz). She won

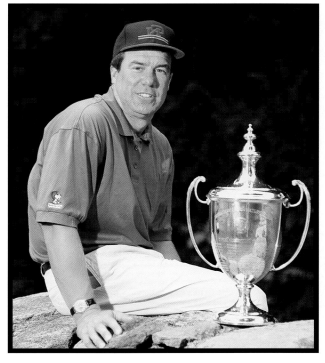

Jerry Courville Jr.   *Darrell Kestner*

in 1987 and 1988, following her mother, who won in 1971. Karen was the WMGA Match Play champion in 1989, U.S. Women's Amateur runner-up in 1988, and with Margaret Platt of the Westchester Country Club one of the stars of the victorious 1991 Curtis Cup team. The Morris County Golf Club member now plays on the LPGA Tour.

Without question, the 1990s have belonged to two outstanding champions, both of whom have won U.S. Mid-Amateur titles. Jeff Thomas, who won his national title in 1993, has been MGA Player of the Year in 1993, 1994, and 1996, has won a record eight New Jersey Amateur titles, as well as the 1996 Ike Championship and Sunnehanna Amateur. In 1996, Thomas came within one match of winning his second national title, losing in the finals of the U.S. Amateur Public Links. Jerry Courville Jr., son of Met Area legend Jerry Courville Sr., won the Ike in 1990 and 1991, and his record-setting Player of the Year season in 1995 also included his national title, a spot in the U.S. Open at Shinnecock Hills, a victory in the Met Amateur, a coveted place on the 1995 Walker Cup team, and an invitation to the 1996 Masters. His continued fine play also secured Courville a birth on the 1996 World Amateur Team.

MGA PLAYERS OF THE YEAR

YEAR	WINNER
1976	Richard Siderowf
1977	Jimmy Dee
1978	Jimmy Dee
1979	George J. Zahringer III
1980	George J. Zahringer III
1981	H.P. Van Ingen Jr.
1982	George J. Zahringer III
1983	Jonas Saxton
1984	Jonas Saxton, George J. Zahringer III
1985	Mark Trauner
1986	George J. Zahringer III
1987	George J. Zahringer III
1988	Ralph Howe III
1989	George J. Zahringer III
1990	John C. Baldwin
1991	John C. Baldwin
1992	George J. Zahringer III
1993	Jeff Thomas
1994	Jeff Thomas
1995	Jerry Courville Jr.
1996	Jeff Thomas

Similarly the professional ranks have been ruled in recent years by two stars, Deepdale's Darrell Kestner and Westchester Country Club's Bruce Zabriski. Kestner, a West Virginia native known for his extraordinary putting skills counts three Met Open conquests among his many titles (1982, 1987, 1995) and is one of only five players in history to claim this many Met Opens. It makes him the only player with a good shot at tying Alex Smith's record of four. Winner of two (1982 and 1986) National Assistant titles, Kestner captured the 1996 National Club Pro title and is the only player ever to have won both. Zabriski's second Met Open win in 1996 came by way of a record-tying 12-stroke victory at Stanwich, one of the finest Met Open performances ever. Zabriski has also been recognized three times by the PGA of America as their Player of the Year, including 1996.

Despite the fact that the breeding ground for golf's best players may have shifted to somewhat warmer climes over the years, the historical achievements and memorable performances documented here reaffirm the Met Area's prominence among the game's great players, past and present. ❍

*16th hole at Atlantic Golf Club,
Bridgehampton, New York.*

Golf Clubs
of
Long Island

including New York City

*The statistical information and course and
slope rating for each course were
those in effect for the 1996 golf season.
The "Forward" tee ratings listed for
each club are women's ratings.*

BETHPAGE STATE PARK

"Tillie's Last Hurrah"

A former Bethpage golfer, who was in London during World War II and witnessed the effects of the German bombing, likened what he saw to a familiar scene back home: "I've seen no bomb craters that I've studied as anxiously as I have that bunker guarding number two of the Black Course. They do come bigger. When the ruins are cleared away plenty of them look more like the third hole from tee to green."

The hazards referred to in this letter are just two of many that confront golfers on perhaps the sternest publinx test in the country, the Black Course at Bethpage State Park, located on the Nassau-Suffolk border in the middle of Long Island. The "Black Monster" likely was the last course created by A.W. Tillinghast. Within two years of its opening, "Tillie" had completely divorced himself from golf and was operating an antiques store in Beverly Hills.

The Black is something special, as if the architect were given "carte blanche" to let his creative juices run wild one last time. For Tillinghast, this meant a trip back to his roots as a young architect, for there is a striking resemblance between Bethpage Black and Pine Valley, the archetype of penal architecture designed by Tillinghast's close friend of many years, George Crump, and which Tillinghast watched evolve. While the Black is less severe than Pine Valley, to the average public-course golfer it is every bit as foreboding and unforgiving, seldom allowing a mishit shot to go unpunished.

In 1695, an Englishman named Thomas Powell purchased a large tract of land on the road joining Jericho on the north with Jerusalem to the south. A passage from St. Matthew's gospel (21:1) provided the obvious name:

"and as they departed from Jericho, a great multitude followed Him, and when they drew nigh unto Jerusalem and were come to Beth'phage, unto the Mount Of Olives."

Literally translated, Beth'phage meant "house of figs," but Powell gave it a looser interpretation as "land of fruit or plenty."

The seeds for golf were planted in 1912 when Benjamin Yoakum, a wealthy railroad magnate, purchased 1,368 acres of rolling woodland and farmland. In 1923, the Lenox Hills Country Club opened on land leased from Yoakum. It was organized as an inexpensive club offering high-class golf to its members at a nominal seasonal fee, and featured a semiprivate 18-hole Devereux Emmet course that would become the basis for Bethpage's Green Course.

Yoakum died in 1930, and four years later the

BETHPAGE STATE PARK
Farmingdale, NY
YEAR FOUNDED: 1934

BLACK COURSE

ARCHITECT:
A.W. Tillinghast

COURSE OPENED: 1936

TEES	PAR	YARDAGE
Forward	71	6556
Middle	71	6556
Back	71	7065

TEES	COURSE RATING	SLOPE
Forward	78.9	146
Middle	73.1	140
Back	75.4	144

GREEN COURSE

ARCHITECTS:
Devereux Emmet
A.W. Tillinghast

COURSE OPENED: 1923

TEES	PAR	YARDAGE
Forward	71	5903
Middle	71	6262

TEES	COURSE RATING	SLOPE
Forward	73.3	125
Middle	69.8	121

RED COURSE

ARCHITECT:
A.W. Tillinghast

COURSE OPENED: 1935

TEES	PAR	YARDAGE
Forward	70	6198
Middle	70	6537
Back	70	6756

TEES	COURSE RATING	SLOPE
Forward	76.0	131
Middle	72.0	125
Back	73.0	127

BLUE COURSE

ARCHITECTS:
A.W. Tillinghast
Alfred Tull

COURSE OPENED: 1935

TEES	PAR	YARDAGE
Forward	72	6213
Middle	72	6513
Back	72	6684

TEES	COURSE RATING	SLOPE
Forward	75.5	130
Middle	71.4	124
Back	72.2	126

YELLOW COURSE

ARCHITECTS:
A.W. Tillinghast
Alfred Tull

COURSE OPENED: 1958

TEES	PAR	YARDAGE
Forward	71	5680
Middle	71	6171
Back	71	6316

TEES	COURSE RATING	SLOPE
Forward	72.2	123
Middle	69.5	120
Back	70.1	121

The long, sandy par-three 17th hole — Black Course.

Bethpage Park Authority was created by New York State Parks Commissioner Robert Moses. During 1934, in the depths of the Depression, construction of a new club-house and three public courses began as a Work Relief project, employing as many as 1,800 men.

The Blue and Red courses opened in 1935, as did the revised Green course, all the work of Tillinghast. So too did the new clubhouse, a rambling Colonial-style building approached via a tree-lined road that ends with a small circular drive paved with Belgian blocks. But Tillinghast took his time refining the Black Course, waiting another year before the public got its first look at what was to become a Met Area legend.

The Blue and Red courses hosted the 1936 USGA Public Links Championship, won by movie extra Paul Abbott. Later that year, the Metropolitan PGA held its annual championship over the Blue; defending champion Paul Runyan of Metropolis retained his title with a 1up decision over Charlie Lacey of Pine Valley.

The Blue underwent a major facelift in 1958, supervised by Alfred Tull, when a fifth course, the Yellow, was added to the park. Holes formerly on the Blue became part of the Yellow, and the new holes built filled out both courses.

All five courses fell into disrepair. In 1982, the Black underwent a six-month refurbishing. Bunkers were restored to their original shape and filled with new sand.

The "Black was back" and able to host the 1984 MGA Public Links to rave reviews. Over the next few years the other four courses were renovated, and by the fall of 1987, it was the Black's turn again, and it is now able to host major area events with its head held high.

From its championship markers, the Black stretches to 7,065 yards with a par of 71, long enough to challenge even the best players. But the course plays tougher because its greens are relatively small and tightly bunkered. Consequently, the Black is a stern test of long–iron play. It also demands accuracy from the tee, necessary for finding the best position in the treelined fairways for attacking the flags.

-WARNING-
THE BLACK COURSE IS AN EXTREMELY DIFFICULT COURSE WHICH IS RECOMMENDED ONLY FOR HIGHLY SKILLED GOLFERS

But if one feature gives the course its character, it is the bunkering. At least eight greens are so tightly protected that the golfer has virtually no unobstructed entrance, almost no chance to roll a shot onto the carpet. Three holes call for heroic drives over massive bunkers if the player desires any kind of shot to the green. Add to this thick, often knee-high rough infested with bunkers and mounds, rough that would not seem out of place at Shinnecock Hills, The National, or Garden City.

A sign at the first tee warns the unwary of the course's difficulty. Most regulars usually play one of the other Bethpage courses.

Among the many classic holes on the Black is the fourth, a short par five bisected, in the Tillinghast tradition, by a huge, steep-faced cross bunker. The bunker, 150 yards from the green, poses a definite threat to the average player's second shot. Then the approach must float in feathersoft over a huge, high-lipped front bunker; go too far and chance a steep drop into an old quarry filled with sand and rough.

The fifth ranks among the strongest par fours in America, calling for a drive over a small rough-infested hill and a huge angled bunker. Taking a greater risk on the tee shot can lead to an easier uphill approach to a saucer-like green surrounded by rough and three huge bunkers.

The tee shot on 12 is possibly the most demanding on the course. The hole is a dogleg left, with tall trees standing watch at the corner. However, the hole gets its character from the huge, cross bunker 240 yards out in the drive zone. Play short or right of the bunker and the hole becomes a par five.

The 5th hole of the Black Course is one of the country's strongest par fours.

The 8th hole of the Black Course is reminiscent of Pine Valley #14.

The 15th is a backbreaker, a long par four that rises 50 feet over its last 35 yards to a small two-tiered green tightly guarded by three bunkers.

The 17th is an imposing par 3, one of the most challenging one-shotters in the Met Area. The long-iron tee shot must carry a pair of massive front bunkers whose high lips conceal a shallow, figure-eight-shaped green. This 17 is not unlike 17 at Pebble Beach —give or take an ocean.

For years, the name Al Brosch was synonymous with Bethpage golf. A graduate of Farmingdale High School, Brosch was Benjamin Yoakum's private caddie at Lenox Hills, and later became the Bethpage professional. Brosch won 10 Long Island Opens and eight Long Island PGA titles. He also won six Met PGA championships, the first in 1938, the last 21 years later in 1959. In 1951, he became the first player to shoot 60 on the PGA Tour.

The Black hosted many important matches, with perhaps the most famous an exhibition on September 29, 1940, that matched Sam Snead against Byron Nelson. Snead won with a superb 68, but he had his problems with the course. Snead is said to have once walked off the Black in disgust, calling it an "unfair test of golf" after his second shot sailed over the fourth green.

The Black Course hosted the first Ike Tournament in 1953; it remains the only public course to have hosted this event while doing so a second time in 1994 (Ed Gibstein the winner). The Red Course hosts the Long Island Open each year, while in 1989, the Black became the first public course to host the Met Open. Defending champ Bobby Heins edged amateur George Zahringer III in a three-hole aggregate playoff after the pair had tied at 210. Zahringer called the Black "The best layout I ever saw, public or private. There is a uniqueness to every hole, and it's gorgeous. You could certainly play any national event here, without question."

The USGA has taken notice, announcing in 1996 that the Black course will host the 2002 U.S. Open. After the Open the world will know what Long Island's golfers have known for years, that the Black course, "Tillie's Last Hurrah," is truly something special. ○

GARDEN CITY GOLF CLUB
"The Old Man's Grave"

As he walked to the 18th tee at Garden City during the semifinals of the 1908 U.S. Amateur, Walter Travis found himself one down to archrival Jerry Travers. Garden City's home hole a relatively short par three over a pond to a devilishly bunkered green. It had already earned a reputation as a giant killer, a hole where any score was possible. Travis was about to discover that firsthand, although he should have been on guard: Garden City was his home club.

Travis' tee shot found the six-foot-deep bunker to the left of the green—the "Travis bunker," as it was called, because it was he who installed it in 1906, then adamantly refused to remove it even though the majority of the membership thought it unnecessarily harsh. Travis' ball refused to be removed that day, remaining in his bunker after two attempts to hit out proved futile. Travers, who had safely found the green with his tee shot, went on to defeat Max Behr in the finals, while Travis no doubt remained on the scene to accept the condolences of his fellow members. "Well, that's one time the Old Man dug his own grave," one of them supposedly said.

While Travis was learning the basics of the game, the Garden City Company (which owned and operated the village of Garden City) decided to establish a golf course to spur the growth of their model community, created by A.T. Stewart in 1869. The Island Golf Links was a nine-hole, public-subscription course for residents and guests of the Garden City Hotel. The architect was Devereux Emmet, a neophyte in golf design, but an excellent player familiar with the best courses at home and abroad. He was assisted by George L. Hubbell, manager of the Garden City Company.

The Links opened in 1897. It earned high praise and proved very popular. Emmet expanded it to 18 holes by the fall of the following year. The layout of the holes remains basically the same today as it was then.

The course can be described in one word: natural. Findlay Douglas called it, "the nearest thing to St. Andrews" he had ever seen. The signature of the course then, as today, was thick rough and grassy mounds. Holes typically demand a drive

1899

**GARDEN CITY
GOLF CLUB**
Garden City, NY

YEAR FOUNDED: 1899

ARCHITECTS:
Devereux Emmet
Walter Travis

COURSE OPENED: 1897

TEES	PAR	YARDAGE
Middle	73	6506
Back	73	6882

TEES	COURSE RATING	SLOPE
Middle	72.0	135
Back	73.7	139

"The Bottomless Pit" in 1900.

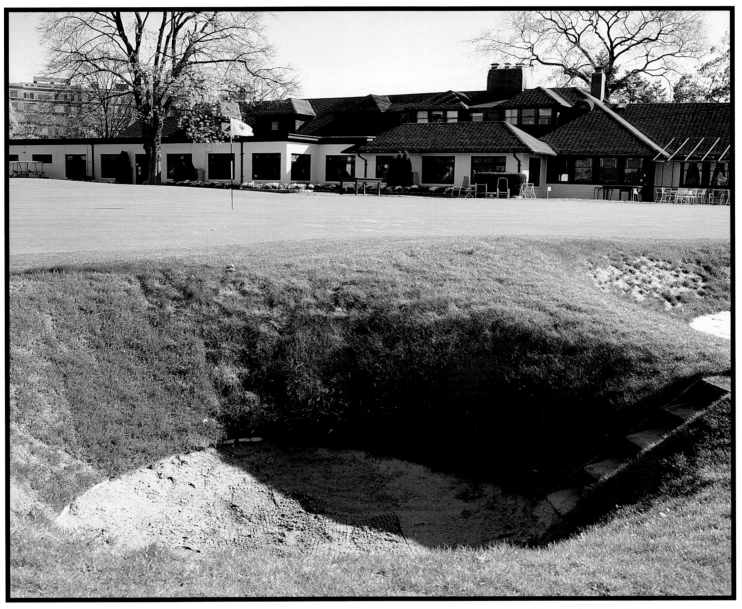

The pot bunker fronting the 18th green.

of 150 yards over rough to reach the fairway, then another carry into the green. Besides intimidation, the rough provides camouflage, hiding trouble, greens, and the proper line of play. The style of hazards reflects Emmet's penchant for cross bunkering and Travis' preference for more penal features, such as deep pot bunkers.

The opening hole is unusual. Its serpentine fairway is difficult to find, hidden by vast expanses of rough, mounds, and bunkers. The player has a choice: a drive left must clear only 100 yards of rough, but then calls for a carry over a pair of bunkers fronting the green; the more ambitious 200-yard carry straight ahead leaves a short, wide-open pitch.

The second is a short par three with a do-or-die carry over the "bottomless pit," a byproduct of the excavation

that provided sand and gravel for the village's streets long before the course was built. Three bunkers (including a tiny pot) within the pit protect the left front, while three others encircle the right and rear.

The drive on the straightway eighth hole must carry 130 yards of rough to reach a fairway that ends abruptly 100 yards from the green. A wide gully, crossed by a road protected behind by a long flat trap, precedes an elevated green that is flanked on both sides by difficult bunkers and is hugged in back by a very deep one. History was made on this hole during the 1913 U.S. Amateur, in the semi-final match between Jerry Travers and Francis Ouimet. Trailing by two holes going to the second tee in the afternoon, Ouimet rallied to catch his rival, then edged ahead at the

WALTER TRAVIS

Australian-born Walter Travis came to this country as a boy. He didn't take up golf until his 30s, playing his first rounds at the Country Club in Flushing, joining the Oakland Golf Club in 1896, then becoming a charter member of the new Garden City Golf Club in 1899. By that time, he had twice reached the semifinals of the U.S. Amateur (1898 and '99), and twice been eliminated by the long-hitting Scot, Findlay Douglas.

Travis was a notoriously short hitter, a fact generally attributed to his slight physique and the age at which he took up the game. To compensate, he was extremely accurate and consistent, and a short-game wizard. He is still regarded as one of the greatest putters of all time. He also was a stickler for the Rules, and usually had little to say to an opponent, preferring to concentrate his attention on his game and the long black cigar that became his trademark.

When the U.S. Amateur came to Garden City in 1900, Travis gained revenge over Douglas with a 2-up victory in the finals. He successfully defended his title the next year at Atlantic City, then won for a third time in 1903 at nearby Nassau. In 1904, a 42-year-old Travis put America on the map with a stunning upset in the British Amateur, the first victory ever by a foreigner. He used a center-shafted "Schenectady" putter (named for the city where it had been made) that had been given to him on the eve of the tournament by Edward Phillips of Apawamis. The Royal & Ancient eventually banned center-shafted putters from British tournaments. Ironically, Travis never again putted well with the Schenectady, although he had used one in 1902 when he finished tied for second in the U.S. Open.

Along with his three U.S. Amateur championships, Travis captured four Met Amateur titles. He also participated in the longest match in Amateur history, taking 41 holes in 1908 to eliminate collegiate champion Henry Wilder in a second-round match.

Travis' last victory came in the final tournament of his career, the 1915 Met Amateur at Apawamis, when he holed a 30-foot putt on the last green. He was 54 years old at the time, and defeated old rival Jerry Travers en route to the finals. During his later years, Travis devoted considerable energy to the editorship of *The American Golfer*, the magazine he founded. The "Grand Old Man" died in 1927.

The club maintains a collection of Walter Travis memorabilia in its "Travis Room."

seventh. On the eighth, he placed his 180-yard approach eight feet from the stick and looked on the verge of pulling further ahead. But Travers responded by placing his approach a mere 10 inches from the cup, a shot that not only won the hole, but turned the tide of the match.

The usual expanse of rough in front of the 16th tee conceals a bunker in the center of the fairway and another pair cutting into the fairway from the right. The ideal drive avoids these hazards and finds the right side of the fairway, leaving an open shot into the green; the more conservative tee shot to the left places an expanse of rough, mounds, and sand between the player and the green, which is protected on the right by four bunkers.

Garden City's home hole is perhaps its most (in)famous. The one-shotter plays across Lake Cornelia, a man-made pond that once was part of the excavation site, to a huge sloping green in front of the clubhouse. A small, eight-foot-deep pot bunker sits dead center in front of the green, with a larger bunker to its right. A narrow sand pit encircles the back of the green, and to the left lies the deep "Travis bunker." The bunkers give this hole the feeling of the 11th at St. Andrews, the famous Eden.

The Club became private in 1899, when the present name was adopted. As the reputation of the course grew, many leading players joined. Herbert Harriman, who won the inaugural Met Amateur, held at Garden City in the spring

The second hole, crossing the Bottomless Pit, today.

of 1899, joined immediately thereafter; he won the U.S. Amateur later that same year. Charles Blair Macdonald and his son-in-law, Henry James Whigham, the country's first two amateur champions, became members in 1900. With Travis, the club listed four U.S. Amateur champions among its members within two years of its inception. Garden City was indeed the hub of golf in the Metropolitan Area.

And it has remained a key player in the region, hosting one U.S. Open (1902), four U.S. Amateurs, one Met Open, six Met Amateurs, an Ike, and a Walker Cup.

Travers won his fourth Amateur at Garden City in 1913. During qualifying, he took a seven at the treacherous 18th, shanking two iron shots into Lake Cornelia; he survived a 12-man playoff to qualify. Ouimet, his 3&2 victim in the semifinals, would rebound a few weeks later to make golf history by upsetting Harry Vardon and Ted Ray in the U.S. Open at The Country Club in Brookline, Mass.

In the 1936 U.S. Amateur, Johnny Fischer overcame a three-hole deficit in the finals to defeat Jock McLean. Fischer evened the match on 18 with a long birdie putt, then won the title with another birdie, from 30 feet, on the first extra hole.

In September, 1924, the Walker Cup matches were held at Garden City. The American team, which included Ouimet, Bobby Jones, Chick Evans, and Jess Sweetser, defeated their British rivals 9-3. Jones missed a downhill, six-foot putt on the final green in foursomes play, resulting in his only loss ever in international team competition.

Travis' memory lives on in many ways at Garden City. Perhaps the best is the amateur match-play tournament that bears his name. The Travis Memorial, held each May, began in 1902 as the Spring Invitational Tournament: The Old Man won that year and the next seven as well, and one last time in 1914 at age 53. The tournament has become one of the most prestigious invitational events in the United States, and a fitting tribute to one of our greatest players. ○

Member John M. Ward, a member of Major League Baseball's Hall of Fame and founder of the Long Island Golf Association.

Nassau Country Club

"Birth Of A Bet"

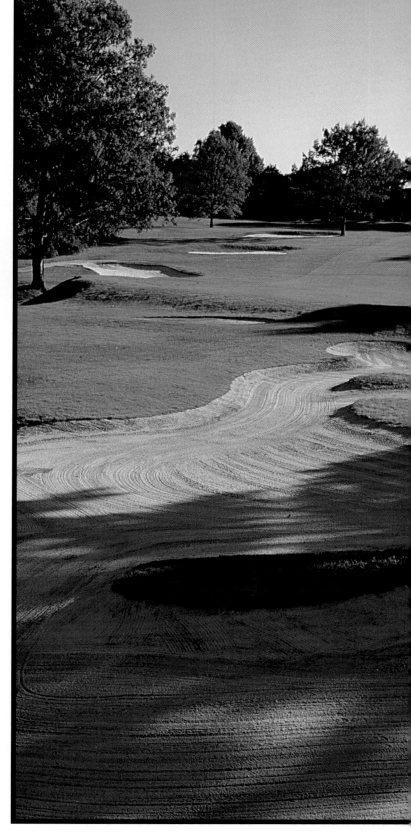

In an article in *The New York Times* in 1957, Findlay Douglas explained the origins of the "Nassau" bet:

"At the turn of the century, inter-club matches were very much in vogue, with the results reported to the local newspapers. Many a prominent socialite and/or businessman would be embarrassed when a defeat by a score such as 7&6 became public knowledge. To avoid such embarrassment, J.B. Coles Tappan, a Nassau member, proposed the three-point match, with the front and back nines worth one point each, and the full 18 holes the other. With this format, the worst possible thrashing would be recorded painlessly as a 3-0 loss, and a player off his game one nine might be able to save one point with a better performance on the other side. So, originally the Nassau bet was a scoring system named for the club of its origin. Later it would become a very popular betting system as well."

Had the timing been slightly different, golfers today would be playing a $5 Queens instead. The club known today as Nassau was originally the Queens County Golf Club, the first to take root on the North Shore's Gold Coast. The name was changed on January 1, 1899, coinciding with the formation of Nassau County out of what had been the eastern part of Queens County.

The Club's patriarch was Charles Pratt, whose Long Island oil business became part of John D. Rockefeller's Standard Oil empire. The founder of Pratt Institute in Brooklyn, Charles Pratt died in 1891, but not before acquiring more than 800 acres in Glen Cove on which he, his six sons, and one of his two daughters built their estates.

Queens County Golf Club was organized on October

NASSAU COUNTRY CLUB

Glen Cove, NY

YEAR FOUNDED: 1896

ARCHITECTS:
Members
Devereux Emmet
Seth Raynor
Herbert Strong

COURSE OPENED: 1899

TEES	PAR	YARDAGE
Forward	72	5545
Middle	70	6275
Back	72	6648

TEES	COURSE RATING	SLOPE
Forward	72.9	126
Middle	70.7	131
Back	72.4	134

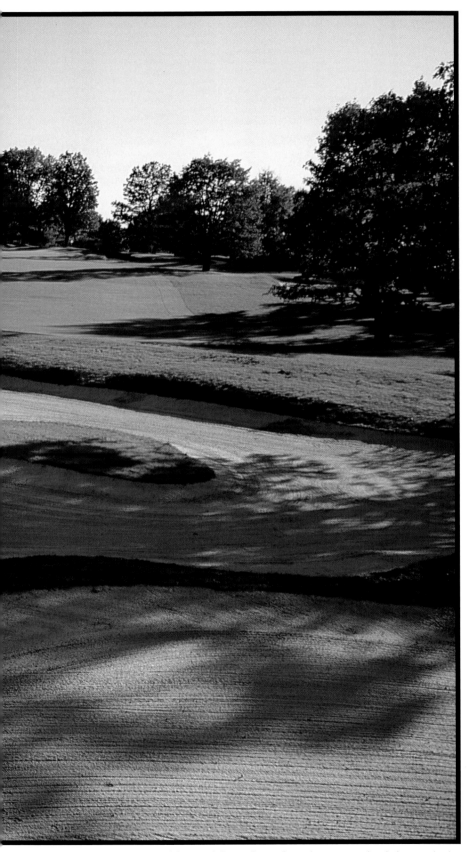

The second shot on the par-five 15th must contend with this cross bunker.

CALAMITY JANE

An old Quaker graveyard sits between the ninth green and 10th tee at Nassau Country Club. The story is told that assistant professional Joe Merkle found a battered putter in that graveyard one night, bandaged it up, and named it "Calamity Jane." Ultimately, that putter would fall into the hands of Bobby Jones on the eve of the 1923 U.S. Open. Jones won that Open and four more, and Calamity Jane became possibly the most famous golf club of all time.

In truth, Calamity Jane originally belonged to Jim Maiden, Nassau's professional from 1908-46, and brother of Stewart Maiden, Jones' mentor at East Lake in Atlanta. Calamity Jane was shafted by Maiden himself, and he gave the club its name, as was his custom with all clubs. Perhaps the inspiration came from a quote found in Robert Browning's "History Of Golf:" "What greater calamity can befall a golfer than a short putt missed. What greater averter of calamity could there be than a long putt holed." The real Calamity Jane was a notorious cattle rustler in the old West, with calamity the fate that typically befell her enemies.

While playing upstate one day, Maiden's caddie misplaced the club, which found its way into another bag. En route back to Nassau by railway express, its hickory shaft split. Maiden gave the wounded club to Merkle, who saved its life, winding it with its now distinctive twine wrapping.

When he arrived on Long Island for the 1923 U.S. Open at Inwood, Jones visited Nassau. Bobby was off his game, particularly his putting. After a practice round, Jones waited on the final green while Jim Maiden retrieved a putter from his shop. On his first stroke, Jones drained a 40-footer. Finding that he could hole six-footers with ease, Jones asked to borrow the putter. He never gave it back. Jones won the Open the following week with the original, made a copy the following year, and used Calamity Jane II through his Grand Slam in 1930.

The original Calamity Jane is on display at Augusta National, with the first copy at the USGA's Golf House museum. Jones made six more copies and gave them to friends. One of these is on display at Calamity Jane House, the halfway house at Nassau's 10th tee.

JERRY TRAVERS

Long before Bobby Jones walked Nassau's fairways, many of golf's elite tested their skills there. Perhaps the most notable was Jerome Dunstan Travers, four-time U.S. Amateur champion (1907, 1908, 1912, and 1913), who won the 1915 U.S. Open at Baltusrol as an amateur.

Travers first played golf at age nine on the front lawn of his family's estate in Oyster Bay. In 1900, at age 13, he began playing regularly at the old Oyster Bay course. Soon after the family joined Nassau in 1902, young Jerry caught the eye of Nassau professional Alex Smith, who approached one afternoon after watching the teenager hit some balls and challenged him to appear at the practice tee the following morning if he wished to make something of himself as a golfer. Travers accepted, and Smith gave him his first lesson that day. The following season, Travers made his first appearance in the U.S. Amateur, held at Nassau, but bowed out in the second round. He also advanced to the finals of the club championship, but lost. In 1904, Walter Travis astounded the world by winning the British Amateur using his now-famous, center-shafted Schenectady putter. From that moment, Travers eagerly anticipated their first meeting in competition.

That came in September in the finals of the Nassau Invitational. Travers earned the right to meet Travis by defeating fellow Nassau member Findlay Douglas 2&1 in the semifinals. Yet Travers felt that his putting was not up to par, and on the eve of the finals switched from a cleek putter to a Schenectady. The match with Travis turned into a battle of the Schenectadies, with both players wielding hot putters. Travers came from behind to even the match on 17, then won with a 12-foot birdie putt on the third extra hole. In addition to his national titles, Travers took the Met Amateur on five occasions — 1906, 1907 (at Nassau), and three in a row, 1911-1913.

24, 1895, and play began that fall on a six-hole course, the first work of Tom Bendelow, who was retained as the pro to teach the game to the Pratts and their friends. By the following summer, the club was incorporated and formally opened with a gala celebration and a nine-hole Bendelow course.

The original location, two miles from the present site, proved inconvenient in the pre-automotive era, so in 1898 the Club purchased land adjacent to the railroad station. The new 18-hole golf course was designed by a committee of members and opened in 1899. The first clubhouse at the new site, designed by Stanford White and similar to his work at Shinnecock Hills, burned to the ground in 1909. The present Georgian brick clubhouse with stained glass windows was completed in 1913.

Nassau's course has been revised several times over the years, notably in 1915 when several new holes were built, again in 1920 (by Devereux Emmet), then finally in 1925 (Herbert Strong) when the present alignment appears to have taken shape. Perhaps the most recognizable hole on the old course was the 17th, called "Pond," a 150-yard par three requiring a 70-yard carry over the water hazard that crosses the current eighth fairway.

The course today is unique in that it includes 14 par fours, three short holes, and one par five. Its reputation rests on its long par fours—particularly holes 6, 7, 8, 11, and 12—which provide a stern test.

The approach across the pond on #8.

The fifth is a gem of a par three in the Raynor style. The plateau green is set above a 15-foot-deep bunker, with similar bunkers left and right and a severe drop-off behind. The putting surface is two-tiered, the upper deck like a balcony curving around the bowl-like main section.

The "lake hole," number eight, is the most dangerous. The fairway rolls downhill toward the lake, which is within reach of longer hitters. Trees and out-of-bounds are close by on the left. The approach typically is played from a down-hill lie over the water, which angles across the fairway from right to left.

The 15th is the only par five on the course, a double dogleg to the left in the Emmet style, with a patch of rough, sand, and mounds (called "the pit") bisecting the fairway at the second turn.

Nassau has hosted two USGA events—the 1903 Amateur, won by Walter Travis, and the 1914 Women's Amateur, won by Mrs. H. Arnold Jackson (nee Kate Harley). Locally, Nassau has hosted eight Met Amateurs, the most of any club, as well as three Met Opens. The 1962 Met Open featured a dramatic duel between Miller Barber and Tom Nieporte that took five rounds to resolve in Barber's favor.

Having hosted the 1996 Met Amateur, won by Ken Bakst, Nassau enters its second century building on one of the great traditions in Met Area golf.   ○

Alex Smith, Travers' mentor, was Nassau's first professional. The Scot from Carnoustie—known as "Miss 'Em Quick" Smith for the speed with which he lined up and played his putts—came to the Club in 1901 and remained for eight years. At first, he seemed destined to play in the shadow of Willie Anderson, four-time U.S. Open champion between 1901 and 1905, with Smith twice the runner-up. But the tide turned when Smith beat Anderson in a playoff for the inaugural Met Open in 1905 at Fox Hills. The following summer, Smith ended Anderson's reign as national champion, in the process becoming the first player to break 300, his 295 seven shots clear of the field. Smith also won the 1910 U.S. Open, outlasting his brother Macdonald Smith and American-born Johnny McDermott in a three-way playoff. Smith added three more Met Open titles, in 1909, 1910, and 1913, giving him four, still the record for that event.

NATIONAL GOLF LINKS OF AMERICA

"Macdonald's Classic Course"

At the turn of the century, the few American golf courses that existed had been built by "golfing illiterates," and could hardly be compared to the great championship tests in the British Isles. Or so thought one Charles Blair Macdonald, who was determined to do something about it in the grandest of fashions.

Macdonald thought himself chosen by divine edict to supervise and govern the growth of the game in the United States. A big man, Macdonald also had a huge ego, and was stubborn and humorless as well. But he was intelligent, articulate, and a stickler for the Rules of golf. Above all else, he was devoted to St. Andrews and everything the Royal & Ancient represented in golf.

In 1872, Macdonald's father, a wealthy man of Scottish descent, sent his son from Chicago to Scotland to be educated at St. Andrews University. It was there he was introduced to golf and developed into a fine player, nearly equal to the best of the day. Upon graduation, he returned to a golfless United States, a time he described as the "dark ages."

In time, golf made it to the U.S., and Macdonald was asked to build a nine-hole layout for the fledgling Chicago Golf Club, which he expanded to 18 holes in 1893, making it the first 18-hole course in this country. He also became involved with the formation of the USGA in 1894, and after a few false starts, won the first "official" U.S. Amateur Championship the following year.

Player, prophet, and protector of the game, Macdonald's lasting contribution will be as an architect. While helping the game grow, he dreamed of building a "classic" course in this country, and figured the Atlantic coastline was the ideal location. In 1900, his business brought him to Wall Street and the die was cast.

In 1901, Macdonald conceived the idea of "transatlantic translation,"

Charles Blair Macdonald statue at National.

whereby he would build a course in this country, including holes that, if not direct copies, embodied the principles of the great holes abroad. His goal was to "build a course that would serve as an incentive to the elevation of the game in America."

He traveled abroad in 1902 and again in 1904, soliciting reaction and suggestions from leading figures in the game and devising a plan. In 1904, an agreement was drawn up incorporating the National Golf Links Of America. Seventy subscribers from around the country contributed $1,000 apiece—before a site was chosen—for a share in a club, which, since its inception, has been one of the most exclusive in the country.

After a four-month stay in Great Britain in 1906, Macdonald returned with surveyor's maps and sketches of the great holes and interesting features of others. He then searched the east coast from Cape Cod to Cape May for the ideal terrain. In the spring of 1907, he found a 205-acre site on the south fork of Long Island, along Sebonac Neck, fronting both Peconic Bay and Bull's Head Bay. "A God-endowed stretch of blessed seclusion," he called it.

The land was of great scenic beauty and Scottish flavor, covered by a dense growth of bayberry, huckleberry, and blackberry bushes. Under the direction of engineer Seth Raynor, the ground was cleared and much soil was moved to create the "natural" settings Macdonald desired.

The official opening took place in September of 1911, and featured an invitational competition won by Harold Hilton, fresh from his victory in that year's U.S. Amateur.

The National was an immediate sensation on both sides of the Atlantic. Bernard Darwin was lavish in his praise, commenting in 1922 that "those who think it is the greatest golf course in the world may be right or wrong, but are certainly not to be accused of any intemperateness of judgment."

From the moment it opened, the

Looking down from the 17th tee, with Peconic Bay in background.

course had an enormous influence on American architecture. It was not an uncommon sight to see delegates from around the country studying The National, taking voluminous notes that they would bring back home. Here is just a taste of what they saw:

"Alps" (the par-four third hole) is Macdonald's version of the famous 17th at Prestwick in Scotland, and almost certainly the toughest hole on the course, not simply due to its extreme length but also because it plays into the prevailing breeze. The drive must cross a large bunker that angles across the beginning of the fairway, challenging the player to cut off as much as he dares. The blind second shot must carry a huge rough-covered saddle-back hill (the Alps) to a wide, rolling green (18,000 square feet) 20 yards past a long bunker. Macdonald offers the average player the

NATIONAL GOLF LINKS OF AMERICA
Southampton, NY

YEAR FOUNDED: 1904

ARCHITECT:
Charles Blair Macdonald

COURSE OPENED: 1911

TEES	PAR	YARDAGE
Forward	73	5811
Middle	73	6409
Back	73	6779

TEES	COURSE RATING	SLOPE
Forward	74.3	133
Middle	72.7	137
Back	74.3	141

alternative of playing the hole as a par five, following the fairway to the right around the hill. Once finished, players ring a bell announcing that the green is clear.

"Redan" (four) copies the famous 15th at North Berwick, Scotland, and is one of the great par threes in America. The green is set on a right-to-left angle to the tee behind a gaping bunker at least 20 feet below green level. An equally ferocious bunker lies in wait at the right rear of the green, which falls away from the shot. A Redan hole appears on most Macdonald courses, the name coming from a fortification that was stormed by the British at Sevastopol in 1855 during the Crimean War.

The "Short" (six) also became a Macdonald staple, a short par three totally surrounded by bunkers, with a large horseshoe-shaped ridge (the "donut") in the center of the green. Darwin described it as "a most terrifying little hole, the green fiercely guarded by a timbered bunker and the hole cut in a hollow shaped like a horse-shoe—a little paradise to which the roads from all other parts of the green are beset with shocks and switchbacks worthy of Coney Island."

"St. Andrews" (seven) is an adaptation of the "Road Hole," the 17th at The Old Course. Although Macdonald didn't have railroad sheds or a hotel protecting the corner of his dogleg par five, he did fill that area with a large expanse of scrub-filled bunkers, and added a surprise bunker left-center in the fairway to catch the unwary golfer hoping to play it safe. A 10-foot-deep pot bunker sits to the left-front of the shallow green, which is angled to the fairway and backed along its full length by a huge bunker, Mac-donald's "road." The ideal approach is a bump-and-run shot played into the opening of the green from the right side of the fairway.

The windmill

"Bottle" (eight) is a par four and the unsung hole at The National. Modeled after a hole at Sunningdale outside London, its character is defined by a series of bunkers that angle across the fairway from the left rough. The golfer may attempt to carry the bunkers to allow a better look at the tightly bunkered, elevated green. More likely, he will choose to fade his drive to the lower part of the fairway and have a limited view of a plateau green behind a nest of deep bunkers.

"Eden" (13) pays homage to the famous par three 11th at St. Andrews. Play revolves around a pair of greenside bunkers: "Strath," a severe pot front and right; and "Hill," larger and left. On the tee, the normal reaction is to avoid Strath, often pulling the shot into Hill. Since the green slopes sharply from back to front, anything less than a delicate explo-sion from Hill may run into Strath. And therein lies the greatness of the design.

"Cape" (14) is the best known of Macdonald's original creations at The National. This par four requires a mod-erate carry over a pond to a tumbling fairway that bends slightly right en route to a green that is almost totally surrounded by sand. Unlike later adapta-tions of this design, this Cape offers little incentive to gamble off the tee and try cut-ting the corner of the dogleg.

The water in front of the tee of "Punchbowl" (16) is the least of the problems. The ideal line on the par four requires a good poke to clear a large bunker on the right side of the fairway. The more conservative drive to the left may roll down into a deep grassy bowl or worse, stop on the inner side of the bowl, from which a full shot is vir-tually impossible. There is a similar hazard on the right to catch a pushed or sliced drive. The green, set in a small punchbowl 20 yards behind a huge cross bunker, cannot be

The intriguing eighth, which gives the golfer an option from the tee.

Looking around the Alps at the third green and bell tower.

seen from the fairway. (Back in 1919, a member thought that a windmill would look rather nice sitting on the hillside overlooking the green, so Macdonald had a 50-footer built and left the bill in the member's locker.)

In 1986, "Peconic" (17) was rated by *GOLF Magazine* as the 10th best hole in the country, quite an accolade for a relatively short par four. From the elevated tee, the golfer has a beautiful view of Peconic Bay. When he focuses his attention on the task at hand, he will once again face a choice: The ideal drive must be on the left side of the fairway, but must carry a morass of rough and bunkers requiring a solid stroke of at least 200 yards; the more conservative drive to the right must skirt a couple of fairway bunkers, and leaves an approach that will have to carry a large inverted bunker that hides the putting surface from sight.

"Home" (18), a par five, plays slightly uphill past the clubhouse on the left, with Peconic Bay at the foot of the hill along the right. Two large bunkers in the left rough force most drives to the right. Then the second must carry a cross bunker and thread its way through a series of traps. Should either the second or third shot be pushed, or the final approach played too firmly, the ball will likely take a "sheer drop into unspeakable perdition," to quote Darwin, who praised the hole as the finest finish in the world. Arnold Palmer once tempted "perdition," trying to draw his second shot around the flagpole that stands at the edge of the cliff in front of the clubhouse. Arnie's ball was never seen again.

Other players have found how dangerously close the three-story, gray stucco clubhouse comes into play. The story is told of the golfer who hooked his second shot on 18 onto the roof, walked up to the second floor, into an occupied bedroom, climbed out the window, and played his ball from the rain gutter back to the fairway. That is the true spirit of Macdonald, who strictly believed in "play it as it lies."

The clubhouse formally opened in 1912. The original intent had been to use the old Shinnecock Inn, located near the 9th green and 10th tee, but it burned to the ground before the course was finished. The new clubhouse, built on the high ground overlooking Peconic Bay, is famous for two things: a world-renowned luncheon and the life-size statue of Macdonald in the library, which, legend has it, the great man commissioned and then billed the membership.

The first Walker Cup matches were held at The National in 1922. The American team won by a score of 8-4, no surprise since all eight team members—Bobby Jones, Francis Ouimet, Jess Sweetser, Chick Evans, Robert Gardner, Jesse Guilford, Max Marston, and W.C. Fownes— were or would become U.S. Amateur champions.

Macdonald spent most of his last 30 years at The National—his home was on the hillside across Bull's Head Bay—tinkering with the course, trying to make it perfect. Late in life he admitted that, even then, he was not sure the course was "beyond criticism." He died in 1939, and was buried in nearby Southampton.

Nothing would have pleased Macdonald more than to have been called the "father of American golf." But he was too stern, too gruff, too uncompromising to win that prize. Yet looking objectively at his life and accomplishments, there is no doubt that no one else came close to matching his contributions to the sport in its early years in this country.   ○

SHINNECOCK HILLS GOLF CLUB

"The French Connection"

During the winter of 1890-1891, a young Scottish golfer named Willie Dunn was in southern France building a golf course at Biarritz, a favorite watering spot of the rich and famous. Three Americans from the exclusive Southampton colony also were in Biarritz, enjoying a winter respite. William K. Vanderbilt, Duncan Cryder, and Edward Mead had heard about golf and its popularity in Britain, and asked Dunn if he might demonstrate the game for them. He took the trio to the famous "chasm hole," a 125-yarder across a deep ravine, and hit several balls, all of them onto the green, some quite close to the hole. "This beats rifle shooting for distance and accuracy. It is a game I think would go in our country," exclaimed Vanderbilt. So were planted the seeds that ultimately grew into one of America's greatest championship courses, Shinnecock Hills.

Before leaving France, the three Americans determined to build a golf course in Southampton, one they believed would be the first in their country, and converted fellow Southamptonite Samuel Parrish to their cause. That summer they contacted the Royal Montreal Golf Club for help in designing a course. The club granted its professional, Willie Davis, a month's leave of absence, and he designed what, due to budgetary restrictions, turned out to be a 12-hole layout.

Beatrix Hoyt

Davis employed a crew of 150 Shinnecock Indians from the nearby reservation for the difficult task of building the course. He later recalled:

"Except for several horse-drawn roadscrapers, all the work was done by hand. The fairways were cleaned off and the natural grass left in. The rough was very rough, with clothes-ripping blueberry bushes, large boulders, and many small gullies. The place was dotted with Indian burial mounds and we left some of these intact as bunkers in front of the greens. We scraped out some of the mounds and made sand traps."

Shinnecock Hills Golf Club was formally organized in August of 1891 and incorporated on September 21, becoming the first such legal entity in the country.

The clubhouse was completed in June of 1892, the first building of its kind in the United States, and quickly became a focal point for the Southampton social set. It was designed by Stanford White, the most fashionable architect of the day. A "jack of all arts," and a favorite in New York social circles, White is among those credited with bringing the Renaissance (of architecture) to America. His previous credits included Penn Station and the original Madison Square Garden, where he lived in a "tower studio."

White was destined to gain even more notoriety in death. He was murdered in 1906 by the husband of his former lover during a performance at the Garden. The ensuing trial was one of the most sensational in the city's history.

Golf quickly became a fad at Southampton, especially among women. The original 12-hole course became so crowded that another nine holes (the Red Course) were laid out in 1893 just for the ladies.

By October of 1891, word of the Southampton course reached John C. Ten Eyck of St. Andrew's in Yonkers. Ten Eyck visited Samuel Parrish at his New York office and invited him to St. Andrew's for a game, marking the first time players from different clubs played together in America.

Willie Dunn reentered the picture in 1895 when he expanded the 12-hole course to 18, the second of its kind in the country (behind the Chicago Golf Club). Dunn served

SHINNECOCK HILLS GOLF CLUB

Southampton, NY

YEAR FOUNDED: 1891

ARCHITECTS:
Willie Davis
Willie Dunn
Charles B. Macdonald
Howard Toomey
William Flynn

COURSE OPENED: 1931

TEES	PAR	YARDAGE
Forward	70	5375
Middle	70	6248
Back	70	6821

TEES	COURSE RATING	SLOPE
Forward	72.1	124
Middle	72.1	135
Back	74.6	145

From behind the 18th green at sunset.

a couple of years (1894-1895) as Shinnecock professional.

The railroad from New York, two and a half hours away, intersected the new course, coming into play on four holes on the front nine. It also carried many pilgrims to the end of Long Island to study the first legitimate golf course in the region, (re)designed as it was by a famous Scottish professional.

The U.S. Amateur and Open championships of 1896 were the second such pair to be held under the auspices of the USGA, and were staged concurrently at Shinnecock (a practice discontinued after 1897). The Amateur was by far the more important event. It was the first of back-to-back titles captured by H.J. Whigham, son-in-law of C.B. Macdonald, founder of neighboring National. A recent graduate of the Scottish links, Whigham used an unusual "wooden putter" to great effect, running his short approaches onto the greens rather than pitching them as his rivals did.

The Open was merely a one-day "add-on" to the Amateur, and was won by James Foulis, professional at the Chicago Golf Club. Among the contestants were Davis, Dunn, and two Shinnecock Indians, John Shippen and Oscar Bunn, both 21 years old and former members of the work crew that built the course five years earlier. Shippen, in contention until a disastrous 11 on the short par-four 13th, where his tee shot found a sandy road, eventually tied for fifth place. The son of a black minister and a Shinnecock woman, he was the first black to compete in the U.S. Open. But Shippen's participation led to a rebellion of the white professionals, who refused to play until USGA President Theodore Havemeyer threatened to conduct the tournament with just the two Shinnecock entrants.

The galleries for the championships were predominantly female, and for good reason. Shinnecock Hills could be considered the birthplace of women's golf in the U.S. It was

The 11th, one of America's great short par threes.

the women's enthusiasm that led to the rapid growth of the Club. They had the Red course to themselves, although they could earn the privilege of playing the White by submitting three attested scores from the Red to prove their readiness.

The White course measured just 4,423 yards, a weakness that was exploited during the '96 championships. That was corrected by 1901 when the Red course was abandoned, leaving more land for the White course. In 1916 Macdonald and Seth Raynor authored a significant revision in the course. The present seventh, ninth, and 17th holes date to this time.

The first four U.S. Women's Amateur titles were won by ladies from Shinnecock Hills. Mrs. C.S. Brown won at Meadow Brook in 1895. Then Beatrix Hoyt, America's first female teenage phenomenon, won three consecutive titles (1896-1898), was the medalist five consecutive years (1896-1900), then abruptly retired from competitive golf at age 20 less than two months after losing on the 20th hole in the semifinals in 1900 at her home course. In 1899, Hoyt helped organize

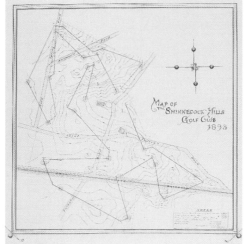

the Women's Metropolitan Golf Association, although she never played in any of its competitions.

In 1928, Suffolk County extended Sunrise Highway through the Hamptons. The right-of-way cut through the old course, so the club engaged the team of Toomey & Flynn to design a new one. Future architect Dick Wilson supervised the construction, which was completed by 1931. All but a few of the present holes took life at this time.

Located between the Atlantic Ocean and Peconic Bay, both within two miles, the links course is usually buffeted by strong winds, with the prevailing breeze from the southwest. Under these conditions, the longer par fours generally play downwind, the shorter ones into the breeze. The sandy terrain is dotted with nearly 150 bunkers, although on most holes they do not front the greens, giving the golfer the option of playing a run-up under the wind.

The challenge to the longer hitters comes in finding the flat areas in the often severely undulating terrain. For the average player, simply reaching the island fairways can be a challenge. Most tee shots must carry a sizable expanse of rough and sand. Many of the tees on the longer holes are elevated, offering the player a panoramic view of the hazards he must battle. And there is rough—thin, whispy, reedlike, often knee-high, capable of altering the path of the clubhead—lurking alongside the fairways, placing an even greater premium on accuracy. The course is an outstanding example of both the penal and strategic schools of architecture.

There are many outstanding holes at Shinnecock Hills. Here are but four.

The sixth, a long par four, is a rugged test, especially for the average player, who can barely see the fairway beyond a vast expanse of mounds, sand, and high rough. The fairway angles to the right, then bends around a pond 50 to 75

yards short of the green. The average player most likely will be forced to play to the left, short of the pond, then approach directly over a deep greenside bunker. Once called the "Pond Hole," the sixth was the centerpiece of the new course when it opened in 1931. Dunes extended from tee to green along the right, but there was an "oasis of fairway" on that side that offered the better player the chance of getting home in two, if he dared a 200-plus-yard drive over a "mass of tumbling dunes" that preceded the target. It was this same characteristic that made the "Channel Hole" at Lido so famous.

The ninth bends left, forcing the longer hitters to cut the corner to avoid driving through the fairway. From the landing area, the fairway rolls through a series of dramatic wavelike undulations before reaching the foot of the dramatically elevated green. The embankment leading up to the green is covered with rough and four bunkers. The green sits on a plateau in front of the clubhouse, well above the fairway and seemingly unprotected.

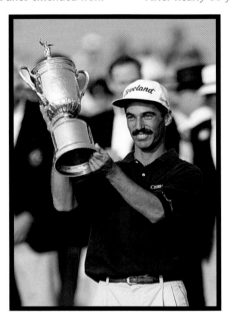

1995 U.S. Open Champion Corey Pavin.

The 11th is a superb little par three that requires a "do or die" shot to a heavily-bunkered, severely-contoured green. Four bunkers, set some 15 feet below the putting surface, guard the front and right side of the green, which falls away to the right and rear. A chip from beyond or to the left of the green may easily run right through the putting surface. *GOLF Magazine* rated this hole among the 100 best in the country in 1986.

From its highly elevated tee near Charlie Thom's (Shinnecock professional from 1906-1961) cottage, the 14th plays down into a valley, then up a tree-lined fairway that narrows as it approaches the green. The drive must be

accurate, avoiding bunkers left and right some 200 yards from the green, and the second shot must be threaded through a very narrow entrance to a green set beyond four bunkers. (Another of *GOLF*'s best 100 holes.)

After nearly 80 years out of the tournament limelight, Shinnecock Hills hosted the 1977 Walker Cup, won by the American team 16-8. In 1986, the U.S. Open came for the second time—giving the world its first extended viewing of the course. After a wet, blustery first day that would have been considered awful by British Open standards, the players and the weather settled down. The final day belonged to Raymond Floyd, who, at 43, became the oldest player to win the U.S. Open championship. His 75-68-70-66= 279 left him the only player under par, and his 111 putts established a new Open record. Victory did not come easily, however, for it was not until the 14th hole of the final round that Floyd surged to the front, vaulting over nine players who had led him with nine holes to play.

Shinnecock Hills was chosen to host the Centennial U.S. Open in 1995, a championship that will be remembered for Corey Pavin's decisive 4-wood approach in gusting winds to within six feet on the 72nd hole, sealing a two-stroke victory over Greg Norman. Pavin's final-round 68 for 280 led Norman by two and Tom Lehman by three. Neal Lancaster fired an Open-record 29 on the back nine to close with 65 and a tie for fourth.

More than a century (and three golf courses) after its founding, Shinnecock Hills remains one of America's treasured golf courses, capable of testing the world's leading players.   ❍

ATLANTIC GOLF CLUB

"Play Me"

ATLANTIC GOLF CLUB
Bridgehampton, NY

YEAR FOUNDED: 1990

ARCHITECT:
Rees Jones

COURSE OPENED: 1992

TEES	PAR	YARDAGE
Forward	72	5296
Middle	72	6573
Back	72	6940

TEES	COURSE RATING	SLOPE
Forward	72.4	128
Middle	72.3	132
Back	74.0	136

For more than a century, the Hamptons at Long Island's East End have been a fashionable place for New Yorkers looking to beat the heat of Summer in the "Big Apple." The residents of the region have been keenly aware of the threat to their ecological and social stability presented by overcrowding, and so have vigorously resisted new development.

One consequence of this is the small number of private golf courses, and newcomers to the Hamptons have come to learn that obtaining membership in a private club is nearly impossible to obtain.

Lowell Schulman, a successful real estate developer in Westchester County, was one such person who loved the enticing summer breezes and beautiful beaches of the East End. Schulman, who possessed an extensive collection of golf memorabilia and a deep love for the game's traditions, found the area's lack of golf courses and available memberships disconcerting.

During a weekend in the Hamptons in 1988 Schulman decided on the spot to

The short par-three 11th.

build his own course. That very weekend, he looked at a parcel of land which, he said, cried out, "Play Me." The spot was the 203-acre Equinox Farm of Francesco Calesi, off Scuttle Hole Road north of Bridgehampton. As farmland, it was just marginal, and was slated for residential development. But its glacial topography, ridges and swales, wetlands, deep kettle ponds, and distant view of the ocean four miles away excited Schulman. He summoned architect Rees Jones, who agreed that a world-class course could be built on the land—and, indeed, that many of the holes were already there, just waiting to be crafted.

Calesi needed little persuading that a golf course was better than more housing. Not surprisingly, Schulman moved quickly. Despite the high cost of the land and expected development costs, there was little trouble attracting future members willing to invest in what promised to be something truly special.

Schulman did, however, encounter resistance from environmentalists, so he engaged Tom Julius and Dave Schonberger as project managers to shepherd the project through the environmental approval process. Julius prepared what might be the most comprehensive environmental study ever for a golf course. Permission to build the course was finally obtained in February of 1990, but Jones' routing had to be changed several times to satisfy environmental concerns. Despite the delays and required changes, Atlantic is today a shining example of how a golf course can not only exist in harmony with the environment, but actually enhance the land's environmental quality.

Atlantic opened in 1992 to rave reviews, winning *Golf Digest's* "Best New Private Course" award. In its short history, it has gained national prominence and praise, not an easy accomplishment considering the stature of its famous neighbors— Shinnecock Hills, National, and Maidstone.

Atlantic's clubhouse came a year later. Designed by Jaque Robertson in the traditional, understated East End shingled style, it features deep porches offering a striking view out over the 18th hole.

In 1995, Atlantic hosted its first major championship, the Met Open. The tournament resolved into a battle between two of the leading professionals in the region, Darrell Kestner and Bruce Zabriski. Kestner prevailed, but only after a three-hole-aggregate playoff. The pair finished on even terms after the regula-

From behind the first green.

tion 54 holes at eight-under-par 208. These fine scores are a bit misleading, however, as Atlantic did not have its expected ally, the wind, on hand for the three days of the tournament.

Most of the holes on the links-like course are lined by a stunning variety of knobs, mounds, and moguls, creating bowl–like settings. Perhaps the most fearsome shot is the drive on the par-five 13th hole, which must carry 200 yards over a forested gully well below the fairway. Just as demanding is the tee shot on 14, a 90-degree-right dogleg

Rees Jones and Lowell Schulman

par four with two large bunker complexes set in deep rough where the tumbling fairway turns. Similarly the long par-four fifth requires a solid tee shot over a winding, sinewy bunker guarding the angled entrance to the fairway.

The greens are framed by mounding and moguls to accentuate the target, and feature subtle rolls rather than bold contours. Most of the greens are protected by large bunkers that partially close entranceways, creating a dogleg effect on approaches. But from the appropriate side of the fairway, the path is open for a British-style bump-and-run approach under the wind. The foreign flavor is heightened by the seaside grasses, blowing in the breeze, that give Atlantic so much of its character and look.

For a new course Atlantic has a remarkable feel of "always being there." In many respects, it recalls golf's British heritage, which makes for an easy fit with its historic and Scottish-flavored neighbors.　　　○

THE CREEK CLUB

"The Best Of Both Worlds"

THE CREEK CLUB
Locust Valley, NY

YEAR FOUNDED: 1922

ARCHITECTS:
Charles Blair Macdonald
Seth Raynor

COURSE OPENED: 1923

TEES	PAR	YARDAGE
Forward	71	5480
Middle	70	5980
Back	70	6454

TEES	COURSE RATING	SLOPE
Forward	72.0	127
Middle	69.9	127
Back	71.5	130

The Creek Club was organized in 1922 by a committee of 11 distinguished Long Island sportsmen: Vincent Astor, George Baker Jr., Marshall Field, Clarence Mackay, J.P. Morgan, Herbert Pratt, Harry Payne Whitney, John Ryan, Harvey Gibson, Frank Crocker, and Charles Blair Macdonald, who designed the golf course. They named their club after Frost Creek, an inlet of Long Island Sound that was to play a significant role in the character of the first five holes on the back nine. The species of bird that inhabits the marshes between the 13th and 14th holes has been adopted as the club's logo, and is called the "Creek bird."

The Club's brick Colonial clubhouse, featuring a dining room on a closed-in porch overlooking Long Island Sound, was unveiled in 1927. A stable was turned into the Club's Dormie House, a male retreat overlooking the first tee.

The Creek was one of the few clubs in the United States to have bathing and yachting facilities on its property, as well as a 1,200 foot beach, swimming pool, and casino for dining and dancing. Members were able to anchor their yachts at the Beach Club, and

The view from the sixth tee, showing #6 (left), #16, and #17 (right), with Long Island Sound as a backdrop.

The long par-three 11th hole.

commence their round at the tenth tee.

The course, built by Seth Raynor, offers the "best of both worlds"—a mix of parkland holes and seaside links. The club also built a tide gate to insure a constant water level on the seaside holes, which offer splendid views of Long Island Sound.

None more so than at the sixth tee, where the golfer can enjoy one of the most breathtaking vistas in Met Area golf, with both Greenwich and Stamford in sight across the Sound. The hole plays from a tee elevated far above a tumbling fairway. The angled punch-bowl green is set behind a huge, mounded bunker in front.

At the 10th, the course reaches the beach, which parallels the left side of the fairway from drive zone to green. Like many "Cape" holes, the drive demands a carry over water, here an inlet that crosses the fairway from left to right, giving long hitters the tantalizing option of going for the green if the wind is right. The par-three 11th plays back across the inlet to one

Joe Dey

of the largest and longest greens in the Met Area.

The 13th and 14th holes pack a powerful one-two punch. The former turns nearly 90 degrees to the right beyond the drive zone, leaving all but the longest hitters with a long carry over a forest of reeds to a lightly-bunkered green. Much of the 14th fairway is hidden by the reeds, which demand a do-or-die carry; the hole bends right, then crosses Frost Creek before rising to an elevated, sloping green.

Prominent among The Creek's members was Joseph C. Dey, Jr., who served the USGA as Executive Secretary from 1934 to 1968, then became the first commissioner of the Tournament Players Division of the PGA, from 1968 to 1973. Dey was elected to the World Golf Hall of Fame in 1975, the same year he became only the second American to be named captain of the Royal & Ancient at St. Andrews. And where better to play the Royal & Ancient game than on the picturesque, challenging links at The Creek. ❍

ENGINEERS COUNTRY CLUB

"The Flight Of The Bumblebee"

ENGINEERS COUNTRY CLUB
Roslyn Harbor, NY

YEAR FOUNDED: 1917

ARCHITECTS:
Herbert Strong
Devereux Emmet
Frank Duane

COURSE OPENED: 1918

TEES	PAR	YARDAGE
Forward	73	5636
Middle	70	6330
Back	70	6656

TEES	COURSE RATING	SLOPE
Forward	73.0	126
Middle	70.5	125
Back	71.9	128

Engineers was established in 1917 by members of the Engineers Club of Manhattan, a swank social group comprised of wealthy, blue-blooded engineers. They purchased the 210-acre Willett Manor House and estate in Roslyn Harbor, which featured a boat house and jetty on Hempstead Bay. The rambling brick and frame manor house, overlooking the water, was converted into a clubhouse, but leveled by fire on November 2, 1917, just after the inaugural ball. Rather than rebuild, the extensive stables on the grounds were converted into an unusual, but thoroughly modern, clubhouse.

The engineers engaged architect Herbert Strong and gave him a simple mandate: Build 18 holes unlike any others in the country. He had the course ready for the 1918 season, and served as the club's golf professional for two years.

Engineers hosted two national championships in its first four years. The first was the 1919 PGA Championship, the second edition of that event. Jim Barnes repeated—he had won in 1916, before World War I interrupted—defeating Fred McLeod 6&5 in the finals. The professionals and tournament officials were lavish in their praise of the course and club facilities, so the club was offered the next year's U.S. Amateur.

Bobby Jones was on hand in 1920 as a carefree 18 year old feasting on pie-a-la-mode at lunch between rounds. According to Jones, it was after this event that he began to take the game more seriously, worrying if he would ever break through and win a major tournament.

In the finals of the Amateur, Chick Evans played superb golf to defeat Francis Ouimet 7&6: During one 19-hole stretch, Evans needed just 71 strokes. Two matches early in the championship have received more attention in retrospect than the finals. In the second round, Evans was fortunate to get by Reggie Lewis of Greenwich: One down going to 18, Evans pulled his drive into a bunker, then left his recovery in the rough 100 yards short of the green. Lewis was just over the green in two, seemingly in position to close out the match. Evans pitched to 14 feet, then Lewis, with just a fair chip, put his ball inside Evans'. To prolong the match, Evans had to sink his putt, and Lewis miss his—which is exactly what happened! Evans eventually won on the 41st hole, one of the longest matches in Amateur history.

Jones advanced to the semifinals, where he was eliminated by Ouimet 6&5. He later considered that match his "last trouncing as a kid," with an incident on the seventh green during the afternoon round ending his childhood. As he was about to putt, a bee landed on his ball. Jones chased it away, but it returned. He chased it again, and this time it came to rest on the green nearby. A gallery official placed his megaphone over the bee, which promptly escaped through the mouth-

The treacherous approach to the 16th green.

The (in)famous 14th hole, then (70 years ago) and now, in semi-retirement.

piece, and flew back to Jones. Bobby chased the bee around the green, finally persuading it to leave. He returned to his ball and three-putted, falling another hole behind at a crucial juncture in the match.

Spurred by the publicity of two national championships, Engineers took its place among the leading American clubs, its facilities considered among the most luxurious in the country. Devereux Emmet remodeled the course in 1921, rebuilding several greens and giving the 18th hole its dogleg. It was regarded as one of the toughest courses in the country, the "last word in golf construction, or even a couple beyond that," to quote one journalist of the era. Some thought Engineers the finest course in the country; others felt it was no more than a "bag of tricks."

It certainly is an old-fashioned course, replete with several blind shots, that has undergone little revision over the years. On many holes, greenside bunkers are set away from the putting surface, many well ahead of the green. A number of greens are at ground level, and most of the putting surfaces are severely undulating. The 16th is one of the great short par fours in the Met region. The tee is well below fairway level, and the drive must avoid a pair of bunkers left and a drop-off to trees, waste bunkers, and out-of-bounds right. The fairway drops into a ravine in front of the green, with trees narrowing the approach from both sides. A brook curls through the ravine, with out-of-bounds just to its right. Two bunkers front the green in the ravine, and there is another to the right of the green.

Encroaching trees tighten the 18th fairway, as does a fairway bunker to the left. From there the hole rolls down hill into a gully before rising to a green bunkered left and rear. The putting surface breaks to the right rear from a mound at the left side. Behind the green the terrain rises to shrubs and out-of-bounds.

Engineers' glory days ended with the Depression. By 1932 only a small group of original members remained, so the Club closed. A bank ran Engineers until 1938, at first as Roslyn Harbor Country Club, then as Engineers, before operating it as a public course called Rolling Hills. In 1946, as Engineers, the course hosted

the MGA Public Links Championship.

In 1952, a group from the Oceanside Golf & Country Club joined with several individuals from the north shore to purchase Engineers. The new members made extensive renovations, and the club reopened in 1952. But on January 20, 1954, a fire leveled most of the old clubhouse. After a difficult year in makeshift facilities, the Club unveiled its ultramodern new clubhouse in 1955.

The golf course has changed little over the years. In 1970, local architect Frank Duane designed the present par-three third hole, causing the elimination of the short, though (in)famous 14th, the old "2 or 20" hole situated between the present 14th green and 15th tee. The 90-yard par three played over a frontal bunker to a tiny plateau green perched precariously atop a steep hilltop. Two bunkers protected the right side, one was left, and another pair sat at the rear of the green (preventing errant shots from rolling 90 feet down the hillside into formidable rough). It was once written about the 14th that "more malediction, praise, and lamentation has been bestowed upon this particular creation than any other short hole in existence." Two golfing immortals, Bobby Jones and Gene Sarazen, went for "double figures" on this hole. A "bag of tricks?" How about "an engineering marvel?"   ○

FRESH MEADOW COUNTRY CLUB

"A Tale Of Two Clubs"

**FRESH MEADOW
COUNTRY CLUB**
Great Neck, NY

YEAR FOUNDED: 1922

ARCHITECT:
Charles Alison

COURSE OPENED: 1923

TEES	PAR	YARDAGE
Forward	74	5873
Middle	70	6448
Back	70	6700

TEES	COURSE RATING	SLOPE
Forward	74.0	129
Middle	71.3	130
Back	72.4	133

Late in the summer of 1921, representatives of the Golf Course Construction Company approached the Unity Club, a social organization serving Brooklyn, with a proposal to purchase 106 acres of farmland in Queens and build an 18-hole golf course. The idea appealed to the club even though the vast majority of its members knew little about the sport and the round-trip between Flushing and Brooklyn would have turned a round of golf into an all-day affair.

By late November, interest was lagging, and the Company was entertaining other offers. Encouraged by Nathan Jonas, a respected community leader and member of the Unity Club, the deal was consummated. Although the new club was named for an area northeast of Flushing, it was located just south of what is now the Long Island Expressway, near 183rd Street.

From the beginning, Fresh Meadow traveled first class. The members wanted their course to be one of the country's great examinations of golf, up to testing the leading players in major competition. To this end, they engaged A.W. Tillinghast to design the course, which opened in 1923. The following newspaper report is typical of the reception it received:

"News of the Tillinghast Course" in Flushing, New York, had started to spread throughout the golfing world. When the course was officially opened large numbers of golf celebrities and experts came from far and near to test its rigors. What they found was a course in exquisite condition, as though it had been groomed for a decade, and of scenic delight. It contained holes of fascinating variety, some fairways finding their way through groves of towering trees, others with water obstacles on the way to the greens; doglegs with treacherous sand traps as they curved around corners to the left and to the right; out-of-bounds galore to plague the 'hooker' and 'slicer' alike; the famous Tillinghast pear-shaped greens fiercely trapped. All these features created one of the finest tests of golf anywhere."

The new course was dedicated on September 8, 1923. Nine days later, the clubhouse burned to the ground. Typical of the membership, it was rebuilt on an even grander scale, and opened late in 1924.

Gene Sarazen was hired as professional in 1925. The Squire brought along his mentor, Al Ciuci, to teach and run the shop. Ciuci remained until 1972.

Fresh Meadow gained national prominence during the 1930 PGA Championship. Tommy Armour won the title after a back-and-forth struggle with Sarazen in the finals.

With the 1931 U.S. Open scheduled at his home club, Sarazen resigned his position at Fresh Meadow and took a similar position at nearby Lakeville. Sarazen believed the "home pro jinx" had cost him the 1930 PGA, and he was taking no chances.

The picturesque 13th hole.

Sarazen is said to have played conservatively during the first two rounds, a tactic that seemed all the more questionable in light of his mastery of his newly devised sand iron. He considered himself even money to get up–and–down from any greenside bunker. Nonetheless, Sarazen found himself seven strokes back heading for the ninth tee Saturday morning. A birdie there touched off one of the great finishes in Open history. Throwing caution to the wind and shooting for the flag on every hole, Sarazen played the final 28 holes in 100 strokes, finishing the tournament with rounds of 70-66 to equal the Open record of 286.

In the 1940s, the realities of advancing civilization arrived on Fresh Meadow's doorstep, bringing the threat of increased real estate taxes. A move was in the Club's best interests, so in 1946 the property in Flushing was sold and the financially troubled Lakeville Club purchased. Tillinghast's great course soon became a housing development.

Lakeville's genesis began in the early 1800s, when the area around Lake Success became a fashionable summer resort for New Yorkers and Long Islanders, a recreational center featuring dense forests, babbling streams, and ponds. It once had been the home of the Matinecock Indians, a tribe of the Algonquin nation. Matinecock graves have been found behind a small church on Community Drive, off to the right of today's 12th tee.

Lakeville was another Nathan Jonas creation, 171 acres of rolling, heavily-wooded land where he planned to build a private estate. Instead, he used it to form the Lakeville Golf & Country Club for the enjoyment of his friends in the entertainment world, including Irving Berlin, Eddie Cantor, and Oscar Hammerstein. Charles Alison designed the golf course, producing an outstanding layout, "one of the most beautiful and exclusive clubs in America." One golf writer termed Lakeville "the peer of American inland courses." It opened on Memorial Day, 1925.

The clubhouse was as magnificent as the course. Situated on the highest point of the property, the Colonial-style stucco building's features were of unusually large dimensions. On the grounds were flowering gardens, a marble swimming pool framed in evergreens, and a toboggan slide.

The Depression eroded club membership. The Club was reorganized in 1933, but eventually fell into the hands of financial institutions. During the war, Lakeville was leased to nearby Glen Oaks, whose grounds were taken over by the U.S. Navy. After the war, Glen Oaks returned home and Lakeville was sold to Fresh Meadow.

The wave-like bunkering leading to the 18th green.

Fresh Meadow is a delightful parkland course. Its fairways follow the natural roll of the forested terrain, the trees intruding dangerously close to fairways. Several tees are elevated well above the fairway, presenting vistas hardly conducive to keeping one's eye on the ball. Almost every hole spotlights the artistry of Alison's bunkering. The deep-faced "alisons" that gained him everlasting fame in Japan are in evidence.

The 11th is a beautiful par three. The elevated tee is well above the green, which is set in a natural amphitheater. Tall dogwoods tower over the green, which is flanked by three artistically shaped bunkers.

The 12th is one of Long Island's great par fours. From an elevated tee, it plays into a valley once used by the local Indians for councils. A forest close on the left threatens the drive, as does a bunker right. The hole then doglegs left around protruding trees and climbs sharply to an elevated green protected by a pair of bunkers on the right. A bit of hillside falls in front of the green, confusing the golfer trying to judge distance remaining to the pin.

The 13th is a beautiful par three played from a raised tee over water to an elevated green surrounded by bunkers. In the middle of the lake is an island complete with a pagoda and a large weeping willow.

The home hole is a classic example of Alison's bunkering. A row of three high-lipped bunkers rise like a wave across the fairway about 75 yards ahead of the green, with a stream lurking behind. It is a fitting finish to an exquisite golf experience. ○

Gene Sarazen

INWOOD COUNTRY CLUB

"A Career Shot"

As he waited in the 18th fairway preparing to hit his approach to the final green at Inwood, Bobby Jones must have had a feeling of "deja vu." It was Sunday, July 15, 1923, and he had been in the same position the day before, looking to win his first U.S. Open. He had blown his first chance. Would he do it again?

Only 21 years old, Jones was a veteran. He had played the major championships for seven years, but was still without a title to show for his considerable efforts. He'd had the tournament within his grasp when he set up to play his approach to 16 on the final day of regulation play. But he pushed that shot out-of-bounds, then pulled another that luckily deflected off a mound and rolled onto the green. He carded a bogey there, then another at 17. On the home hole, playing into the wind, he hooked his approach behind a bunker left of the green, near the present 11th tee, then chunked his recovery into the sand. With a double bogey on a hole he had previously birdied twice, Jones walked

From behind the 18th green today.

off the course a dejected young man, filled with self-doubt and no longer the tournament leader.

The new leader was Bobby Cruickshank, a Scot from Edinburgh, but he too faltered down the stretch. Needing a birdie to tie, Cruickshank rallied, fading his 2-iron to within six feet at 18 and draining the putt to set up the next day's 18-hole playoff.

More than 8,000 fans watched the back-and-forth affair, the contestants halving only three of the first 17 holes. Cruickshank managed to stay close with some remarkable scrambling, and the two men stood even on the 18th tee.

It was the melodrama on 18 that earned Inwood its place in golf history. The par-four played to 425 yards over a gaping water hazard, a lagoon that crossed the fairway just in front of the green. Trying to hit a low shot into the wind, Cruickshank duck-hooked his drive 150 yards behind a clump of trees on the left, and had no choice but to lay up short of the lagoon.

Jones drove long but into the right rough. Preparing to play to the green, he was in the driver's seat—as he had been the day before. But his shot would not be easy: His 250-yard drive had found a depressed lie on bare ground. He faced a 190-yard shot into the wind and over the hazard. If he gambled and lost, a mishit likely would bury his hopes in a watery grave. Jones did not hesitate. He coolly played a 190-yard mid-iron (equivalent of a 2-iron today) that rose majestically into the breeze before settling down softly within six feet of the cup. He won the title with a two-putt par.

Jones's brilliant pressure shot was honored in 1987 by *GOLF Magazine* as the first in its "Shot Of The Century" series; a plaque was placed alongside the 18th fairway, near the spot from which the shot was struck. 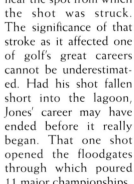 The significance of that stroke as it affected one of golf's great careers cannot be underestimated. Had his shot fallen short into the lagoon, Jones' career may have ended before it really began. That one shot opened the floodgates through which poured 11 major championships.

That Inwood would someday play such a significant role in the history of golf certainly was not expected from its pedestrian beginnings. The Club started life as an engagement gift from Jacob Wertheim to Emma Stern. Emma enjoyed golf, but had no place to play, so Jacob leased a potato farm in Inwood in 1901 and engaged Dr. William Exton and Arthur Thatcher to build a nine-hole course. The fact that it still resembled a potato farm did not bother the membership of the new club, which grew to 80 that first year. Most of them knew little to nothing about golf. In fact, 50 of them resigned after the first year, as did the club's professional, who left to pursue a more lucrative career as a hack driver.

The next spring, the Club contacted A.G. Spalding and brothers for assistance in finding a new professional. Spalding was the major supplier of golf equipment and also acted as a clearinghouse for professional athletes. The man ticketed for the Inwood job turned up hopelessly drunk the morning of his interview, so Spalding substituted a sore-armed former baseball player named Edward

Eriksen, who knew nothing about golf. With little choice, Inwood hired Eriksen, and things worked out far better than expected. Eriksen remained at Inwood for nine years and developed into a highly respected golf instructor. He also re-designed the nine-hole course; seven of his holes remain, with modifications. as part of today's course. He added a second nine as the membership grew.

A farm building on the grounds was converted into a locker room in 1902 and served as Inwood's clubhouse until 1917 when the present clubhouse, a white-columned Georgian structure, was com-pleted. It offers a good view of the course and nearby Kennedy Airport, with the Manhattan skyline in the distance.

Herbert Strong came to Inwood in 1912 as golf professional. The following year, he finished fifth (by three strokes) in the historic U.S. Open won by Francis Ouimet. While at Inwood, Strong's interests turned to architec-ture, and he remodeled the course into near-ly its present form. Following Strong came Jack Mackie, a Scot who began his 34-year tenure in 1917. Mackie was one of the founding fathers of the PGA as well as an amateur architect; his revision of the Eriksen/Strong course hosted the 1921 PGA and the 1923 U.S. Open.

Mackie was succeeded in 1950 by Vic Ghezzi, the 1941 PGA champion and member of the PGA Hall Of Fame. Others who have graced the Inwood pro shop include Ellsworth Vines, who was elected to the Tennis Hall of Fame in 1962 while Inwood's golf professional, and Jimmy

INWOOD COUNTRY CLUB
Inwood, NY

YEAR FOUNDED: 1902

ARCHITECTS:
Edward Eriksen
Herbert Strong
Jack Mackie

COURSE OPENED: 1902

TEES	PAR	YARDAGE
Forward	73	5786
Middle	72	6364
Back	72	6647

TEES	COURSE RATING	SLOPE
Forward	74.5	130
Middle	71.8	128
Back	73.1	131

Wright, six-time Met PGA Player of the Year.

The many-fathered layout is an old-fashioned course, mixing a Scottish seaside flavor with a beautiful parkland setting. Located on an inlet of Jamaica Bay, it is con-stantly exposed to the winds. The bunker-ing retains the character of an earlier era: Irregularly shaped hazards lurk alongside several fairways; many greenside bunkers are set away from the putting surface and complemented by mounds, sharp drop-offs, and severe rough around the collar. The foundation for a good score must be laid over the first five holes, all of which offer birdie opportunities.

A lake fronts the two-tiered 10th green. Two large bunkers flank the green, each preceded by a large mound, so the hole appears shorter than its yards. During the club's 40th anniversary celebration in 1941, Ben Hogan took a five after his tee shot fell short into the water.

In the 1921 PGA Championship at Inwood, Walter Hagen defeated Long Jim Barnes 3&2 in the 36-hole final. It was the first of Hagen's five PGA titles.

Inwood has hosted a pair of Met Opens. In 1968, Jerry Pittman's 274 was eight strokes ahead of runner-up Jimmy Wright. Pittman set a new course record with a 65 in the third round. During an 11-hole span in the final round, he and playing partner Wright carded an amazing 14 birdies! Even Bobby Jones would have found it difficult keeping pace.   ❍

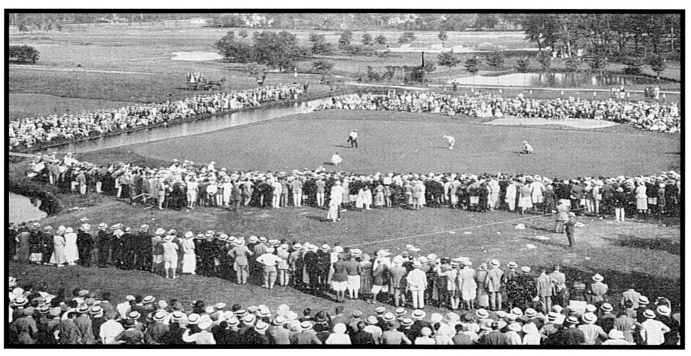

A crowd gathered at the 18th green during the 1923 U.S. Open.

MAIDSTONE CLUB

"The Great American Links"

Regarded as the "father of inland golf," it is ironic that Willie Park's major contribution to American golf was a links, The Maidstone Club, hard by the Atlantic Ocean on Long Island's south shore, among the dunes and marshes near the beach at East Hampton.

Maidstone was named for the town in Kent, England, from which East Hampton's 17th-century settlers emigrated. The name was resurrected in 1891 when the Club was founded. At the time, East Hampton was a close-knit, conservative little community, summer home to a colony of artists and writers including John Howard Payne, who penned "Home, Sweet Home." The rich began to arrive toward the end of the century, when the sport of the day was tennis, and Maidstone was founded as a tennis and bathing club, a family club, for the summer residents of East Hampton.

Golf first came to Maidstone in 1894 as a primitive three-hole course, probably nothing more than a meadow in its natural state. The first nine-hole course opened in 1896; situated entirely on the village side of Hook Pond, it was designed by the Scottish professional Willie Tucker.

The facilities expanded to a full 18 holes in 1899. The new course, designed by member Adrian Larkin in close consultation with Willie Park Jr. and Park's brother Jack, included seven holes "on the very margin of the waves," east of the present clubhouse site.

In 1919, the members began discussing a new clubhouse on the dunes overlooking the ocean. The issue was brought to a head in 1922 when a fire leveled the old clubhouse near the third green. Around the same time, a large plot of duneland between Hook Pond and the ocean was purchased, allowing for a pair of 18-hole courses. The Club then decided to build the English-style stucco clubhouse overlooking the ocean, as well as beachside cabanas and an Olympic-size pool.

The clubhouse as seen from the 18th tee.

MAIDSTONE CLUB

East Hampton, NY

YEAR FOUNDED: 1891

ARCHITECTS:
Willie Tucker
Adrian Larkin
Willie Park Jr.

COURSE OPENED: 1896

TEES	PAR	YARDAGE
Forward	72	5461
Middle	72	6006
Back	72	6390

TEES	COURSE RATING	SLOPE
Forward	72.1	128
Middle	70.8	131
Back	72.5	134

Willie Park was called upon once again to redesign Maidstone's layout. He responded with 12 new holes on the recently acquired duneland, and combined these holes with the first three and final three holes on the existing course to create the West Course which remains virtually intact today. Park also drew up plans for expanding the remaining holes into the East Course, which was constructed in 1930.

Park's new holes were critically acclaimed. Bernard Darwin, the British writer and golfer, told American journalist Grantland Rice, a Maidstone member, that "the dunes holes (6 through 10) were the finest stretch he had ever seen in America."

Like most clubs, Maidstone had its difficulties during the Depression, compounded by the violent, unexpected hurricane of 1938, which closed the course for the 1939 season. After World War II, Maidstone reduced its overhead, cutting back to 27 holes by selling some land to the east of the clubhouse along the beach, property that housed some of the Club's original ocean-front holes.

Today, members enjoy the best of all worlds-a strikingly beautiful golf course ranked among the 100 best in the world by *GOLF Magazine*, and a beach club rated the best in the Met Area by *The Met Golfer*.

Maidstone is every inch a links course. The terrain is relatively treeless, swept by the winds that typically blow from the southwest off the Atlantic. The rough is made rougher by gorse-type brush, while reeds and cattails grow near the ocean and Hook Pond. Park used the linksland well: Golfers face fearsome carries over marshland vegetation from on at least half the tees. But even on a bad day, the beauty makes the struggle with nature worthwhile.

In 1986, *GOLF Magazine* listed the 100 greatest golf holes in the United States. Two of Maidstone's dunes holes–9 and 14–were included. The ninth would not seem out of place in Scotland or Ireland. From its tee high atop the dunes, the hole plays over a stretch of gorse and beach

The short 14th, with the ocean as a backdrop.

The pool and beach club.

grass down to a fairway set in a valley nestled between two large dunes, with the ocean off to the right. For the average player, the key is the large crossbunker halfway between the landing area and green, forcing a critical decision on the second shot. The fairway rises beyond the bunker to a green perched well above a waste area.

The short par-three 14th plays from a dune-top tee over a wasteland of sand and scrub to an elevated green carved into a dune, with the ocean as a backdrop.

Close akin is the eighth, a short, semi-blind par three, its green set alongside a large sand dune bordering the ocean. It demands an accurate pitch over the edge of the dune, with all sorts of vegetation to be carried. A large bunker comes from the right side across the front.

In both name and flavor, Maidstone maintains its strong British heritage and its cherished position among the Hampton's great foursome of clubs.　　　　○

MEADOW BROOK CLUB

"A Good Game For Sundays"

Devereux Milburn

The Meadow Brook Hunt Club was incorporated in 1881, and leased land that sprawled from Merrick Avenue to Mitchell Field, and from Old Country Road to Hempstead Turnpike. This was where the elite came to play and watch polo, on unmatched facilities that hosted many important matches and the greatest players in the world.

The Club hosted polo's annual U.S. Open from the early 1900s until 1953. The Meadow Brook team of Harry Payne Whitney, Devereux Milburn, Monty and Larry Waterbury helped the United States win the Westchester Cup in 1909, 1911, and 1913, ending England's domination of the sport.

On a sparkling Sunday afternoon in the summer of 1888, Horace Hutchinson, the British Amateur champion of 1886-1887, paid a visit to Meadow Brook to demonstrate another pastime popular in England. He came dressed in a scarlet coat with green velvet collar, brass buttons, tight-fitting knickers, golf hose, and high gaiters, and carried a putter and six clubs. Holes were cut in the soil with a carving knife. We don't know how Hutchinson performed, but his play did not capture the imagination of the hunt set. Nor did their own attempts at striking the ball win many converts. Perhaps the most favorable comment Hutchinson heard that day was that golf might make "a good game for Sundays."

Despite the initially cool reception, a golf committee was authorized in 1893, and by 1894, a nine-hole course had been completed. The next year, Meadow Brook was the scene of a $1,000 grudge match between member Winthrop Rutherford and Charles Sands, runner-up earlier that year in the first U.S. Amateur championship, a finish Rutherford considered a fluke. A sizable gallery attended, the local press was on hand, and large sums reportedly were wagered on the outcome. Sands won, taking 195 strokes for 34 holes. To add insult to injury, while the match was progressing, thieves dressed in red hunting coats entered the clubhouse and stole money and jewels from the lockers, most notably Rutherford's.

In November of 1895, in the absence of an official USGA women's championship, Meadow Brook decided to sponsor such an event, albeit unofficial. Neither rain nor fog deterred the 13 contestants, who played the nine-hole course once before lunch, then again in the afternoon. Mrs. Charles Brown of Shinnecock Hills emerged a two-stroke winner with a total of 132 that included scores ranging from 3 to 14. Contributing to the high scores was the fact that, in the absence of ladies tees, the contestants had to play from the men's markers.

Despite the celebrity of big-money matches and national championships, the original Meadow Brook course was short-lived.

The members remained more interested in polo. By 1905, the course was abandoned, with the club's golfers playing at Nassau or Piping Rock.

By 1916, crowded conditions at those clubs brought golf back to Meadow Brook, which leased the J. Clinton Smith estate across the road. Devereux Emmet was chosen to design a new 18-hole course. He utilized the brook that gives the Club its name, placing ten greens beside it. One par three of 120 yards called for a tee-to-green carry over water to an island green.

The old course lasted until the early 1950s, its last hurrah coming when the club hosted the Goodall Round Robin. Cary Middlecoff won in 1953, and Sam Snead took top honors in 1954 and 1955.

In the early 1950s, Parks Commissioner Robert Moses condemned the property so that the Meadowbrook Parkway could connect the middle of Nassau County with the south shore beaches. Golf had no problem moving to the

MEADOW BROOK CLUB
Jericho, NY

YEAR FOUNDED: 1881

ARCHITECT:
Dick Wilson

COURSE OPENED: 1955

TEES	PAR	YARDAGE
Forward	72	5644
Middle	72	6758
Back	72	7101

TEES	COURSE RATING	SLOPE
Forward	73.2	126
Middle	73.0	133
Back	74.6	137

John Baldwin

The 8th green with 9th hole in background.

new site in Jericho, but the uprooting brought down the curtain on the club's glory days in polo.

In 1953, ground was broken in Jericho. Dick Wilson designed a new course of championship proportions, which was ready for play in 1955. This configuration lasted until 1967, when the Club sold off considerable acreage near Jericho Turnpike. Wilson then returned to revise the course, building six new holes.

With one exception, every two- and three-shot hole at Meadow Brook is a dogleg. Most of them turn left, creating an advantage for the player with a controlled draw who can avoid the numerous bunkers set in the corners. And with some of the largest greens in the country, Meadow Brook also places a premium on lag putting.

Lee Trevino won the Northville Long Island Classic in 1994 and 1995.

The eighth is Meadow Brook's centerpiece, a 615-yard par five that doglegs left, then right. Byron Nelson called it the "best extra-long par five in the country." The drive must flirt with three bunkers guarding the first bend if the golfer is to have any chance of clearing the treeline protecting the final bend with his second.

Numerous local and national events have been staged at Meadow Brook, including the 1977 Met Open, 1987 Met Amateur, and 1979-1982 Western Union International on the LPGA Tour. The Senior Tour has been holding the Northville Long Island Classic there since 1987. The roster of winners includes Lee Trevino (1994-1995), Raymond Floyd, George Archer (1990-1992), and Gary Player. The seniors have had high praise for Meadow Brook. Billy Casper, two-time U.S. Open champion, called it "one of the greatest courses I've ever played," one that "could house a National Open easily."

Among the prominent golfing members: Herbert Harriman won the US Amateur and inaugural Met Amateur, both in 1899; Robert Sweeny Jr., was the 1937 British Amateur champion; Peter Van Ingen, the 1981 Met Amateur titleholder; and John Baldwin, recent MGA president (1993-1994), won the 1967 Met, Long Island, and New York State Amateurs (the only player with that triple), the 1986 Ike, 1990 Met Amateur, and two MGA Player of the Year awards.

For Baldwin and his predecessors at Meadow Brook, golf is a great game for *any* day of the week.   ○

OLD WESTBURY GOLF & COUNTRY CLUB

"In The Shadow Of The Tower"

**OLD WESTBURY
GOLF &
COUNTRY CLUB**
Old Westbury, NY

YEAR FOUNDED: 1961

ARCHITECT:
William Mitchell

COURSE OPENED: 1962

TEES	PAR	YARDAGE
Forward	72	5775
Middle	72	6476
Back	72	6961

TEES	COURSE RATING	SLOPE
Forward	74.2	132
Middle	71.5	126
Back	73.8	130

Above is an average of three nines

I t rises 187 feet above ground level, 392 feet above sea level. Its top is the highest point in Nassau County. At one time it was a beacon for ocean liners, and during World War II, the United States Air Force used it to watch for enemy aircraft. It is the Whitney Tower, designated an historical landmark in 1986. Its windmill had blades 30 feet in diameter, which drew water from a well 570 feet deep to serve the Whitneys on their fabulous estates. Today, the tower watches over the Old Westbury Golf & Country Club, three nines of challenge and beauty known as Woods, Overlook, and Blue Grass.

William C. Whitney purchased the property in 1887, and began building the estate and stables that would house many great thoroughbreds, including an undefeated steeplechaser named Shillelah, whose tombstone can be seen in the trees to the left of the fourth tee of the Blue Grass course. When Whitney died in 1904, the estate passed to his son Harry Payne Whitney, and "The Manse" became a favorite gathering place for the elite of turfdom and society. One of the leading polo players of his day,

Whitney housed his polo ponies on the grounds, and maintained living quarters for his polo-playing guests.

In 1942, the estate was inherited by Cornelius Vanderbilt "Sonny" Whitney, who demolished the old mansion, the remains of which are now buried beneath the lake by the ninth green of the Woods course. He then built the mansion that is now the Old Westbury clubhouse.

In 1961, the newly-formed golf club purchased 200 acres from the estate, including the mansion house, the tennis house, the polo buildings, the stables, and the tower. According to its bylaws, "the purpose of the club is to operate and maintain a non-profit, non-sectarian country club," a noble attempt to overcome racial and religious prejudice.

Much credit for the Club's success must go to its first president, Arthur Weber, who also served the Metropolitan Golf Association as president (1987-1988). As chairman of

From behind the 9th green on Woods.

The par-three 5th on Overlook.

the Green Committee, Weber used his extensive knowledge of chemical engineering to bring the golf course into superb condition. The architect was William Mitchell, who had the course ready for play on July 4, 1962.

Old Westbury's 27 holes share several characteristics, even though the 12 holes to the north of the clubhouse (the Woods nine and the final three holes of the Overlook nine) were carved from a dense forest, while the 15 holes to the south were laid out over farmland. Accuracy is always in demand, to avoid the trees and position the approach, which typically must cross a large bunker at the entrance to the green. Most greens are elevated, making getting up and down difficult.

Number two on Overlook may be the most difficult par on the property. It is a long, uphill par four with a very small green, and usually plays against the prevailing wind. Four trees give this hole its character: the first two narrow the landing area for the drive, the other pair flank the fairway just short of the green.

The seventh hole on Overlook, located behind the clubhouse, is one of the premier par fours on Long Island, a dogleg left that leaves little room for error. The drive, played from an elevated tee, must be threaded down a narrow treelined fairway that drops off sharply to the right. Three fairway

The Tower

bunkers add to the tension. From there, the hole plays slightly uphill and to the left.

The ninth on Woods is a moderate par four known for giving average players fits. Its narrow treelined fairway plays uphill all the way to a wide, shallow green perched on a knoll behind a steep-faced bunker. A pond juts into the fairway from the right near the green, creating a serious problem for the short hitter.

In 1983, Old Westbury hosted the Met Open, won by defending champion Darrell Kestner. The professionals played Woods and Overlook, as did the contestants in the 1991 Ike, in which Jerry Courville Jr., came from far behind over the final nine to catch Jeff Thomas. Courville won in a three-hole aggregate playoff.

Befitting a former Whitney estate, there are indoor and outdoor tennis courts and an Olympic-size swimming pool. The mural-decorated tennis house was a backdrop in the movie "Sabrina Fair," which starred Audrey Hepburn.

The polo stables now store maintenance equipment, and the old racing stables and dormitory near the club entrance have been renovated and are used by the New York Institute of Technology as a classroom facility. And the tower overlooks one of the most picturesque settings in Met Area golf.   ○

PIPING ROCK CLUB
"Peace Pipe"

In "The Great Gatsby," F. Scott Fitzgerald immortalized the fabulously wealthy denizens of Long Island's north shore, which was known as the "Gold Coast." Theirs was a time of elegance and splendor, private yachts, formal gardens, and castles surrounded by polo fields. A typical summer day started with a morning round of golf, then lunch on the terrace at the Piping Rock Club. In the afternoon, off to a game of polo at the Meadow Brook Club, then to a dinner party that more often than not would last into the wee hours.

Perhaps the most famous Gold Coast party took place in 1924 in honor of the Prince of Wales, who was visiting Long Island for the Westchester Cup polo matches at Meadow Brook. The party took place at Harbor Hill, the Roslyn estate of Clarence Mackay, and was attended by 1,200 guests.

Mackay, builder of several transoceanic cables, was among the founders of two of the north shore's outstanding clubs, Piping Rock and Creek. Piping Rock, the older of the two, was organized in 1909 to "supplement existing clubs" in the area, Meadow Brook in particular. But the membership rosters overlapped considerably because the two clubs served different purposes: Meadow Brook was primarily a gentleman's polo and hunt club; Piping Rock was a family-oriented country club. Not that there was a lack of interest in polo at Piping Rock. There were two playing fields to the north of the clubhouse and a practice field in the valley to the south.

The Club's name was taken from a well-known rock which lent its name to a large section of Locust Valley. The rock is located on a hill on the north side of Piping Rock Road, on what once was the main trail between Oyster Bay and Mosquito Cove (Glen Cove). It was used by the Matinecock Indians as a resting place, a spot for tribal leaders to meet and smoke the peace pipe.

The Club's founding fathers purchased a large tract of land including several miles of roads and bridle paths, and along with polo fields, planned to build a one-mile turf course for flat and steeplechase racing (encircling the polo fields), a two-mile hunt course, tennis courts, and a swimming pool at the beach club. A golf course would be built if there was the demand.

Piping Rock opened formally in 1912, the year the golf course was being built. Charles Blair Macdonald was the architect, assisted as always by Seth Raynor. It was one of the few contracts Macdonald accepted, but he was never happy with the course. His fierce loyalty to golf clashed with the primacy of the club's other sport. Horses thundered

PIPING ROCK CLUB

Locust Valley, NY

YEAR FOUNDED: 1909

ARCHITECTS:
Charles Blair Macdonald
Pete Dye

COURSE OPENED: 1912

TEES	PAR	YARDAGE
Forward	71	5487
Middle	71	6343
Back	71	6723

TEES	COURSE RATING	SLOPE
Forward	72.5	128
Middle	71.3	131
Back	73.0	134

across his fairways and his front nine was "sacrificed to the polo fields;" the holes had to be routed clockwise around the fields, inhibiting his use of the terrain.

The recent work of Pete Dye, completed in 1987, coupled with an outstanding job by course superintendent Richard Spear, transformed a good, old-fashioned course into an outstanding modern layout, faithful to the original Macdonald concept.

Piping Rock features contrasting nines. The front rolls over relatively level terrain, with the old polo fields usually in view. The back side plays over more rugged territory, making use of more of Macdonald's deep bunkers.

Typical of a Macdonald design, a number of the holes are based on famous precedents. The par-four eighth is a rendition of the Road Hole, (#17) at St. Andrews. The green is set on an angle to the approach, circling around a pot bunker front and left, making for an exceptional pin placement at the left rear. A pair of bunkers right and rear perform the same function as St. Andrews' road.

The par-four 12th is Prestwick's Alps hole. The fairway is in a valley and bunkered on both sides. The approach to the green is blind, over a ridge and a bunker, to a green set in a rim of mounds with a deep bunker down below the left side.

The 14th is a strong par four of 450 yards. From an elevated tee, it offers a choice: a long carry over a pair of bunkers to the right center of the fairway, or to the left, avoiding a bunker in the rough.

Two outstanding players served Piping Rock as head professional in recent years. Tom Nieporte came in 1962, fresh off the PGA Tour, where he won twice. While at Piping Rock, Nieporte won the 1966 Met Open, 1967 Bob Hope Desert Classic, and numerous other local titles.

Jim Albus continued the tradition of being an outstanding teacher also capable of playing with the best local professionals and the best of his generation. Albus came to Piping Rock in 1976, and has won two Met Opens and two Met PGA titles; he was elected to the Met PGA Hall of Fame in 1996. In 1991, Albus captured the Senior Tournament Players Championship over the likes of Jack Nicklaus, Gary Player, and Lee Trevino, marking an end to his club days and the beginning of his new life on the Senior Tour of "Gold Coast" proportions. ❍

Right: 10h hole. Inset: Former Piping Rock Club Professional turned Senior PGA Tour star Jim Albus when he won the Met Open in 1984.

BROOKVILLE COUNTRY CLUB

"In The Swing"

View from behind the fifth green.

**BROOKVILLE
COUNTRY CLUB**
Glen Head, NY

YEAR FOUNDED: 1922

ARCHITECT:
Seth Raynor

COURSE OPENED: 1922

TEES	PAR	YARDAGE
Forward	73	5613
Middle	72	6293

TEES	COURSE RATING	SLOPE
Forward	72.1	120
Middle	70.6	123

In 1919, E.H. Crawford came to Glen Cove to manage the vast Pratt estate. Within two years, he had interested a number of successful artisans from the surrounding North Shore communities in forming an inexpensive, informal golf and country club.

Early in 1922, the club purchased an estate consisting of both open meadows and virgin woodlands, across the road from the Piping Rock Club and bordered by a number of impressive estates. The original clubhouse, a converted homestead located at the northeast end of the present parking lot, lasted until 1967 when the present clubhouse was built.

Brookville's golf course was designed by Seth Raynor. Work began in the spring of 1922, and Raynor had nine holes ready for play by the middle of July. The second nine holes, cut from the woods, opened two years later.

Like many clubs, Brookville suffered during the Depression and World War II, eventually losing the property at public auction. But within two years, a small syndicate of members was able to buy back their club, which was eventually sold back to the full membership. As times improved after the war, the membership included a number of musicians from the Big Band era, who often entertained at club parties.

The course is notable for the settings of its greens, several set atop natural rises, another in a bowl, still others protected by cross bunkers and swales. Perhaps the most memorable holes are a number of relatively short par fours. Both the second and fourth are extremely tight doglegs requiring precise placement off the tee. The ninth plays to a rising fairway, then downhill to a partially blind, punchbowl green with a collar of rough in front and bunkers to either side; the shape of the bowl steers the incoming shot from right-front to left-rear.

The drive zone for the par-four 15th hole is divided by rough and includes a deep swale about 100 yards from the green, which does not allow view of the putting surface. The short pitch to the green must avoid a long crossbunker, a large bunker on the right, and still another to the left that wraps around the back.

Also worth mentioning is the long, uphill, par-three third, with its dramatic two-tiered green guarded by deep bunkers on either side. The landing area of the par-five home hole tilts towards a large fairway bunker on the right, beyond which the hole rolls through two swales to an elevated, sloping green.

The course has recently undergone a major renovation by Gil Hanse that in part will restore the Seth Raynor flavor. ○

CHERRY VALLEY CLUB
"Cherry Blossom Time"

G arden City's public Salisbury Links, created in 1907, proved very popular. So popular that by 1915, the course had become congested. In May, 1916, the Garden City Company, which owned the property, decided to reorganize it as a private club, naming it Cherry Valley Golf Club after the road, lined with wild cherry trees, that ran through the property (and was closed when the Club went private).

While still a community club, the Salisbury Links played host to the 1913 Met Open, won by Alex Smith. It was his fourth Met Open title, still a record for the event.

In 1927 the U.S. Women's Amateur came to Cherry Valley. Miriam Burns Horn of Kansas City defeated local heroine Maureen Orcutt of White Beeches in the finals.

The Cherry Valley course of 1927 had evidenced a dramatic change from the original layout, and at the same time was somewhat different from the present course. The architect for the revision was Devereux Emmet, and the changes he made in 1916 were extensive, including the elimination of the double green that served two holes. The course originally extended into the present Adelphi University property and across Cambridge Avenue.

Emmet's course remained intact until 1959, when the membership purchased the property and sold off some land south of First Street to finance the deal. Architect Frank Duane was engaged to replace the two holes lost, and did so by building the present 4th, 5th, and 17th, at the same time combining two holes into the present par-five second. Also at this time, the nines were reversed. After Duane was done, only five holes from the original Salisbury Links remained.

The golf course retains an old-fashioned flavor. Perhaps the most vivid impression is of the unusual bunkering—cross bunkers, like the angled bunker that must be carried to reach the landing area on the par-five third; and long, serpentine bunkers extending more than 100 yards in length, like those bordering the second on the right and the eighth on the left. Another defining characteristic is the tall love grass, blowing in the breeze between fairways. Not to mention the steeple of the Cathedral of the Incarnation across the street, which can be seen from many holes and provides the line on the par-four 15th.

Cherry Valley has had some prominent members over the years, among them E.H. Driggs Jr., winner of the 1927 and 1944 Met Amateurs, the inaugural (1923) and two subsequent New York State Amateurs, and three Long Island Amateurs; Joseph Donahue, president of the MGA (1980-1982), who won the club championship three times; and T.S. Tailer, Jr., who listed Cherry Valley as his home club when he won the 1932 Met Amateur.

During the first half of 1996, the clubhouse was completely remodeled, topped off by a striking new clock tower. In addition, rows of cherry trees have been planted along both sides of the entrance road, a nice touch that recalls the club's early days. ❍

CHERRY VALLEY CLUB
Garden City, NY

YEAR FOUNDED: 1916

ARCHITECTS:
Walter Travis
Devereux Emmet
Frank Duane

COURSE OPENED: 1907

TEES	PAR	YARDAGE
Forward	73	5178
Middle	72	6349
Back	72	6705

TEES	COURSE RATING	SLOPE
Forward	72.3	127
Middle	70.4	123
Back	72.0	127

The 15th green with the cathedral spire in the background.

COLD SPRING COUNTRY CLUB

"Kahn's Game"

**COLD SPRING
COUNTRY CLUB**
Cold Spring Harbor, NY

YEAR FOUNDED: 1947

ARCHITECTS:
Seth Raynor
Robert Trent Jones

COURSE OPENED: 1923

TEES	PAR	YARDAGE
Forward	73	5667
Middle	71	6158
Back	71	6395

TEES	COURSE RATING	SLOPE
Forward	73.4	126
Middle	70.0	129
Back	71.0	131

Otto Herman Kahn was a man of enormous wealth, charm, and generosity. The German-born banker, financier, railroad baron, philanthropist, and patron of the arts was called "The King of New York." He sponsored many struggling actors and theatrical groups, and his contributions helped create and establish the Metropolitan Opera.

Kahn purchased a 443-acre tract of land in Cold Spring Harbor in 1914. There he built "Oheka" (from the first letters of his names), the second largest private residence in the United States, on the highest point on Long Island–a man-made mountain that took two years to "grow." The 127-room mansion featured a ballroom with a 60-foot ceiling and a grand dining hall that could seat 250. Designed by the noted architect William Adams Delano, Oheka was completed in 1919.

Otto Kahn

Kahn's parties at Oheka were frequent, elegant, even legendary. Kahn had been excluded from the greatest of all North Shore parties, one given by Clarence Mackay to honor the Prince of Wales, so he decided to get even. He let it be known that someone of the highest nobility would be a guest at Oheka, and that he planned to honor him with a gala party. After much jockeying for invitations, and a round of introductory speeches, in marched a chimpanzee, nattily clad in a tuxedo, to take the seat of honor!

Kahn decided to build a private golf course and hired Seth Raynor. Supposedly Kahn would watch his guests and local professionals play, note where their drives landed, and overnight a bunker would appear on that spot.

Kahn died of a heart attack in 1934, beginning a period of uncertainty for the property. It was a retreat house for the New York City Sanitation Department, then a military academy, before its recent $1.5 million restoration, paid for by member Gary Melius, to its "Gatsby Era" grandeur.

The course enjoyed a better fate. In 1947, a group of 15 men, many of them former members of the defunct Willow Brook Country Club in Lynbrook, formed the Cold Spring Country Club and purchased the course. They converted the Kahn stables into a clubhouse, and engaged Robert Trent Jones to build the present fifth and sixth holes, replacing the first and last holes of the original course, two short par fours.

Cold Spring is a lovely, yet challenging, parkland course that retains the Raynor signature, including holes named "Short" (#3), a classic "Road" (#9), a "Redan" (#11), an "Eden" (#13), and a "Biarritz" (#17). Perhaps most memorable of all is the 10th, a gem of a short par four. A tree-lined road crosses the hole 120 yards from the tee, demanding quick elevation on the drive. The fairway sits in a bowl, without a view of the green, which is itself situated in a hollow, surrounded by moguls, and preceded by rough and three bunkers. Clearly professionally designed, with little influence from the King. ○

The picturesque 13th.

DEEPDALE GOLF CLUB

"One Man's Playground"

**DEEPDALE
GOLF CLUB**
Manhasset, NY

YEAR FOUNDED: 1926

ARCHITECT:
Dick Wilson

COURSE OPENED: 1956

TEES	PAR	YARDAGE
Forward	70	5391
Middle	70	6322
Back	70	6623

TEES	COURSE RATING	SLOPE
Forward	71.5	119
Middle	71.3	132
Back	72.6	135

I n 1925, William K. Vanderbilt II, one of Long Island's most avid sportsmen, decided to convert some of the rolling acreage near his former summer estate at Lake Success into a very private golf course for him and a few friends. Vanderbilt engaged Charles Blair Macdonald—who was doing very few courses since finishing The National—and his protégés, Seth Raynor and Charles Banks, to turn the 200-acre tract into the latest word in golf courses.

Vanderbilt's plan was not impulsive; the acreage had been under "scientific treatment" for two years to guarantee good fairways. The course opened in the spring of 1926, and was spectacular. Its Redan and Alps holes were said to have been even better than those at The National. Vanderbilt's friends soon approached him with the idea of organizing a golf club with a small, select membership, a place for weekday play when there was no time for the two-hour train ride out to Southampton and The National. On October 26,1926, the Deepdale Golf Club was incorporated.

Because Vanderbilt had sold his mansion south of the lake to the fledgling Glen Oaks Club in 1924, a new clubhouse was needed. The Spanish-style stucco building, with outside stairways and a piazza overlooking the lake, opened late in 1926. The Club quickly had 250 members. Included on its roster over the years were eight presidents of the USGA, including George Walker, donor of the Walker Cup.

In 1954, the Long Island Expressway was routed through the northern part of the course. Dick Wilson was hired to create a new 18-hole course on the old site, but when this proved inadvisable, the club purchased the W.R. Grace estate, 175 acres of densely wooded, rolling terrain in Manhasset, while selling the old facilities to the new Lake Success Country Club. Two holes from the old course survive at Lake Success (the seventh and ninth) as does a mural in the clubhouse depicting the original layout.

Wilson's new course and the Grace-mansion-turned-clubhouse opened in 1956. In typical Wilson style, 11 holes are doglegs.

William K. Vanderbilt II

The fairways are tight—unforgiving woods line almost every one—and both its esthetics and challenge are enhanced by the artistically-sculpted bunkering, which is often supplemented with tall stands of love grass.

Among the most notable of the many fine holes are the 8th and 15th, long par fours that dogleg left before climbing to well-bunkered, hilltop greens. The home hole rises to the landing area, then turns left and crosses the club's entrance road en route to a green tucked behind a bunker at the left front. Most recognizable to commuters is number 10, which tumbles down a steep hill toward the Long Island Expressway.

Deepdale twice hosted the Met Amateur. In 1972, future PGA Tour professional George Burns defeated Jerry Courville Sr., in the finals; in 1986, Deepdale member George Zahringer III bested John Baldwin.

Today, Deepdale offers its members an idyllic setting and one of the best tests in the Met Area. ○

The 11th hole.

FISHERS ISLAND CLUB
"Treasure Island"

FISHERS ISLAND CLUB
Fishers Island, NY
YEAR FOUNDED: 1925
ARCHITECT:
Seth Raynor
COURSE OPENED: 1926

TEES	PAR	YARDAGE
Forward	72	5393
Middle	72	6103
Back	72	6544

TEES	COURSE RATING	SLOPE
Forward	71.0	118
Middle	70.9	130
Back	72.9	134

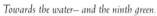
Towards the water— and the ninth green.

With water visible from every tee and green, comparisons with Pebble Beach are inevitable. But its island setting, with distant views of Long Island, Block Island, and the Connecticut/Rhode Island shoreline 100 miles from Manhattan set it apart. It is the Fishers Island Club, and its links-style course is currently ranked among the top 100 in the world by *GOLF Magazine*.

The island was a thriving resort destination as early as the late 1890s, with three hotels and the Hay Harbor Club, which sported nine holes of golf, all toward the western end of the island. To the east lay 1,800 acres of farmland owned by Ferguson's Fishers Island Farms Company, which controlled the ferry from New London, one of the hotels, and the cottages around the club.

In 1925, Ferguson's hired the men that created the Mountain Lake Club in Florida to develop the same sort of community/club. That team included landscaper Frederick Law Olmstead Jr. (his father had laid out Central Park in New York City) and course designer Seth Raynor. The close ties between the two clubs lasted until Mountain Lake closed in 1963; they even shared much of their memberships, which alternated between one in the summer, the other for the winter months.

The original plans for Fishers Island called for two golf courses, the first to be built mid-island, the other to follow at the eastern end, with homesites scattered throughout. Raynor chose two sites and laid out two courses on paper, the present course and "an even more spectacular course" mid-island; but plans for the latter were discarded in 1926 in favor of more desirable home sites.

Raynor died in January, 1926, so the work was completed by his assistants, Charlie Banks and Ralph Barton. The course and clubhouse opened in July, 1926, by which time the Club had attracted 180 members.

The course features spectacular ocean views on many holes, with water a serious threat on at least a dozen of them. On an unforgettable course, two of the most memorable holes are numbers three and four. The fourth is a moderate-length par four that after a long drive to an elevated fairway demands a blind approach over a tall peak to a punchbowl green perched at water's edge. The fifth is a long par three, rising sharply from tee to green, with the ocean in front of the tee and along the right.

Only slightly less noteworthy are the short par-five eighth, with water and duneland to both sides off the tee; the short par-three 11th, with the ocean hard to the right; and the short, uphill, par-five 18th, that starts with a long carry over an inlet.

The original clubhouse was massive, too large for the ultimate size of the seasonal membership. The club attempted to demolish it with explosives in 1963 to no avail, only to have it burn down later that year. The smaller, unpretentious clubhouse is more in keeping with the very private nature of the club. Fisher's Island—a rare combination of tranquility, beauty and fine golf.   ❍

The dramatic 5th hole.

GARDEN CITY COUNTRY CLUB

"Airmailed"

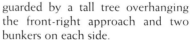

When the decision was made to convert the Salisbury Links into the private Cherry Valley Club in 1916, many were excluded. And so a group of residents from the Estates section of Garden City, led by Gage Tarbell, builder of the Westchester-Biltmore Hotel, organized the Garden City Country Club.

The new club leased an estate west of Nassau Boulevard and asked Walter Travis to design a championship 18-hole course, which opened in 1917. Immediately to the west of the new course was farmland. To the south, wilderness. Two blocks north was the former site of the Nassau Boulevard Air Field where, in 1911, the first airmail flight in American history took off on a flight all the way to Mineola.

The modern course closely resembles Travis' original, with a few alterations. Trees were planted on the relatively barren terrain in the early 1930s. Drainage areas in front of the third and fifth tees were the result of a county water reclamation project in 1941; the excavated earth was used to build up the 12th green and form the ridge that separates the sixth and seventh holes. A 1980s rejuvenation by architect Brian Silva stayed within the course's character.

The greens are highly undulating, featuring bold ridges and spines, and surrounded by mounds and bunkers, many of which extend out into the narrow entrances. Number three is the postcard hole, a moderate-length par four with a pond off the tee that empties into a brook running along the left side of the hole. The fairway falls sharply right to left, away from three bunkers high in the drive zone. The sloping green is

The clubhouse

guarded by a tall tree overhanging the front-right approach and two bunkers on each side.

At the par-five 12th (called Iwo Jima), a nest of three bunkers sits in the fairway about 150 yards from home. The green sits high on a plateau, built up with the dirt removed from the ditches on the front nine. There is a bunker in the face of the rough-covered rise into the green, and another at the feet of the rise. A tempting—but risky—green to go for in two!

In 1936, the 25th anniversary of the first airmail flight was celebrated and reenacted. The 14th fairway substituted for the Nassau Boulevard Air Field, which no longer existed; a plane landed and took off with the mail, headed for Roosevelt Field.

Garden City has hosted one Met Open (1950) and two Met Amateurs. Frank Strafaci was an easy winner of the 1954 Amateur, his record-setting seventh, at his home club. The 1969 final matched two of the giants of recent years, with Dick Siderowf edging Jerry Courville Sr. 2&1. By then, news of the outcome travelled by wire.

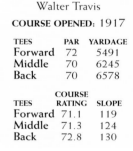

GARDEN CITY COUNTRY CLUB
Garden City, NY

YEAR FOUNDED: 1916

ARCHITECT:
Walter Travis

COURSE OPENED: 1917

TEES	PAR	YARDAGE
Forward	72	5491
Middle	70	6245
Back	70	6578

TEES	COURSE RATING	SLOPE
Forward	71.1	119
Middle	71.3	124
Back	72.8	130

View from third tee.

GARDINER'S BAY COUNTRY CLUB

"Spoiled Children Of Fortune"

During the final quarter of the 19th century, an effort was made to turn Shelter Island into a summer resort comparable to Newport. Situated between Long Island's north and south forks, Shelter Island is just seven miles long and four miles wide, accessible by ferry from either Greenport or Sag Harbor.

The Manhanset Manor House was built in 1873, and by the early 1890s had 300 guest rooms as well as tennis courts, stables, a baseball diamond, and a fine restaurant. The Manor offered all of life's finer amenities to the "spoiled children of fortune," who arrived daily on steamboats from New York and New London.

The Shelter Island Club was organized in 1895 to supplement the hotel's offerings with a nine-hole golf course. The first clubhouse was the Derring homestead, built in 1782, which is located to the right of the present eighth fairway. In 1904 the golf course was expanded to 18 holes and the name changed to Manhanset Manor Country Club. The facilities extended from Greenport Harbor to Gardiner's Bay.

**GARDINER'S BAY
COUNTRY CLUB**
Shelter Island Heights, NY

YEAR FOUNDED: 1951

ARCHITECTS:
C.A. Fox
Seth Raynor

COURSE OPENED: 1896

TEES	PAR	YARDAGE
Forward	71	5377
Middle	70	6124
Back	70	6359

TEES	COURSE RATING	SLOPE
Forward	71.2	117
Middle	68.2	119
Back	69.3	121

In 1910, the Manhanset Manor House was struck by lightning and burned to the ground. In its place, the Derring Harbor Casino was built, organized in 1915 by a group of wealthy New York bluebloods. Also at this time, the golf course was revised by Seth Raynor. Eight new holes were built, heading to and from the Casino, which served as the clubhouse, Raynor's course bears little resemblance to the present one. Perhaps the closest to an original hole is 11, which is played at 240 yards across a ravine to a punchbowl green. That ravine was known as "Echo Valley" because numerous boulders deflected the anguished cries of trapped golfers. The present hole plays at just 184 yards over a couple of trees that have grown midway.

The Club experienced financial troubles, and in 1918 found new ownership and changed names to Derring Harbor Golf Club. In 1926, the present clubhouse was built and the course completely revised, creating the present alignment of holes.

The Depression, three hurricanes, and World War II conspired against the Club, forcing it to close its doors in 1942. The course became a bean farm, and might still be one today had not the Shelter Island Lions Club interceded in 1950, helping the new Gardiner's Bay Country Club incorporate and lease the land. The golf course was restored and stability came to Shelter Island. A strong junior program is likely to guarantee a healthy future.

Gardiner's Bay is a course of mixed messages: from the deep gully that crosses the 9th, 11th, 12th, and 17th holes to the relatively flat terrain through the middle of the back nine; from the old-fashioned bunkering that surrounds the ground-level third green and the signature Seth Raynor bunkering at the 12th, 13th, and 17th holes to the modern-style, member-designed raised fourth green; and from the challenge of cutting the corner at the sixth hole to the unreachable turn at the eighth. Overall, Gardiner's Bay reflects the century-long journey from resort to delightful summer retreat. ◌

The short 9th hole. Inset: Nesting osprey on Shelter Island, incorporated in the Club's logo.

GLEN HEAD COUNTRY CLUB

"Ladies Day"

Glen Head Country Club is the result of a union of two Glen Head-area clubs from a bygone era. For a membership, it reached out to Sound View; for a golf course, to Women's National.

Marion Hollins

Most of Glen Head's founders took up golf at Sound View, playing there through 1947, when the course was sold to become Great Neck Estates. They purchased the former Women's National Golf & Tennis Club. The golf course, unused for several years, was rejuvenated, and some 80 bunkers eliminated to make it more enjoyable for the average club player.

Women's National had opened in 1924, fulfilling the women-only dream of Marion Hollins, the daughter of H.B. Hollins, first president of the MGA. Miss Hollins, possibly the most influential woman of golf's first half century in America, won the U.S. Women's Amateur in 1921 and the WMGA championship three times. The Glen Head site was acquired in 1922, and Devereux Emmet hired to design and build the course; both Charles Blair Macdonald and Seth Raynor consented to help with suggestions. The objective was to create a course that would "bring out the best in women's golf without sacrificing length or hazards."

Hollins visited England and Scotland in 1922-23, studying scores of courses and taking detailed notes on holes and features she liked, passing them along to Emmet on her return.

Ernest Jones, recognized as one of the great golf teachers despite losing a leg during World War I, held sway as professional at Women's National while developing an excellent reputation as a teacher of ladies. But like so many others, Women's National suffered through the Depression and in 1941 merged with the Creek Club. Both golf courses remained in play that year, but that proved financially impossible in 1942, so operations ceased at Women's National.

By 1948, the course was recultivated and the new club fully operational in the old clubhouse. The course has undergone only minor changes over the years, most notably the creation of the alternate par-three 15th, which can be used in place of the 16th hole on occasion.

Glen Head's course sits in a parkland setting, on land sloping away from the centrally located clubhouse. Many holes play over rolling ground, with trees a constant factor. Most of the greens are protected by at least one large, gaping bunker, while many feature steep falloffs to the sides or behind.

Supposedly Emmet's favorite hole was the fourth, an imposing par three played from a slightly elevated tee to a plateau green nearly encircled by huge, deep bunkers. The par-three 16th features a sloping, table-top green set above a huge bunker, with four fingers reaching into the sand. Another bunker guards the right rear. Truly a fair challenge. These two holes are perhaps most reminiscent of the original hazards at Women's National. ❍

GLEN HEAD COUNTRY CLUB
Glen Head, NY

YEAR FOUNDED: 1948

ARCHITECT:
Devereux Emmet

COURSE OPENED: 1924

TEES	PAR	YARDAGE
Forward	74	5829
Middle	71	6231
Back	71	6506

TEES	COURSE RATING	SLOPE
Forward	74.4	128
Middle	70.5	126
Back	71.7	129

The uphill 6th hole finishing in front of clubhouse.

GLEN OAKS CLUB

"Pipe's Dream"

Looking back from the 9th green, Blue course.

GLEN OAKS CLUB
Old Westbury, NY

YEAR FOUNDED: 1924

ARCHITECT:
Joe Finger

COURSE OPENED: 1971

TEES	PAR	YARDAGE
Forward	72	5660
Middle	72	6660
Back	72	6995

TEES	COURSE RATING	SLOPE
Forward	73.6	126
Middle	73.1	132
Back	74.7	136

Above is an average of three nines

In 1924, 25 men organized as the Glen Oaks Club and purchased 165 acres of the William K. Vanderbilt II estate, south of Lake Success. The Vanderbilt mansion, high on a hilltop, became their clubhouse.

The original course was designed by an obscure English architect named Wilfred H. "Pipe" Follett, a noted golfer and editor/writer for the (now defunct) *Metropolitan Golfer*. Glen Oaks was a scenic beauty, carved through virgin forest over hilly terrain.

In 1927, construction of the Northern State Parkway shaved 40 acres off the property while isolating another 18, including the clubhouse site, from the rest of the grounds. The course was redesigned and a new clubhouse constructed on the highest point in Queens County.

During World War II, the Club's property, which was across Lakeville Road from the Sperry Corporation, became a very sensitive security risk. The government took charge in 1942, allowing the Hazeltine Corporation to use the Club for its war work. The members leased the financially troubled Lakeville Club, where they played for the remainder of the war, after which the government moved out and the members returned.

By the late 1960s, more room was needed but there was no where to grow at the Queens location. In 1968, the Club sold its original property to Sigmund Sommer—who built the North Shore Towers complex on the site—and purchased 250 acres in Old Westbury.

Joe Finger, author of the Monster at the Concord

Hotel, was given the new course commission. Work began in 1970; it was playable by Labor Day, 1971.

Glen Oaks has 27 holes (the Red, White, and Blue nines), which play through narrow corridors of trees. The greens are large throughout, while water is a serious factor on the Blue nine, where major hazards come into play on three holes. The final hole on the Blue is the club's centerpiece. It doglegs around a pond, demanding a carry of at least 230 yards to clear the hazard (or choose the long way around), then rises abruptly to an elevated back-to-front green. The hole has been rated by *Newsday* among the best on Long Island.

The Metropolitan PGA Championship has twice been held at Glen Oaks. In 1976, Jimmy Wright claimed the title by playing what he called the best competitive round of his career, a final round 65 on an overcast day punctuated by treacherous, swirling winds. Wright's round included seven birdies and no bogies, and was eight shots better than his nearest competitor. In 1986, Glen Oaks assistant professional Don Reese's 209 was five strokes better than runner-up Jim Albus.

The current pro is Tom Joyce, a veteran of four U.S. Opens and two PGA Championships, and winner of both the Long Island and Westchester Opens.

The striking, modern clubhouse encompasses 110,000 square feet, mostly on a single floor. The club's luxurious Olympic-size swimming pool and eight tennis courts certainly would have caught William K. Vanderbilt's eye. ○

HEMPSTEAD GOLF & COUNTRY CLUB

"The Survivors"

When the private Cherry Valley Club was formed in 1916, supplanting the public Salisbury Links, the members of the Midland Golf Club moved their shingle to the new Salisbury publinx in what is now Eisenhower Park. In 1920, several of the surviving Midland members joined with a group of Hempstead businessmen to form the Hempstead Golf Club. Many of them were members of the Morton Masonic Lodge, which dated back to 1797 and counted among its members over the years signers of the Declaration of Independence and two governors of New York.

The new club purchased 122 acres of farmland and woods, and engaged the noted English greenkeeper Peter Lees to lay out a golf course. Lees first molded the farmland, and had nine holes ready for play on September 17, 1921, when an official opening-day match was played in a downpour. All 18 holes were ready by the start of the 1923 season. Lees' design was altered significantly when A.W. Tillinghast carved seven new holes from the woods for the 1927 season.

Hempstead's course has two personalities. The holes cut through the trees are relatively flat, but tight; the others are more open and rolling. All are heavily bunkered, an aspect of the course that has recently undergone a marvelous restoration at the hands of local architect Stephen Kay.

To score well at Hempstead, the golfer must survive five long par fours on the front side, sidestep a pair of potentially dangerous short par fours (numbers 9 and 12), then stay below the cup on the treacherous 15th green. Its dance floor is a tilting, two-tiered terror, cascading down the hillside in front of the halfway house.

The fourth is Hempstead's centerpiece, a long par four with an echelon bunker set on a left-to-right angle across the right entrance to the fairway, requiring a carry of 180 yards at its farthest point. For the average player, the second shot must contend with another large bunker, centered in the fairway about 50 yards from home.

HEMPSTEAD GOLF & COUNTRY CLUB
Hempstead, NY

YEAR FOUNDED: 1920

ARCHITECTS:
Peter Lees
A.W. Tillinghast

COURSE OPENED: 1921

TEES	PAR	YARDAGE
Forward	72	5896
Middle	72	6389
Back	72	6567

TEES	COURSE RATING	SLOPE
Forward	73.8	127
Middle	70.8	124
Back	71.6	126

The Hempstead clubhouse was a farmhouse, expanded several times over the years. The front of the building dates back to 1756, and was occupied by Tories during the Revolution. Inside the clubhouse in 1935, Hofstra University was founded by a group of club members.

Hempstead has been the venue for four MGA championships over the years. Judge Joseph Gagliardi of Winged Foot captured the 1951 Met Amateur at Hempstead; Ed Sullivan had a really big show, taking the low net prize in the qualifying round with a 77-9=68. The club also has hosted the 1946, 1949, and 1996 Met Juniors; the 1949 winner was the club's own Billy Edwards, his third of a record five consecutive MGA Junior titles.

The club's committment to junior golf today recalls the founders' persistent pursuit of golf as young men.   ❍

Approach to the cascading 15th green.

HUNTINGTON COUNTRY CLUB

"Oysters Roosevelt"

**HUNTINGTON
COUNTRY CLUB**
Huntington, NY

YEAR FOUNDED: 1910

ARCHITECT:
Devereux Emmet

COURSE OPENED: 1911

TEES	PAR	YARDAGE
Forward	73	5684
Middle	70	6210
Back	70	6357

TEES	COURSE RATING	SLOPE
Forward	73.1	126
Middle	70.5	132
Back	71.2	133

Among the first half-dozen golf clubs on Long Island was Oyster Bay Golf Club, which was established in 1894. Its membership was small yet exclusive, including many names from New York's upper social strata, among them architect Devereux Emmet and Theodore Roosevelt. The Club leased farmland on the Berry Hills, and sported a nine-hole course. The Club lasted barely more than a decade, but made its mark as the place where both Jerry Travers and 1899 U.S. Women's Amateur champion Ruth Underhill learned the game.

Shortly after Oyster Bay was disbanded, some of its remaining members founded the Huntington Country Club in 1910. Many of the original members made Huntington their summer residence; others lived year-round on the grand estates in the vicinity. In fine Oyster Bay tradition, the new Club chose Emmet to design and build its golf course, which opened in 1911. The next significant change to the course took place in 1929 when the present 10th hole was built, combining a par four to a green at the top of the hill with a par three down to the present green into one hole. At the same time the present

14th and 15th holes were developed, fourteen had been a par four played to a punchbowl green at the foot of "Cardiac Hill"; 15 had been a short par four up the hill.

Huntington is highly flexible, the first nine holes laid out in three triangles, each coming back near the clubhouse, which allows play to start at four points. The course is heavily bunkered, both greenside and in the fairways, including four crossbunkers. High fescue grass in the rough adds to the authenticity of the old-fashioned course.

The second hole sets the tone, needing a carry of 170 to 190 yards to clear a deep crossbunker and reach the higher elevation of the fairway. The hole bends to the right, with out–of–bounds the length of the hole on that side.

The aforementioned 10th is a long par four to a down-hill fairway that kicks to the right toward woods and out–of–bounds. The second shot will traverse a huge bunker across the left side of the fairway, beyond which the hole drops sharply to lower ground.

The second shot on the par-five 15th must carry a rising expanse of rough (Cardiac Hill) that once included three rows of bunkers called "the Maginot Line," then avoid a pair of bunkers to either side at the top of the hill.

The Huntington clubhouse was built specifically for the Club in 1910, and was enlarged for the first time in 1922. Perilous times during the Depression almost dragged the Club under during World War II; at that time, the course was opened to the public for a $1 green fee, and membership dropped to 40.

Besides tennis and paddle tennis, Huntington members can take advantage of their "winter club," one of just two in the Met Area. The ice rink, to the left of the first fairway, is used for skating and hockey. There is also a separate winter clubhouse and dining at the main clubhouse during the winter season. ❍

The picturesque 13th hole.

HUNTINGTON CRESCENT CLUB

"New Moon"

Approach shot on 5th hole.

**HUNTINGTON
CRESCENT CLUB**
Huntington, NY

YEAR FOUNDED: 1931

ARCHITECT:
Devereux Emmet

COURSE OPENED: 1931

TEES	PAR	YARDAGE
Forward	71	5390
Middle	70	6137
Back	70	6403

TEES	COURSE RATING	SLOPE
Forward	72.2	126
Middle	70.0	129
Back	71.2	131

The Huntington Crescent Club is a direct descendant of the Crescent Athletic Club of Brooklyn. The 1,500 "new moons" who founded the CAC in 1888 were primarily interested in lacrosse, baseball, and track. In 1896, they built a nine-hole course adjacent to the anchorage off Bay Ridge, on the east cliff of the Narrows overlooking New York Bay; it was expanded to 18 three years later. Even then, the property was the target of developers, so the Club began looking for greener pastures.

In 1930, they purchased an estate in Huntington, 300 acres of rolling woodland, formal gardens, with a frontage on Huntington Bay. Unfortunately, the plans for 24 tennis courts, fields for soccer, cricket, baseball, lacrosse, and polo, a toboggan slide, a yachting anchorage, and cabanas at the beach were stifled by the Depression. But not the golf course.

The architectural team of Emmet, Emmet, and Tull designed two 18-hole golf courses: The shorter East Course opened on July 4, 1931; the stronger West Course followed in the spring.

The '30s and '40s were difficult years. The beach was sold, a good portion of the remaining property was developed, and the West Course was all but destroyed. Only the front nine of the East Course remains relatively intact; the back includes holes from the old West Course.

What remains is a pretty parkland setting, featuring numerous swales, gullies, and elevated tees and greens. Some of the greens are fiercely bunkered, while others are relatively unprotected.

The fourth is a short, but testing, par four. The tee is elevated well above the fairway, which angles sharply right in the drive zone, with a tall tree at the corner, a bunker at its feet, and another bunker at the far side of the turn. The green is nearly surrounded by long, narrow bunkers, one of which protects the right front, leaving only a narrow entrance.

The fifth is a dogleg-left with a bunker on the right. From the landing area, the hole runs downhill through a gorge and across a patch of rough before rising to a table-top green bunkered at the front corners and behind.

The drive at the par-five seventh must fly over a deep, rough-infested gully ("Death Valley") to a rolling fairway that turns to the right, around a bunker at the corner, 175 yards from the green, which has a sizable burial mound right of center.

Today's descendants of the new moons enjoy a variety of sporting facilities including tennis courts and an Olympic-size swimming pool. The estate mansion still stands and serves as the clubhouse, and the beach is close by, a reminder of the founders' grandiose plans. ❍

LaTourette Golf Course

"New York's Finest"

For many years, the LaTourette Golf Course on Staten Island has been recognized as the crown jewel of New York City's public-course network. But had the original owner of the property—his ghost, actually—gotten his way, the property may have remained farmland.

Back in the 1830s, David LaTourette's 500-acre farm was the largest piece of privately-owned land on the island. (The present clubhouse dates back to that era.) In 1928, New York City purchased 120 acres of the farm for $3,500 per acre with the intent of building a public course.

The first nine holes, designed by John R. Van Kleek, opened in the spring of 1929. That seminal course included the original versions of the present 15th through 18th holes, and concluded with three consecutive par threes, including a finishing hole that ran away from the clubhouse. The trouble began in 1935 when the second nine opened and a major addition, containing the restaurant, was built onto the clubhouse. This disturbed the ghost of David LaTourette, who is said to have haunted the building at the time.

The completion of all 18 holes also led to the founding of LaTourette Golf Club, an MGA member club at a public facility.

Among LaTourette's more notable holes are the third, a short par three that is all carry over a pond to an elevated, reverse-L-shaped, two-tiered green. Trees overhang the full length of the hole, and swirling winds are usually a factor.

The most difficult par is the fifth hole, a long, downhill par four with trees hanging over the right side of the green. A hump in the center of the green divides the putting surface into two parts and demands a precise final approach.

Perhaps the most demanding shot on the course is the first one on the par-four eighth hole. From the blue tees, the tee shot must carry almost 240 yards to reach the rising fairway, the first 175 yards over a pond. Not only must the drive be long, it also should favor the left side to set up the best approach to the angled green.

The LaTourette pro shop was the first "office" for Jim Albus, who was head professional there from 1969-1980, after finishing his military service. Albus, winner of two Met Opens, went on to Piping Rock and then to great success on the Senior PGA Tour.

Since 1988, LaTourette and the American Golf Corporation, which took over management of the facility in 1985, have been annual hosts to the New York City Amateur, a 54-hole competition that now attracts an international field (it was restricted to city residents its first year). Among the winners have been George Zahringer III, Jerry Courville Jr., and Jeff Thomas, who was the first repeat winner (1995-'96).

A fitting tribute to the city's most demanding layout. ❍

**LATOURETTE
GOLF COURSE**
Staten Island, NY

YEAR FOUNDED: 1928

ARCHITECT:
John R. Van Kleek

COURSE OPENED: 1929

TEES	PAR	YARDAGE
Forward	72	5493
Middle	72	6322
Back	72	6692

TEES	COURSE RATING	SLOPE
Forward	70.9	115
Middle	69.6	118
Back	71.3	121

The LaTourette clubhouse.

MIDDLE BAY COUNTRY CLUB

"Nomad's Land"

**MIDDLE BAY
COUNTRY CLUB**
Oceanside, NY

YEAR FOUNDED: 1955

ARCHITECT:
Alfred Tull

COURSE OPENED: 1931

TEES	PAR	YARDAGE
Forward	73	5529
Middle	72	6505
Back	72	6821

TEES	COURSE RATING	SLOPE
Forward	72.4	117
Middle	72.1	129
Back	73.5	131

The tee shot at the 8th hole.

The early golfers of Baldwin and Oceanside, on the south shore of Long Island, were a nomadic lot. In 1919, they played at Milburn Country Club east of Grand Avenue in Baldwin. Milburn had financial troubles in 1941 and was reorganized as the Willow Brook Country Club. In 1931, the semiprivate Oceanside Golf & Country Club was formed by Joseph Weinstein, who offered one-year memberships. The course was highly respected and chosen to host the 1938 Metropolitan PGA Championship, won by Al Brosch.

Oceanside made it through the Depression and war years in one piece. Trouble came in 1951 when the county condemned club property west of Waukeena Avenue for use by Oceanside High School. A group of 149 members left the Club and purchased the old Engineers Country Club. The few members who stayed behind continued to play over what became a public nine-hole golf course. The old clubhouse remained, but was separated from the course by the road.

Willow Brook's property was condemned in the early 1950s, partly to make room for Baldwin High School. The members contacted

Weinstein, offering him the nucleus of a new club if he would add a second nine holes to the old Oceanside course. Alfred Tull reworked the old holes and laid out the new ones on a landfill, finishing by 1955.

Typical of the seaside courses on the south shore, the terrain is flat and relatively treeless. Golfers have to contend with persistent wind and water, which is a serious factor on eight holes. In 1988, David Postelwait added mounding to give the course a more modern look and protect the sand in the bunkers, which was being scattered by the winds.

The eighth is a short par four that curves left around the bay that gives the course its name. The left side of the fairway is flanked by a long waste bunker at water's edge, while the right side is lined with mounds and bunkers. The back-to-front putting surface is closely guarded by five additional bunkers, two long ones across the front and three smaller ones at the sides.

Middle Bay hosted the 1974 Met Open, in which Bob Bruno of Pelham won with a seven-under-par 209. He hit an 8-iron over a clump of trees right of the 18th fairway to within 10 feet for a winning birdie. In the end, like the early golfers of the region, Bruno found safe passage to the home green. ○

Aerial view of the golf course and bay.

THE MILL RIVER CLUB

"A Noble Experiment"

The Mill River Club on Long Island was conceived by founder William S. Roach with the explicit purpose of being diverse, as a "truly balanced, nonsectarian club." It has been a glorious social experiment proving that people of different races and creeds can mingle and enjoy each other's company.

Roach was a man for all seasons. He started his career in Hollywood as a reporter for *Variety*, later becoming a camera guru for Disney. A bomber pilot during World War II, Roach earned his law degree from Columbia. He was a patron of the arts and an avid golfer. He also believed that all men were created equal.

In 1964, he purchased Appledore, a Gold Coast estate located one mile north of Northern Boulevard between Planting Fields Arboretum and the SUNY Old Westbury campus. Roach quickly established the membership and funding. Two wings were added to the mansion to accommodate a large dining room, locker rooms, and grill. The pro shop had been a four-car garage.

For his golf course, Roach turned to a relative unknown named Gerald Roby, who had worked for William Mitchell. Roby did the Mill River job for his old friend, then retired.

The facilities opened on May 29, 1965. To help establish the golf program, Roach hired 1952 PGA champion Jim Turnesa, who served as golf professional for about five years. The entrance road to the club is named in his honor.

The course features some rugged territory, tight, tree-lined fairways that tumble through some abrupt elevation changes. The 11th is the centerpiece, a long par four over a gully to a landing area set in a narrow saddle hemmed in by trees tight on both sides. The green is on a plateau, with a pond on the left a threat to the player laying up on his second shot.

Number 14 is an exacting, picturesque, short par five that doglegs to the right, with out-of-bounds left beginning just beyond the bend. The fairway rolls downhill and kicks left through the blind target area for the second shot. The large, rolling green is perched on a plateau behind a huge bunker.

Mill River remains true to Bill Roach's goal, and thrives on its diversity. It has been recognized by the National Conference of Christians and Jews, and its policy also was noted in the *Congressional Record*.   ❍

**THE MILL
RIVER CLUB**
Oyster Bay, NY

YEAR FOUNDED: 1964

ARCHITECT:
Gerald Roby

COURSE OPENED: 1965

TEES	PAR	YARDAGE
Forward	72	5513
Middle	72	6194
Back	72	6595

TEES	COURSE RATING	SLOPE
Forward	72.4	126
Middle	70.4	131
Back	72.3	134

Approach to 18th green.

MONTAUK DOWNS STATE PARK

"Miami Beach North"

If the vision of one man had not head-long into the Depression, the East End of Long Island may have been changed forever.

That man was Carl Fisher, who built Miami Beach from a tangle of mangrove swamps. Fisher liked what he saw when he first visited Montauk on his yacht in the mid 1920s, and soon the "Miami Beach of the North" was on the drawing board. Fisher purchased 9,000 acres and drew up plans for a golf course, marina and yacht club, polo fields, tennis courts, and a luxurious 200-room hotel to be called Montauk Manor. Montauk was to become a point of departure for Long Islanders traveling to Europe by boat, replacing the trip back into Manhattan with a railroad ride to the end of the island.

Fisher employed 800 men daily to build roads, lay water pipes, and build Tudor-style homes on the hillsides. But the stock market crashed in 1929, and Carl Fisher's dreams crashed with it. Still, enough of his projects were completed to make Montauk a meeting place for the rich and royal.

The Montauk Downs State Park opened in 1927 with an 18-hole course, a natural links designed by an Englishman, Captain H.C. Tippett, likely with an assist from Charles B. Macdonald. Their course rolled through a "cluster of rounded hills and valleys, with here and there a gash of a ravine cutting across the landscape." There wasn't a level hole to be found, nor was there a trace of artificiality. The terrain was barren linksland, "as close an approach to the famous seaside links of the British Isles as may be had anywhere."

The course survived the Depression, the famous hurricane of 1938, and World War II, but was replaced by the present Robert Trent Jones course in 1969. The hotel was converted to condominiums in 1974, and the course was taken over by the state in 1978.

Where once the land was bare,

The long par-three 12th hole.

trees abound today. The enduring impression of the course is of the many long par fours, most of which play uphill to elevated greens. Two par fives challenge the longer hitters with the option of going for the green in two over water. The seventh cascades out of the woods down to a lake, while the 13th features a lateral water hazard along the right side that crosses in front of the elevated green.

A pair of the par threes retains some linksland flavor. The second is relatively short, but plays straight uphill over treeless terrain to a green perched atop the highest point on the property. A huge bunker guards the right side, extends across the front, and leaves only a small entrance. From the back of the elevated tee, the 12th hole demands a 200-yard carry over rugged terrain to a raised, heavily bunkered green. Against the prevailing breeze, a driver may not be enough to get home.

Montauk Downs averages 50,000 rounds each year, a remarkable number considering its remote location.

MONTAUK DOWNS STATE PARK

Montauk, NY

YEAR FOUNDED: 1927

ARCHITECT:
Robert Trent Jones

COURSE OPENED: 1969

TEES	PAR	YARDAGE
Forward	72	5797
Middle	72	6289
Back	72	6762

TEES	COURSE RATING	SLOPE
Forward	74.2	132
Middle	71.2	130
Back	73.3	135

THE MUTTONTOWN CLUB

"Twins"

The approach to the 18th green.

An intriguing Gold Coast legend tells of the two sisters who lived in twin estates on opposite sides of Northern Boulevard in Muttontown. The nearly identical mansions would later become parts of country clubs: The one south of the highway became Charter Oaks (then Fox Run, before the club's demise); the one to the north was reborn as The Muttontown Club.

The northern mansion was called "The Chimneys" because it had 13 of them—servicing 26 fireplaces—sticking out of the slate roof. The 44-room, red-brick Georgian house and 125 acres of rolling hills eventually was sold to Howard C. Brokaw, a prominent member of the international set (and the Piping Rock Club), a former Princeton football star who made his fortune manufacturing U.S. Army uniforms during World War I.

Brokaw made it known that upon his death, he wanted his property to become a country club. It took just a few months after his passing in 1960 to fulfill his wish. The estate was sold to Robert Leibowitz, son of a state Supreme Court Justice, and Louis Goldberg, who sold it the next year to the members of the newly formed Muttontown Club. They brought in Alfred Tull to design the golf course, which opened in May, 1962.

Muttontown is a typical North Shore layout of rolling hills and mature trees. The greens are large and well bunkered. The first hole is one of the strongest openers on Long Island, a sharp dogleg-right par four with trees closely guarding the turn. From the back tees, it takes a drive between 215 and 235 yards to leave a clear, although blind, second shot downhill to a sloping green.

The picturesque final hole calls for an accurate drive to avoid fairway bunkers left and trees right. But that is not all, as the approach is over a large pond to a two-tiered green.

In more recent years, additions have included a new dining wing (on land that once had been formal gardens), tennis courts, and an Olympic-size pool. A brick garage has been converted into an attractive pool house, while Brokaw's study is now the 19th hole, allowing the former owner to keep abreast of each day's happenings. ❍

**THE
MUTTONTOWN
CLUB**

East Norwich, NY

YEAR FOUNDED: 1960

ARCHITECT:
Alfred Tull

COURSE OPENED: 1962

TEES	PAR	YARDAGE
Forward	74	5815
Middle	71	6410
Back	71	6755

TEES	COURSE RATING	SLOPE
Forward	73.3	127
Middle	70.8	124
Back	72.4	128

NORTH HEMPSTEAD COUNTRY CLUB
"Declaration Of Independence"

**NORTH HEMPSTEAD
COUNTRY CLUB**
Port Washington, NY

YEAR FOUNDED: 1916

ARCHITECTS:
Ed Eriksen
A.W. Tillinghast
Charles Banks
Robert Trent Jones

COURSE OPENED: 1916

TEES	PAR	YARDAGE
Forward	73	5477
Middle	70	6112
Back	70	6293

TEES	COURSE RATING	SLOPE
Forward	71.6	124
Middle	70.2	126
Back	71.0	129

George Washington visited Roslyn in the 1790s in gratitude for the area's support during the Revolution. Indeed, it was the north shore farmers who first declared their independence from Great Britain in 1775, separating themselves from the loyalist, land-owning gentry of Hempstead. That schism eventually led to the creation of the Town of North Hempstead in 1784 and the naming of Port Washington in 1857.

When a new golf club was organized early in 1916, it took the name North Hempstead and as its home an estate along Middle Neck Road (now Port Washington Boulevard). The entrance was an old country road cut through rows of ancient elms, and the land was shared with all types of wildlife, including quail, foxes, and ducks.

The first golf professional was Ben Nicholls, brother of Gil, a two-time Met Open winner. Together, the brothers designed the first North Hempstead course, 18 holes lying flat in a cow pasture and opened in 1916.

Ben Nicholls was succeeded by George McLean, his brother's archrival, who represented North Hempstead in the inaugural PGA Championship in 1916, and he by Ed Eriksen, who came to North Hempstead in 1919. Between 1920 and 1922, Eriksen completely revised the course, reportedly act-

U.S. Women's Amateur Champion Alexa Sterling, a member in the 1920s.

ing on the advice of A.W. Tillinghast. Charles Banks introduced the picturesque par-three second hole in 1930. In 1957, another revision became necessary when the club's lease on 7.5 acres expired. So Robert Trent Jones was engaged to build four new holes (11, 12, 13, and 17), which opened in 1958.

Today it is a course of tree-lined fairways with sizable undulations, challenging the average player for sufficient length to reach the level areas. The greens also are highly contoured.

Banks' second is the most photogenic hole, a short par three across a pond to a raised green surrounded by bunkers. The putting surface is divided into two sectors by a sizable front-to-back spine.

Less pretty but more troubling is the eighth, a three-shot par five with a large rock protecting the right entrance to the green. The drive is played through a chute to a steeply-rising fairway; the objective on the second shot is to clear a second crest and a stretch of rough on its backslope, simplifying the shot to the green, which is tucked on a plateau behind three deep sand-faced bunkers—and the rock.

The Depression ended the Club's expansive period. The maintenance budget was slashed so the course began to resemble the cow pasture it once had been. Because of gas rationing during World War II, many members travelled to the Club by railroad, concluding their journey on the Club's Tally Ho (a horse-drawn carriage) from the Plandome station. Others came with the milk man and left on a hay wagon.

A notable crowd hung out at North Hempstead, including sportswriters Grantland Rice and Ring Lardner, "Toonerville Trolley" cartoonist Fontaine Fox (the first club champion), and Clarence Buddington Kelland, who helped write the 1952 Republican Party platform. Had Kelland lived two centuries earlier, he might have had a hand in writing the Declaration of Independence.   ❍

The hazards approaching the 8th green.

NORTH HILLS
COUNTRY CLUB
"A Tree Grows In Manhasset"

The watery par-three 12th.

In 1919, the Belleclaire Country Club built its 18-hole course in Bayside, Queens, hemmed in by Horace Harding Boulevard, Bell Boulevard, and Rocky Hill Road. The club was sold for development in 1927, and a nucleus of its members moved on to found the North Hills Golf Club in Douglaston later that year.

The North Hills course was laid out over extremely rolling and scenic terrain by the father-son team of Willie Tucker Sr. and Jr. It opened on Labor Day, 1927. The palatial Spanish Mission-style clubhouse was regarded by some as the crowning achievement of architect Clifford C. Wendehack's career.

Prominent among the early golfers was George Voigt, winner of both the Long Island Amateur and Open in 1928. In 1930, Voigt led Bobby Jones by two holes with five to play in the semifinals of the British Amateur, the first leg of Jones' Grand Slam.

North Hills failed during The Depression and was run by a bank, which operated the facility as a public course before selling it back to the members after the war. By 1960, city real estate taxes had taken their toll so the club sold its land to the city and Cathedral College. Property was purchased in Manhasset, and Robert Trent Jones was hired late in 1960 to design a new 18-hole course, which was ready by the spring of 1963.

Members will tell you that North Hills has "more trees than any other golf course in the universe," placing a constant premium on accuracy. The hilly terrain assures that many approach shots will be played from difficult lies.

Typical is the long par-four second, which bends sharply left away from water on the right, then plays uphill to a green with an eight-foot pitch from left rear to right front. *Newsday* has rated the long par-four 10th among the toughest holes on Long Island. A large tree stands over the corner of the right dogleg at the crest of a hill, blocking most shots from that side of the fairway. From there, the hole rolls downhill and to the right, toward a crowned green.

Mal Galletta, now an active octogenarian, has been the club's most accomplished golfer, winning 19 club championships between 1944 and 1986, the last at age 75. He also won the 1944 North & South Amateur and the 1946 Long Island Amateur. His son, Mal Jr., is a three-time winner of the Long Island Open; grandson Mal III won the Long Island Amateur before turning professional.

North Hills has been an active tournament host since the move to Manhasset, including five Ike Championships (1977 and 1981-1984). The first edition of the LPGA Tour's Western Union Classic was held there in 1978: Judy Rankin won at nine under par and Nancy Lopez stumbled at the start, four-putting the treacherous second green.

The annual 18-hole invitational tournament, begun in 1972, features individual and team competitions. The roster of winners includes Gene Francis, Jerry Courville Sr., and, most prominently, Jerry Courville Jr., who has won four times. Obviously, a straight shooter. ❍

**NORTH HILLS
COUNTRY CLUB**
Manhasset, NY

YEAR FOUNDED: 1927

ARCHITECT:
Robert Trent Jones

COURSE OPENED: 1963

TEES	PAR	YARDAGE
Forward	72	5663
Middle	72	6039
Back	72	6472

TEES	COURSE RATING	SLOPE
Forward	73.0	125
Middle	69.6	125
Back	71.6	129

NORTH SHORE COUNTRY CLUB

"The Sands Of Time"

North Shore Country Club began life as an annex to New York City's Harmonie Club, which itself was formed in 1852 as a home-away-from-home for recent immigrants. "Harmonie" translates from German as "get together," and the new club offered its members the chance to gather for "songfests, literary readings, and general conviviality."

In 1913, Harmonie purchased the Glenwood Country Club and its 18-hole golf course. Glenwood had opened the year before, with a major attraction its anchorage in Hempstead Harbor. The club had its own private beach, complete with a boathouse, pier, and wooden catwalk up to the circa-1860s clubhouse. Many members arrived by private yacht.

Once the original Glenwood course proved inadequate, A.W. Tillinghast was engaged in 1915 to revise it, but in the end retained only five holes from the existing 18. Working on the rugged, rolling terrain, he laid out a

George Sands

number of tight doglegs with strategic trees guarding their elbows. The two par threes at the turn, the "Redan" ninth and a picture-postcard 10th—with a deep ravine between tee and green—are outstanding.

Notable among the longer holes are the sixth, a long par four, its fairway slanting steeply from right to left, and the par-five 16th, which calls for a careful draw around the 90-degree turn if the long hitter wants any chance to get home in two. Everyone remembers the eighth, a relatively short par four with a large lake in front of the green.

North Shore received its baptism of fire in 1919 as host to the Met Open. The winner was Walter Hagen who, in one round, drove the green at the par-four 11th by cutting across the corner (the trees were much smaller then).

George Sands is the club's most prominent (and enduring) member, which he has been since 1920. Now in his 90s, Sands has given himself to golf. He has been president of the Metropolitan Golf Association (1974-1975), was a cofounder of the Ike Tournament, and helped establish the Long Island Caddie Scholarship Fund (1962) and Long Island Seniors Golf Association (1951). In 1985, the MGA honored him with its Distinguished Service Award; the Metropolitan Golf Writers followed suit in 1987. In 1991, the Long Island Golf Association instituted the George E. Sands Distinguished Service Award, and honored its namesake as its first recipient.   ❍

NORTH SHORE COUNTRY CLUB
Glen Head, NY

YEAR FOUNDED: 1913

ARCHITECT:
A.W. Tillinghast

COURSE OPENED: 1912

TEES	PAR	YARDAGE
Forward	75	5684
Middle	72	6288
Back	72	6617

TEES	COURSE RATING	SLOPE
Forward	72.6	125
Middle	71.2	128
Back	72.3	130

From behind the 8th green.

OYSTER BAY TOWN GOLF COURSE

"World Class"

**OYSTER BAY
TOWN
GOLF COURSE**
Woodbury, NY

YEAR FOUNDED: 1989

ARCHITECT:
Tom Fazio

COURSE OPENED: 1989

TEES	PAR	YARDAGE
Forward	70	5109
Middle	70	5795
Back	70	6351

TEES	COURSE RATING	SLOPE
Forward	70.4	126
Middle	69.0	126
Back	71.5	131

In 1928, Andrew Mellon purchased a 121-acre estate known as "Woodlands," just north of Jericho Turnpike in Woodbury, and gave it to his daughter Alicia and her husband as a wedding gift. It became their summer retreat. The 38-room, two-story Italian-style mansion was designed by William Adams Delano, and the grounds included numerous century-old trees.

The Town of Oyster Bay purchased the estate in 1979, and had the idea of building a public course in 1984. They turned to George and Tom Fazio to design it. The Fazios labeled the site "world class," one of the best pieces of property they ever had to work with. George died early in the project, and the finished product can be attributed almost entirely to his nephew Tom. The course opened for play in April of 1989, and each year has provided upwards of 50,000 rounds of challenging public golf.

The fourth is the most memorable hole. It's a par four that plays down into a hidden fairway, turns slightly to the right around a spectacular bunker complex, and marches uphill to a green 50 feet above the fairway.

Oyster Bay's finish is as strong as it is picturesque. The 16th is a slight dogleg to the right, climbing to an elevated green cut into a hillside; the drive must carry the edge of a lake to reach the preferred left side of the fairway. Number 17 is a dogleg right that plays through a chute of trees to a narrow landing area overlooking the green, which is elevated beyond a collar of rough. The left side of the 18th fairway is flanked by a long bunker complex; it takes a good poke to reach the corner of this dogleg left. The greens at both 17 and 18 are tiered, with bunkers protecting the left-rear lower decks—clearly the most challenging pin placement on either surface.

The renovated Mellon mansion makes a grand clubhouse, with a pro shop, lockerrooms, grill room, and three private dining rooms. A world-class facility, it is a gift that keeps giving to the residents of Oyster Bay. ❍

The approach to the fourth green.

PINE HOLLOW COUNTRY CLUB

"Utopia Bound"

The approach to the first hole.

**PINE HOLLOW
COUNTRY CLUB**
East Norwich, NY

YEAR FOUNDED: 1955

ARCHITECT:
William Mitchell

COURSE OPENED: 1955

TEES	PAR	YARDAGE
Forward	72	5521
Middle	71	6359
Back	71	6731

TEES	COURSE RATING	SLOPE
Forward	71.5	121
Middle	70.5	129
Back	72.3	131

When it opened in 1955, Pine Hollow was the first new private club on Long Island in a quarter-century. Its small syndicate of owners invested more than $1 million to purchase the 133-acre estate of Consuelo Vanderbilt Balsan and create a golfing Utopia. Their plan was to create a luxurious private club, then sell it to the membership for a substantial profit. The sale went through in 1960.

The 42-room, French Norman-style mansion was built in 1934 for $750,000; Consuelo, a great–granddaughter of Cornelius Vanderbilt, purchased it in 1939. Among the first of the great estates to be fully air conditioned, it also featured a swimming pool, tennis courts, formal gardens, marble fireplaces, sculptured gold-bronze dolphins for sink faucets, and a direct phone line to Europe. Its guests over the years included Winston Churchill, Charles de Gaulle, and the Duke of Windsor.

The new owners added a two-story wing for locker-rooms, a dining room, grill room, and cocktail lounge.

They also engaged William Mitchell to build a championship course, his first of several on Long Island. More than 1,000 trees and shrubs were transplanted to help frame the holes.

The Club opened in April of 1955 and the syndicate moved quickly to put its name in the headlines. In June, 1958, Pine Hollow hosted the Pepsi-Boys Club Open, the first PGA Tour event held on Long Island. With a purse of $60,000, it was that year's richest Tour event. Arnold Palmer led all the way, with rounds of 66-69-67-71=273, 11 under par.

Among Pine Hollow's golf pros was Larry Laoretti, who is remembered as a raconteur who conducted an annual trick-shot demonstration. Laoretti left the club ranks to join the Senior Tour, and he won the U.S. Senior Open at Saucon Valley, Pennsylvania, in 1992.

Pine Hollow has recently undergone major renovation. The mansion now has larger, more modern dining facilities. On the course, architect Gil Hanse rejuvenated the bunkering, adding considerably to the course's playability and esthetics. Both the 10th and 15th holes now dogleg to the left around dramatic clusters of bunkers that narrow the drive zones.

The course also retains an old-fashioned flavor, such as at the 14th, a short, difficult par three. Its plateau green is perched above a huge, deep bunker dotted with two islands of dense grass. The sharply sloping putting surface also is bunkered once right and twice left, and a deep pot bunker waits behind the green.

The 16th is a beautiful, short par four that rises then drops precipitously to a hidden landing area flanked on the right by four bunkers. The hole tumbles through another swale before rising to a plateau green set above three deep bunkers. Hanse's work has brought Pine Hollow closer to the golfing utopia originally envisioned. ❍

Larry Laoretti

PLANDOME COUNTRY CLUB

"Backup Plan"

Plandome Country Club was an afterthought, a fallback position. In 1928, the founding fathers purchased part of the Leeds estate hoping to develop the property for home-sites. When the stock market crash of 1929 intervened, the land was used for a golf club instead. Fortunately so, for Plandome is among the most challenging and picturesque courses in Nassau County.

Orrin Smith was commissioned to lay out the course. Perhaps best known for designing a private course for Henry Ford in Michigan, Smith had Plandome ready for play by May, 1931.

Smith's back nine has undergone considerable change over the years (the front nine is basically unchanged), with perhaps six holes remaining intact, including the extra hole, a par three between the 17th green and 18th tee that once was a regular part of play.

George Lawrence's painting of the 3rd hole.

The 10th through 13th holes are of more recent vintage. Severely rolling terrain creates a series of uphill, downhill, and sidehill lies, and a deep gully crosses five holes.

The first hole may be the stiffest opener in the Met Area. It starts from an elevated tee, then sweeps up and around to the right, with the fairway falling sharply toward the tree line on that side. The tilted green rises above the fairway, separated by a wall of rough.

The 13th is a beautiful hole. The drive must be carefully directed to the right-center of a two-level fairway that kicks severely left toward trees and out-of-bounds. The approach is played across a gully.

The 18th is a short par four calling for a 175-yard carry from an elevated tee to clear a pair of cross bunkers and reach the fairway. The pond along the right is not on club property, and is out-of-bounds. A stand of willows separates the green from the water, forcing the tee shot to the left for a clear approach.

Plandome began life as an English-style, golf–only club. Country club facilities came later. The Leeds farmhouse, a three-story, 20-room, white clapboard structure, was enhanced and served as the clubhouse. It was destroyed by fire in 1958, and replaced by the present building.

Plandome's junior program has produced a number of outstanding players, among them two-time MGA Player of the Year John Baldwin and former PGA Tour player George Burns.

One name that stands out among the Club champions is that of Bobby Riggs, who no doubt could have won several club titles had that been conducive to winning bets. Needless to say, the hills of Plandome are alive with Riggs stories. Riggs is said to have hit his tee shot on the home hole into the swimming pool to win a bet. There are numerous spots on the course where he practiced shots that later would serve him well. Riggs' opponents never got a second chance. ❍

PLANDOME COUNTRY CLUB
Plandome, NY

YEAR FOUNDED: 1929

ARCHITECT:
Orrin Smith

COURSE OPENED: 1931

TEES	PAR	YARDAGE
Forward	74	5400
Middle	71	6135
Back	71	6450

TEES	COURSE RATING	SLOPE
Forward	71.3	122
Middle	69.6	127
Back	71.6	132

RICHMOND COUNTY COUNTY CLUB

"The Outerbridge Crossing"

**RICHMOND
COUNTY
COUNTRY CLUB**
Staten Island, NY

YEAR FOUNDED: 1888

ARCHITECT:
Members

COURSE OPENED: 1897

TEES	PAR	YARDAGE
Forward	74	5809
Middle	71	6351
Back	71	6636

TEES	COURSE RATING	SLOPE
Forward	73.6	127
Middle	70.8	126
Back	72.1	128

Richmond County Country Club was organized in 1888, the same year St. Andrew's was formed. Within a decade, the club had compiled a distinguished history associated with three popular sports of the day—fox hunting, lawn tennis, and golf.

Most of the club's founders were members of the Richmond County Hunt, which had been organized in 1887 to formalize an organization that had been active on Staten Island for nearly a decade. As housing developments began to dot the island's landscape, fox hunting became less practical and ceased by 1915.

Golf came in 1894, led by George Hunter, George Armstrong, and James Park, Englishmen who began playing over the Fox Hills in the fall of 1893. Hunter and Armstrong were members at St. Andrew's, and participated there in the "unofficial" amateur championship of 1894. Staten Island was a summer retreat at the time, and Richmond County a summer club.

The pioneer golfers laid out a nine-hole course, and Hunter donated a medal, which has been awarded to the medalist in the qualifying round for the club championship since 1895. It is one of the oldest medals in continuous competition in American golf.

The club moved in 1897 to its present site on the Dongan Hills to accommodate the growing number of golfers. A nine-hole course went in immediately, and a second nine followed the next season. The present clubhouse was part of a lavish estate, built in the 1840s by a shipping magnate who liked to watch from his porch as his ships entered New York Harbor.

Lawn tennis became popular in 1899. A quarter-century earlier, the sport was imported to this country from Bermuda by Mary Outerbridge, the sister of two of the club's founders. Eugene Outerbridge took the lead in forming a national organization to govern the sport, helping found the United States Lawn Tennis Association in 1881.

The golf course was revised in 1956 when logistical and financial considerations led to the sale of the first and 18th holes, both par threes and the only two holes on the clubhouse side of Todt Hill Road, which had become a busy thoroughfare. The present 11th and 12th holes replaced them, and a pro shop-caddie house was constructed. The sale separated the clubhouse from the course, an inconvenience the membership endured gracefully.

Despite one hole that falls off the face of the earth and the longest (644 yards) par five in the Met Area, the course derives its character from the dramatic undulation of its greens. A seemingly ever-present creek crosses or borders 10 holes. And while relatively short, the course is no pushover.

The third is the once-famous "Wee Drap" hole, a short par three that falls 200 feet from tee to green. A pond fronts the green, a pair of bunkers waits behind.

Played from an elevated tee that offers a spectacular view of the Lower Bay, the tenth drops precipitously in the drive zone before rising sharply, then proceeding—and proceeding slightly downhill with a moderate pitch to the left before reaching a pair of cross bunkers 100 yards from home. A deep swale precedes the green.

In 1989 New York State manifested its interest in Staten Island's green belt by purchasing the golf course, then giving the Club a 99-year lease at an annual rent of $1. This has allowed the Club to finance considerable course improvements and cover annual maintenance costs, as well as build a modern clubhouse adjacent to the golf course.   ❍

Wee Drap today.

ROCKAWAY HUNTING CLUB

"The Grandaddy Of Them All"

ROCKAWAY HUNTING CLUB
Cedarhurst, NY

YEAR FOUNDED: 1878

ARCHITECTS:
Devereux Emmet
A.W. Tillinghast

COURSE OPENED: 1916

TEES	PAR	YARDAGE
Forward	71	5463
Middle	70	5866
Back	70	6251

TEES	COURSE RATING	SLOPE
Forward	70.4	119
Middle	69.1	126
Back	70.9	129

Rockaway Hunting Club is the oldest country club in the United States, although not originally a "country club" in today's sense of the word. Its principal clientele was the horse set, and it featured fox hunting and steeplechase racing.

In 1877, a group of young men from Bayswater in Far Rockaway took part in a "chase" between Lawrence and Valley Stream, enjoying themselves immensely. They organized a club in Bayswater in 1878, but by 1884, residential development had forced a move to the present location in Cedarhurst. There the members built a clubhouse considered the largest, most luxurious on Long Island, that overlooked Reynolds Channel, Long Beach Island, a polo field, and a four-mile steeplechase course.

Rockaway's initial fame came in polo, creating a bitter rivalry with Meadow Brook Hunt. By 1888, the two clubs were so superior to all others that a handicap system was created. The world-champion Rockaway team was headed by Foxhall Keene, who was rated the best all-around player in America for eight years.

Golf has been played at the club almost from the start, and today it is the sport of choice. The first course consisted of a few primitive holes suggested in 1891 by John Reid and John Ten Eyck of St. Andrew's. By 1895, the club boasted a full nine-hole layout designed by Willie Dunn, which was extended to 18 holes by Tom Bendelow in 1898.

Devereux Emmet built a new 18-hole course in 1915, crossing Woodmere Channel and extending to Reynolds Channel. Another revision in 1926, by A.W. Tillinghast, included the highly-acclaimed ninth hole, which *GOLF Magazine* rated among the nation's 100 best in 1986.

The character of the course is shaped by large bodies of water, severely undulating, multilevel greens, and afternoon sea breezes. The final three holes on the front nine play along the water. Seven is a "Cape" hole, with the drive played over Woodmere Channel and the green set just short of Reynolds Channel, which runs from tee to green along the right side of number eight. The ninth is crescent-shaped, curving to the right around Reynolds Channel; marshes and an inlet of the Channel must be carried off the tee, while another inlet is in play on the second shot—especially after a short drive.

Although a number of members were accomplished in a variety of sports, the greatest athlete in club history was Foxhall Keene. During the late 1890s, he took a brief respite from polo and developed into one of the top golfers in the Met district. He was a regular competitor in regional and national tournaments, but not with the expected success. He did compete in the 1897 U.S. Open, and advanced to the quarter-finals of the 1898 U.S. Amateur. Truly, a man for all seasons. ❍

The waterside 9th hole.

ROCKVILLE LINKS CLUB
"Humm Dinger"

View from alongside 15th green.

L ate in the summer of 1984, John Humm Jr., 25-time club champion of Rockville Links between 1946 and 1981, led defending two-time champion Ed McGoldrick after the first round of their 36-hole final. Sensing that the critically ill McGoldrick was fatigued, Humm suggested they continue their match the following morning, when McGoldrick fired a 68 to come from behind and win the championship 2up. McGoldrick's courageous performance deprived Humm of the chance to establish a new national record for championships at one club. Sadly, McGoldrick passed away a few months later.

The Rockville Centre Country Club was formed in December, 1922. The first order of business was to put together a parcel of 113 heavily wooded acres, then the Club turned to Devereux Emmet for a design. It has been said that more than 1,000 trees were felled, while heavy underbrush and blueberry bushes were cleared away. The first nine holes were ready by July 1, 1924, but Emmet quit after the first season, and it was the club's professional/greenkeeper, Harry O'Brien, who completed the back nine in 1926.

The remaining trees give Rockville Links its character. They are a forbidding, unforgiving presence on most holes, and watch closely over the turns of the numerous doglegs. With few exceptions, the terrain is flat, and the course heavily bunkered.

The postcard hole is the short, par-three fifth, which plays over a pond to a relatively flat green bunkered right front and left rear. Another, smaller pond waits at the green's left flank.

Unlike any other hole on the course, the fairway of the par-four 15th is flanked by bunkers and mounds left and right. From there the land rises abruptly before falling into a gully leading to the plateau green.

Joe Turnesa became club professional in 1938, remained with the Club through the war years, and retired after the 1947 season. During his tenure, Turnesa won a pair of Long Island Opens, putting one-handed on both occasions. Mike Turnesa Jr., Joe's nephew, is the Club's current professional, and his son, Marc, won the MGA Junior Championship in 1994.

In the 1953 Met Open at Rockville, only one player, Pete Cooper, bested par. His 284 for four rounds topped Pat Cici by four strokes.

The original clubhouse, which faced DeMott Avenue, was moved to its present location in 1924. A porch was built, surrounding much of the exterior, and lockers were built upstairs. Today, the upstairs locker rooms are a club hallmark as is John Humm's record. ○

**ROCKVILLE
LINKS CLUB**
Rockville Centre, NY

YEAR FOUNDED: 1922

ARCHITECT:
Devereux Emmet

COURSE OPENED: 1924

TEES	PAR	YARDAGE
Forward	73	5731
Middle	72	5731
Back	72	6257

TEES	COURSE RATING	SLOPE
Forward	73.4	127
Middle	68.0	122
Back	70.3	128

SANDS POINT GOLF CLUB

"The Governor's Ball"

The long par-five 14th hole.

**SANDS POINT
GOLF CLUB**
Sands Point, NY

YEAR FOUNDED: 1927

ARCHITECT:
A.W. Tillinghast

COURSE OPENED: 1928

TEES	PAR	YARDAGE
Forward	72	5618
Middle	72	6348
Back	72	6644

TEES	COURSE RATING	SLOPE
Forward	73.7	127
Middle	70.8	124
Back	72.2	127

Sands Point was rich long before it garnered a reputation as focal point of Long Island's "Gold Coast" society. Besides good soil and natural resources, it has long been rumored that part of Captain Kidd's treasure is buried nearby.

It was another captain who first found the area profitable. Captain John Sands arrived in 1695. Eighty years later, his descendants led the North Shore farmers who split from the large landowners of loyalist Hempstead in what has been called the first American "declaration of independence."

At the end of the 19th century, Sands Point's independence ended with the extension of the Long Island Railroad. With the promise of a direct ride to Manhattan, prominent New Yorkers began summering in Sands Point. In no time, Sands Point was on a par with Newport as America's summer social capital. Eventually, the warm-weather guests settled in, building the mansions immortalized in "The Great Gatsby."

In August, 1925, the Harbor Hills Park Corporation purchased the Julius Fleischman estate. Included in the sale was a nine-hole golf course, called Harbor Hills, and a world-class polo facility that had welcomed the great players of the world and nurtured a world-championship team.

Two years later, Vincent Astor, Cornelius Vanderbilt, Bernard Baruch, Irving Berlin, Walter Chrysler, Harry Guggenheim, E.F. Hutton, John Hay Whitney, Marshall Field, with future New York Governor Averill Harriman at the helm, turned Harbor Hills into the Sands Point Club. Although polo remained the primary activity until World War II, golf took on increasing importance. A.W. Tillinghast was engaged in 1927 to revamp the original nine and complete an already started second nine—without touching the polo field!

Tillinghast suggested, and got approved, a radical revision that would produce an outstanding course worthy of the property. It opened in 1928. Then and now, deep greenside bunkers and multiple fairway hazards make the course difficult, with racy greens and well placed trees adding to the challenge. (For the past decade, the Club has been working to restore the original layout, particularly the shape, depth, and exact location of Tillinghast's bunkers.)

Sands Point greets golfers with a tall maple 100 yards off the first tee. It must be carried or skirted to reach the ideal position in the right center of the fairway on the dogleg-left par five.

The fourth fairway rises and falls while kicking left toward an out-of-bounds line. A final fall into a gully precedes the climb to a severely sloping, left-to-right green. Tall trees overhang the right side on the approach.

The 14th is an heirloom, a par five of nearly 600 yards. The landing area kicks left, away from a pair of bunkers and intruding trees, but toward another bunker and out-of-bounds along Middle Neck Road. The ideal second shot is over the crest of the hill to a relatively flat area about 150 yards from home, after which the hole drops even more precipitously.

Harriman's righthand man during the Club's first 15 years was Captain Ernest Carter, the secretary and general manager who devoted his life to Sands Point. Carter was an outstanding golfer, a champion in his native Ireland, quarterfinalist in the 1934 Met Amateur, club champion at Sands Point in 1940, and longtime holder of the course record for members with a 65 set in 1929. Captain Carter treated Sands Point as his own personal treasure. ❍

SEAWANE GOLF & COUNTRY CLUB

"Getting A Bead"

In 1914, an Indian grave was discovered on the Hewlett estate of John N. Auerbach. Among the findings were skeletal remains, arrow and spear heads, and a large quantity of copper beads known by the Indians as "sewan." Auerbach anglicized the name for the beads to Seawane, chose it for his estate, and then it was used for the founding of the Seawane Club in 1927.

The fledgling club engaged Devereux Emmet to lay out an 18-hole golf course, which he carved out in true links style, much of it on land reclaimed from the marshes. The course lies on flat, treeless terrain, exposed to the winds off the ocean. Undermining play are two deep-water canals, numerous crossbunkers in the fairways, bunkers in front of greens, and bold contours, mounds, and swales on the greens.

For their clubhouse, the membership modernized Auerbach's three story Victorian country estate. The club was easily accessible by boat via the canals and nearby Lake Kathellen, a deep body of water that provided a fine anchorage for motor boats.

William D. Richardson

The Club fell on hard times, and eventually the course and clubhouse fell into disrepair. The downward spiral continued until 1960, when residents of Hewlett Harbor purchased the club from the remaining members.

The third hole introduces the golfer to the canal system, which borders the right side from tee to green. Lake Kathellen is immediately behind the green, and very much in play. The drive on the fourth hole must cross the canal, which returns to the right of the green.

The 16th is a par four with one canal on the left, another crossing in front of the green buttressed by a wall of rocks. The green is protected by three bunkers and framed by mounds.

The long, par-five 17th has an entirely different flavor. Suddenly appearing 150 yards from the green is a large waste area of sand, mounds, and grass.

Since 1948, Seawane has hosted the Richardson Memorial, which honors the late William D. Richardson, a reporter for *The New York Times* from 1921 to 1957. The tournament is conducted by the Long Island Golf Association and contested at match play in flights of 16 after an 18-hole qualifying round. The list of winners includes the best of the Met Area: Humm, Galletta, Strafaci, Siderowf, Courville, Francis, Burns, Zahringer, and Baldwin among them. The winners are rewarded handsomely, although not with copper beads.   ❍

SEAWANE GOLF & COUNTRY CLUB

Hewlett Harbor, NY

YEAR FOUNDED: 1927

ARCHITECTS:
Devereux Emmet
Alfred Tull

COURSE OPENED: 1927

TEES	PAR	YARDAGE
Forward	73	5602
Middle	72	6192
Back	72	6531

TEES	COURSE RATING	SLOPE
Forward	73.1	124
Middle	70.1	124
Back	71.6	127

The canal crossing the 16th hole.

SOUTHWARD HO COUNTRY CLUB

"Windmills On Your Mind"

Horace Havemeyer

**SOUTHWARD HO
COUNTRY CLUB**
Bay Shore, NY

YEAR FOUNDED: 1923

ARCHITECT:
A.W. Tillinghast

COURSE OPENED: 1923

TEES	PAR	YARDAGE
Forward	72	5596
Middle	71	6182
Back	71	6524

TEES	COURSE RATING	SLOPE
Forward	73.1	124
Middle	70.2	128
Back	71.8	131

F or several generations, the name Havemeyer has been closely identified with the sugar industry. Several members of the family shared the nickname, "The Sugar King." Among them was Theodore Havemeyer, one of the organizers and first president of the USGA.

With wealth and leisure, Henry Havemeyer, Theodore's brother, indulged his taste for the country life by building an estate on Long Island's Great South Bay. His son, Horace, a founder of the Timber Point Club, proved to be the saving angel of the Southward Ho Country Club.

In 1923, Southward Ho was organized

The windmill

with 140 acres of land and buildings. On the property, not far from the clubhouse, was a working windmill, which graces the club's logo. It was replaced by a new windmill in 1996. Like the old windmill, it is played as a hazard to the right of the tenth fairway.

A.W. Tillinghast designed Southward Ho's golf course, its greens closely resembling those of Winged Foot, pear-shaped, pitched back-to-front, with bunkers pinching in at the front corners. The terrain is generally flat, with only a scattering of trees on most holes. But there are bunkers everywhere, including a few almost completely encircling their greens. Knee-high rough flanking the fairways leaves the average player with little option but to recover back to safety.

Southward Ho's centerpiece is the eighth hole, a relatively short par four that is long on danger. The tee shot must be played with rifle accuracy through a long chute of mature trees, with a poke of more than 200 yards needed to clear the corner of the 90-degree right dogleg. That is followed by a pitch over a pond to a two-tiered green guarded by three bunkers. (Gone are the former island green at the par-three ninth and Tillinghast's signature wasteland of sand, rough, and mounds that once bisected the fairway on the par-five 11th.)

The Depression proved difficult for Southward Ho, and in 1934 it went bankrupt. It was reorganized and run by the bank as the South Bay Golf Club. Toward the end of World War II, the Club found itself in a precarious situation until Horace Havemeyer saved the day—and the club. He bought the Club and gave it a 10-year option to purchase, which it did in 1954. In recognition of his role as club savior, the Havemeyer Tournament was instituted in 1951. It became the Havemeyer Memorial after his death in 1956, and remains an important stop on the spring calendar for many of the area's top amateurs. ○

ST. GEORGE'S GOLF & COUNTRY CLUB

"Dragon Tales"

ST. GEORGE'S GOLF & COUNTRY CLUB
Stony Brook, NY

YEAR FOUNDED: 1915

ARCHITECT:
Devereux Emmet

COURSE OPENED: 1917

TEES	PAR	YARDAGE
Forward	71	5457
Middle	70	6218

TEES	COURSE RATING	SLOPE
Forward	71.4	124
Middle	70.4	128

According to legend, a fierce dragon once ravaged the countryside. To appease the monster, the people decided that a human sacrifice—the king's daughter—was necessary. St. George happened by in the nick of time, slayed the dragon, and won the princess.

The real St. George was a victim of the religious persecution inflicted by Roman emperor Diocletian against the Christians in the 4th century. He actively protested Diocletian's horrors until he himself was tortured to death.

The legend of St. George that made it to Suffolk County involves St. George's Manor in Setauket, a quiet and restful summer resort hotel that attracted a wealthy clientele of New York businessmen. Among those who frequented the manor were the founding fathers of the St. George's Golf & Country Club, which was founded in 1915. As their logo, they chose St. George, armed only with a golf club, fighting the dragon.

While there are no dragons at St. George's today, the members are subject to a form of persecution even more sinister than their namesake had to endure—putting greens with undulations that at times are severe, other times just subtle, with nary a straight putt on any of them.

The central figure in the Club's history was Devereux Emmet, a lifelong resident of Long Island. Emmet had an estate in nearby St. James overlooking Stony Brook Harbor. He maintained a nine-hole course there, a good test of golf with hazards such as haystacks and pig pens. It was where several of St. George's founders first played golf.

Before designing the course, Emmet served on a committee of four that selected the site. He later served as Chairman of the Green and Tournament/Handicap Committees. And although the original plans called for 36 holes, only 18 were built; styled after a Scottish links, they opened in 1917.

The overwhelming feature is the endless variety of subtle rolls and breaks in the putting greens. Six holes call for carries over sand, and the grass-faced bunkers typically are deep. Emmet made maximum use of the tumbling terrain in his routing.

From the elevated tee on the par-four third, the golfer can take the narrow high road to the right or the low road to the left, with severely sloping real estate in between. The approach shot, usually played from an uneven lie, must be aimed to the right side of the green to play the prevailing tilt.

The tee shot on the par-four fourth must be played up and over a steep rise. Then the fun begins. The green is completely encircled by three deep bunkers, one set amongst half a dozen moguls. Most of the trouble cannot be seen from the fairway.

It is said that the dragon itself is buried under the 15th green, a putting surface even St. George likely would three-putt. ○

The downhill approach to the third green.

VAN CORTLANDT PARK GOLF COURSE

"The House Of The Philistines"

Golf writers A. Hedley, Grantland Rice, C. Sharps, and H. B. Martin playing for the N.Y. Newspaper Golf Club's championship at Van Cortlandt in 1913.

America's first public golf course was built at the instigation of a group of wealthy men who were hoping to have New York City build them a private course of their own. This group of public benefactors hailed from the exclusive Riverdale colony on the Hudson River and their target was Van Cortlandt Park in the Bronx, created in 1888 on the estate of Oloff Van Cortlandt, a wealthy Dutchman who fathered two New York City mayors.

Although the men of Riverdale never got their private course, they convinced Parks Commissioner James Roosevelt of the benefits of a public golf links in a city park. No doubt they were the architects of the nine-hole course, which opened in the summer of 1895. They formed their own club, the Mosholu Golf Club, but within five years they were driven from the course by "the Philistines."

The original course concluded with a conversation piece—a hole 580 yards long. The tradition of extreme length has passed the test of time at Van Cortlandt: The present course includes two 600-yard par fives, the second and 12th, situated side by side, with the 12th hole retracing the old ninth.

The first public golf tournament held in America was played at Van Cortlandt in 1896, sponsored by the private St. Andrew's Club for golfers not members of USGA clubs. An Australian novice named Walter Travis finished ninth, shooting 110 for two rounds, playing the long ninth hole in 10 and 13 strokes. Actually, no one managed less than eight on the hole.

In 1899, the course was expanded to 18 holes by Tom Bendelow, who remained for two years as club professional/greenkeeper. He added holes one through seven on the high ground opposite the railroad station. Within two decades, the "hill holes" would move to their place at the end of the round.

The course remained unchanged into the 1930s. In those days, players arrived by railroad or subway, exiting within one block of the first tee; a season's pass cost $10; and a weekend round took six hours—after a five-hour wait! But according to one expert, the course was "at least the equal, if not better than, the average private links of the time."

Among Van Cortlandt's stalwarts were newspapermen such as Grantland Rice and H.B. Martin, who formed the New York Newspaper Golf Club. At least four other MGA clubs played out of Van Cortlandt in those days. One, the Lakeside Golf Club, survives to this day.

In 1916, Van Cortlandt hosted a 72-hole tournament for pros. Jim Barnes came out on top, his 67-69-67-73=276 lowering the world record for 72 holes by two strokes, despite poorly kept greens that "made putting a hazard."

Golf in the park changed in the mid-1930s when the Major Deegan Expressway and Mosholu Parkway were routed through the grounds, disrupting six holes. In 1949 the course was expanded across the railroad tracks with four new holes designed by William Mitchell, and later revised by Geoffrey Cornish.

Conditions declined in the 1960s, 70s and 80s as the city neglected its parks and golf courses in the face of financial pressure. The American Golf Corporation took over management of Van Cortlandt in 1992, giving it a facelift with numerous capital improvements and remedial projects. The clubhouse has been renovated, tees and greens irrigated, new sand placed in the bunkers, and cart paths built. ○

VAN CORTLANDT PARK GOLF COURSE
Bronx, NY

YEAR FOUNDED: 1895

ARCHITECTS:
Tom Bendelow
William Mitchell

COURSE OPENED: 1895

TEES	PAR	YARDAGE
Forward	70	5029
Middle	70	6002
Back	70	6096

TEES	COURSE RATING	SLOPE
Forward	68.0	108
Middle	67.7	108
Back	68.6	110

WESTHAMPTON COUNTRY CLUB

"The Thrill Of It All"

WESTHAMPTON COUNTRY CLUB
Westhampton Beach, NY

YEAR FOUNDED: 1890

ARCHITECT:
Seth Raynor

COURSE OPENED: 1916

TEES	PAR	YARDAGE
Forward	72	5345
Middle	70	6229
Back	70	6457

TEES	COURSE RATING	SLOPE
Forward	71.7	125
Middle	71.6	132
Back	72.7	134

Sailing was the staff of life in the Westhampton of 1890, with sailboat racing "the thrill of it all" and the main activity at the Westhampton Country Club. The Club hoped to establish a sizable place for social gatherings; to provide a location for a baseball diamond; and to create an organization to further the sailboat races that were the focal point of summer activities. The ball games and boat races were the subject of large wagers, as well as an intense rivalry with the nearby Quogue Field Club.

The desire for a golf course was inhibited by the lack of available land. A nine-hole course was laid out at nearby Quiogue Point in 1896, with several holes along Quantuck Bay. At the same time, the club began to acquire land near the clubhouse, and a new nine-holer was built there before 1900.

By 1915, the golfers wanted 18 holes, so the club leased the present property. The original clubhouse was moved across Moniebogue Bay to its new site during the winter chill. Seth Raynor, a native of Southampton who was just beginning to design courses on his own after years of working with C.B. Macdonald, was given the assignment.

Westhampton retains an old-fashioned flavor, especially in the placement of many of its fairway bunkers, which reflect shot lengths in the pre-irrigation era. But it is the high rough, perpetually blowing in the seaside breeze, that makes a round memorable.

The signature hole is the par-three third. The punch-bowl green is surrounded by rough and nine symmetrically-placed bunkers: four on the high ground out front; a pair on either flank; and one at the back.

The 1920s were golden years for Westhampton golf. For a while at the end of the decade, there were 11 men playing at or near scratch. Among them was Eugene Homans, the man Bobby Jones defeated in the finals of the 1930 U.S. Amateur to complete his Grand Slam.

Toward the end of the decade, the Club hired Charlie Banks to design "one of the finest golf courses on Long Island" at Oneck Point, south of the existing course. But when the Depression hit, the club found itself overextended. Oneck Point was abandoned in 1933, and in 1944 the club reorganized under the name Ketchaboneck and began operating on a minimum budget. The members repurchased their facilities in 1950 and took back their name the next year.

Today, Westhampton is a summer club, sharing its membership with other Met Area clubs. The McBrides from Arcola have dominated the club championship in recent years, just as the Dears from Morris County did a generation ago. ○

16th hole as painted by member George Lawrence.

WHEATLEY HILLS GOLF CLUB

"For Whom The Bell Tolls"

When the Island Golf Links became the private Garden City Golf Club in 1899, the Garden City Company allowed a group of residents to continue playing on a plot of land between Cathedral and Franklin Avenues. The new group called itself the Midland Golf Club, and its members built their own nine-hole course and clubhouse.

The Midland course lasted until 1907, when the land was taken back for residential development. But the Garden City Company created yet another public course, called Salisbury Links, a few blocks to the west, with the Midland golfers forming the nucleus.

Salisbury became popular—and congested. The Midland membership contemplated starting their own club, and although the idea was voted down, a splinter group formed Wheatley Hills in 1913.

Wheatley Hills leased a 100-acre farm and engaged Devereux Emmet to design an 18-hole course, which was completed by late 1914. A farmhouse became the clubhouse, and an old ship's bell, which had been used to signal the area's farm workers to meals and quitting time, was used to salute the club champion. It now sits to the side of the practice putting green, rung to signal the start of "shotgun" tournaments.

In 1931, the Northern State Parkway was built, cutting across the eastern end of club property and destroying a few holes. Emmet and Alfred Tull built nine new holes, including six on the back side. (This was not the club's first run-in with a highway. In its early years, the property was bisected by the Long Island Motor Parkway, which divided the golf course into two nearly equal halves connected by a tunnel between the ninth green and tenth tee.)

Today, Wheatley Hills is a pretty parkland course with rolling tree-lined fairways and no water hazards. Most of the greens tilt back to front; some are tightly bunkered, others unprotected.

The par-four second hole plays down to a fairway then up a sharp rise to the green. Two bunkers left and one right flank the landing area for the approach, 25 yards short of the wide-open fall-away green.

The 16th drops into a glade guarded by a pair of bunkers on the right between 75 and 125 yards from home. The table-top green is protected across the front by a large bunker, with a small pot at the right entrance, a third bunker on the right side, and another pair in the bank behind the sloping putting surface.

The 1975 Met Amateur, played at Wheatley Hills, was won by Bill Britton. Now a touring professional, at that time Britton was a 19-year-old publinxer. Among the club champions is PGA Tour player George Burns.

The Club's history is closely tied to that of two men. Willie Klein was the golf professional from 1925-1957 and winner of three Long Island Opens, including the first two (1922-1923). Member Gene Francis was seven-time Long Island Amateur champion.

The Club's bell serenaded both on many occassions. ❍

WHEATLEY HILLS GOLF CLUB

East Williston, NY

YEAR FOUNDED: 1913

ARCHITECTS:
Devereux Emmet
Alfred Tull

COURSE OPENED: 1914

TEES	PAR	YARDAGE
Forward	74	5379
Middle	72	6366
Back	72	6822

TEES	COURSE RATING	SLOPE
Forward	71.6	125
Middle	71.1	129
Back	73.2	133

The dramatic 2nd hole

THE WOODCREST CLUB

"Born Again"

The watery par-three 14th.

The picturesque parkland course at the Woodcrest Club is the second life for a historic piece of land that had been a dairy farm. The farmhouse and stables of the old Lewis Farm were located near the present 10th green, and reached from Underhill Boulevard.

The farm buildings were torn down soon after the property was purchased in 1915 by James A. Burden, owner of Burden Iron. He converted the 120 acres into a magnificent estate called "Woodside." His brick and stone English Georgian manor house, which would become the Woodcrest clubhouse, was designed by William Adams Delano, architect of the White House. The paneling in the building was imported from English castles.

Burden employed a staff of 45 for the daily operation of his estate, which included a prize-winning rose nursery (near the 16th green) and a polo field (between the second and seventh greens). The Prince of Wales stayed at Woodside during his visit for the 1924 Westchester Cup polo matches between the United States and Great Britain, one of the great social events in "Gold Coast" history. Franklin and Eleanor Roosevelt were frequent house guests of the Burdens during FDR's presidency.

Following Burden's death, his widow remarried, and upon the death of her second husband, Richard Tobin, she sold the estate in 1962 to the fledgling Woodcrest Club, begun by Pat Tiso, professional at nearby Pine Hollow. The Club immediately added a large dining room to the mansion, decorated with massive chandelier wall fixtures imported from Vienna.

For their golf course, the founding fathers turned to William Mitchell, who built a number of outstanding courses on Long Island around this time, including Old Westbury and Pine Hollow. He had Woodcrest ready in 1963. For a number of years, Woodcrest was home to its annual Tournament of Club Champions.

The right-angle, right-dogleg par-four first hole is one of the strongest openers on Long Island. Two scenic par threes, the 8th and 14th, have ponds extending from tee to green.

The strongest hole on the course may be the 12th, a scenic par four with a pair of tall, mature trees standing sentinel over both sides of the landing area. The home hole, which bends sharply to the right with water in the corner of the dogleg, offers interesting possibilities for players forced to gamble in an attempt to catch up. The home green is located on what used to be the lawns of an estate that once hosted princes and presidents. ○

THE WOODCREST CLUB
Syosset, NY

YEAR FOUNDED: 1962

ARCHITECT:
William Mitchell

COURSE OPENED: 1963

TEES	PAR	YARDAGE
Forward	72	5655
Middle	72	6180
Back	72	6479

	COURSE	
TEES	RATING	SLOPE
Forward	73.1	123
Middle	70.5	127
Back	71.8	130

THE WOODMERE CLUB

"The Longest Short Course"

The watery par-three 11th hole.

In June, 1982, Ben Crenshaw stepped out of a helicopter to play Woodmere's 16th hole as part of a Met Area "Dream 18." He put his tee shot into the water fronting the green, and then, after pitching onto the wrong level, added to his embarrassment with three putts. In just a few minutes, Crenshaw learned what local golfers know all too well. Although short on yardage, Woodmere is a challenging layout. The late Claude Harmon summed it up best in 1957, calling Woodmere "the longest short course" he had ever played. (After a few drinks in the men's grill, Harmon revised his opinion to "the toughest golf course on the East Coast!")

Woodmere was formed in 1908 as a tennis club, and it was not until moving to its present location in 1910 that an 18-hole golf course was built, on land once used for several holes of the neighboring Rockaway Hunting Club's original course.

The fourth hole was the centerpiece of the old course, a long par four of about 400 yards with a 20-foot-high crossbunker in the drive zone. Beyond the bunker the fairway sloped right, and the three-tiered green featured a "valley of sin" through the middle. The club offered a $500 prize to anyone who could carry the bunker off the tee and stay in the fairway!

The course underwent a major facelift in the late 1940s, when the club bought a large parcel of land from Rockaway Hunting Club. Robert Trent Jones was commissioned to build a new back nine. The green settings were rejuvenated in 1986-87 when Brian Silva reshaped the bunkers and added greenside mounding.

The course rolls gently over flat terrain, with few trees of significance after the fifth hole. It's the greens that golfers remember. Most are severely undulating, five are flanked by sizable water hazards, and many are guarded by bunkers set amidst mounds, recalling the styling of an earlier era.

The fourth is an unusual, double-dogleg par four. The ideal drive is a draw around a tall tree standing at the left edge of the fairway. The hole rises gently and turns sharply right in the last 50 yards. Trees to the right obstruct any shot from that side of the fairway.

The 16th is the prize, a solid par three with water fronting the green and four bunkers behind. A horseshoe-shaped ridge runs through the dance floor, so putts fall away in all directions.

The tee shot on the home hole must carry a wide expanse of Woodmere Channel and avoid a bunker to the left. The two-tiered green is set on a left-to-right angle to the approach, tucked behind a bunker across its right front.

Woodmere has hosted three Met Opens, the most newsworthy the 1965 affair when Jerry Pittman fired an impressive 69-68-67-71=275, three strokes better than Jimmy Wright and Wes Ellis. Few golfers have taken such liberties with Woodmere's challenging layout.

THE WOODMERE CLUB

Woodmere, NY

YEAR FOUNDED: 1908

ARCHITECTS:
Jack Pirie
Robert Trent Jones

COURSE OPENED: 1910

TEES	PAR	YARDAGE
Forward	71	5474
Middle	70	5967
Back	70	6385

TEES	COURSE RATING	SLOPE
Forward	71.6	118
Middle	69.7	128
Back	71.7	131

BELLPORT
COUNTRY CLUB
Bellport, NY

YEAR FOUNDED: 1916

ARCHITECT:
Seth Raynor

COURSE OPENED: 1916

*Owned by Bellport as a
private club, this is a well bunkered
links style course with small, fast
greens. The fairways are tight, but
there are few trees. The lasting
impressions are the ever-present
wind and the lovely views of
Bellport Bay and Fire Island.*

TEES	PAR	YARDAGE
Forward	72	5282
Middle	71	5973
Back	71	6234

TEES	COURSE RATING	SLOPE
Forward	69.2	112
Middle	68.9	115
Back	70.1	118

BERGEN POINT
GOLF COURSE
West Babylon, NY

YEAR FOUNDED: 1972

ARCHITECT:
William Mitchell

COURSE OPENED: 1972

*One of Long Island's
wind-swept linksland type courses,
this popular Suffolk County Park
facility can play a very long 6,637
yards. With water on a majority
of the holes, accuracy is more than
a passing concern.*

TEES	PAR	YARDAGE
Forward	71	5707
Middle	71	6197
Back	71	6637

TEES	COURSE RATING	SLOPE
Forward	71.9	117
Middle	69.1	112
Back	71.1	116

BRENTWOOD
COUNTRY CLUB
Brentwood, NY

YEAR FOUNDED: 1923

ARCHITECT:
Devereux Emmet

COURSE OPENED: 1925

*Brentwood is a reasonably priced
daily fee course. This popular
Town of Islip municipal course
features small greens and
towering pines.*

TEES	PAR	YARDAGE
Forward	74	5093
Middle	72	5835
Back	72	6173

TEES	COURSE RATING	SLOPE
Forward	68.4	111
Middle	67.8	118
Back	69.3	121

BRETTON WOODS
COUNTRY CLUB
Coram, NY

YEAR FOUNDED:
unknown

ARCHITECT:
unknown

COURSE OPENED:
unknown

*This nine-hole executive
course is the centerpiece of
a residential development.
The well maintained fairways
are narrow and tree lined, and
the greens are small and sloping.*

TEES	PAR	YARDAGE
Forward	30	1847
Middle	30	1847

TEES	COURSE RATING	SLOPE
Forward	59.7	92
Middle	57.8	91

THE BRIDGEHAMPTON
CLUB
Bridgehampton, NY

YEAR FOUNDED: 1924

ARCHITECT:
Willard Wilkinson

COURSE OPENED: 1924

*The conditions at this old
nine-hole course can rival those of
any other, regardless of size. The
course is surrounded by trees, yet is
hilly and open. Nevertheless, blind
approach shots exist to five of its
small, fast greens.*

TEES	PAR	YARDAGE
Forward	36	2688
Middle	35	2846

TEES	COURSE RATING	SLOPE
Forward	67.6	119
Middle	67.8	122

CALVERTON LINKS
Calverton, NY

YEAR FOUNDED: 1994

ARCHITECT:
Cole Hayes

COURSE OPENED: 1994

*This youthful beauty
features doglegs, modest elevation
changes and a nicely manicured
appearance. A dual-tee nine
holer, it fits within its one-time
farmland like a glove. One of the
Met Area's best miniature courses is
located on the premises.*

TEES	PAR	YARDAGE
Forward	36	2217
Middle	36	2682
Back	36	3036

TEES	COURSE RATING	SLOPE
Forward	65.6	108
Middle	66.2	113
Back	69.4	119

THE CEDARBROOK CLUB
Old Brookville, NY

YEAR FOUNDED: 1960

ARCHITECT:
Albert Zikorus

COURSE OPENED: 1960

*The terrain here is moderately
rolling, and the conditioning excellent. An experiment of five years
ago, "The Superintendent's
Revenge," with sadistically placed
tees and cups to take the measure of
the members, will not be repeated
soon. Cedarbrook has been a
popular host for LIGA events.*

TEES	PAR	YARDAGE
Forward	75	5780
Middle	72	6368
Back	72	6658

TEES	COURSE RATING	SLOPE
Forward	74.9	129
Middle	71.7	126
Back	72.9	129

CHERRY CREEK
GOLF LINKS
Riverhead, NY

YEAR FOUNDED: 1996

ARCHITECTS:
Charles Jurgens, Sr.
Vincent Sasso

COURSE OPENED: 1996

*Cherry Creek celebrates its first
birthday in 1997. A links style
course with rough to match, it is
also heavily bunkered and features
Long Island's longest hole, the 644-
yard par six 18th. It features beautifully sculpted elevated green complexes.*

TEES	PAR	YARDAGE
Forward	73	5800
Middle	73	6600
Back	73	7200

TEES	COURSE RATING	SLOPE
Forward	72.1	122
Middle	70.8	116
Back	73.4	120

CLEARVIEW GOLF COURSE

Bayside, NY

YEAR FOUNDED: 1925

ARCHITECT:
Willie Tucker

COURSE OPENED: 1925

Clearview started life as a private golf and yacht club of which New York Governor Al Smith was a member. It is well named for the views available of Long Island Sound and the Throg's Neck Bridge. This busy, popular place with gently sloping fairways offers some forgiveness for shots a little off target.

TEES	PAR	YARDAGE
Forward	70	5497
Middle	70	6263

TEES	COURSE RATING	SLOPE
Forward	70.4	115
Middle	69.2	114

COLONIAL SPRINGS GOLF COURSE

East Farmingdale, NY

YEAR FOUNDED: 1995

ARCHITECT:
Arthur Hills

COURSE OPENED: 1995

One of Long Island's premier public layouts, this 27-hole Arthur Hills design occupies previously flat terrain, leased from Pinelawn Cemetery. Each nine is an outstanding challenge with strong finishing water holes.

TEES	PAR	YARDAGE
Forward	72	5467
Middle	72	6036
Back	72	6780

TEES	COURSE RATING	SLOPE
Forward	70.5	119
Middle	70.0	120
Back	71.7	124

Above is an average of three nines.

CRAB MEADOW GOLF CLUB

Northport, NY

YEAR FOUNDED: 1964

ARCHITECT:
William Mitchell

COURSE OPENED: 1965

Crab Meadow is known in Huntington and beyond for its well-maintained greens and bunkers, gently rolling fairways and nice views of Long Island Sound. The popular, semi-private operation limits morning play to residents and guests.

TEES	PAR	YARDAGE
Forward	72	5772
Middle	72	6294
Back	72	6557

TEES	COURSE RATING	SLOPE
Forward	72.6	120
Middle	69.7	116
Back	70.9	118

EISENHOWER PARK GOLF COURSES

East Meadow, NY

YEAR FOUNDED: 1917

Eisenhower Park features three straightforward courses. The Red course, though relatively flat, presents the greatest challenge. It is a descendant of Salisbury No. 4 and was the site of the 1926 PGA Championship, won by Walter Hagen. The newer Blue and White courses by Robert Trent Jones have elevated, well bunkered greens.

WHITE COURSE

ARCHITECT:
Robert Trent Jones

COURSE OPENED: 1950

TEES	PAR	YARDAGE
Forward	72	6269
Middle	72	6269

TEES	COURSE RATING	SLOPE
Forward	71.6	116
Middle	69.2	117

BLUE COURSE

ARCHITECT:
Robert Trent Jones

COURSE OPENED: 1951

TEES	PAR	YARDAGE
Forward	72	6026
Middle	72	6026

TEES	COURSE RATING	SLOPE
Forward	69.6	109
Middle	68.0	112

RED COURSE

ARCHITECTS:
Devereux Emmet
Robert Trent Jones

COURSE OPENED: 1924

TEES	PAR	YARDAGE
Forward	72	5449
Middle	72	6349
Back	72	6756

TEES	COURSE RATING	SLOPE
Forward	70.7	111
Middle	69.7	117
Back	71.5	121

DIX HILLS PARK GOLF COURSE

Dix Hills, NY

YEAR FOUNDED:
unknown

ARCHITECT:
unknown

COURSE OPENED:
unknown

This nine-hole executive-size layout offers very nice conditions, especially the greens, for its many players. It has a good deal of appeal for walkers with its moderate terrain.

TEES	PAR	YARDAGE
Forward	64	3764
Middle	58	3764

TEES	COURSE RATING	SLOPE
Forward	60.9	90
Middle	57.2	83

DOUGLASTON GOLF COURSE

Douglaston, NY

YEAR FOUNDED: 1927

ARCHITECT:
Willie Tucker

COURSE OPENED: 1927

On the short side, due to seven par threes, Douglaston occupies some rugged terrain and is nonetheless an adequate challenge. Offering great views of the New York skyline, this course is the successor to North Hills Country Club. The Spanish-style clubhouse is one of architect Clifford Wendehack's finest.

TEES	PAR	YARDAGE
Forward	67	4602
Middle	67	5140
Back	67	5585

TEES	COURSE RATING	SLOPE
Forward	66.3	107
Middle	64.2	107
Back	66.2	111

DYKER BEACH GOLF COURSE

Brooklyn, NY

YEAR FOUNDED: 1928

ARCHITECT:
John R. Van Kleek

COURSE OPENED: 1928

*Located in the shadows of the Verrazano Narrows Bridge, the Brooklyn public course is one of New York City's oldest and best. It's a shotmaker's course with undulating greens. This former training ground of the Strafaci brothers is a direct descendant of Dyker Meadow Golf Club, an MGA charter member. *See Lost Courses.* *

TEES	PAR	YARDAGE
Forward	72	5696
Middle	71	6260
Back	71	6548

TEES	COURSE RATING	SLOPE
Forward	70.4	115
Middle	69.2	114
Back	70.5	116

FOREST PARK GOLF COURSE
Forest Park, NY

YEAR FOUNDED: 1896

ARCHITECTS:
Tom Bendelow
Lindsay Ervin

COURSE OPENED: 1896

Originally called Oak Ridge, Forest Park is enjoying refurbished tees, greens and fairways—not to mention a new clubhouse. The Queens layout continues its reputation for fine playing conditions.

TEES	PAR	YARDAGE
Forward	67	5431
Middle	67	5431
Back	67	5840

TEES	COURSE RATING	SLOPE
Forward	70.4	116
Middle	65.7	108
Back	67.5	111

FOX HILL GOLF & COUNTRY CLUB
Baiting Hollow, NY

YEAR FOUNDED: 1968

ARCHITECT:
Robert Trent Jones

COURSE OPENED: 1968

Fox Hill is a challenging, well-fescued Robert Trent Jones design. Under new management in the 1990s, the course has blossomed into one of Eastern Long Island's most demanding courses. The four holes leading to and from the clubhouse are picturesque and challenging.

TEES	PAR	YARDAGE
Forward	72	6605
Middle	72	6365
Back	72	6838

TEES	COURSE RATING	SLOPE
Forward	73.0	126
Middle	71.8	124
Back	73.8	130

GLEN COVE GOLF CLUB
Glen Cove, NY

YEAR FOUNDED: 1970

ARCHITECT:
William Mitchell

COURSE OPENED: 1971

Glen Cove is a well-conditioned executive size course which offers lovely views of Long Island Sound, fine fairways, fast greens and reasonable rates for daily fee players. Mal Galetta, Jr., the former Long Island Open champion, is the head professional.

TEES	PAR	YARDAGE
Forward	66	4048
Middle	66	4602
Back	66	4866

TEES	COURSE RATING	SLOPE
Forward	62.8	98
Middle	63.2	108
Back	64.4	111

GOVERNORS ISLAND GOLF COURSE
Governors Island, NY

YEAR FOUNDED: 1903

ARCHITECT:
Fred Roth

COURSE OPENED: 1903

At this printing the future of the course on Governor's Island is uncertain since the federally-owned island off the foot of lower Manhattan was slated for evacuation as of August 31, 1996. Play of the nine holes circles around the star-shaped fort of Revolutionary War vintage. Nowhere else in the Met Area can such close-up views of the city be found.

TEES	PAR	YARDAGE
Forward	62	3813
Middle	62	3813

TEES	COURSE RATING	SLOPE
Forward	64.0	92
Middle	60.0	88

HAMLET GOLF & COUNTRY CLUB
Commack, NY

YEAR FOUNDED: 1994

ARCHITECT:
Stephen Kay

COURSE OPENED: 1994

Stephen Kay did a complete remake of the former site of Commack Hills Country Club. Still progressing is the residential development. Water is a serious threat on six holes. Most challenging is the water fronting the green at the short par-five 15th. The Waldbaum's Hamlet Cup in late summer is a major prep for the U.S. Tennis Open.

TEES	PAR	YARDAGE
Forward	70	5388
Middle	70	6203
Back	70	6427

TEES	COURSE RATING	SLOPE
Forward	71.1	127
Middle	70.1	130
Back	71.1	132

HAMLET WIND WATCH GOLF CLUB
Hauppauge, NY

YEAR FOUNDED: 1990

ARCHITECT:
Joe Lee

COURSE OPENED: 1990

Working on a site that had been Colonie Hill Golf Club, architect Joe Lee used the real Colonie Hill—site of the hotel and the second highest spot on Long Island, to create this popular layout. property contains 15 acres of water within which the 18 holes meander. Course features are bent grass greens and tees. Wind Watch hosts a John Jacobs Golf School.

TEES	PAR	YARDAGE
Forward	71	5135
Middle	71	6138
Back	71	6405

TEES	COURSE RATING	SLOPE
Forward	69.5	121
Middle	69.7	125
Back	71.0	128

HAMPTON HILLS GOLF & COUNTRY CLUB
Westhampton, NY

YEAR FOUNDED: 1964

ARCHITECT:
Frank Duane

COURSE OPENED: 1964

This hidden gem is one of Frank Duane's finest designs. Gracing the hills of Westhampton, it features outstanding twin par 4s at the 7th and 17th. Both holes play from elevated tees across water back up to elevated greens.

TEES	PAR	YARDAGE
Forward	71	4912
Middle	71	6159
Back	71	6634

TEES	COURSE RATING	SLOPE
Forward	69.4	118
Middle	70.7	130
Back	72.9	134

HAUPPAUGE COUNTRY CLUB
Hauppauge, NY

YEAR FOUNDED: 1960

ARCHITECT:
unknown

COURSE OPENED: 1960

Hauppauge is a membership public course, open to non-members weekdays and late weekend afternoons. The course is generally level. Water builds up with six possible encounters on the final nine.

TEES	PAR	YARDAGE
Forward	74	6022
Middle	72	6280
Back	72	6525

TEES	COURSE RATING	SLOPE
Forward	75.5	131
Middle	69.9	120
Back	71.0	122

HAY HARBOR
GOLF CLUB
Fishers Island, NY

YEAR FOUNDED: 1898

ARCHITECT:
Members

COURSE OPENED: 1898

Hay Harbor, Fisher's Island's original resort course, is a 9-hole layout in which golfers face two of the most difficult tests on the first two holes: the 425- yard opener and the watery 395-yard second.

TEES	PAR	YARDAGE
Forward	76	5900
Middle	68	6210

TEES	COURSE RATING	SLOPE
Forward	72.8	118
Middle	69.0	111

HEATHERWOOD
GOLF CLUB
Centereach, NY

YEAR FOUNDED: 1965

ARCHITECTS:
Charles & Fred Jurgens

COURSE OPENED: 1965

Originally a 9-holer in the 1950s, Heatherwood became 18 in 1965. One who masters the par threes has the key. Of the 12, five are 200 yards or longer. The 13th, a short par 4, features a treacherous green from which a putt may trickle into a pond.

TEES	PAR	YARDAGE
Forward	60	3465
Middle	60	4109

TEES	COURSE RATING	SLOPE
Forward	58.5	91
Middle	58.6	95

HOLBROOK
COUNTRY CLUB
Holbrook, NY

YEAR FOUNDED: 1992

ARCHITECT:
unknown

COURSE OPENED: 1992

The tree-lined fairways here provide isolation from adjoining holes. Excellent conditioning along with four water holes allow a pleasantly challenging experience. Shots missing the raised greens require difficult recoveries from the native, sandy terrain.

TEES	PAR	YARDAGE
Forward	71	4736
Middle	71	5978
Back	71	6252

TEES	COURSE RATING	SLOPE
Forward	66.9	119
Middle	68.5	126
Back	69.8	128

INDIAN HILLS
COUNTRY CLUB
Fort Salonga, NY

YEAR FOUNDED: 1965

ARCHITECTS:
Steve Christoff
Charles & Fred Jurgens

COURSE OPENED: 1965

This narrow hilly test, with sloping greens and high rough features spectacular North Shore views of Long Island Sound. Of particular note is the view from the treacherous, short par-four 12th, where an errant shot can bound into the beach. Seven other chances to reach water lie within the course.

TEES	PAR	YARDAGE
Forward	72	5368
Middle	72	6209
Back	72	6572

TEES	COURSE RATING	SLOPE
Forward	71.7	126
Middle	71.5	132
Back	73.1	135

INDIAN ISLAND
GOLF COURSE
Riverhead, NY

YEAR FOUNDED: 1973

ARCHITECT:
William Mitchell

COURSE OPENED: 1973

Wind and out-of-bounds add to the difficulty at this Suffolk County Park course. The demand for accuracy off the tees and on approach shots increases on the back nine. Beautiful Flanders Bay scenery awaits on several holes. The par five 15th is locally regarded as Long Island's answer to the 18th at Pebble Beach.

TEES	PAR	YARDAGE
Forward	72	5524
Middle	72	5976
Back	72	6353

TEES	COURSE RATING	SLOPE
Forward	72.8	126
Middle	69.3	121
Back	71.0	124

ISLAND HILLS
GOLF CLUB
Sayville, NY

YEAR FOUNDED: 1927

ARCHITECT:
A.W. Tillinghast

COURSE OPENED: 1927

This South Shore Tillinghast gem built in the 1920s remains a fine test. When built, it was among the Island's longest at 6,779 yards. After World War II it was purchased by a group of members from Willow Brook Country Club in Baldwin.

TEES	PAR	YARDAGE
Forward	72	5583
Middle	72	6366
Back	71	6532

TEES	COURSE RATING	SLOPE
Forward	71.3	116
Middle	70.4	120
Back	71.2	122

ISLAND'S END
GOLF & COUNTRY CLUB
Greenport, NY

YEAR FOUNDED: 1961

ARCHITECTS:
G. Heron & C. Martin

COURSE OPENED: 1961

Island's End is the easternmost golfing experience available on Long Island's North Fork. An 18-holer since the late 1960s, It is worth the trip for its gently rolling terrain, undulating greens, and perfect views of the Sound from the par-three 16th—the Connecticut shore is visible on a clear day. Afternoon breezes add to the challenge of this popular daily fee course.

TEES	PAR	YARDAGE
Forward	72	5131
Middle	72	6307
Back	72	6639

TEES	COURSE RATING	SLOPE
Forward	68.8	116
Middle	70.1	115
Back	71.6	118

KISSENA PARK
GOLF COURSE
Flushing, NY

YEAR FOUNDED: 1933

ARCHITECT:
John R. Van Kleek

COURSE OPENED: 1933

Kissena Park is the perfect place for those who prefer a view of the Manhattan skyline to that of water hazards. Small greens make for exacting approach shots. It's a challenge for all, and a great course to hone one's par-three game.

TEES	PAR	YARDAGE
Forward	64	4425
Middle	64	4425
Back	64	4727

TEES	COURSE RATING	SLOPE
Forward	63.9	98
Middle	60.9	93
Back	61.7	94

LAKE SUCCESS GOLF CLUB

Lake Success, NY

YEAR FOUNDED: 1957

ARCHITECTS:
Orrin Smith
Albert Zikorus

COURSE OPENED: 1957

This municipally-owned and operated private club is located on the former site of the Deepdale Golf Club, which moved when the Long Island Expressway consumed some of the property. Lake Success opened in 1957 with a revised course on which only the seventh and ninth holes are originals. The clubhouse remains in service—with a mural depicting the original 18-hole Deepdale design.

TEES	PAR	YARDAGE
Forward	72	5673
Middle	70	6061
Back	70	6293

TEES	COURSE RATING	SLOPE
Forward	72.6	126
Middle	69.5	126
Back	70.7	128

LAWRENCE VILLAGE COUNTRY CLUB

Lawrence, NY

YEAR FOUNDED: 1924

ARCHITECT:
Devereux Emmet

COURSE OPENED: 1924

Postcard type views are ever-present here with the Atlantic beach near by and boats moving along Bannister Creek. The course is tree-lined and flat, but with no less than 12 water holes. A completely rebuilt clubhouse was unveiled in 1996.

TEES	PAR	YARDAGE
Forward	71	5477
Middle	70	6252
Back	70	6528

TEES	COURSE RATING	SLOPE
Forward	72.5	122
Middle	70.7	126
Back	72.0	129

LIDO GOLF COURSE

Lido Beach, NY

YEAR FOUNDED: 1978

ARCHITECT:
Robert Trent Jones

COURSE OPENED: 1949

A public course since the Town of Hempstead took over in 1977, Lido is a flat, heavily bunkered layout with elevated tees and greens. Water is a factor on six holes, and wind presents new experiences each day. The 16th, which is a replica of the famous Channel Hole (see Lost Courses) and the watery 17th, are most challenging.

TEES	PAR	YARDAGE
Forward	72	5603
Middle	71	6387
Back	71	6868

TEES	COURSE RATING	SLOPE
Forward	71.4	114
Middle	71.3	124
Back	73.5	128

MARINE PARK GOLF COURSE

Brooklyn, NY

YEAR FOUNDED: 1962

ARCHITECT:
Robert Trent Jones

COURSE OPENED: 1962

The Manhattan Skyline is the backdrop for this New York City Park facility. Essentially a flat course with larger-than-average greens, the lack of trees gives this, the longest of the city courses, a true linksland touch. It is a great example of how to rejuvenate a landfill.

TEES	PAR	YARDAGE
Forward	72	5323
Middle	72	6609
Back	72	6866

TEES	COURSE RATING	SLOPE
Forward	68.8	108
Middle	70.1	111
Back	71.3	113

MERRICK ROAD PARK GOLF COURSE

Merrick, NY

YEAR FOUNDED: 1967

ARCHITECT:
Frank Duane

COURSE OPENED: 1967

This nine-hole course with narrow fairways and sloping elevated greens ocucpies level terrain and offers a strong challenge and outstanding views of East Bay and Jones Beach. Operated as a daily fee facility by the Town of Hempstead, an annual play of 75,000+ nine-hole rounds is typical.

TEES	PAR	YARDAGE
Forward	36	2845
Middle	36	3115

TEES	COURSE RATING	SLOPE
Forward	72.0	113
Middle	69.6	108

MIDDLE ISLAND COUNTRY CLUB

Middle Island, NY

YEAR FOUNDED: 1965

ARCHITECT:
Baier Lustgarten

COURSE OPENED: 1965

Middle Island features three equally-difficult nines. The Spruce is long, but open, the Oak is oak lined and tight, and the Dogwood has elevations and doglegs. The second hole on the Oak is Long Island's longest par 4 at 484 yards. The average length of the six par fives is a generous 558 yards.

TEES	PAR	YARDAGE
Forward	71	5875
Middle	71	6617
Back	71	6992

TEES	COURSE RATING	SLOPE
Forward	74.1	128
Middle	71.7	125
Back	73.4	128

Above is an average of three nines.

MOSHOLU GOLF COURSE

Bronx, NY

YEAR FOUNDED: 1914

ARCHITECTS:
John R. Van Kleek
Stephen Kay

COURSE OPENED: 1914

It's an indian name meaning "smooth stones" or "small stones" which prevailed in Tibbett's Brook. Mosholu was built as an 18-holer in the northeast corner of Van Cortlandt Park in 1914 to ease congestion at the Van Cortlandt layout. It has since been reduced to nine holes.

TEES	PAR	YARDAGE
Forward	70	6382
Middle	71	6382

TEES	COURSE RATING	SLOPE
Forward	76.2	133
Middle	70.5	124

NISSEQUOGUE GOLF CLUB

St. James, NY

YEAR FOUNDED: 1968

ARCHITECT:
C.K. Martin

COURSE OPENED: 1968

The club occupies a former secluded peninsula estate jutting into Smithtown Bay, the Nissequogue River, and St. James Bay. The course is dramatically undulating with tree-lined fairways which rise and fall abruptly. Many greens are tightly bunkered, others contured with a variety of ridges, bowls and tiers. The waterside second is one of Long Island's premier par threes.

TEES	PAR	YARDAGE
Forward	72	5451
Middle	72	6039
Back	72	6531

TEES	COURSE RATING	SLOPE
Forward	71.3	124
Middle	70.7	128
Back	73.0	133

NORTH FORK COUNTRY CLUB

Cutchogue, NY

YEAR FOUNDED: 1912

ARCHITECT:
Donald Ross

COURSE OPENED: 1912

Today's first seven holes along with 17 and 18 was the original Donald Ross nine-hole course built in 1912. By 1920, an additional nine was built. Several attractive water holes must be negotiated in the middle of the course. Former members include Jack Tuthill, the former PGA Tournament Director, and James Hand, twice the club champ and later the USGA President in 1984-85.

TEES	PAR	YARDAGE
Forward	72	5114
Middle	71	6015
Back	71	6160

TEES	COURSE RATING	SLOPE
Forward	68.7	120
Middle	69.8	125
Back	70.4	126

PINE HILLS COUNTRY CLUB

Manorville, NY

YEAR FOUNDED: 1974

ARCHITECTS:
Roger Tooker
Anthony Marino

COURSE OPENED: 1974

Water comes into play on eight holes here. This public facility is very popular as 55,000 rounds in a 364 day season attests. It provides an outlet for those with cabin fever. The Fred Alfano Memorial, a long-standing amateur event, attracts many— even an occasional celebrity.

TEES	PAR	YARDAGE
Forward	73	5115
Middle	73	6230
Back	73	6829

TEES	COURSE RATING	SLOPE
Forward	70.3	119
Middle	71.3	124
Back	74.0	129

NOYAC GOLF & COUNTRY CLUB

Sag Harbor, NY

YEAR FOUNDED: 1963

ARCHITECT:
William Mitchell

COURSE OPENED: 1964

This hidden gem on the South Fork's north shore, just west of Sag Harbor is one of the East End's toughest tests. The course is carved from dramatically undulating, tree-lined terrain. Particularly memorable is the par-five 14th, which cascades downhill through a maze of bunkers over its last 125 yards.

TEES	PAR	YARDAGE
Forward	72	5601
Middle	72	6311
Back	72	6866

TEES	COURSE RATING	SLOPE
Forward	73.0	125
Middle	72.1	132
Back	74.5	136

THE PONDS AT LAKE GROVE GOLF CLUB

Lake Grove, NY

YEAR FOUNDED: 1995

ARCHITECT:
Buddy Johnson

COURSE OPENED: 1995

Attractive features of this public, executive course are accessibility and pace of play—generally three-plus hours for 18 holes. This gently rolling layout offers six par fours and twelve par threes with water on six holes. Fairways are narrow, separated by trees and mounding.

TEES	PAR	YARDAGE
Forward	60	3300
Middle	60	3500

TEES	COURSE RATING	SLOPE
Forward	56.6	85
Middle	56.9	88

PELHAM BAY/ SPLIT ROCK GOLF COURSES

Bronx, NY

YEAR FOUNDED: 1899

The real Split Rock is a large, glacial boulder the size of a small car. It actually has a deep split in it, and lies outside the course between the Hutchinson River Parkway and the New England Thruway. Split Rock, a tighter course with a demanding back nine, was a CCC project of the 1930s built adjacent to the older, open Pelham Bay course.

PELHAM BAY

ARCHITECT:
Lawrence Van Etten

COURSE OPENED: 1899

TEES	PAR	YARDAGE
Forward	73	5634
Middle	70	6405
Back	70	6691

TEES	COURSE RATING	SLOPE
Forward	70.4	113
Middle	69.6	114
Back	70.9	116

SPLIT ROCK

ARCHITECT:
John R. Van Kleek

COURSE OPENED: 1934

TEES	PAR	YARDAGE
Forward	71	5509
Middle	70	6239
Back	70	6691

TEES	COURSE RATING	SLOPE
Forward	71.7	122
Middle	70.3	122
Back	71.9	125

PENINSULA GOLF CLUB

Massapequa Park, NY

YEAR FOUNDED: 1946

ARCHITECT:
Maurice McCarthy

COURSE OPENED: 1946

All one's clubs get into the act at Peninsula. Though water hazards are lacking, with two of the six par four holes over 400 yards, this nine-holer is no pushover. A very active member group and outside play keeps things hopping.

TEES	PAR	YARDAGE
Forward	37	3012
Middle	37	3277

TEES	COURSE RATING	SLOPE
Forward	74.5	127
Middle	71.6	123

PORT JEFFERSON COUNTRY CLUB AT HARBOR HILLS

Port Jefferson, NY

YEAR FOUNDED: 1955

ARCHITECTS:
Devereux Emmet
Alfred Tull

COURSE OPENED: 1924

Formerly known as Belle Terre, Port Jefferson's memberships are taken largely by residents. Lies are rarely level and fairways are generally tight. The 18th is a strong par 5 with water fronting the green. The clubhouse offers a spectacular view of Long Island Sound.

TEES	PAR	YARDAGE
Forward	74	5713
Middle	72	6349
Back	72	6793

TEES	COURSE RATING	SLOPE
Forward	73.5	127
Middle	70.6	126
Back	72.6	130

QUOGUE FIELD CLUB

Quogue, NY

YEAR FOUNDED: 1900

ARCHITECTS:
R.B. Wilson
Stephen Kay

COURSE OPENED: 1900

Views of the Great South Bay loom throughout this water and wetland laced nine holer. The layout lost nine holes to a hurricane of World War II vintage. Superb conditions invariably prevail.

TEES	PAR	YARDAGE
Forward	72	5230
Middle	72	6256

TEES	COURSE RATING	SLOPE
Forward	70.6	118
Middle	69.9	123

ROCK HILL COUNTRY CLUB

Manorville, NY

YEAR FOUNDED: 1966

ARCHITECT:
Frank Duane

COURSE OPENED: 1966

Wind is the unseen factor here. What's seen are hills, dogleg holes and fine conditioning. The tight, target golf needed going out eases up for the back nine but finishes with a demanding closer at 18.

TEES	PAR	YARDAGE
Forward	72	5390
Middle	71	6465
Back	71	7050

TEES	COURSE RATING	SLOPE
Forward	71.4	121
Middle	70.7	126
Back	73.4	131

ROLLING OAKS COUNTRY CLUB

Rocky Point, NY

YEAR FOUNDED: 1961

ARCHITECT:
Arthur Colocci

COURSE OPENED: 1962

Rolling Oaks Country Club, formerly Tall Tree Golf Club, features challenging small sloping greens. The popular public-access course also boasts narrow fairways separated by tall hardwoods

TEES	PAR	YARDAGE
Forward	65	4350
Middle	65	4715

TEES	COURSE RATING	SLOPE
Forward	67.0	111
Middle	63.0	105

SAG HARBOR GOLF CLUB

Sag Harbor, NY

YEAR FOUNDED: 1919

ARCHITECT:
unknown

COURSE OPENED: 1919

A modest three-hole layout at birth, Sag Harbor has since added six more. Until recently, it boasted Long Island's only sand greens. The course is flat with tiny, undulating greens. A links-flavor course, with views of Gardiner's Bay, Sag Harbor never closes unless nature makes play impossible.

TEES	PAR	YARDAGE
Forward	72	4030
Middle	70	5500

TEES	COURSE RATING	SLOPE
Forward	62.0	104
Middle	65.8	115

SHELTER ISLAND COUNTRY CLUB

Shelter Island, NY

YEAR FOUNDED: 1898

ARCHITECT:
unknown

COURSE OPENED: 1898

Lovingly dubbed "Goat Hill" by many regulars, Shelter Island is a rugged 9-holer with six par 4s and three par 3s. It is hilly with excellent greens. Blind shots on seven holes are good reasons not to bet with locals on your first trip.

TEES	PAR	YARDAGE
Forward	34	2103
Middle	33	2512

TEES	COURSE RATING	SLOPE
Forward	63.5	105
Middle	63.8	107

SILVER LAKE GOLF COURSE

Staten Island, NY

YEAR FOUNDED: 1929

ARCHITECT:
John R. Van Kleek

COURSE OPENED: 1929

This is one of New York City's most popular and therefore busiest courses. The fairways are narrow, but length is not the only factor in a course's difficulty. It is hilly and scenic. PGA Tour pro Bill Britton cut his golfing teeth here.

TEES	PAR	YARDAGE
Forward	69	5202
Middle	69	5736
Back	69	6128

TEES	COURSE RATING	SLOPE
Forward	68.6	119
Middle	66.1	105
Back	67.8	110

SMITHTOWN LANDING COUNTRY CLUB

Smithtown, NY

YEAR FOUNDED: 1971

ARCHITECT:
Arthur Poole

COURSE OPENED: 1971

This hilly layout with small greens is available only to Smithtown residents on weekends and holidays. Master Professional Michael Hebron's instructional school and the Met PGA Junior Classic have made this a popular destination. A nine-hole par three course complements the regular 18.

TEES	PAR	YARDAGE
Forward	72	5263
Middle	72	5858
Back	72	6114

TEES	COURSE RATING	SLOPE
Forward	70.1	126
Middle	68.3	127
Back	69.4	129

SOUTH FORK COUNTRY CLUB

Amagansett, NY

YEAR FOUNDED: 1948

ARCHITECTS:
Members
Frank Duane

COURSE OPENED: 1948

A 12-hole course before World War II, it was plowed under during the war for potato farming, then rebuilt as a dual-tee nine-holer in 1948. Fairways are narrow and separated by rough—the greens are small, elevated and sloping. The membership is acting to expand to 18 holes. The views are of the Atlantic and local farmland.

TEES	PAR	YARDAGE
Forward	72	4877
Middle	72	5815

TEES	COURSE RATING	SLOPE
Forward	68.5	117
Middle	68.7	126

SOUTH SHORE GOLF COURSE

Staten Island, NY

YEAR FOUNDED: 1927

ARCHITECT:
Alfred Tull

COURSE OPENED: 1927

Rolling hills and tree-lined fairways turn this busy layout into flaming color each fall. Well bunkered greens, narrow fairways and prime conditioning give this course a country club atmosphere. South Shore is a regular on the three-course rota for the annual Staten Island Classic.

TEES	PAR	YARDAGE
Forward	72	5555
Middle	72	6315

TEES	COURSE RATING	SLOPE
Forward	69.8	114
Middle	68.6	113

SOUTHAMPTON GOLF CLUB

Southampton, NY

YEAR FOUNDED: 1925

ARCHITECTS:
Seth Raynor & Charles Banks

COURSE OPENED: 1927

Founded as a semi-private course for local businessmen, who remain the nucleus of today's thriving private club. Much of the terrain is gently rolling, with subtle hazards. Exception is the fourth, which appears on all lists of the East End's top holes. Under long time professional Bob Joyce, the club has nutured such fine player's as PGA star John Adams and two time Met Open champ Bruce Zabriski.

TEES	PAR	YARDAGE
Forward	71	5446
Middle	70	5965
Back	70	6287

TEES	COURSE RATING	SLOPE
Forward	72.1	124
Middle	69.8	126
Back	71.3	129

Nissequogue's picturesque second hole.

SWAN LAKE GOLF CLUB

Manorville, NY

YEAR FOUNDED: 1979

ARCHITECTS:
Charles & Fred Jurgens

COURSE OPENED: 1979

This semi-private club could be Long Island's answer to Augusta National for its lack of rough and its huge greens. Water is a frequent challenge. The conditioning is excellent for such a popular layout.

TEES	PAR	YARDAGE
Forward	72	5245
Middle	72	6338
Back	72	7011

TEES	COURSE RATING	SLOPE
Forward	69.0	112
Middle	69.5	115
Back	72.5	121

THE TAM O'SHANTER CLUB

Brookville, NY

YEAR FOUNDED: 1963

ARCHITECTS:
Steve Christoff
Robert Trent Jones

COURSE OPENED: 1963

The clubhouse sits atop a hill from which the opening and closing holes run, and overlooks land that had been a potato farm until 1961. Seven water holes are located within the heavily bunkered layout. The greens are large and sloping and the fairways bordered with menacing rough.

TEES	PAR	YARDAGE
Forward	74	5788
Middle	72	6475
Back	72	6875

TEES	COURSE RATING	SLOPE
Forward	71.4	120
Middle	70.7	128
Back	72.5	131

SPRING LAKE GOLF CLUB

Middle Island, NY

YEAR FOUNDED: 1966

ARCHITECTS:
Charles & Fred Jurgens

COURSE OPENED: 1966

Spring Lake features moderate elevation variations. The greens on the Thunderbird course are large, and the course is long. The watery first hole on the Sandpiper nine may be the most intimidating opener in the Met Area. Superb conditioning is the hallmark of this beauty.

THUNDERBIRD COURSE

TEES	PAR	YARDAGE
Forward	72	5732
Middle	72	6455
Back	72	7048

TEES	COURSE RATING	SLOPE
Forward	72.2	124
Middle	70.5	123
Back	73.2	128

SANDPIPER NINE

TEES	PAR	YARDAGE
Forward	72	5214
Middle	72	6106
Back	72	6500

TEES	COURSE RATING	SLOPE
Forward	69.9	122
Middle	69.4	125
Back	71.2	128

SUNKEN MEADOW STATE PARK

Kings Park, NY

YEAR FOUNDED: 1968

ARCHITECT:
Alfred Tull

COURSE OPENED: 1968

If nine holes is all you want to do, Sunken Meadow is the place for you. Within walking distance of the North Shore, this may be Long Island's favorite place to walk nine holes on gently rolling terrain. The Blue nine is the most challenging of the three.

GREEN-BLUE COURSE

TEES	PAR	YARDAGE
Forward	71	6185
Middle	71	6185

TEES	COURSE RATING	SLOPE
Forward	70.4	112
Middle	68.7	111

GREEN-RED COURSE

TEES	PAR	YARDAGE
Forward	72	6165
Middle	72	6165

TEES	COURSE RATING	SLOPE
Forward	70.3	113
Middle	68.5	112

RED-BLUE COURSE

TEES	PAR	YARDAGE
Forward	71	6100
Middle	71	6100

TEES	COURSE RATING	SLOPE
Forward	70.0	112
Middle	68.2	112

TIMBER POINT
GOLF COURSE
Great River, NY

YEAR FOUNDED: 1923

ARCHITECT:
Charles Alison
William Mitchell

COURSE OPENED: 1925

*The largest of Suffolk County
Park's four layouts, Timber
Point, with 27 holes, may also be
the busiest with an average of
475 rounds daily. Water appears
on 19 holes, several of which
border the Great South Bay.
Gibraltar, the spectacular
180-yard par-three, 5th on
the Blue course, plays uphill to
a green overlooking the Bay.*

WHITE-RED COURSE

TEES	PAR	YARDAGE
Forward	74	5358
Middle	72	5944
Back	72	6441

TEES	COURSE RATING	SLOPE
Forward	70.5	117
Middle	68.5	115
Back	70.8	119

RED-BLUE COURSE

TEES	PAR	YARDAGE
Forward	74	5455
Middle	72	6187
Back	72	6642

TEES	COURSE RATING	SLOPE
Forward	71.7	119
Middle	70.3	118
Back	72.3	123

BLUE-WHITE COURSE

TEES	PAR	YARDAGE
Forward	72	5367
Middle	72	6093
Back	72	6525

TEES	COURSE RATING	SLOPE
Forward	71.2	119
Middle	69.8	118
Back	71.7	122

TOWERS
COUNTRY CLUB
Floral Park, NY

YEAR FOUNDED: 1976

ARCHITECTS:
W. H. Follett
Frank Duane

COURSE OPENED: 1925

*For the residents of North Shore
Towers, this is golf "in the round."
The course, occupying the former
Glen Oaks site, circles three
residential towers. Though of
modest length, full use is made of
the hilly terrain providing classic
settings for the greens.*

TEES	PAR	YARDAGE
Forward	71	5373
Middle	71	5578
Back	71	5782

TEES	COURSE RATING	SLOPE
Forward	69.7	114
Middle	65.5	109
Back	67.2	113

The Village Club
of Sands Point

VILLAGE CLUB OF
SANDS POINT
Sands Point, NY

YEAR FOUNDED: 1924

ARCHITECT:
unknown

COURSE OPENED: 1924

*Originally owned by Isaac
Guggenheim, it was believed to be
his private course until purchased
by IBM in 1953. They used it
through 1994. It is now operated
by Sands Point primarily for its
resident members. Its lack of water
holes is offset by rolling terrain and
a view of Manhattan from the
ninth fairway.*

TEES	PAR	YARDAGE
Forward	72	5503
Middle	72	6251

TEES	COURSE RATING	SLOPE
Forward	69.8	116
Middle	69.1	120

WEST SAYVILLE
GOLF COURSE
West Sayville, NY

YEAR FOUNDED: 1970

ARCHITECT:
William Mitchell

COURSE OPENED: 1970

*This busy Suffolk County Park
course typically registers 55,000
rounds annually. The flat, walkable layout with elevated greens
offers views of the South Shore and
Fire Island. Tall sea grass comes
into play on several holes.*

TEES	PAR	YARDAGE
Forward	72	5387
Middle	72	6130
Back	72	6715

TEES	COURSE RATING	SLOPE
Forward	70.1	120
Middle	69.5	122
Back	72.1	127

The spectacular setting at Fox Hill's first and tenth greens.

4th hole (Lower Course) at Baltusrol Golf Club, Springfield, New Jersey.

Golf Clubs of New Jersey

including Orange and Rockland Counties, New York

The statistical information and course and slope rating for each course were those in effect for the 1996 golf season. The "Forward" tee ratings listed for each club are women's ratings.

117

BALTUSROL GOLF CLUB

"In The Shadow Of The Mountain"

**BALTUSROL
GOLF CLUB**
Springfield, NJ

YEAR FOUNDED: 1895

ARCHITECT:
A.W. Tillinghast

COURSES OPENED: 1922

UPPER COURSE

TEES	PAR	YARDAGE
Forward	73	5895
Middle	72	6449
Back	72	6866

TEES	COURSE RATING	SLOPE
Forward	74.8	133
Middle	71.0	128
Back	72.9	131

LOWER COURSE

TEES	PAR	YARDAGE
Forward	75	5963
Middle	72	6599
Back	72	7195

TEES	COURSE RATING	SLOPE
Forward	75.8	134
Middle	72.3	132
Back	74.9	140

Jack Nicklaus in 1980.

Baltusrol holds the distinction of being the only club to have hosted U.S. Opens on three distinct golf courses. Baltusrol also is unique in that its founding father, Louis Keller, did not play golf. But Keller, who created the New York Social Register, did have many friends who played, so in 1890 he bought 477 acres at the foot of New Jersey's Baltusrol Mountain, and five years later engaged George Hunter to lay out a nine-hole course. He then invited a select group of friends to join his new club.

Baltusrol takes its name from the mountain that forms the Club's northwestern boundary, which itself had been named for a farmer—Baltus Roll—who lived near where the clubhouse now sits. One evening in 1831, two thieves broke into Roll's house, dragged him outside, beat him, and left him to die in a snowbank while they ransacked the house, apparently in search of money. The murder and subsequent trial was the story of the year in the New York press.

The original clubhouse was a converted farmhouse that burned to the ground in 1909. The story is often told of the member who returned home to New York one morning explaining to his wife that he had been detained in New Jersey and had spent the evening at the Club. She responded by handing him the morning paper, its headlines telling of the previous night's fire. The present clubhouse, built in the English Manor House style, was ready a year later.

Baltusrol's original nine-hole course was expanded to a full 18, now referred to as the "Old Course," prior to the 1898 season. Very little from that course remains in play today. In 1901 it hosted the U.S. Women's Amateur, won by Genevieve Hecker. That championship returned in 1911,

and was won by Margaret Curtis.

In 1903, Willie Anderson captured the U.S. Open at Baltusrol, where he had been professional for one year before the turn of the century. The U.S. Amateur came the next year, when 20-year-old H. Chandler Egan, a Harvard sophomore, trounced 16-year-old Fred Herreshoff in the finals. Tournament favorite Walter Travis, the British Amateur champion, bowed out in the second round, the victim of sharpshooting George Ormiston, who holed out full shots at both the 12th and 17th holes.

The final major contested over the Old Course was the 1915 U.S. Open, which also was the final major won by Jerry Travers. He almost lost the tournament on the 10th tee in the final round, when, using a driving iron, he sliced one out-of-bounds (loss of distance—no stroke—in those days), then hooked his second try into deep rough. Facing elimination, Travers hit a beautiful par-saving pitch to within two feet.

At the time, 10 was the pre–eminent hole on the Old Course, making at least one appearance on the cover of a national magazine. A short par four, it played from a tee on the mountainside to an island green surrounded by a moat (now the green on the present 16th hole of the Lower Course, with the water replaced by sand and rough).

Travers' winning margin came on the par-five 15th, where he gambled on carrying the sand with his second shot, and succeeded—just barely. His shot caught the lip of a bunker, but carried through and stopped 10 yards short of the green. He pitched close and holed his putt for the winning birdie.

The majestic clubhouse.

Aerial view showing bunkering on 17-Lower, with 17-Upper to left

The approach to 5-Lower.

By 1918, the Old Course had become antiquated and overcrowded, so an additional 172 acres to the west were purchased, and A.W. Tillinghast hired to design two new courses. His task was complicated by the country's war efforts, and made even more difficult because the new courses were to be built atop the Old Course on a timetable that would allow play to continue during construction. The work was not finished until June of 1922.

The two courses are very different. The Upper, which lies closer to the mountain, is hilly and uses the sloping ground to dictate the strategy for each shot. The (often unseen) influence of the mountain is especially prevalent on the highly-contoured putting surfaces: There is no such thing as a straight putt, especially on the first six greens!

Johnny Farrell conducting one of golf's first junior clinics.

The Lower gives a more open appearance, despite more than 120 bunkers. The greens are large and are easier targets to hit, provided the tee shot is placed precisely.

Most lists of the world's great par threes include the fourth hole of the Lower. The tee shot is all carry over a pond to a green that is four times wider than it is deep and fronted by a three-foot high stone wall. Three bunkers just over the back dare the player to overclub: The slippery explosion from one of these bunkers, played from a downhill lie toward the pond, is truly frightening.

Played at full length, its tee set back in a narrow chute of trees, 17 on the Lower is 630 yards, making it the longest hole in U.S. Open history! The second shot must carry the "Sahara Desert," a huge expanse of bunkers crossing the fairway approximately 380 to 420 yards from the championship tee. The final approach must carry a nest of five bunkers fronting the elevated green.

Both courses finish strong. Lower 18 is a par five that plays from an elevated tee set in a chute to a tree-lined fairway crossed by water where it doglegs left. The green is elevated and guarded by a deep bunker right and a nasty little bunker front and center.

Upper 18 also starts in a tight chute. The long par four finishes at the clubhouse, protected by a number of bunkers well short of the dance floor. It is a much tougher par than its counterpart on Lower.

The Lower tasted national competition first, hosting the 1926 U.S. Amateur, won in an upset by George Von Elm over Bobby Jones. Ten years later, the U.S. Open was contested on the Upper, and it appeared "Lighthorse" Harry Cooper, one of the great shotmakers of the time, would finally capture the national championship. But Cooper was denied, despite eclipsing the Open record by two strokes. Tony Manero finished nearly an hour behind Cooper with a 67 for 282 to beat the old record by four strokes and overcome a six-shot deficit. For Manero, who learned the game caddying at various Westchester clubs, it would be his only significant win.

The U.S. Amateur returned to the Lower Course in 1946, its first renewal after the war. Ted Bishop defeated "Smiley" Quick in the finals on the 37th hole.

The 1954 U.S. Open was a landmark event in several respects. It was the first Open to be televised nationally, and also the first in which the fairways were roped off, forcing spectators to watch from the sidelines. The man of the hour proved to be Ed Furgol, a 10-year veteran of the Tour with just one previous title. Furgol, whose left arm was crooked as the result of a childhood accident, did all he could to lose the tournament on the final two holes. He sliced his drive at 17 into deep rough, then skulled his second toward the Sahara; but the ball rolled through the middle of the hazard and into the fairway on the other side, setting up an easy par. On the final hole, Furgol duck-hooked his drive into the trees. His only apparent escape was back toward the tee until he noticed a narrow opening leading to the 18th fairway of the Upper Course, which had not been designated out-of-bounds. A punched 8-iron into the Upper Course led to a tournament-winning par.

The grave of Baltus Roll.

The women staged their Open on the Lower Course in 1961. Mickey Wright fired a near-perfect 69-72 on the final day to win convincingly.

The men returned to the Lower for the 1967 Open. Despite amateur Marty Fleckman leading after both the first and third rounds, the contest came down to virtual match play between Jack Nicklaus and Arnold Palmer the last two rounds. With Palmer unable to buy a putt on Sunday, Nicklaus took charge with five birdies on the front nine. Needing one more birdie to break the Open record of 276, Nicklaus responded with a monumental one-iron that soared 230 yards, but just barely carried the bunker fronting the final green. Nicklaus drained a 22-foot putt for the record-setting birdie and later described his play (71-67-72-65=275) as "just about my finest ever."

Thirteen years later, the U.S. Open returned and, once again, attention focused on Nicklaus, who was paired all four rounds with Isao Aoki. Nicklaus' opening 63

tied the Open record, and paved the way for record 36-, 54-, and 72-hole totals, but after three rounds the two were tied. They battled to the wire, with Nicklaus' long birdie putt on 17 the crushing blow. His 63-71-70-68=272 remains the Open record, while Aoki's 112 putts erased the standard set by Billy Casper at Winged Foot in 1959. It was Nicklaus' fourth Open victory, and placed him in the select company of Willie Anderson, Bobby Jones, and Ben Hogan.

In 1985, the U.S. Women's Open came to the Upper Course for the first time. Kathy Baker made it her first professional victory.

Nicklaus' 36- and 72-hole records and the more recent 54-hole record were tied during the 1993 Open by Lee Janzen, who fired 67-67-69-69=272 to edge Payne Stewart by two strokes. A birdie at 14 and a chip-in birdie at 16 provided the winning margin in their head-to-head confrontation.

One other Open has significance to Baltusrol. In 1928, Johnny Farrell defeated Jones in a 36-hole playoff at Olympia Fields. Farrell was Baltusrol's professional for nearly 40 years, from 1934 through 1972. Besides his Open victory, Farrell won seven consecutive tournaments (and 10 in all) in 1927. He also was recognized as the "best dresser" on Tour. During the 1950s, he hosted golf's first national television show," Swing Into Sports."

Since Farrell's retirement until 1996, the shop has been overseen by Bob Ross, winner of the National Club Professional of the Year Award in 1980.

The mountain still stands tall over Baltusrol, one hundred years after its birth, and the amphitheater below has witnessed many of the greatest moments in American golf history.   ○

The severely bunkered par three 7-Upper.

PLAINFIELD COUNTRY CLUB

"The Legacy Of Dornoch"

PLAINFIELD COUNTRY CLUB
Plainfield, NJ

YEAR FOUNDED: 1890

ARCHITECT:
Donald Ross

COURSE OPENED: 1921

TEES	PAR	YARDAGE
Forward	74	5685
Middle	72	6435
Back	72	6859

TEES	COURSE RATING	SLOPE
Forward	74.3	135
Middle	72.0	132
Back	73.6	136

When Donald Ross moved from Dornoch, Scotland, to this country at the turn of the century, he brought with him a naturalist philosophy, thinking that golf holes should be designed to fit into natural settings, with boldly-contoured greens atop plateaus. From his greenside style followed the truism that a "Ross course" be a severe examination in inventive chipping. No course typifies the Ross style better than Plainfield, but it took 30 years to bring him into the picture.

The Club was organized in 1890 by a group of Wall Street brokers as the Hillside Tennis Club. With two tennis courts, it quickly became a focal point in the social life of the affluent community, and soon would add more courts and a small clubhouse.

Five years later, the Club moved within town, and, with some misgivings, built a rudimentary nine-hole course. Golf quickly became the predominant activity, membership continued to grow, and the move was made in December, 1897 to the present site, 100 acres of rolling countryside, replete with numerous natural hazards. The property, bisected by Raritan

Leighton Calkins

Road, is believed to have been the scene of the Battle Of The Short Hills, a Revolutionary War skirmish between Colonial and British armies as Washington retreated from New York. These same hills were to figure into Ross' plan 150 years later.

An 18-hole Tom Bendelow course opened in 1898. Although it bore no resemblance to the present course, it played over terrain near the present clubhouse, as well as the practice area and the West nine across Raritan Road. It underwent considerable lengthening and revision during its lifetime.

The Club changed its name to Plainfield in 1904. Foremost among those signing the documents was Leighton Calkins, a former member of the Executive Committees of both the USGA and the MGA, and a mayor of Plainfield who made headlines for nude sunbathing. Calkins formalized the junior golf program previously advocated by H.B. Hollins of Westbrook, the first president of the MGA, and the first three MGA Junior Championships (1912-1914) were contested at Plainfield. Calkins also devised a handicap system that is the basis for what we use today. It was adopted by the MGA in 1905, and by the USGA in 1911. Calkins, who wrote extensively about golf, is credited with introducing the term "par" into the golf vernacular.

In 1916, Plainfield purchased additional land and engaged Ross to build a completely new 18-hole course east of Raritan Road. Construction was delayed by World War I, and the course was not formally unveiled until September of 1921. Nine holes from the old course were preserved, and called the "West-9." The rise and fall of the terrain and the relative absence of trees made it resemble the heathland of Scotland, and was quite similar to Gleneagles, the world-famous golf resort.

The most significant change to the course over the years was the 1930 cre-

The Plainfield clubhouse.

The picturesque par-three third hole.

ation of the "Tunnel," a sequence of three holes (13 through 15) cut through virgin forest at the extreme northeastern corner of Club property, supposedly according to topographical plans prepared by Ross.

Plainfield is a Ross masterpiece. The rolling terrain seldom gives the player a level stance. Six water hazards and nine cross-bunkers complicate the straight and narrow path from tee to green. Out-of-bounds comes into play on nine holes, most often to the right. But in true Ross fashion, the greens are king: Seven are perched atop knolls, often demanding a semi-blind approach; many are dramatically contoured, featuring severe slopes, swales, terraces, and crowns.

The first three holes—two long par fours and a par three over water—have been called the toughest start in New Jersey. The opener can be a back-breaker, especially for the player likely to miss his first shot right into a wall of trees and out-of-bounds.

The third is a pretty par three of moderate length played slightly downhill to a ground-level green set on a left-to-right angle to the shot. A pond at the right front of the green and a deep bunker at the left rear combine to give the hole a slight "Redan" flavor.

A great short par four, the fourth plays sharply uphill, demanding a long, well-placed drive to carry to the top of the hill and remain in the fairway. A good drive leaves

The phalanx of bunkers crossing the 18th hole.

only a short pitch to a tightly bunkered green that falls off sharply back and right.

The 11th is a little par three with dramatic Scottish undertones, downhill over sand to a saucer-shaped green whose back-to-front slope is the steepest on the course. A shot hit slightly short likely will roll back off the putting surface into a bunker.

Number 17 is the toughest, and most strategic, of the four doglegs. The tee shot must carry trees at the corner or be faded around the corner over a nest of bunkers. A long, straight drive over the bunkers easily can run through the fairway; out-of-bounds to the immediate right adds to the risk. From the fairway, the hole rises slightly uphill through an isolated valley to a table-top green set behind two bunkers at the left front and a moderate pot bunker to the right.

To help create some needed cash flow during the Depression, the Club began operating the West nine as a semi-public facility, a practice that continues to this day.

John Cook

The West-9, known today as Plainfield West, has produced some outstanding amateurs, most notably Jeff Thomas, three time MGA Player of the Year, and winner of the 1993 U.S. Mid-Amateur Championship.

Most prominent among the early golfers was Charley Whitehead, who captured six State Amateur titles in seven years (1936-1942), and capped his streak by becoming the first amateur to take the New Jersey Open, in 1942. Runner-up Vic Ghezzi had won the National PGA Championship the previous year.

Through the years, Plainfield has been a gracious host to numerous regional events, including three Met Opens and five Met Amateurs. Wes Ellis established the 72-hole record at 283 with a five-stroke victory over former Masters and PGA champion Doug Ford in the 1963 Met Open, part of Ellis' "Jersey Slam" that season.

Plainfield's reputation as a "green monster" was established in the 1957 Met Open, also won by Ellis, but with

The approach from the left side of the 7th fairway.

ing professional. In an awesome display, McGovern never went past the 13th hole in any match, and had 23 birdies over the 73 holes he played. For two weeks following the win, he wore both the Met Amateur and Met Open crowns.

In 1978, Plainfield hosted the U.S. Amateur Championship. One semifinal pitted 18-year-old Bobby Clampett, the year's dominant amateur, against Scott Hoch. Even after 18, Clampett pushed his drive on the first extra hole onto the sixth tee, then hit a green he couldn't see with a wide hook. That kept the gallery buzzing until the next hole when Clampett once again pushed his drive into trees. This time he found no miracle in his bag. In the finals, 20-year-old John Cook took command early and came home a 5&4 winner over Hoch.

a score of 296. More than half the field failed to break 80 in the final round. Although played at the end of a rather wet September, with the rough high and the final day quite windy, the field included at least 20 former or future Tour players. Ellis' winning 296 was the highest score to win the Met Open since 1927, and has not been approached since.

The 1988 Met Amateur belonged to Jim McGovern, who was playing his last amateur tournament before turn-

There was an international flavor to the U.S. Women's Open in 1987. Laura Davies of England, Japan's Ayako Okamoto, and American veteran JoAnne Gunderson Carner were deadlocked after 72 holes at 3-under-par 285. Davies won the playoff with a 71.

Whether hosting a national championship or a top local event, Plainfield has consistently sparkled as one of the Met Area's greatest tests of golf. A true Ross gem.   ○

Looking from behind the green at the par-five 16th.

THE RIDGEWOOD COUNTRY CLUB

"Jersey's Finest"

THE RIDGEWOOD COUNTRY CLUB
Paramus, NJ

YEAR FOUNDED: 1890

ARCHITECT:
A.W. Tillinghast

COURSE OPENED: 1929

EAST-CENTER COURSE

TEES	PAR	YARDAGE
Forward	74	6000
Middle	72	6415
Back	72	6749

TEES	COURSE RATING	SLOPE
Forward	75.9	135
Middle	71.5	133
Back	73.1	136

EAST-WEST COURSE

TEES	PAR	YARDAGE
Forward	74	5992
Middle	72	6539
Back	72	6938

TEES	COURSE RATING	SLOPE
Forward	75.1	134
Middle	71.9	135
Back	73.7	139

WEST-CENTER COURSE

TEES	PAR	YARDAGE
Forward	74	5910
Middle	72	6538
Back	72	6879

TEES	COURSE RATING	SLOPE
Forward	74.9	135
Middle	72.0	135
Back	73.6	138

In 1890, the only set of golf clubs in New Jersey belonged to William Rosencrantz, who lived in the Hermitage, the former estate of Aaron Burr in Ho-Ho-Kus, a small village a mile north of Ridgewood. Rosencrantz had been introduced to the game while in England, then began hitting golf balls on the Hermitage lawns upon his return. In 1891, he and some curious neighbors built the first golf course in New Jersey, a simple two-hole layout in a meadow across the street from his home.

Two years later, the Ho-Ho-Kus Golf Club was formally organized and the course expanded to six holes. Another three holes were added in 1897, but as there was no room for further expansion, many of the 53 members became dissatisfied with the course, not to mention the lack of a clubhouse.

George Jacobus

In 1901, the Club moved to what is now called "Veterans' Field" in the heart of Ridgewood, changed its name to Ridgewood Golf Club, and began play on a nine-hole course. But by the end of the decade, the village's rapid growth meant another move was in order.

The Club purchased 100 acres on a hill in the southwestern part of town and in 1911 work began on 18 holes known in club annals as the "Billy Goat" course. Donald Ross made some revisions to the roller-coaster layout in 1914, calling the site one of the most beautiful in the country.

Pretty soon, this course was being squeezed by housing developments and high taxes. The final move took place in 1927, to a heavily-wooded tract in Paramus where a new 27-hole golf course, designed by A.W. Tillinghast, and a Clifford Wendehack clubhouse opened on Decoration Day, 1929.

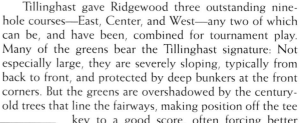

Tillinghast gave Ridgewood three outstanding nine-hole courses—East, Center, and West—any two of which can be, and have been, combined for tournament play. Many of the greens bear the Tillinghast signature: Not especially large, they are severely sloping, typically from back to front, and protected by deep bunkers at the front corners. But the greens are overshadowed by the century-old trees that line the fairways, making position off the tee key to a good score, often forcing better players to club down for accuracy. The trees also isolate each hole, creating a scene of splendid tranquility.

Many of Ridgewood's holes are memorable. The fairway on the par-five 3-East is interrupted 300 yards off the blue back tees by a series of rough-covered mounds. The second shot is best played to the left to open up the approach to one of Tillinghast's finest greens—long and narrow, angled to the fairway, cascading from back to front, and surrounded by nine bunkers.

The drive on the dogleg-left 9-East must favor the right side to open up the green and avoid trees along the left. The entrance to the huge, level green is protected by a large bunker at the left front. A pond to the right further complicates the approach, and brings the bunker more into play.

The opener on Center is a Cape hole, a sharp dogleg-left over a lake just in front of the tee. The approach is complicated by a long cross-bunker angling across the fairway and ending 50 yards from the green.

Known to the members as the "Five and Dime" hole ("if you don't get a five, you'll get a ten."), 6-Center is a gem of a short par four. A slight rise precedes the fairway, concealing much of the danger. The hole curves to the right, with the ideal line over a long diagonal bunker in the right rough. The fairway ends abruptly 50 yards from home, the terrain rising through a collar of rough. The small, narrow, plateau green is surrounded by six bunkers; the two front and one right side are well below the putting surface, which has a ridge and falls from a high left side.

Number 5-West is a classic example of Tillinghast artistry. The drive must carry a nest of mounds on the right, beyond which the fairway widens. Then the hole plays slightly left and uphill to a severely sloping, multi-level green perched atop a knoll. The narrow entrance is watched over by matching beech trees and flanking bunkers.

The "five and dime" 6-Center

Another wonderful hole, 8-West is one of the premiere par fives in the Met Area. It can be described as a double-dogleg to the left, but that doesn't tell the complete story. Out-of-bounds parallels the left side, yet the drive must be played with a draw to avoid running through the first bend. The ideal second shot fades between a tall tulip tree on the right and a fairway bunker on the left. The green breaks severely toward a deep bunker lurking precariously on the left.

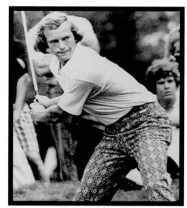

Jerry Pate

Many great players have walked these fairways. Among the best known was George Jacobus, the Club's professional for 51 years until his death in 1965. Although slight of build, Jacobus was one of the longest and straightest hitters in the game. In 1928, he played nine consecutive holes at Ridgewood in 10-under par, and on another occasion hit his tee shot 392 yards to drive the green on the par-four 17th hole at the old course, considered an American record for 32 years.

Jacobus became the first American-born professional (and ex-caddie) elected president of the PGA of America.

He took office in 1932 and served for seven years. His reign was tumultuous, coming at the start of a divisive 30-year conflict between the club professionals and touring professionals.

Jacobus also was responsible for bringing Byron Nelson to Ridgewood as a playing assistant in 1935. With Jacobus' help, Nelson developed a new swing that was more suitable for the steel shafts coming into vogue at that time. Nelson has said the 1936 Met Open at Quaker Ridge, where he defeated Gene Sarazen, Johnny Farrell, Craig Wood, and others, was the turning point in his career.

Ridgewood member Marge Mason won at least 30 state and regional titles, including the United States Women's Senior Amateur in 1967. Together with Maureen Orcutt and Carolyn Cudone, she dominated ladies' golf in New Jersey for a quarter of a century.

The first event of national interest held at Ridgewood was the 1935 Ryder Cup, won by the United States team, 9-3. Walter Hagen served as playing captain of the victorious Americans.

Nearly 40 years later, Ridgewood hosted the 1974 U.S. Amateur Championship, won by Jerry Pate playing in his first (and last) Amateur, just 22 months before his famous 5-iron from the rough won him the U.S. Open. Pate eliminated local hero George Burns, Bill Campbell, and Curtis Strange en route to his final match up with Texan John Grace. Three down after 20 holes, Pate fought back, capping his comeback with a miraculous wedge shot from the right rough at 7-West that helped him take a two-hole advantage.

Lee Trevino

The LPGA Tour visited for the 1981 Coca-Cola Classic. Kathy Whitworth won the $125,000 event in sudden death over Alice Ritzman. Whitworth recorded an 8-under-par score of 211, coming from seven strokes behind over the final 11 holes.

The prestigious U.S. Senior Open Championship was played over Ridgewood's Center and West nines in 1990–the "rookie" year for Lee Trevino and Jack Nicklaus. The week-long perfect weather was interrupted on Sunday, when a one-hour thunderstorn delay stopped play. Trevino was already safely in at 275, 13 under par, and watched from a TV trailer as Nicklaus uncharacteris-

tically bogied the 17th hole, thus eliminating any chance of catching the leader. Trevino won the Championship, and the trophy, by two shots over Nicklaus.

Al Mengert of Echo Lake stormed to the 1960 Met Open title at Ridgewood, lowering the West-East record three times with scores of 69-68-67-69=272. Mengert finished 12 strokes clear of runner-up Wes Ellis in capturing the middle leg of his "Jersey Slam." Ten years later, Jim Albus and Jimmy Wright deadlocked at 288 after four rounds of the Met Open. Albus' one stroke margin of victory came on the playoff's 17th hole, the par-three 8-Center.

The 1938 Met Amateur at Ridgewood resulted in a classic final-round matchup. Frank Strafaci won his first of a record seven Met Amateur trophies with a 3&1 decision over the reigning U.S. Amateur champion, Willie Turnesa.

Ridgewood also has hosted the 1994 Met Open (won by Charlie Cowell), and the 1952 (Joseph Marra) and 1985 (George Zahringer III) Met Amateurs.

Its not surprising that many of these great players and almost anyone who plays Ridgewood agrees with senior golf writer Arthur "Red" Hoffman, who terms the course "Jersey's Finest." ❍

The approach to 9-East, with clubhouse in background.

CANOE BROOK COUNTRY CLUB

"A Flower A Day"

The clubhouse entrance and flower display.

Just outside the main entrance to Canoe Brook's clubhouse is a floral display unlike any other in the Met Area. Each day, an evergreen shrub is transplanted from the Club's greenhouse, replacing the one on display the previous day. The shrubs are unusual in that they have been cut to proclaim the date. In the year 2001, they will mark the centennial of one of New Jersey's most prestigious clubs.

In the middle of the 19th century, the area around Summit, New Jersey, became a popular summer resort, attracting prosperous New Yorkers, many of whom worked on Wall Street. With its 600-foot elevation, Summit was an ideal escape from the heat of the city. Eventually, many of these summer visitors bought land and built permanent homes in Summit.

Carroll P. Bassett, a Summit resident and pioneer in the utilities industry, hatched the idea that would become Canoe Brook Country Club, which took its name from a tributary of the Passaic River. The Passaic Valley has numerous waterways, and canoes were a likely mode of travel a century ago.

The Club purchased 133 acres to the north of Morris Turnpike in Short Hills. Jack Vickery designed an 18-hole course, with nine holes on either side of Canoe Brook

Road. The first nine were ready for play by the fall of 1902; the second nine was completed in 1908. A farmhouse on the property was converted into a clubhouse and formally opened on November 1, 1902.

In 1916, the course received a facelift at the hands of Walter Travis. The heavily bunkered course measured 6,611 yards, 300 yards longer than the "big" courses of the day, and was recognized as a superior test of golf.

As the 1920s began to roar, Canoe Brook was in an expansive mood, and thinking about a second course. In March of 1921, the Club bought 129 acres south of Morris Turnpike in Summit. Charles Alison designed the South Course, which opened for play in the spring of 1924. Fourteen holes were carved from virgin forest, which provided superb settings for golf holes of unsurpassed beauty. Six holes had water in play.

Resistance to the new course was immediate. It was called "an incorrigible monster with death lurking for any shot that strayed three feet from the narrow fairways." Members preferred the North Course, their "Garden Of Eden," and ridiculed the South as "Siberia," with "jungle-like" rough. After nearly selling the new course in 1925, the Club retained Major Jones, Baltusrol's longtime greenkeeper, as a consultant to devise a salvage plan. By 1930 the ugly duckling had been transformed into a lovely swan, and was considered the Club's "championship" course.

The reputation of the South Course grew. The USGA actively sought it out as the site for the 1936 Women's Amateur Championship, which was won by 19-year-old

CANOE BROOK COUNTRY CLUB
Summit, NJ
YEAR FOUNDED: 1901

NORTH COURSE

ARCHITECTS:
Jack Vickery
Walter Travis
Alfred Tull
Robert Trent Jones
Rees Jones

COURSE OPENED: 1902

TEES	PAR	YARDAGE
Forward	72	5775
Middle	72	6591
Back	72	7066

TEES	COURSE RATING	SLOPE
Forward	74.5	133
Middle	72.3	135
Back	74.8	138

SOUTH COURSE

ARCHITECTS:
Charles Alison
Robert Trent Jones
Rees Jones

COURSE OPENED: 1924

TEES	PAR	YARDAGE
Forward	72	5599
Middle	72	6400
Back	72	6691

TEES	COURSE RATING	SLOPE
Forward	72.9	128
Middle	71.9	130
Back	73.2	133

Around the corner at the 3rd hole of the South Course.

The North lies on high ground to the north of Route 24, while much of the South crosses lower ground south of the highway. The feature holes on the North are the eighth, a strong par four with water and bunkers short and right of the green; the par-five 11th, which passes through a bottleneck in the drive zone before dropping to lower ground, bending left, and crossing a brook en route to an angled green; and the par-three 16th, which demands rifle accuracy between mature trees that overhang both sides of the hole.

The South has five par threes, including the 10th, which has water from tee to green and sand surrounding the green. Also of note are the sharp dogleg-left third, which calls for an accurate lay-up off the tee to split the fairway bunkers, and the claustrophobic fifth, which drops sharply and to the right through a narrow opening in the drive zone.

Canoe Brook re-entered the national spotlight in 1983, hosting the Women's Amateur once again, this time over the North Course. Joanne Pacillo edged Sally Quinlan 2&1 for the title. The tournament returned for the third time in 1990 when Pat Hurst edged Stephanie Davis on the first hole of sudden death after the pair finished even after 36 holes. Defending champ Vicki Goetze won the qualifying medal with 144.

As time marches on, Canoe Brook regularly adds to its already-significant history. Only the flowers remain a constant, although they change every day!   ❍

Pam Barton, who earlier that summer had captured the British Women's Amateur. In the finals, Barton came from four down to defeat local favorite Maureen Orcutt 4&3. A heroine as a nurse during World War II, Barton lost her life in a 1945 plane crash.

In 1948, Canoe Brook rejected an offer to sell the North Course. The following year, they traded 46 acres (including seven holes) west of Canoe Brook Road for equal acreage east of the road. Alfred Tull designed eight new holes, which were completed early in 1952. The new North Course quickly became known as one of the sternest tests in the Met Area.

In the late 1960s, the state decided to widen Morris Turnpike, cutting a wide swath through the heart of Canoe Brook and cutting use of the South Course for four years. In 1978, Robert Trent Jones Sr. was called in to rebuild what are now the first three holes on the North Course and six holes on the South. More recently, Rees Jones worked on both courses, rebuilding and enlarging the tees, repositioning the bunkering in the tradition of the original architecture, and enlarging the holding ponds. He changed the character of just one hole, 14-North, where the lake now extends to the front of the green, making this par three the signature hole on the course.

From behind the 10th green on the South Course.

ESSEX COUNTY COUNTRY CLUB

"Where East Became West"

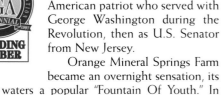

**ESSEX COUNTY
COUNTRY CLUB**
West Orange, NJ

YEAR FOUNDED: 1887

ARCHITECTS:
A.W. Tillinghast
Seth Raynor
Charles Banks

COURSE OPENED: 1918

TEES	PAR	YARDAGE
Forward	73	5680
Middle	71	6539
Back	71	6851

TEES	COURSE RATING	SLOPE
Forward	73.4	128
Middle	71.5	126
Back	72.9	128

Few people in the Met Area know there once were mineral springs in the hills of New Jersey, and that the fashionable hotel that developed there had close ties to golf's roots in the state. It was a direct antecedent of the state's oldest country club, and witnessed the birth of the New Jersey State Golf Association.

In 1820, mineral springs were discovered in a wooded ravine on a farm owned by Dr. John Condit at the foot of the eastern side of First Mountain in the Oranges. Condit was an American patriot who served with George Washington during the Revolution, then as U.S. Senator from New Jersey.

Orange Mineral Springs Farm became an overnight sensation, its waters a popular "Fountain Of Youth." In 1821, the Orange Springs Hotel was built as a health resort. But in the early 1830s, the water's flow diminished and the resort's popularity waned.

The hotel changed hands frequently during the next four decades, during which time it came to be known as the Mansion House. In 1868, it was purchased by Major Benjamin Hutton, a wealthy New York merchant, who renamed the grounds Hutton Park. In 1887, at a meeting in the house, a group from Essex County Hunt formed the Essex County Country Club, the first such entity in New Jersey. The intent was to offer a wider variety of social activities and outdoor sports to the hunt club's membership. Until then, polo was the sport of choice, with Essex County engaging in hotly contested matches against local clubs such as Meadow Brook and Rockaway Hunting.

Essex County purchased the Mansion House in 1889, the same year Thomas Alva Edison joined the club. Edison was an active social member, even demonstrating his "talking movie machine" at the club in 1913. Edison also played some golf in his younger days, but had little time for the game.

In 1895, the Club formally approved the construction of a nine-hole golf course, laid out in Hutton Park by a young Scot named Alex Findlay, who became the Club's first professional. Findlay's course was extended to 18 holes in 1897.

On the evening of June 1, 1900, Essex County hosted a meeting at which the New Jersey State Golf Association was formed. Representatives from 10 clubs—Essex County, Morris County, Baltusrol, Montclair, North Jersey, Hillside, Golf Club of Lakewood, Englewood, Jersey City, and Yountakah—participated. The first New Jersey Amateur Championship was played on the Hutton Park course later that summer, with Archibald Graham of North Jersey becoming the first State champion.

Crowded conditions at Hutton Park forced the Club to add to its golf facilities. A.W. Tillinghast was hired in 1916 to build an 18-hole course, called the West or Upper Course, at the top of First Mountain, a couple of miles away.

In the mid 1920s, the Club began selling off its Hutton Park property while buying more land on the mountain west of the course. In 1925, Seth Raynor was hired to replace the Upper Course with two new courses. After redesigning the Upper Course (to be renamed the East), incorporating seven of the Tillinghast holes (the first six and the ninth). Raynor died suddenly of pneumonia, and Charles Banks completed the project, also building a second course, called the West.

A striking feature of the East Course are the elevated greens guarded by deep bunkers. The long par fours are exceptional, challenging even the low-handicap player

The dramatic par-three 11th.

From behind the cross bunkers on the 5th hole.

with a variety of hazards that transcend length. The Club's elevated setting brings the wind into play. No surprise, then, that the back nine has been called "the toughest in the state, bar none," including Pine Valley: There is little room for error on any of the holes.

From the championship tee—set well above the fairway in a chute of trees—the par-five eighth requires a huge drive to the left center of the fairway, just short of a lake, before the long hitter can even think about going for the green in two. A hanging lie may force a more conservative decision, as may the deep bunker protecting the right front of the green.

The 11th is a long-iron par three played over a vegetation-filled gully. The green is set on an angle behind a deep bunker on the right. A ridge running front to back separates the portion of the green behind the frontal bunker from the rest of the putting surface.

The par-four 14th runs slightly uphill around a couple of fairway bunkers to a punch-bowl green hidden behind a huge bunker. The figure-eight-shaped putting surface sits on an angle behind that bunker, its two halves separated by a burial mound.

Essex County's par-four home hole is one of the great finishes in the state. The tee is well above the fairway, with the championship markers set behind a pair of sentinel trees. Unless the drive is long and straight, the average player may have no choice but to lay up behind a series of bunkers scattered about the fairway. The well-bunkered green, which has distinct front and back levels, sits atop a small hill.

As golf facilities expanded on the hill, the Club became segmented. Social members still enjoyed the old clubhouse and its facilities in Hutton Park; the golfers played golf, then went home. There was no clubhouse on the hill, simply a locker room. By the early 1940s, change was inevitable. A new clubhouse was unveiled on July 4, 1942, and the old Mansion House demolished the following year. The old course soon disappeared, the Hutton Park property became a residential neighborhood, and Essex County became primarily a golf club.

The West Course began operating as a public facility in 1939. It was sold to the Essex County Park Commission in 1979, which renamed it the Francis Byrne course leaving Seth Raynor's East Course the Club's only layout.

One of the Club's first professionals was David Hunter, who served from 1903 through 1931. He came to the United States from Prestwick, Scotland, where his father, a crony of Old Tom Morris, had been professional. (David was born in the Prestwick clubhouse.) He was the first player to break 70 in the U.S. Open, shooting a 68 during the first round in 1909 at Englewood (which he followed with an 84 in the second round).

"Long Jim" Barnes, who counted four majors among his conquests, was the professional at Essex County from 1939 to '42, during which time he won his last championship, the 1939 New Jersey Open.

Essex County has hosted two major MGA events, the 1946 Met Amateur, won by Frank Strafaci, and the 1987 Ike, which was captured by Mike Kavka. The 1951 New Jersey Open at Essex County resulted in the only 1-2 amateur finish in the tournament's history, with Chet Sanok edging Billy Dear by one stroke.   ꙮ

METEDECONK NATIONAL GOLF CLUB

"Bound For Glory"

METEDECONK NATIONAL GOLF CLUB

Jackson Township, NJ

YEAR FOUNDED: 1984

ARCHITECT:
Robert Trent Jones

COURSE OPENED: 1987

TEES	PAR	YARDAGE
Forward	73	5319
Middle	72	6684
Back	72	7180

TEES	COURSE RATING	SLOPE
Forward	72.2	131
Middle	72.9	136
Back	75.3	141

In 1987, it was a rare event indeed when a new golf course opened in the Met Area. And it was front-page news when Robert Trent Jones, the dean of American architects, predicted that his latest creation would, in a short time, rank among the 25 best courses in the country.

In both cases, the subject was Metedeconk National, the first private golf club organized in New Jersey in almost 20 years.

Metedeconk National holds title to 1,200 acres in Jackson Township. The Club was the dream of Richard Sambol and his son, Herb. Their goal was simple — to create a club strictly for golf, with an exclusive national membership. Jones and his right-hand man, Roger Rulewich, a past president of the American Society of Golf Course Architects, examined the property and informed the Sambols that they could build a world-class course on the site, giving the project added impetus.

The Club's name is taken from the nearby Metedeconk River, part of which flows through Club property. The river was named for a tribe of the Leni Lenape Indians that inhabited much of New Jersey. The Indian word "Metedeconk" can be translated roughly as "warriors of peace."

The golf course was built on a 400-acre tract that included 250 acres of wetlands that could not be disturbed. The course was built around the wetlands—front nine to the west, back nine to the east—to act as a buffer between future development on the property and the natural habitat.

Construction began in December of 1984. Holes were cleared, four ponds were created both as playing hazards and reservoirs, and five long bridges were built over the wetlands. The course opened in September of 1987.

Metedeconk is rugged. Water comes into play on seven holes. Pine trees, oak trees, and wild underbrush isolate each fairway. The added dimension that places this course in a special category is the rough, specifically the tall, redtipped fescue grass that is cut just once a season and allowed to grow to US Open proportions.

The seventh is the signature hole, a picturesque par four that doglegs to the right around an extended bunker dominating the right side of the landing area. The hole then rolls downhill to a green set behind a bulkheaded lake and a bunker across its left front. The putting surface falls away from the approach on a right-to-left angle.

A great vista awaits at the 16th hole, a short par four with water down the right side from tee to green. From the elevated tee, the player chooses how big a piece of the lake he can cut off.

Richard and Herbert Sambol

Metedeconk's two homecoming holes, 9 and 18, are reminiscent of the ninth at Shinnecock Hills, playing uphill toward the clubhouse, to greens perched above the fairway and guarded by walls of rough. Both putting surfaces are severe, especially the two-tiered ninth.

A prominent member of the Metedeconk National team when construction began was Steve Cadenelli, who played the dual role of Golf Course Superintendent and General Manager up until 1996. Cadenelli is a former president of the Golf Course Superintendents Association of America and is currently overseeing the development of a new course on Cape Cod.

Approach to the par-5 10th.

Metedeconk gained international acclaim in the fall of 1990 with the first Metedeconk International Challenge Cup, the brainchild of the Sambols and T. Finbarr Kiely, a native of Cork, Ireland, and seven-time Metedeconk club champion (1988-1995). In the inaugural competition, a team of eight representing the Golfing Union of Ireland faced off against a similar contingent carrying the MGA banner in singles, four-ball, and foursome play. The MGA team, with Jerry Courville

Sr. as nonplaying captain, won.

In 1996, Metedeconk hosted the Ike Championship with eight time New Jersey Amateur Champ Jeff Thomas winning·to finally capture his first MGA "major".

With that kind of exposure, and with the Sambol family skillfully guiding the Club's development, the high national ranking Jones envisioned will come. In its own backyard, Metedeconk is already recognized as one of the most challenging tests in the Met Area. ○

MONTCLAIR GOLF CLUB

"The Boston Tee Party"

While most of the golf in this country descends directly from Scotland, there is at least one notable exception. Golf came to one section of New Jersey in a roundabout fashion, via Boston from France.

During the summer of 1892, Mr. and Mrs. John Wood Stewart visited some friends at Wellesley near Boston. While there, Mrs. Stewart was invited to play a game of golf over the rolling lawns of the Hunnewells. This was preceded by a demonstration of the game by a young lady from Pau, France, named Florence Boit, a niece of the Hunnewells. Mrs. Stewart fell in love with the new game and brought it home with her to New Jersey.

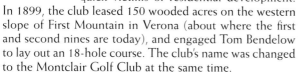

Isaac "Ike" Grainger

In the fall of 1893, the Stewarts and Frederick M. Wheeler, all members of the Essex County Hunt Club, formed the Golf Club of Montclair, which was formally organized in October of 1893. The club's first two courses-nine holes in Erwin Park then an 18-holer across Valley Road in what is now Memorial Park—were quick victims of residential development. In 1899, the club leased 150 wooded acres on the western slope of First Mountain in Verona (about where the first and second nines are today), and engaged Tom Bendelow to lay out an 18-hole course. The club's name was changed to the Montclair Golf Club at the same time.

By 1920, neither the golf course nor the clubhouse was large enough for the growing membership. Donald Ross was engaged to design 27 new holes, which he had ready for play by the spring of 1922. The present Colonial-style clubhouse opened the following year. By October of 1928 the club had accumulated enough land to add a fourth nine, this one designed by Charles Banks and quickly recognized as the Club's premier nine.

All four nines rise and fall with the land, with many holes featuring significant elevation changes. The greens are just as rolling, possibly the most dramatic in the region, featuring an assortment of crowns, tiers, troughs, slopes, and often unbelievable borrows. One frustrated golfer is said to have responded to the inquiry, "How did you make 7 on that hole?" with "Easy-on in 2 and 5 putts."

The Ross stamp is clearly seen on the eighth hole on the No. 2 nine. This short par four runs uphill from tee to

Second hole of the No. 4 nine.

green, with three bunkers cutting left-to-right across the hole ahead of the green, each slightly higher than the one before. The putting surface falls back to front despite an upper deck at the left front.

The Peckman River flows across the lower holes on the west side of the mountain. It has its greatest impact on the fifth hole on the No. 3 nine, a sharp dogleg to the right calling for a fade or lay-up off the tee. The river zigzags in front of the tee, then meanders up the right side, angling out into the landing area before crossing the fairway short of the green, which is perched atop a knoll.

The No. 4 nine begins with a series of memorable holes. The first is a moderate par five that bends 60 degrees to the left and rolls 30 degrees downhill from tee to green. With a long drive down the left side, the punchbowl green can be reached in two despite a huge bunker above the right front corner. Long hitters often use their 3-wood off the elevated second tee to stay short of a pond the crosses the fairway. The green, one of the largest on the proper-

MONTCLAIR GOLF CLUB

West Orange, NJ

YEAR FOUNDED: 1893

ARCHITECTS:
Donald Ross
(Nos. 1,2,3 Nines)

Charles Banks
(No. 4 Nine)

COURSE OPENED:
1922 (Nos. 1,2,3)
1928 (No. 4)

TEES	PAR	YARDAGE
Forward	74	5767
Middle	70	6224
Back	72	6498

TEES	COURSE RATING	SLOPE
Forward	74.7	131
Middle	70.5	126
Back	71.8	128

Above is an average of four nines

ty, is hemmed in by a huge bunker front and left and a long, deep bunker right and rear.

As impressive as Montclair's course is its membership, which has included many outstanding players and administrators. Among them, Jerry Travers, who won two U.S. Amateurs while at Montclair (1907-1910), and later won the U.S. Open (1915); Carolyn Cudone, New Jersey Women's Amateur champion 11 times at medal play, six times at match play, and five times the WMGA winner at match play.

Also, Isaac Grainger, president of the USGA in 1954-55 after a three-year term (1943-45) as president of the MGA. It was Grainger who determined that Sam Snead's ball lay outside that of Lew Worsham on the final green of the 1947 U.S. Open championship, a delay so unnerving to Snead that he missed his short putt and lost the championship. Grainger also called a two-stroke penalty on Lloyd Mangrum for twice replacing his ball on the same green during the playoff for the 1950 U.S. Open championship won by Ben Hogan.

Later came Robert Gardner, who won six Met Amateurs over a seven-year period (1958-64). Gardner also was runner-up to Deane Beman in the 1960 U.S. Amateur, a Walker Cup player, and a three-time winner of the individual championship in the Ike tournament. But he never won his club championship, saying the thought of the treacherous greens made him nervous.

Robert Trent Jones, the quintessential American golf course architect, joined Montclair in the late 1930s, and

MGA Presidents Kenneth Gordon and John F. Kelsey Jr.

has been a member for more than 50 years; Trent's son Rees, a noted architect in his own right, also is a Montclair member.

The U.S. Amateur came to Montclair in 1985. The winner was Sam Randolph, who also won the qualifying medal, his 64 establishing a new course record for the No. 2 and No. 4 nines. Randolph had to overcome back spasms to edge fellow collegian Peter Persons 1-up in the title match.

The Women's Amateur was contested at Montclair in 1973, with Carol Semple topping a field that included Hollis Stacy, the dominant amateur at the time, and later a three-time winner of the Women's Open. Semple went on to win the 1974 British Amateur, becoming the first women in 26 years to hold the two titles simultaneously.

Sounds like a great place for a tee party. ⟳

The punchbowl green on the first hole of the No. 4 nine.

MORRIS COUNTY GOLF CLUB

"Good Goff: Bloomers On The Links"

Findlay Douglas

Golf was nurtured through its infancy in this country as much by women as by men. The ladies of Shinnecock Hills, who had a nine-hole course of their own, were the driving force behind that Club's early success. In New Jersey, the women of a wealthy Morristown colony organized a club of their own in April of 1894. Miss Nina Howland was elected its first president. By summer, they had a clubhouse and a seven-hole course laid out by member John Brinley, the landscape architect responsible for New York City's Botanical Gardens. The course played over and around a deep punchbowl that dominated the terrain.

The ladies celebrated the conclusion of their first season with gala festivities that attracted guests from the upper social strata of New York City, Tuxedo, even Europe. The women played a 14-hole tournament.

Mrs. Arthur James attempted the first shot of the day, and whiffed! After Miss Lois Raymond moved her ball just a few inches on her first swing, she stamped her feet and exclaimed, "Isn't that too mean for anything!"

But the women had already made their fatal mistake: They had taken on approximately 200 men, primarily husbands and fathers, as associate members, anticipating they would make fine caddies. As the Club grew in popularity, the men became more involved. Early in 1896, the men took control, and Paul Revere, a great-grandson of the Boston equestrian, was elected the new president. When offered an honorary presidency, Nina Howland refused, chastised Revere, and never played Morris County again.

The Club retained its close affiliation with women's golf, hosting the first USGA-conducted Women's Amateur in 1896, thereby becoming the first club in New Jersey to host a national championship. In preparation for the tournament, the course was expanded to a full 18 holes. Eight of the 25 contestants qualified for match play, and Beatrix Hoyt of Shinnecock Hills, 16 years and three months old, led the field with 95. She held on to win, and remained the youngest to win the Women's Amateur until

MORRIS COUNTY GOLF CLUB
Convent Station, NJ
YEAR FOUNDED: 1894
ARCHITECT:
Seth Raynor
COURSE OPENED: 1920

TEES	PAR	YARDAGE
Forward	73	5627
Middle	70	6188

TEES	COURSE RATING	SLOPE
Forward	73.0	139
Middle	69.8	132

1971 when she was surpassed by Laura Baugh, who was two weeks younger.

In September of 1898, the U.S. Amateur came to Morris County, attracting thousands of spectators and full media coverage. The galleries were roped off and kept a safe distance from the contestants, perhaps the first time such measures were taken at a major event. Findlay Douglas, a long-hitting Scot just two years out of St. Andrews, dominated the field, never facing a tough match en route to the title.

James Tyng, Morris County's three-time club champion, and the first baseball player to don a catcher's mask, was eliminated in the second round by Foxhall Keene of Oakland. The latter parlayed some inspired golf and the psychological ploy of making his high-strung opponent wait an hour at the first tee. The USGA immediately outlawed such gamesmanship.

Percy R. Pyne II of the host club had an unfortunate experience on the 17th hole during the qualifying round. After making a hole in one there during a practice round the previous day, Pyne hit over the green and his ball came to rest under a fence. Unaware of the unplayable lie rule, young Pyne ran up a total of 17 shots before holing out. He missed qualifying by one stroke.

In 1916, a plan for a new clubhouse and course was

Spectators crossing railroad tracks at the 1898 U.S. Amateur.

The 7th fairway cascading down to the green.

spearheaded by Wynant D. Vanderpool, later a president of the USGA (1924-1925). For their new golf course, Morris County turned to Seth Raynor, who found the site very much to his liking, and responded with a magnificent course, which opened in 1920.

Situated in the hills of northwestern New Jersey, the layout has tree-lined fairways and some severely undulating terrain. The putting surfaces are relatively small and come in a variety of shapes. Several greens cannot be seen from the tee, and the drive must be played over a crest to a landing area that runs downhill.

The foundation for a good score must be built over the first six holes, which are short (but tricky) by modern standards. The challenge begins at the seventh, the most controversial hole. It is a long par four with a high ridge running across the landing area. Many members can't reach the top of the ridge, yet longer hitters must be careful of not hitting too far over it, leaving a downhill lie for the long second shot. From there, the hole takes two precipitous drops, the last some 100 yards from the semi-punch-bowl green.

The home hole also plays over a ridge, this to a semi-blind fairway that falls to the left and toward a lake within reach of the long hitters. The sloping green is set in a cathedral of trees to the side of the clubhouse.

The facilities opened in grand style back in 1920, highlighted by a 36-hole exhibition matching the touring British team of Harry Vardon and Ted Ray against the American amateurs Bobby Jones and Chick Evans, fol-

lowed by a white-tie dinner in the new clubhouse. Evans had won the U.S. Amateur (at Engineers) the week before, adding to the interest in the match. With several top-ranked players planning to be on hand for the occasion, the members decided to stage an informal match-play event. Jones won that tournament, then teamed with Evans to trounce Vardon and Ray 10&9 the following day, thanks to Evans's five consecutive threes starting at the third hole. Thus began the annual "Weekend of Golf," which remains the Club's premier member-guest event.

Former touring professional David Glenz served as Morris County professional from 1982 to 1990, during which time he became the first Met Area pro to win four "majors" in one season—the Met Open, New Jersey Open, New Jersey PGA, and Nissan Classic in 1986.

Perhaps the most accomplished member was Billy Dear, a fierce competitor who won the New Jersey Amateur and was runner-up in the New Jersey Open, both in 1951, and won the MGA Senior in 1970. Dear served as MGA President 1964 to 1965.

Notable among the ladies are Marie and Karen Noble, a mother/daughter combination that accounted for State Amateur championships 25 years apart. In 1988, Karen Noble won the WMGA's Match Play championship and was runner-up in the U.S. Women's Amateur. In 1989, she won both the match- and stroke-play championships of the WMGA, and in 1990 competed successfully in the Curtis Cup matches. She now is a member of the LPGA Tour. The original founding women would be suitably proud.

MOUNTAIN RIDGE COUNTRY CLUB

"Anyone For Softball"

Around the turn of the century, most major cities in America had a men's social organization called the Progress Club. In 1912, a group of men from the Newark branch incorporated as the Mountain Ridge Country Club. Reportedly, they celebrated their grand opening, on May 30, 1913, not with a golf tournament, but with a softball game.

The Club's first site was in West Orange, across Mt. Pleasant Avenue from the current Essex County Country Club. In fact, the original nine-hole Mountain Ridge was laid out by Essex County's longtime professional, David Hunter. After about a decade, it was expanded to a hilly 18-holer designed by A.W. Tillinghast.

In the late 1920s, Public Service of New Jersey won the right to construct a power station adjacent to the club's property. With the accompanying overhead power lines threatening play, the club decided to move farther into the countryside. The West Orange property was sold in 1928, and 253 acres of farmland off Passaic Avenue in West Caldwell purchased in 1929.

For its new facilities, Mountain Ridge turned to two men then at the top of their games. Clifford C. Wendehack designed the Tudor-style clubhouse, while Donald Ross laid out the golf course. Work started in 1929, and the course was officially opened on June 6, 1931, and has remained virtually untouched by any other architect through the years.

The Mountain Ridge fairways are tree-lined but not especially tight. However, their contouring helps bring into play the legendary rough, which is actually fertilized and cultivated. The greenside bunkering, especially those well away from the green, is typical of Ross. Many of the green sites are raised, perched atop natural plateaus in the Ross style.

The eighth is the number-one handicap hole, as scenic as it is difficult. The tee is raised well above a contoured fairway that gives a straightaway hole the appearance of a double-dogleg. The well-bunkered green falls sharply from back to front, with one of the right bunkers extending into the entrance to the green.

Number 16 is a short par three that has been compared to Augusta National's famous 12th. It plays over a pond to a green bunkered twice to the left and once to the right, with the last extending into the entrance. Another interesting par three is the tricky seventh, which plays straight uphill to a punchbowl green hidden behind a pair of bunkers that slant across the front like flippers in a pinball machine.

In 1960, Wes Ellis started a six-year tenure as Mountain Ridge professional, bringing one of New Jersey's best-kept secrets into the regional spotlight. During those years, Ellis dominated the state's pro ranks to an extent never seen before nor since. Ellis won the 1958 Canadian Open and the 1959 Texas Open before coming to Mountain Ridge, then captured the 1961 Crosby and 1965 San Diego Open while representing the Club. In New Jersey, Ellis won four consecutive State PGA titles (1961-1964) firing a remarkable 15-under 273 at his home course in 1962. Ellis completed the "Jersey Slam" in 1963, winning the New Jersey PGA, New Jersey Open, and Met Open. All told, Ellis won three Met Opens (two at Plainfield and one at Winged Foot), a pair of New Jersey Opens, four New Jersey PGAs, and established the course record at Mountain Ridge with a 62.

In recent years, Mountain Ridge has hosted a pair of Met Opens (1966, 1985) and a Met Amateur (1979), with Tom Nieporte, amateur George Zahringer III, and Jerry Courville Sr. the winners, respectively.

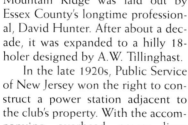

MOUNTAIN RIDGE COUNTRY CLUB

West Caldwell, NJ

YEAR FOUNDED: 1912

ARCHITECT:
Donald Ross

COURSE OPENED: 1931

TEES	PAR	YARDAGE
Forward	75	5986
Middle	71	6571
Back	71	6803

TEES	COURSE RATING	SLOPE
Forward	75.2	131
Middle	71.9	127
Back	73.0	129

The 16th hole

Opening day dedication ceremony, June 6, 1931. Donald Ross is third from right.

The current professional is Mike Burke Jr., who came to the club in 1987. Mike comes from fine golf stock: His father was head professional at Deal Golf & Country Club, and won the 1966 State Open; his mother is a niece of one of the game's great teachers, Bob Toski. Burke won the Met Amateur in 1978, and in 1986 captured both the Dodge Open and Michelob Classic. After a serious injury suffered in a Christmas Eve 1989 auto accident, he won the Ping NJPGA Match Play Championship and NJPGA Player of the Year honors in 1990. But softball has been off limits. ○

SOMERSET HILLS COUNTRY CLUB

"A Contrast In Styles"

When the USGA moved its headquarters, museum, and library from Manhattan to Far Hills, New Jersey, in 1972, several of its officials soon realized an unexpected bonus— their new office was just a few miles from the Somerset Hills Country Club. Nestled in the rolling hills of Somerset County's horse country, just outside Bernardsville, Somerset Hills is one of the state's oldest and most prestigious clubs.

The Club's history begins in 1896, when the Ravine Land and Game Association was formed to hold title to a 365-acre plot along the North Branch of the Raritan River, about five miles west of today's site. The land had been purchased in the fall of 1894 with the intent of forming a country club with golf and tennis. A dam built across the river formed Ravine Lake, which provided swimming, boating, and fishing facilities for the club. A clubhouse was built on a hill overlooking the lake, with construction completed in 1899. The Club quickly became the social center of the region.

The first golf course was a dangerous nine-hole Tom Bendelow layout that included several parallel fairways, even a few holes that crossed each other. There was no room to expand until 1916, when the Club purchased 194 acres from the estate of Frederick P. Olcott off Mine Mount Road. The land included an English-style country home and a private race track. Work began on a Colonial-style clubhouse and six grass tennis courts, while A.W. Till-

The "Dolomites" near the sixth green in 1917.

inghast was retained to design an 18-hole golf course that was finished late in 1917.

Somerset Hills is a course of great beauty and charm, perennially listed among the top 100 courses in the country. Its two nines were created in contrasting styles, the front side originally a links laid out over barren terrain on the old Olcott race track; its predominant features are numerous mounds and small, high-lipped bunkers cut from the sides of mounds. The back nine is heavily wooded with far fewer bunkers and mounds, but with water on four holes.

The course is known for its outstanding collection of par threes. The second hole is a beautiful Redan. Behind three bunkers well in front of the green lurks the huge Redan bunker left front, set below a high mound, and another greenside bunker right front. There's also a high mound at the right rear, and a dangerous fall-off at the left rear. As if the hole needed more character, the green slopes right front to left rear.

The green on the par-three 12th is a peninsula that extends into the pond bordering the left side, so the hole feels much like the 16th at Augusta National.

The 15th is the hole everyone remembers, a dogleg-

SOMERSET HILLS COUNTRY CLUB

Bernardsville, NJ

YEAR FOUNDED: 1899

ARCHITECT:
A. W. Tillinghast

COURSE OPENED: 1917

TEES	PAR	YARDAGE
Forward	72	5643
Middle	71	6218
Back	71	6572

TEES	COURSE RATING	SLOPE
Forward	73.5	126
Middle	70.4	126
Back	71.8	129

right par four that runs downhill from the fairway to the largest green on the course. Guarding the green is a creek that becomes a cascading waterfall at greenside. This hole was honored by *GOLF Magazine* in 1986 as one of the 100 greatest in the country.

Somerset Hills hosted the 1982 Met Amateur, the first of five won by George Zahringer III. The USGA's Junior Girls Championship has been played there twice: Amy Alcott won in 1973, when Nancy Lopez was the medalist, Kim Saiki won top honors in 1983.

The Curtis Cup came to town in 1990. Playing before 4,000 fans, the American team swept all six singles matches the final day to win the Cup, 14-4. On the team was Karen Noble of nearby Morris County, who won both her individual matches.

Another bonus for USGA officials, the luxury of conducting a championship in their own backyard. ○

The waterfall alongside the 15th green.

The second hole, one of the world's most striking Redan holes.

THE TUXEDO CLUB

"Keep Your Eye On The Ball"

THE TUXEDO CLUB
Tuxedo Park, NY

YEAR FOUNDED: 1886

ARCHITECT:
Robert Trent Jones

COURSE OPENED: 1956

TEES	PAR	YARDAGE
Forward	73	5368
Middle	71	6237
Back	71	6693

TEES	COURSE RATING	SLOPE
Forward	70.9	118
Middle	70.7	132
Back	72.7	136

On a rainy day in 1885, two men flagged their train to a halt somewhere in the Ramapo Hills of Orange County, then slogged through a downpour to a wagon. In an hour's time, they were transported to the top of a ridge overlooking what soon would be called Tuxedo Lake. One of the men was Pierre Lorillard, great-grandson of tobacco tycoon Peter Lorillard. His companion was architect Bruce Price. Lorillard planned to develop the area for sporting activities— primarily hunting and fishing—and build an exclusive club and community.

Lorillard organized his club in 1885. Price gathered a work crew of 1,800 and in eight months built "thirty miles of roads, a complete water and sewage system, twenty-two turreted cottages, two blocks of stores, and the clubhouse itself." The total cost was $1.5 million, a considerable sum in those days. The price tag quickly rose to $2 million as the Club built a golf course, race track, and mile-long toboggan slide.

Tuxedo Park soon became a fashionable playground for New York's upper social strata, most of whom also built homes there. The social highlight of the season was the Autumn Ball, which doubled as a season-ending celebration and coming-out party for debutantes. The initial Autumn Ball, in 1886, also marked the first appearance in this country of a tail-less dinner jacket destined to become known as the tuxedo.

The word "tuxedo" is the anglicized Indian name for the lake, "P-tuck Sepo." It means "home of the bear," an appropriate description of what at the turn of the century was called "the most difficult links to negotiate in the country."

Golf was introduced to the Tuxedo colony by Dr. E.C. Rushmore. Unaware of the pioneer group across the river at St. Andrew's, Rushmore sent to Montreal for clubs and balls. A crude six-hole course was laid out early in the summer of 1889.

The members soon expressed a desire for a more sophisticated course, and again turned to their friends in Montreal for help, in the person of Henry Hewat, a Scottish engineer working in nearby Paterson, New Jersey who had previously worked in Montreal. Hewat designed a nine-hole course on the opposite side of the lake from the clubhouse that opened in April, 1892. But due to the course's remote location, the game failed to grow in popularity until 1894, when a new nine-holer was built near the park's north gate. The following quote comes from the May, 1895 issue of *Scribner's* magazine;

"There are nine holes in the course, which crosses Tuxedo Brook four times and furnishes great variety in its hazards of hills, stone walls, railroad embankments lined with blast furnace slag, apple trees, and a combination of terrors in front of what is known as Devil's Hole, consisting of brook, boulders, and road, which has spoiled many a score. The course is known as a 'sporting links,' where straight, long drives are the only hope for preserving the temper, and the hazards are such that they make glad the heart of man when surmounted…"

A deep gully fronted the fifth green and caddies were rewarded with an extra five cents whenever it became necessary to push their player up the hill. The 415-yard 14th, known as the "Rifle Gallery," demanded an extremely accurate drive to a narrow fairway situated between Route 17 and the Erie Railroad tracks.

Tuxedo hosted the country's first interclub team match in the summer of 1894, when a seven-man team from Shinnecock Hills came to play. That October, a contest of grander scale took place among six teams, two each from the home club and St. Andrew's, and one

The main clubhouse, with Tuxedo Lake in the foreground.

each from Shinnecock Hills and Brookline. The match resulted in a tie between St. Andrew's and Brookline that was never resolved—the New Yorkers had to return home to host the "amateur championship." Brookline carried home the trophy, which many years later was donated to the USGA and is now given to the winner of the U.S. Senior Open.

It was during an early St. Andrew's-Tuxedo match that a popular golf axiom first gained popularity. John Ten Eyck of St. Andrew's was paired against Tuxedo president Walker Breese Smith, who announced to his rival on the third tee that the keys to successful golf were "courage" and "keeping your eye on the ball." Smith explained that he derived his courage from Scotch whiskey, which he offered to share with his rival. Then, after teeing his ball, he removed his glass eye, placed it on top of the ball, and smashed it down the fairway. The wealthy Smith carried a box of glass eyes, and he repeated his ritual on every tee. The more serious Ten Eyck was shaken—and soundly beaten that day.

The Tuxedo Park community felt the full impact of the Depression and World War II. By the mid-1940s, many of the fabulous homes that dotted the hillsides were shuttered. In September, 1953, construction of the New York Thruway jolted the Club, cutting a wide swath through the golf course and swallowing all but four holes. But the Thruway and the Tappan Zee Bridge (which opened in 1955) may actually have helped revive the Club, making it more accessible to nearby counties.

In 1953, Tuxedo purchased a farm two miles south of the lake and main clubhouse and hired Robert Trent Jones to design a new course. Nine holes and a new golf clubhouse opened July 4, 1956; the second nine came the following year.

From the first hole, one of the most difficult and intimidating in the Met Area, Tuxedo is a fine example of Jones' blend of the penal, strategic, and heroic schools of architecture. The opener cuts through a forest demanding an accurate tee shot that must carry the top of a ridge. Only then does the green come into view, perched atop a knoll beyond a deep swale. Water comes into play on 11 holes, with five requiring a carry over a lake or stream fronting the green. The three par fives are reachable in two, but only by taking risks with the drive and second shot. Similarly, three short par fours–5,14, and 16–can all be reached with short irons but only if the tee shot is played aggressively and accurately.

Although the "new" course has always been highly regarded and Walter Travis did win the 1902 Met Amateur at Tuxedo, the Club has generally preferred to stay out of the tournament spotlight. In 1986 Tuxedo did host the first Ike championship conducted under the auspices of the MGA. That championship, won by John Baldwin, was part of Tuxedo's Centennial celebration. In 1997 Tuxedo will again host a new MGA event, the Senior Open, this time as part of the MGA's Centennial.

Tuxedo members can avail themselves of a spectacular main clubhouse overlooking Tuxedo Lake and perhaps the broadest range of facilities of any club in the region—including court tennis and racquets, fishing, and sailing—fulfilling Pierre Lorillard's dream of more than a century ago.   ❍

UPPER MONTCLAIR
COUNTRY CLUB
"Cliffside Hose No. 4"

Cadillac NFL Classic.

From humble beginnings in a small firehouse, the Upper Montclair Country Club soon reached for the stars, boasted the best eight-man team in the Met Area, and hosted the richest professional tournaments of their day.

The Club, organized in 1901, began as a merger. One party was a group of golfers who played over a rudimentary five-hole course in a meadow along Grove Street, just across the Garden State Parkway from the present course. They merged with the Upper Ten Club, a social group that met in the Cliffside Firehouse, Hose No. 4. When the firehouse was moved to a location on Bellevue Avenue next to the course, the Club was established. The firehouse/clubhouse had just one shower, no 19th hole, and wooden boxes for lockers.

By 1903, the Club had expanded to nine holes. It evolved over the years, with new nines opening in 1909, 1910, and 1930, the last an A.W. Tillinghast design. This gave the Club 27 holes of its own and nine leased to the adjacent Elmbrook Country Club, which lasted until 1952, when it was sold for residential development.

Highway development twice ate into Club property in the ensuing years. Route 3 came in 1946, causing a major

**UPPER MONTCLAIR
COUNTRY CLUB**
Clifton, NJ

YEAR FOUNDED: 1901

ARCHITECT:
Robert Trent Jones

COURSE OPENED: 1956

TEES	PAR	YARDAGE
Forward	74	5700
Middle	72	6515
Back	72	6855

TEES	COURSE RATING	SLOPE
Forward	73.5	124
Middle	71.3	127
Back	72.9	131

Above is an average of three nines

revision. But this was only a minor inconvenience when compared to the amputation of six holes by the building of the Garden State Parkway in the mid 1950s. Between 1954 and 1958, Robert Trent Jones completely redesigned the 27-hole layout, keeping 18 holes open for play at all times.

Upper Montclair features large, undulating greens, each with several good pin placements, strategic greenside and fairway bunkering, and water in play on 10 of the 27 holes (directly in front of five greens).

The famous hole 3-South is a fixture on lists of the Met Area's best. The hole bends sharply left in the drive zone, then rolls slightly downhill to a boomerang-shaped green protected by a small bunker in front and a pond front and right.

Both 5-West and 2-South, moderate par fives, are guarded by water in a manner similar to 15 at Augusta National. At 5-West, a stream crosses the fairway just in front of the slightly elevated green. At 2-South, the challenge is lofting the second shot over a 50-foot-wide pond in front of the green.

Before it ever staged a professional tournament, Upper Montclair was known throughout the region for the golf played by its members. Consider for a moment the following line-up that Upper Montclair could have fielded in the 1920s:

Jerry Travers was the dominant figure in amateur golf in

One of the Met Area's finest, 3-South.

this country during the years 1906 to 1915. During this span, he won the U.S. Amateur four times, the Met Amateur five times, and the 1915 U.S. Open at Baltusrol. He joined Upper Montclair in 1911 after a brief sabbatical from golf, during which he honed his skills as a playboy. Other members of note were Frank Dyer, winner of the 1923 Met Amateur; Bill Reekie, winner of the 1924 and 1926 Met Amateurs; J. Edward Hale, runner-up in the 1922 Met Amateur; and Stephen Berrien, one of the best young prospects in the region during the mid-1920s, and a future MGA president.

During the past half-century, the most prominent player to represent Upper Montclair has been Chet Sanok, 15-time club champion and the only amateur ever to win both the Met Open (1952) and New Jersey Open (1951 and 1956). He also won the 1975 Ike individual trophy, and twice (1969 and 1975) led Upper Montclair to victory in the team competition.

As a site for professional tournaments, Upper Montclair has been an innovator. The inaugural Thunderbird Classic in 1962 offered the Tour's first $100,000 purse, won by Gene

Littler, who edged Jack Nicklaus by two strokes. During that tournament, Upper Montclair became the first club to rope its fairways from tee to green, perfected a garbage-collection routine that was copied widely, and had the West and South nines completely wired underground for television coverage. The Thunderbird returned to Upper Montclair in 1966 for its final three editions, won by Mason Rudolph, Arnold Palmer, and Bob Murphy.

In 1970 Upper Montclair hosted the first (and only) Dow Jones Open, which offered the first $300,000 purse in Tour history. Bobby Nichols won the $60,000 first prize by dropping an 18-foot birdie putt on the final green.

The LPGA Tour has visited Upper Montclair four times, staging the Coca-Cola Classic in 1979-1980, and the Chrysler-Plymouth Charity Classic in 1983-1984. Five players, including Nancy Lopez and Mickey Wright, tied in 1979; Lopez won the playoff with a birdie at 7-South.

Since 1993, Upper Montclair has hosted the Senior Tour's Cadillac NFL Classic, which pairs senior pros with NFL stars in a unique format that has proven a big hit with fans. ○

ALPINE COUNTRY CLUB

"Big Rock Candy Mountain"

The region around Alpine Country Club has some historical importance. During the American Revolution, as General Washington's army retreated toward Trenton in 1779, British General Howe crossed the Hudson River in pursuit and marched his army along Closter Dock Road. During that march, Howe burned an old grist mill belonging to Miller Demarest and executed two of his sons. The foundation of the mill can be seen off the road between the clubhouse and the first tee.

In 1929, a consortium of millionaires from the worlds of finance and government (including two state senators) got together to form what they hoped would be a club of importance in the golf world. It was initially known as Aldecress, named for the neighboring communities—Alpine, Demarest, and Cresskill—on the western slope of the Palisades where the Club is located.

The Club, which opened in 1931, was the last built in New Jersey by A.W. Tillinghast, and may have been his greatest challenge. The terrain was a mix of trees, swamp, and rock; it took 30 tractors to clear the fairways. Rock taken from the ground was used with railroad ties to help contour fairways and stabilize tee and green sites.

The best-laid (and designed) plans of Aldecress' founders ran headlong into the Depression, and the original Club failed within a few years. The course was opened to the public during that time, and became private again until 1961 when the present Alpine Country Club was organized.

The course, which plays through some difficult terrain along tight, wooded fairways, flashes its claws early. The second and third holes, both moderate-length par fours, are stern tests. The second hole curves to the right with a lake at the corner and in front of the green. A smaller pond on the right side of the third fairway can force longer hitters to lay up off the tee.

Alpine likely is best known for two short and unusual par fours on the back side. The tenth hole plays straight uphill, at an angle perhaps seen nowhere else in the Met Area, to a slanting fairway where the pull of gravity is quite evident. In 1995, this hole had the highest scoring average in the region. The 14th fairway is divided about 180 yards from the tee by a series of bunkers, forcing the average player to make a crucial decision—lay up short and left, or take out the driver and go for it. The green is one of the most difficult and tightly bunkered on the course.

The Club has prospered in its present form. The members recently revitalized their clubhouse at the bottom of the hill, and built a separate golf house at the top next to the first tee and final green. ○

The daunting drive at the 10th.

**ALPINE
COUNTRY CLUB**
Alpine, NJ

YEAR FOUNDED: 1929

ARCHITECT:
A.W. Tillinghast

COURSE OPENED: 1931

TEES	PAR	YARDAGE
Forward	75	5660
Middle	72	6471
Back	72	6711

TEES	COURSE RATING	SLOPE
Forward	73.8	130
Middle	71.9	132
Back	73.0	134

ARCOLA COUNTRY CLUB

"The Scrambler"

Approach to the 17th green with the 18th green in the background.

A famous painting commemorates Napoleon's victory over the Austrians in 1796 at the bridge in Arcola, Italy. In truth, Napoleon's ego far outweighed his skills as a military tactician; his great strength lay in public relations, and Arcola was typical, his "press agents" turning a comedy of errors at Arcola into a great triumph. Napoleon rallied his weary soldiers by risking his own life, seizing a regimental color, rushing to the front lines, and planting it on the bridge. In the panic that ensued, as his subordinates attempted to drag him to safety, Napoleon was dropped from the bridge into the swamps below, then fished out while under enemy fire.

During the 1700s, the Red Mill of Arcola played a central role in the Colonial life of northern New Jersey. It became a popular meeting place for businessmen from throughout the region. The community that developed there came to be known as Red Mills, later changed to Arcola to honor the "little emperor."

All that remains of the old mill site is a bridge crossing Route 4. And all that retains the name is Arcola Country Club, an oasis of green in a desert of asphalt.

Arcola was founded in June of 1909, by a group of founding fathers of the North Jersey Country Club. They purchased a 108-acre site on a knoll in Paramus, extending from Paramus Road to Sprout Brook, and engaged H.H. Barker to design an 18-hole golf course. It was known for small, tightly bunkered greens and "Arcola lies" in the rough—hard pan with the occasional clump of wild grass.

Arcola was beset with highway problems in the mid-1950s when the Garden State Parkway was routed directly through the eastern part of Club property, destroying three holes. At the same time, the Club sold 30 acres bordering Paramus Road, eliminating another five holes. Arcola was fortunate to be able to purchase enough adjacent land to replace the lost holes, then hired Robert Trent Jones to undertake a redesign. Jones produced a lovely, gently-rolling parkland course, with three ponds coming into play on four holes: One guards the seventh green and fronts the eighth tee; another dominates Arcola's best-known hole, the par-three 11th; and the third helps form a beautiful cape hole at the short par-four 13th.

During the Club's first 40 years, its claim to fame was the Arcola Cup, an invitational tournament traditionally held the week before the U.S. Amateur and attracting many of the country's leading golfers. The final edition was held in 1948 and captured by Arcola's own Joe McBride, the Club's most prominent player over the years, and one of the top match players ever in New Jersey. McBride was a relatively short hitter who wore his rivals down with a relentless short game, as superb a scrambler on the links as Napoleon was on the battlefield. ❍

ARCOLA COUNTRY CLUB
Paramus, NJ

YEAR FOUNDED: 1909

ARCHITECTS:
H.H. Barker
Robert Trent Jones

COURSE OPENED: 1909

TEES	PAR	YARDAGE
Forward	74	5795
Middle	72	6525
Back	72	6844

TEES	COURSE RATING	SLOPE
Forward	74.7	126
Middle	71.4	125
Back	72.8	127

BLUE HILL GOLF COURSE

"Come Get Your Thrill"

The postcard hole, formerly No. 10, now No. 8 Woodlands.

W hen Montgomery Maze, a prominent Manhattan realtor, died in 1914, he bequeathed to his son, Montgomery Jr., his summer cottage (called "The Castle") and stables, both built of stone, as well as a stone-age nine-hole golf course to the east. Young Monty, a banker/agronomist, developed the facilities, expanding the course to 18 holes and helping establish a private club called Blue Hill in 1924. The course, designed by local professional Joe Sylvester, opened to the public during the Depression, but the Club remained private until Maze's death in the mid-1960s. In 1967, the course was sold to Orangetown, and has been a very successful public facility: The stables were converted into a pro shop with locker rooms, while the Castle became a restaurant that was expanded in the mid-'80s and is a popular lunch spot for nearby businesses as well as golfers.

A reservoir was built in 1970 on land previously used for holes 11 through 15, so five new ones (1, 2, 3, 6, and 7 of the Lakeside nine) were built, and the rest improved, by architect Frank Duane. In the mid-'70s, two ponds were added between Lakeside's sixth and seventh.

In 1995, nine new holes were added by local architect Stephen Kay, making Blue Hill a 27-hole facility. The new holes are the first through seventh of the Woodlands Nine plus four and five of Lakeside. (Lakeside's former first and second holes are now the last two of Woodlands.) The original nine, now called Pines, remains intact.

Blue Hill gains much of its character from the ridge that crosses the property and defines the drive zone on six holes. A number of greens are boldly contoured, tiered, or slanted. The fairways of the older holes are lined by mature trees, the new holes were cut through virgin forest and swampland.

Lakeside's sixth hole is regarded as one of the toughest in Rockland County. It's a long, uphill par four with two ponds separated by a bunker to the right. Beyond that trouble, the hole rises abruptly to a hidden green.

Woodland's par-three eighth is the course's signature hole. From an elevated tee overlooking the reservoir, it plays to a green fronted by a large bunker, with another pair of deep bunkers on the right.

Number six on the Pines is typical of the old holes. The ridge crosses the drive zone, so a bell is rung to tell players on the tee that the landing area is clear. The green is slightly elevated in front of the clubhouse, and features a major upper tier in the rear.

Superior drainage and the many supportive, enthusiastic golfers—Blue Hill typically hosts some 57,000 rounds per year—allow the course to open earlier each spring and stay open later each fall than any in the county. Blue Hill was also the site for the 1985 MGA Public Links Championship.

BLUE HILL GOLF COURSE
Pearl River, NY

YEAR FOUNDED: 1924

ARCHITECTS:
Joe Sylvester
Frank Duane
Stephen Kay

COURSE OPENED: 1924

TEES	PAR	YARDAGE
Forward	72	5217
Middle	72	6071
Back	72	6373

TEES	COURSE RATING	SLOPE
Forward	70.6	117
Middle	68.6	114
Back	70.0	116

Above is an average of three nines

BROOKLAKE COUNTRY CLUB

"The More Things Change…"

Ralph Guldahl

BROOKLAKE COUNTRY CLUB
Florham Park, NJ
YEAR FOUNDED: 1921
ARCHITECTS:
Herbert Strong
Geoffrey Cornish
Brian Silva
COURSE OPENED: 1923

TEES	PAR	YARDAGE
Forward	74	5746
Middle	72	6678
Back	72	6893

TEES	COURSE RATING	SLOPE
Forward	73.8	125
Middle	72.0	125
Back	73.0	127

Even by the no-holds-barred rules of the Roaring '20s, plans for a 54-hole golf club were grandiose. But few clubs had the kind of property—a magnificent thousand-acre estate—that allowed one's imagination to soar. The founders of Braidburn Country Club (called Brooklake today) envisioned a year-round "haven of rest and recreation," one "without parallel" in the Met Area.

Late in 1921, a group of 35 men called the Madison Brook Country Club purchased 300 acres from the 1,000-acre, Madison, New Jersey estate of the recently deceased Dr. Leslie Ward. Ward, whose ancestors were among the original settlers of New Jersey, was one of the founders of the Prudential Insurance Company. His property, Brooklake Farms, included a magnificent stone mansion, the famous Braidburn Tower with its four-sided clock, and a private nine-hole course with a challenging par of 31.

The new Club was supposed to have three 18-hole courses, including one exclusively for ladies and novices. In 1922, Herbert Strong was hired to design a championship 18 to supplement Ward's original nine, which was to be reserved for the ladies and beginners. Strong's layout, the 18-hole Lake course with four water holes, opened in 1923, at which time the Club was called Braidburn, a Scottish term for two bodies of water coming together. Other facilities included canoeing, fishing, and swimming on the lake; an outdoor swimming pool, and miles of bridle paths—but never more than 27 holes of golf, thanks to the Depression.

Ward's mansion served as the clubhouse until 1935, when it was damaged by fire and the Club shifted operations to the former carriage house. That building was destroyed by fire in 1949, so the mansion was rebuilt as a clubhouse, only to burn to the ground again the following year. Part of the present clubhouse was built on the original foundation.

During the Depression, the original membership sold out in 1942, and Braidburn became a privately-owned, non-equity club. Conditions didn't improve until 1958, when the Club was sold again. The clubhouse was expanded, making it one of the largest in the country at the time. Six indoor tennis courts were built, and in 1972, Hal Purdy designed a nine-hole course that replaced Ward's original layout. Six years

later, the new holes were sold off and developed into a residential neighborhood.

In 1984, the Club was purchased by the present owners, all members of the old Club, and the name changed to Brooklake. They sold the last three holes of the original 18, and engaged Geoffrey Cornish and Brian Silva to design five new holes (including #9, 17, and 18), changing the first hole from a par four to the Met Area's only opening par three.

The tee shot on 10 must cross a lake to reach a fairway that turns left toward an island green. The home hole is a long, narrow par five dominated by a lake that crosses the fairway over the final 100 yards.

Jim Dante, who helped create the New Jersey section of the PGA, was Braidburn's first professional, serving the Club for 15 years. He was followed by Ralph Guldahl, winner of the 1937 and 1938 U.S. Opens. The current professional, Basil Amorosano, has served the Club for the last quarter century.

Brooklake has been an active host of state championships, including four New Jersey Opens, two New Jersey Amateurs, and four New Jersey PGAs.

It looks like Brooklake's somewhat tumultuous past is over, and the Club is now looking ahead to a period of relative calm and progress.

The unique par-three 1st hole.

CRESTMONT COUNTRY CLUB

"The Impossible Green"

The 11th hole.

**CRESTMONT
COUNTRY CLUB**
West Orange, NJ

YEAR FOUNDED: 1922

ARCHITECT:
Donald Ross

COURSE OPENED: 1923

TEES	PAR	YARDAGE
Forward	74	5715
Middle	72	6507
Back	72	6732

TEES	COURSE RATING	SLOPE
Forward	73.8	126
Middle	71.7	128
Back	72.7	130

The New York Athletic Club had Winged Foot, so the Newark Athletic Club decided in 1922 it wanted a golf club of its own. A site was purchased on Second Mountain. Eighteen holes were ready in the spring of 1923, built by Walter Hatch of the Donald Ross organization.

Because this was an athletic club, a complete field and grandstand were built in 1924 to the left of the sixth hole. The facility hosted the International Championships in the fall of 1924, and the Olympic Trials of 1936, with Jesse Owens among the qualifiers.

Although membership originally was restricted to the rolls of the Newark Athletic Club, the Club later admitted members from the general public. The name was changed to the Newark Country Club in 1925, and to the Crestmont Golf Club in 1927.

The clubhouse perches atop a steep incline on Second Mountain. The front nine is relatively flat, except for the holes playing to and from the clubhouse; the back nine is a scenic rollercoaster ride, with several holes doglegging down from elevated tees, then climbing back up to hilltop greens. The Ross influence is clearly stamped on the crowned greens, which feature bold contours and fall off precipitously at the edges. The most dramatic green is on the par-three 11th hole, which plays across a brook up to a well-bunkered plateau green. The dance floor tilts fiendishly back to front, with few level spots, especially on the right side.

Two branches of a creek dominate the sixth fairway, one cutting across the hole then up the left side, where it is joined by the other branch, which crosses the fairway beyond the drive zone. The left side of the landing area is watched over by a tall tree, which is complemented by a bunker right.

The rolling drive zone on the par-four 12th is tightened up by a copse of trees left and fairway countouring on the right. The approach must carry a pond that cannot be seen, 40 yards short of the green.

The 1989 NJPGA Championship was played at Crestmont, and the outcome hinged on the 11th hole. The pin was placed halfway up the right side of the green, and the state's best players couldn't handle it. Rick Hughes of Forsgate, who was one-under going to 11 in the final round, hit his shot to within a foot of the flag, only to watch it draw back some 20 feet. He took a seven! Others met with similar fates, watching hopelessly as their putts rolled up to the hole then back to their feet. Only two of the top 20 finishers managed to two-putt the 11th, including winner Peter Oosterhuis, who holed a tricky six-foot sidehiller for his par. Even Winged Foot's greens couldn't be more difficult. ○

The long par-three 17th hole.

CRYSTAL SPRINGS GOLF CLUB

"The Stone Age"

The Vernon Valley has long been recognized as the premier recreation area in northwestern New Jersey. Since 1991, a site dotted with wetlands and featuring two abandoned limestone quarries has been recognized for a dramatic new golf course that is delighting summer visitors. The quarry pools are deep and their waters crystal clear, and give Crystal Springs its name.

The designer was Robert Von Hagge, a former Tour player who claims to have been the first to use extensive mounding not simply for definition or as a backdrop, but for its dramatic shadowing effect. His course features extensive fairway mounding; multiple tee boxes; large, boldly contoured greens; and the wetlands, which come into play on three holes and border several others.

The 10th, Crystal Springs's signature hole, is a most distinctive par three. The tee sits atop a limestone cliff, 100

From behind the 15th green

feet above the green. The dumbbell-shaped putting surface is 200 feet wide and wraps around a nest of rocks in the rear; the largest target area is the right side, which is flanked by a bunker. The hole derives further character from the 60-foot-deep quarry pool that extends from the far left across the front, creating an imposing carry for a center to left pin placement.

Other noteworthy holes include the par-five third, with a long wetlands carry off the tee and a green circled by sand and flanked by wetlands; the par-five 11th, with wetlands in front of the tee and down the length of the hole on the right, plus another quarry pool left approaching the green; and the 15th, where a bulkheaded green sits behind a water hazard that extends 125 yards into the fairway.

The Club gained instant status in 1991 when David Glenz was hired as head golf professional. Winner of two Met Opens among 13 major regional titles, his activities center around the "David Glenz Golf Academy."

**CRYSTAL SPRINGS
GOLF CLUB**
Hamburg, NJ

YEAR FOUNDED: 1991

ARCHITECT:
Robert Von Hagge

COURSE OPENED: 1991

TEES	PAR	YARDAGE
Forward	72	5201
Middle	72	6451
Back	72	6887

TEES	COURSE RATING	SLOPE
Forward	70.5	123
Middle	69.7	126
Back	72.1	132

The tenth dropping into the quarry.

DEAL GOLF & COUNTRY CLUB

"Forever Young"

*The Deal clubhouse
dating back to 1898.*

In the early 1890s, a wealthy railroad financier and shipping magnate named George Washington Young discovered the Jersey Shore, and purchased 135 acres in West Deal, where he built a magnificent estate. Young was among a pioneer group that established the first golf course at the shore, nine holes designed by Lawrence Van Etten. The "marl pit" that crosses the 12th and 13th holes today—featuring walls 12 to 15 feet high and soft turf on the bottom—was the major hazard on the course even then.

Young and associates played the course for three years before organizing as the Deal Golf Club in 1898. They then built a clubhouse that remains the oldest in continuous use in New Jersey.

Deal expanded its golf facilities in 1899 by building a short nine-hole course exclusively for ladies, and added a second nine to the main course in 1900. By 1903, there were nearly 600 members, including summer visitors: The Club was regarded as the busiest in the country, with a cadre of 175 caddies, male and female.

In 1909, Young married Lillian Nordica, a famous opera soprano, and built a luxurious "bungalow" on his estate, which she used as a rehearsal hall. He christened it in 1910 with a gala party attended by hundreds of famous guests brought from New York City by chartered train. They were entertained by an orchestra, dancers, and the Russian ballet.

Within a few years, Young experienced financial problems and just prior to her sudden death from pneumonia n 1914, Nordica excluded him from her will. Young's problems eventually forced him to sell his estate in 1914 to the Hollywood Golf Club. This cost Deal its fourth, fifth, and

sixth holes, forcing a major revision to the course, overseen by Donald Ross.

Like many Ross designs, Deal is known for its bunkering and highly-contoured greens, which come in a variety of configurations. Most are tightly bunkered, a number are protected in front. Perhaps the most noteworthy is the hidden "valley of sin" green on the par-three eighth, which is angled right to left away from the shot with a deep swale through its midsection.

The picturesque, dogleg-right fourth hole calls for a 200-yard tee shot to the right side of a rolling fairway, taking out of play a copse of trees on the left, short of the green. But a drive slightly off-line to the right will roll down an incline towards a brook, trees, and out-of-bounds. The hole drops sharply to a green set in a hollow behind a deep bunker.

The 1903 Met Amateur was contested at Deal, which at the time was considered the second-longest course in the United States, playing to a staggering 6,495 yards. Its length favored the long-hitting Scot, Findlay Douglas, who overpowered the field.

When the Met Open came in 1910, it was the first time the tournament was not restricted to local players. Still, Alex Smith of Wykagyl came out on top.

Two men figure most prominently in Deal's history. From 1916 to 1942, Francis Arend was Club president as well as golf chairman (running tournaments and assigning handicaps), and financial angel. From 1935 to 1941, the professional was Vic Ghezzi, who represented Deal when he beat Byron Nelson on the 38th hole of the 1941 PGA Championship. Ghezzi, a member of the PGA Hall Of Fame, won 12 times on Tour and was a member of three Ryder Cup teams. ❍

**DEAL GOLF &
COUNTRY CLUB**
Deal, NJ

YEAR FOUNDED: 1898

ARCHITECTS:
Lawrence Van Etten
Donald Ross

COURSE OPENED: 1898

TEES	PAR	YARDAGE
Forward	71	5832
Middle	71	6277

TEES	COURSE RATING	SLOPE
Forward	74.6	128
Middle	70.6	125

DELLWOOD COUNTRY CLUB

"Up, Up, And Away"

Adolf Zukor was one of the pioneers in the movie business. As a young man, the Hungarian immigrant was deeply influenced and inspired by Thomas Edison's film of an elephant switching its tail. As he climbed the corporate ladder to the top of Paramount Studios, he and Edison played key roles in the advent of "talkies."

In 1918 looking for a retreat from Manhattan (and Fort Lee, where the studios were), Zukor purchased a 300-acre estate in New City, in the foothills of the Ramapos, complete with a swimming pool and nine-hole golf course. Two years later, he bought an adjacent 500 acres and built guest houses and a movie theater, calling the complex Mountain View Farm, where he welcomed stars like Charlie Chaplin and Mary Pickford.

Also in 1920, Zukor asked A.W. Tillinghast to build a new 18-hole golf course that remains largely intact to this day. It is best known for small greens, surrounded by bunkers that recently have been restored to their original size and depth.

Dellwood opens with an unusual par four that turns left 250 yards from the tee, at Zukor Road, then climbs 50 feet through a wall of rough to a severely sloping hilltop green. A row of trees extending along the left side demands a drive placed right of center.

The Depression hit the movie industry hard, and by 1933 Paramount was in bankruptcy. Zukor couldn't maintain his estate, so he sold it to New York attorney Bernard G. Nemeroff, counsel for several garment manufacturers. He took over what he renamed the Dellwood Country Club shortly after World War II, and recruited members for his new club primarily from the garment district. Under Nemeroff's benevolent dictatorship, the Club operated smoothly until 1962, when financial woes forced him to offer the membership a 100-year lease on the property.

The dominant golfer in Dell-wood's history has been Al Feminelli, now the professional emeritus. Feminelli came from Old Oaks in 1959 and stayed 32 years. He placed second in the 1964 Met Open and the 1957 and '58 Met PGA Championships. He also played in eight U.S. Opens and a handful of PGA Championships, and was considered by both Ben Hogan and Tony Lema to have been the best long-iron player they ever saw. Feminelli holds the Dellwood course record of 62, and once buried the Tour pros with a 65 at Apawamis in the Pro-Am that eventually evolved into the Thunderbird Classic.

Members today enjoy modern facilities set against a historic backdrop, including a swimming pool surrounded by formal gardens and fountains that recall the splendor of the old Zukor estate.

DELLWOOD COUNTRY CLUB
New City, NY

YEAR FOUNDED: 1947

ARCHITECT:
A.W. Tillinghast

COURSE OPENED: 1920

TEES	PAR	YARDAGE
Forward	73	5555
Middle	71	6433
Back	71	6709

TEES	COURSE RATING	SLOPE
Forward	72.9	127
Middle	71.8	126
Back	73.0	129

The picturesque 7th hole looking towards the Hudson.

ECHO LAKE COUNTRY CLUB

"Getting Together"

The natural amphitheater of Echo Lake's 16th green once was used by the Leni Lenape Indians for tribal ceremonies. In fact, the Club is situated on land purchased from the Lenape in 1664. Much later, two local golf clubs found it mutually advantageous to merge. From that union, Echo Lake was born.

The Cranford Golf Club, organized in 1899, leased land in Cranford south of the railroad tracks and east of town, and built a nine-hole Willie Dunn golf course. Noting the Club's popularity, a group of Westfield residents organized the Westfield Golf Club in 1900. They purchased a farm straddling Old Jerusalem Road, and built their own nine-hole golf course.

Cranford began experiencing growing pains and in 1911 purchased the 160-acre Harper Farm above Echo Lake. Donald Ross designed an 18-hole course, which was opened in the spring of 1913. During the Club's early years at Echo Lake, Max Marston, 1923 U.S. Amateur champion, and E.M. Wild battled head-to-head for the Club championship.

Westfield had no room to expand, but had equity in its land. By 1920, neither club had a large membership, so they began talking about a merger, which was consummated in 1921, when the name Echo Lake was adopted.

Al Mengert was the golf professional for five years, from 1956 to 1960, climaxed by his "Jersey Slam" of 1960—the Met Open, New Jersey Open, and New Jersey PGA. Echo Lake hosted the 1934 Met Open, in which Paul Runyan got up-and-down from a greenside bunker at the 18th hole to win.

Echo Lake today includes 13 original Donald Ross holes. The other five are creations of architects Robert White and Willard Wilkinson. The course has just three par threes and three par fives. It plays over terrain that ranges from flat to steeply sloping. Local knowledge of the slanting terrain is helpful on the approaches to five greens.

The seventh is Echo Lake's postcard hole, a short par three over a pond to a plateau green bunkered twice across the front and twice more at the right front corner and left side.

ECHO LAKE COUNTRY CLUB
Westfield, NJ

YEAR FOUNDED: 1921

ARCHITECTS:
Donald Ross
Robert White
Willard Wilkinson

YEAR OPENED: 1913

TEES	PAR	YARDAGE
Forward	74	5624
Middle	72	6524
Back	71	6620

TEES	COURSE RATING	SLOPE
Forward	72.8	129
Middle	71.4	127
Back	72.2	128

The second hole-short on the card, long on problems.

The best hole is number 16, a mid-length par four that calls for extreme accuracy off the tee to the right-center of the narrow, tree-lined fairway. The hole then turns abruptly left and tumbles downhill, playing over a cross-bunker 40 yards short of the green. The terrain in front of the green kicks downhill and to the left in the general direction of, but nowhere near, the lake that gave the club its name.

SHADY REST

Following the merger, Westfield Golf Club sold its remaining facilities to the Shady Rest Country Club, the first black country club in America, established in 1921. Shady Rest quickly became a magnet for middle-class blacks: Its membership roster included waiters, porters, and janitors as well as doctors, lawyers, and merchants. The Club's golf and tennis tournaments, lectures by famous black leaders, and dances featuring Cab Calloway, Count Basie, and Ella Fitzgerald, attracted members and guests from far and wide. John Shippen, half-black and half-Shinnecock Indian and the first American-born professional to compete in the U.S. Open (1896), was the pro from 1924 to 1960. In 1925, the club hosted the first Black National Championship. In 1964, the facility was sold to the town of Scotch Plains and became the Scotch Hills public course.

EDGEWOOD COUNTRY CLUB

"Red, White, And Blue"

In the years immediately after World War II, the number of private golf clubs in the Met Area remained nearly constant. Few existing clubs had full memberships, and the number of unattached golfers looking to join private clubs did not warrant building new facilities until the 1960s.

But one spot in Bergen County did attract immediate post-war attention. It was a dairy farm, converted in 1946 by owner/builder Robert Handwerg and golf architect Orrin Smith into a 27-hole public facility called the Country Club of New Jersey. In 1953, the owner leased the facility to a group which operated as the Greenwood Country Club, a private club which failed, the owner ending the lease after the 1957 season and operating once again as Country Club of New Jersey in 1958–59.

In November of 1959, 100 men, including most of the Greenwood group and a number of others from Aldecress, organized as the Edgewood Country Club. They signed a 90-year lease on the Country Club of New Jersey's property and set to work upgrading the plant, opening a new clubhouse, and revising several of the original holes in 1960. Edgewood continues to play as three nines, all demanding careful placement of the tee shot to leave clear approaches to small, ferociously bunkered greens. Many holes feature trouble in the form of out-of-bounds, ponds, and creeks.

The fifth on Red is known as the "Willows" because of the trees to the right of the landing area that shape this long, slightly downhill par four. The well-bunkered green is two-tiered.

The par-four sixth on White is a tight driving hole, with lateral water on the right and a narrow fairway that tilts toward the hazard. A pond sits in front of the two-tiered green.

Blue is the shortest nine but has the most dramatic terrain. The seventh on Blue is the course's signature hole, a long par three with a large pond in front of the green, wrapping around to either side.

In 1986, the members purchased the property, and continue to keep a close eye on the conditioning, from the treetops to the flower beds, and, of course the golf course. The members also enjoy a dozen tennis courts and one of the largest swimming pools in New Jersey. ○

EDGEWOOD COUNTRY CLUB
River Vale, NJ

YEAR FOUNDED: 1959

ARCHITECTS:
Orrin Smith
Alec Turnyei

COURSE OPENED: 1946

BLUE-WHITE COURSE

TEES	PAR	YARDAGE
Forward	72	5384
Middle	71	5995
Back	71	6367

TEES	COURSE RATING	SLOPE
Forward	71.4	120
Middle	68.6	118
Back	70.4	124

RED-BLUE COURSE

TEES	PAR	YARDAGE
Forward	72	5374
Middle	71	5994
Back	71	6402

TEES	COURSE RATING	SLOPE
Forward	71.5	119
Middle	68.6	117
Back	70.6	122

WHITE-RED COURSE

TEES	PAR	YARDAGE
Forward	74	5736
Middle	72	6241
Back	72	6601

TEES	COURSE RATING	SLOPE
Forward	72.7	123
Middle	69.6	119
Back	71.3	123

The par-three 7th on Blue.

ESSEX FELLS COUNTRY CLUB

"The Mulligan, Take One"

ESSEX FELLS COUNTRY CLUB
Essex Fells, NJ

YEAR FOUNDED: 1896

ARCHITECTS:
Members
Seth Raynor

COURSE OPENED: 1916

TEES	PAR	YARDAGE
Forward	75	5824
Middle	70	6250
Back	70	6476

TEES	COURSE RATING	SLOPE
Forward	74.9	135
Middle	70.6	123
Back	71.9	125

View of the clubhouse looking back from the 10th green.

It may be necessary to take a mulligan when attempting to explain the origins of that endearing term. There are at least two separate stories: One is Canadian in origin, eventually surfacing in this country at Winged Foot. The other emanates from Essex Fells.

Des Sullivan, golf writer for the *Newark News*, was a Club member, and often played with assistant professional Dave O'Connell. They frequently were joined by John "Buddy" Mulligan, who worked at the Club in the morning while Sullivan and O'Connell practiced, giving them an unfair advantage. To even things up, Mulligan began to demand—and receive—a second chance on the first tee. Word spread among the members, and the bonus shot came to be known as the "mulligan."

In contrast to the spontaneity of the first mulligan stands the founding of Essex Fells. The community was planned to the finest detail by Charles W. Leavitt in the early 1890s. Leavitt bowed out quickly, turning the project over to the Drexels, developers of Philadelphia's "Main Line." They bought 1,000 acres and expanded upon Leavitt's plans. Essex Fells grew, first as a summer retreat, then as one of the more affluent bedroom communities of New York.

By the way, the name comes from the Scottish "fells," meaning "rolling hills," an apt description of the terrain.

The first golfers were a small band from the Drexel organization who played a rudimentary nine-hole course starting in 1896. Within a year, the Drexels realized the attraction of golf, and decided to build a good nine-hole course. They hired Alex Findlay, the professional at Essex County.

Essex Fells Golf Club was organized in 1896 for that purpose. Two rooms in the Water Company's pumphouse served as a clubhouse until a building with a ballroom and wide verandahs was built in 1906. Real estate development forced the Club to move in 1913, when the Drexels leased 112 acres falling east away from Third Mountain. There they built a new 18-hole course, designed by the builders and completed by 1916. A revision carried out in 1924 was orchestrated by Seth Raynor.

The clubhouse perches atop Third Mountain, with seven holes climbing or falling from the hilltop. The yardage at Essex Fells can be deceiving: There are only two par fives—but four huge par fours (holes 1, 8, 15, and 16), each only 10 yards shy of another stroke.

The ninth hole plays straight up the hill, with a pair of imposing, high-lipped bunkers in a wall of rough out front of the green.

The 17th is a short, downhill par four that angles left with a pond on the left of the green and two bunkers right. A drive long enough to pass the downhill terrain is a prerequisite.

Essex Fells enjoyed the national spotlight in 1949 when Babe Didrikson Zaharias carded rounds of 74-70-75=219 to win the inaugural Women's Eastern Open. The "Babe" was one of just three players to break even-80s. The club put up the $3,500 purse for the tournament; the winner's trophy is now used for the women's Club championship.

Essex Fells is the home club of Ann Beard, former president of the WMGA and chairperson of the USGA's Women's Committee. Beard played in five U.S. Women's Opens and three U.S. Women's Amateurs, and won her Club championship 19 times. The MGA honored her in 1991 with the Distinguished Service Award. Ann's daughter, Kendra, is the USGA's Director of Women's Competitions, and has officiated at the U.S. Open, British Open, and Masters. No need for a mulligan here–both Beards have made tremendous contributions to golf. ❍

Ann Beard

FAIRMOUNT COUNTRY CLUB

"A Rocky Beginning"

FAIRMOUNT COUNTRY CLUB
Chatham, NJ

YEAR FOUNDED: 1958

ARCHITECT:
Hal Purdy

COURSE OPENED: 1962

TEES	PAR	YARDAGE
Forward	75	5981
Middle	72	6588
Back	72	6744

TEES	COURSE RATING	SLOPE
Forward	75.6	136
Middle	72.4	132
Back	73.3	133

Fairmount was started in 1958 by seven Manhattan businessmen who were tired of stagnating on Canoe Brook's waiting list. Their hand was forced when a local developer showed an interest in the Noe Farm straddling Southern Boulevard, a site the founders had coveted for several years. So they purchased 180 acres from John Noe.

The farm was a low-lying piece of property, mostly wetlands on the perimeter of New Jersey's Great Swamp, a large wildlife refuge consisting of hundreds of acres that were home to deer, bear, and a variety of birds. At the same time, the swamp was the subject of speculation that the Port Authority would fill part of it in and build a fourth airport for the New York area. To avert any such development, a number of wealthy local residents donated land within the swamp to the Federal Government, with the stipulation that it be designated a wildlife preserve. With the swamp saved, part of Fairmount's border gained a natural and permanent buffer.

The swampy land was a problem, but architect Hal Purdy hoped solving it would give him instant recognition. Work began in the fall of 1960, but weather compounded the problems: The summer of 1961 proved to be the wettest in 25 years, so wet that the construction crew nearly lost a bulldozer in the swamplands. The course finally opened on May 5, 1962.

Even after the course opened, players had to contend with mud and rocks. In the Club's early days, members' families held rock-picking parties that eventually resulted in the elimination of the embedded culprits from the soil.

The front nine, which winds through the woods, is tighter than the back. Water comes into play on 10 holes, including three hazards directly in front of greens. But neither water, trees, nor length really makes Fairmount difficult. It is the greens, which are boldly crowned, falling away to all four sides, and contain an assortment of mounds and contours that baffle even the best putters.

The 11th is the conversation piece, a par five that turns sharply left at the end — over water. The hole plays from an elevated tee to a rolling fairway bunkered along both sides. Up ahead lie two ponds preceding a separate section of fairway, and to the left another pond fronting the green. The average player must decide if the reward of a shorter pitch to the green is worth the risk of attempting to clear the first two ponds on his second shot. Longer hitters have the additional option of going for the green in two.

Fairmount twice hosted the LPGA Tour's Chrysler Plymouth Classic. Nancy Lopez won in 1985 and Becky Pearson won her first and only LPGA title the following year. Fairmount's third hole ranked second toughest on the ladies' tour in 1985. The 11th may have been the most thought-provoking. ❏

The intriguing 11th hole.

FIDDLER'S ELBOW COUNTRY CLUB

"A Bend In The River"

Looking up the 18th (Forest) from the 17th green.

FIDDLER'S ELBOW COUNTRY CLUB
Far Hills, NJ

YEAR FOUNDED: 1965

MEADOW COURSE

ARCHITECTS:
Hal Purdy
Brian Silva

COURSE OPENED: 1965

TEES	PAR	YARDAGE
Forward	72	5368
Middle	72	6260
Back	72	6724

TEES	COURSE RATING	SLOPE
Forward	67.8	118
Middle	69.4	114
Back	71.7	119

RIVER COURSE

ARCHITECT:
Hal Purdy

COURSE OPENED: 1965

TEES	PAR	YARDAGE
Forward	72	5356
Middle	72	6387
Back	72	6731

TEES	COURSE RATING	SLOPE
Forward	72.0	121
Middle	70.8	121
Back	72.4	124

FOREST COURSE

ARCHITECT:
Rees Jones

COURSE OPENED: 1994

TEES	PAR	YARDAGE
Forward	72	5154
Middle	72	6716
Back	72	7128

TEES	COURSE RATING	SLOPE
Forward	68.7	120
Middle	72.4	128
Back	74.3	132

N aming a country club is not as simple as pulling words from a hat and hanging a sign by the road. There often are twists and turns, as was the case with one of the Met Area's more intriguingly named clubs, Fiddler's Elbow.

At a Bedminster Township meeting in 1965 at which the club was incorporated, a Club attorney noticed on an old map that a bend in the Lamington River, one mile south of the future clubhouse, was called Fiddler's Elbow, because it resembled the crooked arm of a man playing a fiddle. The Lamington River, which twists through the property and serves as the border between Somerset and Hunterdon Counties, is a branch of the Black River, which was going to give the Club its name.

Fiddler's Elbow was founded by present owners Ray Donovan and Ron Schiavone. But the idea of limiting it to corporate memberships—unique in the MGA today—is credited to contractor Dave Westergard, who built the original 27 holes. Reflecting the needs of its members, the facilities are ideal for conferences, meetings, and other business functions.

The clubhouse, an English Manor House built of Pennsylvania fieldstone in 1938 (with a two-story addition circa 1968), was once the home of New York investment banker Frederick Mosely. From the early years of the century until the Club took over, the land was used for elaborate fox hunts. Following the death of his wife in 1958, Mosely moved to Boston and the estate became a dairy farm.

Hal Purdy designed the 27-hole complex with the assistance of the Club's long-serving first professional, John Grace. They had the three nines playable in 1965. The Blue and Red nines, which have since been combined to form the River course, were built close to the river, which comes into play on several of the holes. The Lamington also crosses the Green nine, which was married to the Silver nine, designed by Brian Silva in 1990 to commemorate the club's silver anniversary; that combination is called the Meadow course.

The 18-hole Forest Course opened in 1994 to rave reviews. Designed by New Jersey-based architect Rees Jones, it was cut through a forest of white pines and hardwoods.

The Forest course is punctuated by Jones' signature mounding along many fairways and greens. The 12th hole is a strong par four with carries over wetlands both off the tee and into the green.

Both the River and Meadow courses roll through a pretty parkland setting, with trees coming into play on several holes. For beauty and challenge, a pair of par threes stand out: Number three on River crosses wetlands and water; a brook comes into play on Meadow's number four in front and right of the green.

In June, 1995, Fiddler's Elbow became the first facility in New Jersey, golf or otherwise, to be named an Audubon Cooperative Sanctuary by the Audubon Society of New York. With three separate championship courses, Fiddler's Elbow is New Jersey's largest golf facility. ○

FOREST HILL FIELD CLUB

"Field Of Dreams"

**FOREST HILL
FIELD CLUB**
Bloomfield, NJ

YEAR FOUNDED: 1896

ARCHITECT:
A.W. Tillinghast

COURSE OPENED: 1926

TEES	PAR	YARDAGE
Forward	71	5739
Middle	71	6266
Back	71	6503

TEES	COURSE RATING	SLOPE
Forward	73.6	126
Middle	70.4	124
Back	71.4	127

The "Field Club", a product of the late 1800s, was the predecessor of today's "Country Club". The typical field club offered its members a variety of sports such as baseball, football, cricket, field hockey, bowling, shooting, and eventually golf. Forest Hill is one of just two field clubs in the Met Area (Quogue is the other) to survive and keep its original name, as well.

The Forest Hill Tennis Club was founded in 1891 in the Forest Hill section of Newark. It was upgraded to "Field Club" status in 1896 when baseball, football, bowling, and golf were added to its offerings. The Club's first golf course was a nine-holer laid out by Tom Bendelow. A second nine followed in 1906, designed by Willie Norton. The new holes were located across the railroad tracks in Belleville, on the former Hendricks estate, which the Club leased. Deep gullies crossed several fairways, and the course was crossed by Second River and the tracks of two railroad lines. The property was tight, and at least two holes crisscrossed. The Hendricks homestead was used as a clubhouse.

With the lease on the Hendricks property due to expire in 1926, the members purchased a 180-acre tract of virgin forest, north of Belleville Avenue. A.W. Tillinghast was hired to build an 18-hole course, which he accomplished at the expense of some 4,000 trees. The new course opened in 1927. (The original course became Branch Brook, part of the Essex County Park Commission's public network and host to the first MGA Public Links Championship, in 1936.)

Forest Hill's tree-lined fairways fall away from the knoll where the clubhouse is located, giving six holes dramatic elevation changes. Several other holes feature elevated tees or greens or tumbling fairways.

The par-five third turns to the left twice between an elevated tee and plateau green. The tee shot must contend with a quick angle to the left as well as a small pond and out-of-bounds through the fairway. The player going for the green in two faces a second pond beyond the second turn, and a 15-foot-deep bunker below the right

side of the two-tiered green.

The picturesque seventh is the number-one handicap hole, a long par four that rolls uphill and slightly to the right, with a bunker to the right of the landing area. The climb to the green is severe, and the putting surface is flanked by bunkers.

Forest Hill has been a generous host to regional championships over the years, including three Met Opens (1937, 1940, and 1951). Craig Wood, who was the Club professional from 1928 to 1931, took advantage of local knowledge to establish a Met Open record in 1940, firing rounds of 64-66-68-66=264 to beat Ben Hogan by 11 strokes. Hogan was the only other player in a strong field to break par for the 72 holes.

In 1972, John Ruby established a record for the Ike Championship with a 66-67-73=206 score at Forest Hill, winning by eight strokes over Jerry Courville Sr., whose record he eclipsed. Both Wood and Ruby had field days at Forest Hill.   ○

The uphill 7th hole.

FORSGATE COUNTRY CLUB

"Eye Poppin"

**FORSGATE
COUNTRY CLUB**
Jamesburg, NJ

YEAR FOUNDED: 1931

BANKS COURSE

ARCHITECT:
Charles Banks

COURSE OPENED: 1931

TEES	PAR	YARDAGE
Forward	71	5678
Middle	71	6347
Back	71	6577

TEES	COURSE RATING	SLOPE
Forward	72.9	124
Middle	70.4	123
Back	71.4	126

WEST COURSE

ARCHITECTS:
Hal Purdy
Arnold Palmer

COURSE OPENED: 1962

TEES	PAR	YARDAGE
Forward	72	5140
Middle	72	6099
Back	72	6620

TEES	COURSE RATING	SLOPE
Forward	71.6	126
Middle	70.1	123
Back	72.5	127

After playing an exhibition at Forsgate, Sam Snead commented, "These are the most eye poppin' greens and traps I've ever seen." Snead went on to say that, given the chance to place the pins in their most difficult positions, he could set up Forsgate so none of the lead-ing Tour pros could break 75—conceding regulation play from tee to green.

Forsgate was born in 1913 when John A. Forster, the Scotsman who founded Crum & Forster Insurance, purchased the 513-acre site and established Forest Gate Farms (later contracted to Forsgate), New Jersey's largest Grade A dairy farm, which became famous for ice cream.

Forster died in 1931, but not before commissioning Charles Banks to design an 18-hole private playground. The course was completed in 1931, and may have been the last of Banks' career.

The clubhouse, designed by Clifford C. Wendehack, also was completed in 1931. In the mid 1950s, the dining room was opened to the public and the golf course operated on a semi-private basis.

Work started on a second golf course in 1961. Designed by Hal Purdy, it was ready for play in 1962, with major renovations in 1985 and 1995. The latter reworking was done by Arnold Palmer, and involved the creation of the new first and second holes, with the second—623 yards from the tips—one of the longest in the state.

The Purdy course is thought to be the more difficult. Although its bunkers are smaller, the greens are too, and the course is longer and narrower than its neighbor, with water in play on 10 holes.

Forsgate fell on hard times in the late 1970s and early 1980s. In 1984, Matrix Development Group purchased the facility from the Forster family and invested more than $2 million in both courses. Five new holes were built for the Purdy course, and three other greens reworked.

The gaping bunkers, highly contoured greens, and tumbling fairways that Banks created are a far cry from the gently rolling farmland on which the course was built. Banks was at his industrious, fiendish best at Forsgate, moving tons of earth to create sharp undulations on fairways and greens. Since missing the bunkers is of paramount importance, the angle into many of the greens is crucial, placing a premium on driving accuracy.

The par-three third is typical. It is an Eden, playing over a deep hollow before rising to a plateau green set above a 15-foot deep bunker on the right side that is complemented by another deep specimen on the left. The putting surface features a huge spine running back to front through the middle.

Befitting the Club that houses the offices of the New Jersey section of the PGA, Forsgate has maintained a high profile on the tournament scene. The section's stroke-play championship has been contested over the Banks course 12 times between 1948 and 1992. Milton "Babe" Lichardus won three times at Forsgate, 25 years apart.

Forsgate also hosted the LPGA Tour's Coca-Cola Classic for three years (1976-1978). The winners were Amy Alcott, Kathy Whitworth, and Nancy Lopez.

The current Director of Golf is Bill Ziobro, MGA Junior champ of 1966, who in 1970 became one of just two amateurs to win the New Jersey Open. Ziobro also won the New Jersey Amateur that year, and captured the New Jersey PGA in 1976. And so an eye poppin' talent as a youngster has come to hold sway over some of the most eye poppin' greens in the Met Area. ❍

One of Forsgate's finest, to the left of the 8th green.

GLEN RIDGE COUNTRY CLUB

"Forever On Sunday"

**GLEN RIDGE
COUNTRY CLUB**
Glen Ridge, NJ

YEAR FOUNDED: 1894

ARCHITECTS:
Members
Willie Park Jr.
A.W. Tillinghast
Robert Trent Jones

COURSE OPENED: 1913

TEES	PAR	YARDAGE
Forward	72	5669
Middle	71	5842
Back	71	6029

TEES	COURSE RATING	SLOPE
Forward	73.6	132
Middle	69.0	123
Back	69.8	125

The 11th hole, one of the five outstanding par threes.

During golf's formative years in this country, when the typical work-week stretched into Saturday, the issue of Sunday golf was a burning one. In 1904, the members of the Golf Club of Glen Ridge voted 68 to 58 in favor of Sunday play. The vote was called because the owners of three separate tracts of land that made up part of the course would not allow golf on the Sabbath. In effect, the Glen Ridge members voted to abandon part of their golf course in exchange for an extra day of play.

The Golf Club of Glen Ridge was organized in October, 1894, in the home of John Wood Stewart, a prominent member of the Essex County Hunt Club, who the previous year had helped found the Golf Club of Montclair. The first Glen Ridge clubhouse was half the gardener's house on a nearby estate.

The first golf course was a nine-holer that played through "peaceful meadowland" off Ridgewood Avenue, crossing the road twice. The course underwent considerable evolution through 1911, as tracts of land were added or deleted, yet it appears to have straddled Ridgewood Avenue throughout this period. Indeed, the gas lamps that adorn Ridgewood Avenue to this day appear in the Club's logo.

In 1911, the Club purchased additional land one mile north of the original site, where it expanded to an 18-hole course, which was ready for play in 1913. The course consisted of five holes between Ridgewood Avenue and Broad Street, with the other 13 east of Broad. Of these 18, reasonable facsimiles of 10 remain in play today, as course revisions by A.W. Tillinghast (1920s) and Robert Trent Jones (1949-1950) have altered the course significantly.

Glen Ridge rolls gently through narrow, tree-lined fairways, and is best known for its outstanding collection of five par threes, three of which call for demanding carries over water while distracting the golfer with their beauty. The stone-walled brook that loops through the property passes near four greens and marginally affects play on four others; of the aforementioned par threes, the brook passes in front of the fourth green, while the eighth and 11th play side by side across a pond.

It still seems like a lovely place to spend a Sunday afternoon. ❍

GREEN BROOK COUNTRY CLUB

"Land Of The 9pm Sun"

The Green Brook Country Club was built atop the highest of the Caldwell Mountains and faced the afternoon sun. Early Club promotions claimed this gave members an extra half-hour of golf in the summer.

Robert White, the force behind creation of the PGA of America in 1916, designed the course, which opened for play in 1923. Harry Smith, who worked on the construction crew, became the Club's first professional and greenkeeper, serving until 1958.

Green Brook listed 330 members by the end of the decade, but was hit hard by the Depression and World War II. The mortgage was foreclosed in 1940, so the Club was run on a cash-only basis until 1947, when 12 members of nearby Cedar Hill Country Club purchased Green Brook's facilities from the bank. In the early 1950s, the members decided to make it a family club, adding a swimming pool and tennis courts.

The original clubhouse was built in 1925. During the late 1980s, it was extensively renovated with new locker rooms, a dining room and kitchen.

Despite the changes in ownership, White's course remains very much intact. Robert Trent Jones rebuilt a few greens and tees in 1948, and in 1979, Hal Purdy designed the new par-three 17th and added a lake, while the old par-three 10th hole was paved over for parking.

Green Brook offers two highly contrasting nines. The front is tight, wooded, and experiences abrupt elevation changes. The back is flatter and, although tree-lined, not nearly as tight as the front.

The par-five third is a dogleg-left that turns along a high ridge covered with tall rough. Even long hitters lay up short and right of the ridge, then finish with two medium irons. Only two golfers are known to have carried the top of the ridge from the blue tees: Tour star Tony Lema and former Chicago Bear linebacker Dick Butkus.

The par-three fifth drops to a green surrounded by eight bunkers, including two in front above the putting surface.

The drive on nine is the most intimidating shot on the course, playing through a tight chute of trees to a fairway well above tee level. The hole then turns hard to the right and rolls downhill to an elevated, two-tiered green.

Green Brook is in the regional spotlight today as one of its members seeks to establish a new national record. Hank Schinman has won the Club championship 25 times since 1963, leaving him one short of Jerry Courville Sr.'s national record. Should Schinman succeed in his bid, he would bring special attention to one of the Met Area's hidden gems. ○

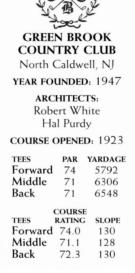

GREEN BROOK COUNTRY CLUB
North Caldwell, NJ

YEAR FOUNDED: 1947

ARCHITECTS:
Robert White
Hal Purdy

COURSE OPENED: 1923

TEES	PAR	YARDAGE
Forward	74	5792
Middle	71	6306
Back	71	6548

TEES	COURSE RATING	SLOPE
Forward	74.0	130
Middle	71.1	128
Back	72.3	130

The ninth hole, with clubhouse behind.

HACKENSACK GOLF CLUB

"Let's Go To The Video Tape"

The unusual target from the 14th tee.

Jim McGovern

Almost from the beginning, golf clubs have provided their members with indoor activities for a rainy day. There is the 19th hole, card rooms, and bowling alleys. The members of the Hackensack Golf Club have a 40-minute film that tells how the course was built in the 1920s. It is especially interesting because the architect was Charles "Steamshovel" Banks, who was known for his use of heavy equipment to move earth.

The Banks course actually is the second in the Club's history. The original was located in Hackensack, at the foot of the western slope of Hackensack Heights. It was a nine-holer designed by Tom Bendelow in 1899. The new club proved very popular, and drew half its members from New York City.

By 1907, the course had been expanded to 18 holes featuring all the latest wrinkles, including punch-bowl greens, elevated stone tees, serpentine sand bunkers, and circus rings (a single bunker encircling a green). In addition, the Susquehanna Railroad ran through the grounds at the base of a 40-foot cut, and was played as a hazard.

By the mid 1920s, increasing real estate taxes forced the Club to move 10 miles to the north to Oradell, to the site of the Kinderkamack Golf Club, which was organized in 1924. The entrance was up the hill from Kinderkamack Road, near the present sixth green. The plan was to merge the two clubs, keeping the Kinderkamack name, and build 27 holes. Instead, construction of a new 18-hole golf course began in 1925, designed by Seth Raynor & Charles Banks. It opened, along with the present clubhouse, a Clifford Wendehack design, in 1928.

Hackensack's fairways are lined with oaks, maples, and pines, and the greens flanked with deep side bunkers. The 14th is Hackensack's conversation piece: It plays from a well-elevated tee to a rising fairway; the golfer on the tee needs all the elevation he can get to carry a tall tree 125 yards out in the center of the fairway, on a line that opens up the best angle to the green and takes bunker across the left front of the green.

No less a golfer than Mountain Ridge professional Wes Ellis called Hackensack's 18th the best finishing hole in the Met Area. It doglegs left around a bunker at the corner, then climbs up the hill toward the clubhouse. The green angles right to left to the approach, and is guarded by a large, deep front bunker.

Hackensack has hosted seven MGA championships over the years, including the 1964 Met Amateur, Bob Gardner's fifth consecutive, and the 1973 Met Open, won by Peter Davison.

Jim McGovern, who grew up in a home adjacent to the course, is the most prominent player in Club history. In 1987, he held off a handful of experienced professionals to win the Met Open at Winged Foot by one stroke, becoming one of just four amateurs to win that title. The following season, he captured the Met Amateur at Plainfield, carding a remarkable 23 birdies in 73 holes of match play. McGovern turned professional in 1988, and won the 1993 Greater Houston Open. He has recently played in both the Masters and U.S. Open.

McGovern's exploits to date would fill a second videotape, doubling the size of the Club's video library. ❍

**HACKENSACK
GOLF CLUB**
Oradell, NJ

YEAR FOUNDED: 1899

ARCHITECTS:
Seth Raynor
Charles Banks

COURSE OPENED: 1928

TEES	PAR	YARDAGE
Forward	74	5757
Middle	72	6646
Back	72	7004

TEES	COURSE RATING	SLOPE
Forward	73.2	128
Middle	71.5	125
Back	73.1	130

HOLLYWOOD GOLF CLUB

"Friendly Neighborhood Rivals"

HOLLYWOOD GOLF CLUB
Deal, NJ

YEAR FOUNDED: 1898

ARCHITECTS:
Isaac Mackie
Walter Travis

COURSE OPENED: 1913

TEES	PAR	YARDAGE
Forward	74	5766
Middle	72	6414
Back	72	6735

TEES	COURSE RATING	SLOPE
Forward	73.9	127
Middle	72.1	132
Back	73.7	135

Hollywood Golf Club traces its roots—and its name—to the now defunct Hollywood Hotel in Long Branch. The Club was incorporated in 1898 by a small group of New York businessmen who spent summers at the northern Jersey shore, the nation's first popular beach resort destination, starting in the 1860s.

The members played a nine-hole Tom Bendelow designed course at the hotel, which was Hollywood's home for three years until an 18-hole layout opened in 1902. The new course served the Club for 11 years, and hosted the 1906 Met Open. But within a few years, the members wanted a longer layout.

They moved to the Club's present home, which had been the Deal estate of railroad financier George Washington Young, who was forced to lease in 1913 to offset financial problems. The course included three of the best holes on the adjacent Deal course. Isaac Mackie designed the new golf course, which opened in 1913, but the membership still wasn't satisfied. So Walter Travis was brought in during 1915 to revise the new course. His major contribution was a complete reworking of the greens and bunkers; Dick Wilson made a similar contribution in 1956.

As it exists today, Hollywood's golf course is a magnificent, old-fashioned test. The gently-rolling course plays along tree-lined fairways, but it is the bunkering and mounds—remnants from a distant era—that give the course its flavor.

The fourth is the postcard hole, one of the most unusual par threes in the area. It plays uphill to an elevated back-to-front green that rises sharply across the front. The green is set in a bowl, surrounded by high mounds and flanked by five bunkers, two of which are carved from dunes.

Formerly called the "Heinz Hole"—for its 57 bunkers scattered from tee to green—the 12th today is simply a brutal par four with but 17 bunkers, most in the fairway between drive zone and green, a

1906 Met Open contestants.

definite threat to the second shot.

In 1906, Hollywood hosted the second edition of the Met Open. The course played long due to heavy rains. The winner was George Low of Baltusrol. The U.S. Women's Amateur followed in 1921, with Marion Hollins proving a popular winner. The victory climaxed her competitive career, and allowed her to turn her attention to other pursuits, the Women's National Golf & Tennis Club in particular.

The cream rose to the top at Hollywood once again in 1925, as Jess Sweetser, considered the equal of Bobby Jones, easily captured the Met Amateur.

The dominant golfer at Hollywood over the years has been Robert Jacobson, Club champion 25 times, once a national record. He took up golf in 1931 at the age of 13, and learned quickly under Club professional Craig Wood. He won his first Club championship the following year, and two years later, he eliminated 1933 U.S. Open champion Johnny Goodman in an early round of the 1934 U.S. Amateur Championship—still one of the biggest surprises in that tournament's history. ❍

The dramatic Scottish-flavored par-three 4th hole.

HOMINY HILL GOLF COURSE

"Home Of Champions"

In 1941, Henry Mercer, a shipping magnate from Rumson, purchased a 230-acre cattle farm called Hominy Hill in Colts Neck, planning to use it as a summer residence. He cultivated purebred guernseys, including Hominy Hill Betty, a national champion who later made headlines by giving birth to twins. Betty was not Mercer's only champion: He also owned the yacht "Wetherly," which he sailed to victory in the 1962 Americas Cup races.

Mercer was a golfer, as were many of his clients, so he decided to convert the farm into a very private—one member—golf club. He spared no expense, engaging Robert Trent Jones to design and build the course, which was completed in the spring of 1965. Unfortunately, Mercer suffered a crippling stroke soon after the course opened, and he was able to play it only a few times before he died in 1974.

In 1976, the Mercer family sold the golf course and its buildings to Monmouth County. The course quickly became the jewel of the county's golf facilities. The property today includes a pro shop, practice fairway, a two-story clubhouse (once a dairy barn), and a conference center built from the renovated Mercer homestead.

Hominy Hill's greens are exceptionally large and rolling for a public course. All but two of the par-four and par-five holes are doglegs, and the landing areas off the tee typically are flanked by clusters of two or three bunkers on either side. The rough is unusually tall and thick, severe punishment for the inaccurate player straining to keep up with the course's demanding yardage.

Hominy Hill's ninth is one of the great par fives in the Met Area. The fairway runs to the left in the landing area, then turns 90 degrees to the right

**HOMINY HILL
GOLF COURSE**
Colts Neck, NJ

YEAR FOUNDED: 1976

ARCHITECT:
Robert Trent Jones

COURSE OPENED: 1965

TEES	PAR	YARDAGE
Forward	72	5794
Middle	72	6470
Back	72	7059

TEES	COURSE RATING	SLOPE
Forward	73.9	128
Middle	71.7	127
Back	74.4	132

before rising over its final 75 yards to the green. A long drive gives the player the option of going for the green by cutting the corner over a lake. A scattering of seven bunkers, including two at greenside, await the shot that carries the water but misses its target. The par-five 14th resembles 15 at Augusta National, with a wide brook crossing in front of the green.

In 1983, Hominy Hill hosted the USGA Amateur Public Links Championship, followed in 1995 by the U.S. Women's Public Links. The course also has been the site for the 1986, 1991 and 1996 MGA/MetLife Public Links Championships.

In 1990, Hominy Hill became the first public facility to host the New Jersey Amateur Championship, won by Jeff Thomas for a record sixth time. Victory did not come easily, as Thomas' scores of 71-73-80-72=296 attest. In fact, Thomas needed birdies on the final three holes to prevail.

The recent championships have served to highlight Hominy's Hill's annual ranking among the country's top public facilities. ○

The direct approach to the ninth green.

KNICKERBOCKER COUNTRY CLUB

"East Side, West Side"

Knickerbocker was incorporated on December 1, 1914, at the home of one Malcolm Mackay on Knickerbocker Road in Tenafly, for the purpose of enjoying golf, tennis, and other sports—on a site slightly more than 10 miles from midtown Manhattan.

The course progressed from the east side of Knickerbocker Road to the west. The first nine holes, on land leased from Mackay for $1 a year, were built "according to a plan" by Donald Ross. They opened July 4, 1915, at which time the Club was negotiating for additional land to the west. Nine new holes, also Ross "designs," were ready by that December, some built on wetlands, others cut through forest. The course featured "long curving holes, deep pits, and sugarloaf mounds" in the Ross style. A third nine was added for the 1925 season, the work of Herbert Strong. A few of the west holes were altered or abandoned at this time; only six holes from that nine remain relatively intact today.

Three years later, the Club spent $69,000 to purchase a house west of the road, intending to make it the new clubhouse. But the Depression ended any such plan; in fact, the house had to be sold at a significant loss. Financial troubles also led to the abandonment of the original nine east of the road in 1938. The remaining 18 holes were used almost as is until 1973, when Geoffrey Cornish repositioned and remodeled six greens, bringing the course to its present configuration. The clubhouse underwent a complete renovation and expansion, completed in 1996.

Knickerbocker has been described as deceptively difficult, the result of narrow fairways, sharp angles, and small greens. The best-known hole is the 12th, which plays from an elevated tee into a wide fairway sliced across by a brook at the end of the drive zone. A large pond hugs the left side of the angled green.

Knickerbocker has had only five proferssionals in more than 80 years. First was a Scot named Willie Collins

The uniquely-bunkered 6th hole.

(1915-'25). Jack Hobens (1926-'41) won the 1908 Met Open at Baltusrol, played in several U.S. Opens while professional at Englewood before coming to Knickerbocker, and was among the founders of the national PGA. He was followed by Willie Walker (1942-'52), brother of Cyril Walker, the Englewood pro who won the 1924 U.S. Open.

Otto Greiner served Knickerbocker for 32 years (1953-'84). During his tenure he won the 1954 Met Open, 1956 New Jersey PGA, and the inaugural Dodge Open in 1964, and played in 10 U.S. Opens. A member of the New Jersey PGA Hall of Fame, Greiner was named NJPGA Professional of the Year in 1973. The man Sam Snead once called "the boldest putter I've ever seen" established the course record 64 the first time he played the course—while interviewing for the head professional position!

Ed Whitman, in the shop since 1985, has been a leading force in New Jersey professional ranks for the past decade, twice winner of the State Open, four-time NJPGA Stroke-Play champion, and holder of several other regional titles. Whitman has been acclaimed NJPGA Player of the Year four times.

Prominent among current members is Dennis Slezak, 1991 Met Amateur champion.

The inaugural New Jersey Open was staged over Knickerbocker's "recently remodeled" course in May of 1921, when Peter O'Hara of Shackamaxon carded 148 for two rounds, three strokes better than amateur Frank Dyer. Wes Ellis won the 1963 NJPGA Championship, his complete performance taking place west of Knickerbocker Road. Only the clubhouse now lies to the east. ❍

KNICKERBOCKER COUNTRY CLUB

Tenafly, NJ

YEAR FOUNDED: 1914

ARCHITECTS:
Donald Ross
Herbert Strong
Geoffrey Cornish

COURSE OPENED: 1915

TEES	PAR	YARDAGE
Forward	74	5851
Middle	72	6410
Back	72	6628

TEES	COURSE RATING	SLOPE
Forward	74.2	129
Middle	71.1	126
Back	72.1	128

MANASQUAN RIVER GOLF CLUB

"Where River Meets Ocean"

Brielle, New Jersey, is an anomaly—a New Jersey shore town with interesting topography, the Old Squan Highlands, which are the highest point on the Atlantic Seaboard from Atlantic Highlands to the north all the way to Florida, commanding panoramic views of the ocean and the Manasquan River.

In 1922, the Manasquan River Golf Club purchased 150 acres of farmland and rolling hills sloping to an 1800-foot waterfront on the river.

A farmhouse, built in 1780, became the original clubhouse. It is believed to be the oldest building in the Met Area used as a golf clubhouse; today it is the ladies locker room.

For their golf course, the members, a mix of summertime and year-round residents, turned to Robert White. He built nine holes in the pastures and swampy meadowlands along the river, which opened for play in 1924, then a second nine (ready in 1926) in the elevated woodlands and laurel-laden ravines overlooking the river. It remains a course with a flavor unlike any other at the Jersey shore, presenting two distinct faces.

The second hole is ranked among the strongest par fours in the state. The hole rises gently through the drive zone, then angles slightly left and falls to a divided fairway separated from the elevated green by a wall of rough.

The featured hole is seven, a nearly 600-yard par five. A drive of 220 yards is necessary to cross a vegetation-filled ravine to reach the crest of a rising fairway that takes a steep plunge 150 yards from the green.

Manasquan River has had notable players among its members, including J. Wolcott Brown, winner of the New Jersey Amateur in 1928 and 1934, the United States Seniors in 1964, and three consecutive MGA Seniors (1967-1969). Long-time member Bob Housen is perhaps the most accomplished, winner of the 1976 Ike Championship (and three-time runner-up), six New Jersey Amateurs (1973, 1978, 1980, 1982, 1986, and 1993, the last at age 53), semifinalist in the 1993 U.S. Senior Amateur and 1981 U.S. Mid-Amateur, and low amateur in the 1988 and 1995 U.S. Senior Opens.

In 1990, the USGA Junior Girls came to Manasquan River. Vicki Goetze, who now plays the LPGA Tour and at the time was the defending U.S. Women's Amateur champion, failed to capture the one title that eluded her during a brilliant junior career. She was defeated 3&2 in the finals by Sandrine Mendiburu, a 17-year-old French girl who became the first foreign winner of the event. The three-time French Junior titleholder won the championship on the greens, taking just 22 putts over 16 holes. ❏

**MANASQUAN
RIVER GOLF CLUB**
Brielle, NJ

YEAR FOUNDED: 1922

ARCHITECT:
Robert White

COURSE OPENED: 1924

TEES	PAR	YARDAGE
Forward	74	5782
Middle	72	6480
Back	72	6703

TEES	COURSE RATING	SLOPE
Forward	74.1	129
Middle	71.5	126
Back	72.5	128

The par-three 15th, near the river.

MAPLEWOOD COUNTRY CLUB

"On The Tee"

The clubhouse overlooking the 18th green.

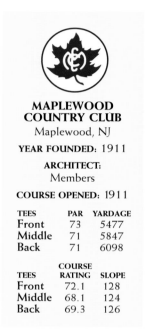

MAPLEWOOD COUNTRY CLUB
Maplewood, NJ

YEAR FOUNDED: 1911

ARCHITECT:
Members

COURSE OPENED: 1911

TEES	PAR	YARDAGE
Front	73	5477
Middle	71	5847
Back	71	6098

TEES	COURSE RATING	SLOPE
Front	72.1	128
Middle	68.1	124
Back	69.3	126

Every bit of golf paraphernalia must begin somewhere. Maplewood's claim to fame is that it was here that the tee made its debut, invented by a member.

In the game's early days, two buckets sat by each tee box, one containing sand, the other water. Using their hands, golfers took a pinch of sand and a few drops of water and formed a small mound on which they placed their ball. This tradition lasted for decades until 1921, when a 60-year-old New Jersey dentist, Dr. William Lowell, took up golf. The tee-building process roughened his hands, a poor condition for a member of his profession.

So Lowell went home one day after a round and whittled himself a wooden peg, cupped at the top. At first, even his playing companions scoffed at the idea. But Lowell persisted with his Reddy Tee, and soon son Ernest saw the business possibilities. The Lowells filed for a patent on May 5, 1922, the documentation stating that the tee was designed to "provide a neat and cheap teeing device, which can be carried in the pockets of players, preventing any soiling of the hands and doing away with the usual rubbing of the hands on the garments worn by the player."

The Lowells formed the Nueblo Manufacturing Company in New York City. Their break came after they gained the endorsement of trick-shot artist Joe Kirkwood

and the flamboyant Walter Hagen, who would stroll down tournament fairways with a Reddy Tee stuck jauntily behind one ear. The wooden tee has been a staple of the game ever since.

Lowell's Maplewood Country Club traces its roots to 1908 when a group of Maplewood residents banded together looking to provide recreational facilities for the youth of the community. They leased 11 acres where they converted a frame barn into a clubhouse. The Maplewood Field Club was formed in 1911 with a baseball diamond and a few golf holes. The golf facilities expanded piecemeal over the next decade, until a full 18-hole course (of unknown authorship) was in place at the end of 1921. The Club's name was changed to the Maplewood Country Club in 1920, and since then, the membership has come primarily from surrounding communities. It remains very much a "town club."

And Maplewood is very much an old-fashioned course, featuring blind shots, tree-lined fairways, and play up and down the centrally located hill.

The eighth is the signature hole, a narrow par three playing to a well-bunkered hilltop green, with a steep fall-off to the left. The 11th is a unique "double spectacles" hole, so-called because of the twin pair of "spectacle" bunkers, the first 50 yards short of the green, the second pair just in front of it. Also memorable is the blind tee shot to the two-tiered 17th fairway.

METUCHEN GOLF & COUNTRY CLUB

"An Electric Circuit"

METUCHEN GOLF & COUNTRY CLUB
Edison, NJ

YEAR FOUNDED: 1915

ARCHITECTS:
Marty O'Loughlin
Charles Laing

COURSE OPENED: 1931

TEES	PAR	YARDAGE
Forward	74	5725
Middle	72	6256
Back	72	6623

TEES	COURSE RATING	SLOPE
Forward	74.6	130
Middle	70.2	123
Back	71.9	126

Before the Metuchen Golf & Country Club was founded in 1915, Thomas Edison, inventor of the phonograph, telephone, incandescent lamp, long-life battery, and other labor-saving devices, played his own games on the land. His experimental electric railroad of 1880 ran along what is now the 15th fairway (roughly through the fairway bunkers toward those at the left of the green), finishing its ride at Pumptown Corners, across the street from where the clubhouse now stands. The Edison Tower, the great man's laboratory in nearby Menlo Park, is clearly visible from the golf course's seventh tee.

Twenty-five years later, the Club's founding members built an $800 clubhouse and a primitive nine-hole golf course, which was notable for its minimal maintenance. The greens were mowed just once a week, and the fairways only when the grass had grown so tall that the members couldn't find their balls.

In 1926, the Club purchased additional land. An 18-hole course was designed and built by Marty O'Loughlin, professional at Plainfield, and a Scot named Charles Laing, the Club's new professional/greenkeeper. The course was unveiled in 1931, with the course playing nine holes away from the clubhouse, then nine back in. The 13th was not the dogleg it is today, and the 14th was a par three across the water. After a reworking in 1953, 14 became the best-known hole, a 400-yard par four with a mature pin oak looming boldly in the middle of the fairway, 150 yards from the green.

The fairway is wider left of the tree, then rolls downhill, ending abruptly well short of the green, where rough left and a pond right intervene.

The land is rolling and heavily treed, but the principal feature of the course likely is the variety of its greens: Each is a different shape, all are contoured. There is even a double green (a la St. Andrews in Scotland), one of just two in the Met Area.

Among Metuchen's members is Al Paskowitz, who has made 27 aces in his career, all but one at his home course, despite suffering seven strokes since 1978. No golfer in the Met Area approaches Paskowitz's record for holes in one. ❍

Looking back from 14th green to the tree in the middle of the fairway.

MINISCEONGO GOLF CLUB
"Happy Valley"

Many Met Area courses are built on "historic acres," whether referring to the region's Native American heritage or its role during the Revolutionary War. Minisceongo's heritage cannot be found in the history books; rather, it is there on display, in the clubhouse and throughout the golf course. The Club is named for the creek that flows through the property.

The Club is the brainchild of local developer/builder

The dramatic 12th hole.

Eric Bergstol, who acquired the land in 1991. Nearly 300 years earlier, the property was a land grant from the King of England to the Concklin family, whose descendants are still in the region. Eventually the family farm and orchards were sold off, so only the family cemetery remained: It is enclosed within a stone wall located between the fourth and 17th fairways; tombstones date back to the 18th century.

The Concklin family cemetery on the fourth hole.

In the 1850s, the buildings became a refuge for children from Manhattan during a diphtheria epidemic. From 1911 to 1972, the Happy Valley Boarding School occupied the premises, giving orphans and other disadvantaged children exposure to an "agricultural education." Next came the Greer-Woodycrest School for the Developmentally Disabled, which closed its doors in 1991. Left behind are two huge stone cisterns (once used to water coach horses travelling between New York and Boston) which can be seen on the golf course, and prehistoric artifacts dating back to 7,000 BC, which are displayed in the clubhouse.

Bergstol engaged the British architect Roy Case, telling him to design a course that "showcases nature's beauty" while protecting the environment. The result, which opened in July, 1994, is a striking, target-style course, with forced carries of 190 to 230 yards on four holes (from the tips), and forests, vast expanses of wetland, and high fescue grass on several other holes. Five sets

MINISCEONGO GOLF CLUB
Pomona, NY

YEAR FOUNDED: 1993

ARCHITECT:
Roy Case

COURSE OPENED: 1994

TEES	PAR	YARDAGE
Forward	72	5475
Middle	72	6028
Back	72	6561

TEES	COURSE RATING	SLOPE
Forward	72.6	121
Middle	70.2	125
Back	72.3	135

of tees give the course flexibility, and allow golfers to choose the degree of challenge best suited to their own games.

The tee shot on the par-four 12th plays up and over an abandoned quarry. The approach heads downhill to a green set behind a pond across its left front. To many, the scene recalls Augusta National's Amen Corner.

The par-four 13th is the ultimate in target golf. The fairway is an island amidst a sea of wetlands; it's a demanding tee shot that must be threaded between trees. Beyond that, the hole angles left across more wetlands and rises to well-bunkered green.

From the back tees, the tee shot on the par-five 15th must carry 230 yards of wetlands. The hole turns sharply to the right at the end, calling for a carefully-placed second shot.

The 18th is a short par five with a stream crossing the fairway in the landing area. The hole gains character from a huge, straight-faced pot bunker at the front left of the green.

Minisceongo is a non-equity private club. The clubhouse is an expanded restoration of the school building/chapel that served a few of the property's earlier clients. ○

MONTAMMY GOLF CLUB

"Palisades Park"

During the 1960s, Ercole Tamburelli, a Bergen County real estate developer, decided to embellish his residential holdings atop the Palisades, 10 miles north of the George Washington Bridge, with three golf courses. Tammy Brook, operating on a lease from Tamburelli, was fully operational by 1964, but sold by his heirs for development in the mid 1980s. Montammy, an 18-hole layout, opened in 1966, followed quickly by Tamcrest, a nine-hole executive course. Besides his money, Tamburelli put a little bit of his name in each club.

Architect Frank Duane was given a splendid piece of property, with severe elevation changes typical of the Palisades but atypical of most New Jersey courses. Duane responded with a dramatic course, one that confronted the golfer with several blind shots and four greenside water hazards.

Among the most distinctive holes is the seventh, a moderate-length par four playing from an elevated tee. Water along the right eventually separates the fairway from the long, shallow green, which is set off to the right.

Montammy boasts a strong set of par threes. The most difficult is the fourth, which plays straight uphill over a large bunker guarding the right-to-left sloping green. The 14th is a short one-shotter with water in front and two bunkers on a rise behind the green.

The 15th is the toughest par on the course. Although relatively level, this par four hides a pond at the left front of the green.

For a number of years starting in the late 1970s, Montammy hosted a Pro-Am for the benefit of a number of local charities. PGA Tour professional D.A. Weibring established a competitive course–record 66 during one of these events. The Club also hosted the 1986 New Jersey PGA Championship, won by David Glenz.

Originally, Montammy was conceived as a men's club, but Tamburelli dropped that idea in favor of the arrangement that lasted 20 years—a private club leased to the membership with an option to buy: They exercised their option in 1986.

In 1996, a major renovation to the clubhouse included the lockerrooms and dining room. Added were the Montammy Room, a new dining facility overlooking the golf course, plus a fitness center, sports bar, and a new halfway house. The members also enjoy tennis and swimming.

MONTAMMY GOLF CLUB

Alpine, NJ

YEAR FOUNDED: 1966

ARCHITECT:
Frank Duane

COURSE OPENED: 1966

TEES	PAR	YARDAGE
Forward	73	5636
Middle	72	6299
Back	72	6691

TEES	COURSE RATING	SLOPE
Forward	73.3	126
Middle	70.5	130
Back	72.3	133

Looking back from the 7th green.

NAVESINK COUNTRY CLUB

"Putting On Ice"

The final two water crossings on the par-five 5th hole.

Only one golf club in New Jersey has an ice skating rink among its amenities. It is the Navesink Country Club in Middletown, just five miles from Atlantic Highlands on the Jersey Shore. It's an appropriate site for a rink because the receding glaciers formed Atlantic Highlands, the highest point on the Atlantic seaboard between Maine and Florida, the rolling nature of the terrain being a consequence.

The modern history of the property dates to 1911, when Amory L. Haskell sold 17 acres to his brother-in-law, Samuel Riker, a descendant of Abraham Van Rycken, after whom Riker's Island was named. Riker built the mansion that one day would become the Navesink clubhouse. He also adorned the grounds with formal gardens and a marble swimming pool and built the long, winding, tree-lined entranceway from Riverside Drive. There also was a glassed-in porch at the east end of the mansion from which Riker and his guests could watch the Americas Cup races, which were held in the ocean off Sandy Hook.

Riker owned 69 acres at his death in 1936, and subsequent owner Charles Lyon, a world-class sailor, expanded the estate to 115 acres, which he sold to the fledgling Navesink Country Club in 1963. Navesink had been conceived as a yearround family club, which set it apart from other clubs in the region at the time.

Hal Purdy designed the course, which was unveiled in 1964. Gaining the most attention were the side-by-side, twin par fives, the fifth and 15th, which cross the same water hazards. The fifth is shorter, but makes up with water what it lacks in length. The tee shot must carry 125 yards to clear the first of three water crossings and reach a narrow, tree-lined fairway. A carefully played second shot of 160 to 200 yards to the right of center will carry the second hazard and leave an open pitch of about 125 yards over a pond.

The fifteenth calls for a drive into the left center of the zigzag fairway to leave a straightaway second shot across the first water hazard to a narrow tree-lined fairway. The shot to the green must traverse a pond complete with fountain and stonework.

The LPGA Tour played the final two editions of the Chrysler-Plymouth Classic at Navesink in 1987 and 1988. Ayako Okamoto won in 1987 with a one-under-par total of 215, a score that was easily eclipsed by Nancy Lopez' scintillating 204 in 1988.

Navesink's clubhouse originally contained 12 luxuriously appointed guest rooms that proved an attraction to the performers who came to the nearby Garden State Arts Center. Many stayed at the Club, playing golf and staging impromptu performances for the members. Among those who roomed at Navesink were Bob Hope, Andy Williams, Pat Boone, Glen Campbell, Peter O'Toole, Rich Little, Johnny Mathis, Robert Goulet, Carol Lawrence, and the comedy team of Rowan & Martin. In typical Navesink fashion, all who visited enjoyed the warm hospitality of the members. ⟲

**NAVESINK
COUNTRY CLUB**
Middletown, NJ

YEAR FOUNDED: 1963

ARCHITECT:
Hal Purdy

COURSE OPENED: 1964

TEES	PAR	YARDAGE
Forward	73	5849
Middle	72	6442
Back	72	6716

TEES	COURSE RATING	SLOPE
Forward	75.8	132
Middle	71.5	126
Back	72.5	128

NORTH JERSEY COUNTRY CLUB

"Captain's Orders"

**NORTH JERSEY
COUNTRY CLUB**
Wayne, NJ

YEAR FOUNDED: 1894

ARCHITECT:
Walter Travis

COURSE OPENED: 1923

TEES	PAR	YARDAGE
Forward	72	5713
Middle	71	6224
Back	71	6540

TEES	COURSE RATING	SLOPE
Forward	74.0	128
Middle	70.7	127
Back	72.2	130

Captain Henry Hewat was among the first serious golfers in New Jersey. A Scotsman, he came to Paterson in 1892 after two years in Canada. He played at St. Andrew's in Yonkers, but the eight-hour round-trip made him wish for a nearby club of his own.

Hewat was an engineer. He'd come to Paterson, the hub of America's textile industry and center for heavy machine manufacturing, to work for Cooke Locomotive Works. His acquaintance with Charles Cooke soon placed Hewat in the leading social and sporting circles, and gained him the acquaintance of Garrett Hobart, later Vice President of the United States from 1897 to 1899 under William McKinley, the first American president to try golf (at Hobart's instigation); John Griggs, Governor of New Jersey (1896-1898) and Attorney General of the United States (1898-1901); and Colonel William Barbour and his cousin J.E. Barbour, whose grandfather was the world's largest manufacturer of linen thread.

*McKinley and Hobart
pictured in Patterson.*

Hewat and these men organized the Paterson Golf Club in April of 1894. They laid out a nine-hole course on a pie-wedge of land known as Chestnut Hill, overlooking the Passaic River. But they had to share the property with baseball players as well as flocks of grazing sheep and cattle that kept the grass short. Play started in March of 1895.

The name North Jersey was adopted in May of 1897. Later that year, the course was expanded to 18 holes with 13 new holes across the river on the Warren Point property of Thomas Barbour, William's father. The transition across the river was completed in 1899 when the original course was abandoned and the remaining new holes built at Warren Point. The Barbour homestead became the clubhouse.

In 1917, a fire destroyed the clubhouse and a proposal to build two new roads threatened to destroy the golf course. The Club purchased more than 200 acres of virgin woodland in Wayne Township five miles from Paterson.

Walter Travis was engaged to design a championship course, and work began late in 1921. Construction proved difficult. More than 30,000 trees were cut down, and the rock-laden terrain proved unyielding. The course was not ready until 1923, the same year a new fieldstone clubhouse, designed by Clifford Wendehack, opened.

Then as now, the course is noted for its rugged terrain, with a number of holes crossed in the drive zone by high ridges. The drive on the second, for example, must carry to the top of a ridge angling across the hole. From the ridge the hole rolls downhill to the green.

The 12th is one of the most unusual par fours in the Met Area. The drive must be played precisely to the top of a narrow landing area that is canted to the right. Beyond the crest, the hole drops nearly 100 feet toward a creek that angles in front of the green.

North Jersey's home hole calls for a long carry over a lake to a tightly bunkered landing area. Beyond the bunkers the hole rises sharply to a hidden fall-away green.

In recent years, the clubhouse has been renovated and expanded (while remaining faithful to the Wendehack style), a new golf course irrigation system installed, and the bunkering revised. North Jersey remains worthy of presidents, vice presidents, and governors. ○

The ninth green with clubhouse behind.

ORANGE COUNTY GOLF CLUB

"Battle Of Midway"

View across the bridge to the 2nd hole.

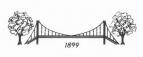

ORANGE COUNTY GOLF CLUB
Middletown, NY
YEAR FOUNDED: 1899
ARCHITECTS:
Members
Robert White
COURSE OPENED: 1899

TEES	PAR	YARDAGE
Forward	73	5927
Middle	72	6401
Back	72	6664

TEES	COURSE RATING	SLOPE
Forward	74.6	130
Middle	71.4	127
Back	72.6	129

Back in 1899, both Goshen and Middletown, neighboring towns seven miles apart, had their golf enthusiasts, although neither had enough to warrant its own course. So they pooled their resources, issuing a public call to all interested to a meeting on April 26 at Midway Park, halfway between the two towns on the trolley line connecting them, but across the Walkill River from the trolley stop.

More than 300 people, male and female, attended the meeting, where the Orange County Golf Club was formed. Henry Bacon, a former congressman, ran the proceedings and was elected the new club's first president, a position that was to be rotated biannually between the two towns. The Club leased some land in Midway Park and a house for annual rent of $450, and hired an "expert" at $40 a month to design a nine-hole golf course; bordered by tall hay, it was ready by the end of May.

In 1925, the Club purchased three plots of land east of the river and hired Robert White to design another nine holes (2 through 10) while revising the old ones. The Club also spent $7,800 for a suspension bridge to connect the two segments of the course. Both the bridge and the new holes opened in 1928. Since then, Albert Zikorus and Steve Esposito have made minor modifications to the course.

The original nine, the "Middletown side" west of the Walkill, features hilly terrain. Holes three through seven on the "Goshen side" are flat. Holes 8 and 10 are a mix, separated by the tough, sidehill ninth.

In fact, 9 and 10 are among the toughest back-to-back holes in the Met Area. Nine is a long, straight par four that slopes right to left from tee to green. Ten plays from an elevated tee to a fairway closely flanked by giant oaks.

Many of the holes feature elevated tees, set on natural perches over the heaving landscape. The most dramatic of these are at the second, which calls for a shot over the river; the tenth; a long par four, and the 14th, a reachable par five.

Number 16 is a short, "delight or disaster" par three, heavily bunkered with a steep drop-off to the right of the green. The 17th is a rolling par four lined with spruce trees and steep drop-offs.

The original clubhouse expanded over the years from a modest farmhouse to a large, attractive building. It was destroyed by fire in 1979; the modern replacement opened in 1981.

The trolley no longer operates, but Goshen and Middletown are closer than ever.

THE POWELTON CLUB

"Southern Comfort"

They came from Charleston and New Orleans in the summer, wealthy Southern planters in search of "good clean air." They arrived in New York by steamer, came up the Hudson, and were transported by coach to the a summer resort hotel called Powelton House, the former residence of Robert Powell. At the same time, Powell was assembling a tract of land that became known as Powelton Farms. The hotel was destroyed by fire in 1870.

The Powelton Lawn Tennis Club was organized in 1882 by Homer Ramsdell, who had assumed ownership of Powelton Farms, and became a charter member of the USLTA. Tennis (still thriving at the club) and its accompanying social life flourished during the 1880s. It was a time of elegance and manners, of grand parties and proper attire.

In 1892, the name was changed to The Powelton Club of Newburgh. A new clubhouse was built and baseball, croquet, bowling, and ballroom dancing were added to the Club's offerings. (That clubhouse was recently used in the movie "Nobody's Fool," starring Paul Newman.)

Club lore asserts that golf was first played in 1892 on a five-hole course designed by Ramsdell's mother, Maud, which would make her America's first female golf architect. The course was expanded to nine holes in the spring of 1897 by member James Taylor. Early golf reflected the origins of the property: Each member was allowed five days a week to play, but on the sixth day, he had to tend the cattle, keeping them off the course and cleaning up after them so that others might play.

Early member G.P. Tiffany; Jerry Travers' father-in-law.

In 1923, Devereux Emmet was retained to revise the original nine and lay out nine new holes.

Although not long, Powelton places a premium on accuracy. The short par fours offer strategic options that invite birdies, but often penalize with bogies or worse. The greens are a mixed bag, with some at ground level and flanked by flat bunkers, others elevated and fiercely guarded by large, deep hazards. The terrain can be severe, and water is a factor on 11 holes—a stream crossing the property feeds four ponds, including the one fronting the postcard par-three seventh hole.

The 12th is the toughest par at Powelton, a long par four ending at a green atop a hill, guarded by a wall of rough, and set on a right-to-left angle to the fairway.

Major alterations were needed in 1985, brought about by the expansion of Interstate 84. The most significant change worked by architects Cornish & Silva was a new 17th hole, ending the Club's use of its heirloom, the double tee that served the 16th and 17th holes. The highways now bring the golfers to Powelton, but that Southern tradition of hospitality remains.   ○

THE POWELTON CLUB
Newburgh, NY

YEAR FOUNDED: 1882

ARCHITECTS:
Members
Devereux Emmet
Geoffrey Cornish
Brian Silva

COURSE OPENED: 1897

TEES	PAR	YARDAGE
Forward	72	5558
Middle	70	6007

TEES	COURSE RATING	SLOPE
Forward	72.2	120
Middle	69.3	127

The devilishly difficult short par four 2nd hole.

PREAKNESS HILLS COUNTRY CLUB

"Horse Sense"

PREAKNESS HILLS COUNTRY CLUB
Wayne, NJ

YEAR FOUNDED: 1926

ARCHITECT:
Willie Tucker

COURSE OPENED: 1929

TEES	PAR	YARDAGE
Forward	72	5722
Middle	72	6429
Back	72	6654

TEES	COURSE RATING	SLOPE
Forward	73.4	132
Middle	71.6	127
Back	72.6	129

The name was taken from the racehorse Preakness, raced by cotton magnate Milton Sanford. Shortly after the Civil War, Sanford bought a farm near Paterson, converted it into a thoroughbred training center, and named it after the horse that established him in the racing game. The horse also gave his name to the middle jewel of the Triple Crown.

The Club was formed in 1926, when the 160-acre Frew estate was purchased. A brochure for prospective members made it clear that Preakness Hills was to be a family club. There would be membership classes for wives and children of members, and a separate tennis membership as well. There were two lakes on the property for bathing, boating, and fishing. One lake also would be used for ice skating, with tobogganing and skiing available on the grounds.

Willie Tucker was hired to design the golf course. Tucker had been a teenage golf professional in his native Surrey, England, then apprenticed in architecture under Willie Dunn. He came to the United States in 1895 to join his brother Sam, head professional at St. Andrew's. The Tucker brothers produced handmade golf clubs sold under the name "Defiance," while Willie, a turfgrass expert, installed and nurtured the turf at Yankee Stadium and the West Side Tennis Club in Forest Hills.

Preakness Hills is set on moderately hilly terrain with tight, tree-lined fairways. Water comes into play on seven holes. Greens are on the large side and individually shaped; many pitch from back to front.

The course is best known for its par threes. Six is the centerpiece, extremely narrow, 222 yards long, with a row of tall trees overhanging the right side, out-of-bounds and a creek bed in their shadows. A sole tree overhangs the left side, about halfway to the green. The putting surface is punctuated by a "burial mound" center rear.

And the home hole is a par three, which plays across a pond to a two-tiered, back-to-front green bunkered twice left, twice more behind, and once right. The putting surface is set in a natural amphitheater in front of the clubhouse.

The short par-four 13th is long on potential disaster. The green is set on a plateau 20 feet above the fairway, guarded by a patch of rough and a bunker short and right at the foot of the hill. The surface is two-tiered—the higher level is left and back—with three putts a foregone conclusion when coming downhill.

Extensive renovation has come to the clubhouse, course, and grounds in recent years. In 1992, *The Met Golfer* recognized the club for "best landscape and floral design."

In 1993, Preakness Hills hosted its first major championships, the Ike and the U.S. Senior Women's Amateur, the latter won by Anne Sander with a three-round score of 230, highest in 10 years. In the Ike, George Zahringer III fired a course-record 65 in the first round to establish a five-stroke lead he nursed to the end. ❍

The 18th hole and clubhouse.

RARITAN VALLEY COUNTRY CLUB

"As You Like It"

In November, 1911, U.S. Senator Joseph S. Frelinghuysen called a meeting at his Somerville estate, The Hill. That night, the Somerville Country Club was organized. It later acquired 151 acres of farmland across the street with a home near the present ninth tee that was converted into a clubhouse. The plan was to offer golf, shooting, tennis, ice skating, and social activities including open-air performances of Shakespeare. The name was changed in 1917 to acknowledge the broad base of the membership and reflect the beautiful countryside.

Work began three years later on the golf course, an 18-hole English-style layout designed by Herbert H. Barker. The holes were given fanciful names such as "Calamity" (number 2), "Majuba " (5, named for a hill in Africa), "Sondhyl" (10, Scottish for the sand hill upon which the green was built), and "Spion Kop" (18, for the numerous bunkers surrounding the old green, now the practice putting green). The picturesque water hole, number 7, was named "Barker" for the architect—it was his favorite.

Gently rolling and relatively short, Raritan Valley resists scoring with small, cleverly bunkered greens. The fourth is a short par four requiring a 150-yard carry over a large pond from an elevated tee. The green is tucked in a corner between a large bunker at the right front and a road on the left.

The seventh is the signature hole, and the second of consecutive par threes. A pond and a stone wall lurk between tee and green, much of which is hidden behind a pair of majestic trees. The sloping front of the green will reject a short shot, while bunkers left, right, and behind strengthen the defenses.

The 16th is the most memorable of Raritan Valley's long par fours, starting with a long water carry from the tee. A crossbunker is placed deceptively short of the

RARITAN VALLEY COUNTRY CLUB

Somerville, NJ

YEAR FOUNDED: 1911

ARCHITECT:
Herbert H. Barker

COURSE OPENED: 1912

TEES	PAR	YARDAGE
Forward	70	5428
Middle	70	6156
Back	70	6364

TEES	COURSE RATING	SLOPE
Forward	72.2	126
Middle	69.6	120
Back	70.5	122

Top: The postcard par-three 7th hole.
Above: The flower gardens at the front of the clubhouse.

green, and a bunker behind gives the appearance of having been cut from a dune.

The course is currently undergoing a major facelift. Four new holes are being built (12 through 14, plus 17).

Members today can enjoy four tennis courts, two squash courts near the ninth tee, and a new, Olympic-size swimming pool complete with water slide. The facilities may have taken on an American flavor, but the golf retains a distinctively old-English style.　❍

ROCK SPRING CLUB
"Prohibition Reaffirmed"

The third hole crossing an old quarry.

In 1887, the Orange Mountain Land Company acquired land at the top of First Mountain in West Orange for residential development. The Orange Mountain Cable Company ran two cable cars operating in a straight line up and down its rocky face. A hotel was built at the summit, offering a panoramic view of Manhattan and Newark, and visitors would drink from the many natural springs on the mountain, including Rock Spring (located near the present 17th tee).

In time, developers converted a swampy area into Cable Lake. They also built an amusement park that featured a merry-go-round, dance hall, carnivals, and wild-west shows—and apparently numerous boisterous parties. The cable cars were succeeded by trolleys, although the first one to attempt the climb slid down the hill into another, causing several fatalities.

Observing the scene from his home near the brow of the mountain was T.H. Powers Farr, a founder of the Essex County Country Club. A devout Baptist who eschewed the parties for which Prohibition became famous, Farr thought the land around Cable Lake would suit a new country club, and a dry one at that. In 1925, he and a group of friends organized the Rock Spring Country Club as a family club, facetiously called "The White Rock Club."

Rock Spring's golf course, which opened in 1928, was designed by Seth Raynor and built after his untimely death by Charles Banks. Its hazards are mild by their standards, but the bunkering-well below the putting surfaces and with steep grass faces-clearly identifies the designers.

The course packs its strongest punch early in the round. The opening hole calls for a 150-yard carry over a corner of Cable Lake. The average player will face a blind approach, downhill to a fall-away green. The lake comes into play again on the second hole, to the left from fairway to green.

The par-three third is a modified Redan supplemented by a scenic view of Manhattan off to the left. It calls for a good carry over a quarry that angles across the hole, finishing to the left of the sloping green, which is guarded by a large bunker across the left front.

Harold Baker, a former Rock Spring member, has earned a special place in the game's history. When faced with the news that a circulatory ailment in his legs would preclude his playing golf, Baker created the first golf cart, a revamped three-wheeled motorcycle that only moved forward and had no muffler. Baker and his "Roar of Rock Spring" were staples of the club scene for a number of years. Rock Spring members have always had a knack for doing things their own way. ❍

ROCK SPRING CLUB
West Orange, NJ

YEAR FOUNDED: 1925

ARCHITECT:
Charles Banks

COURSE OPENED: 1928

TEES	PAR	YARDAGE
Forward	75	6126
Middle	71	6445

TEES	COURSE RATING	SLOPE
Forward	75.3	132
Middle	71.1	124

ROCKAWAY RIVER COUNTRY CLUB

"A River Runs Through It"

**ROCKAWAY RIVER
COUNTRY CLUB**
Denville, NJ

YEAR FOUNDED: 1915

ARCHITECTS:
Tom Gourlay
Devereux Emmet

COURSE OPENED: 1916

TEES	PAR	YARDAGE
Forward	73	5504
Middle	72	6334
Back	72	6609

	COURSE	
TEES	RATING	SLOPE
Forward	72.4	126
Middle	70.5	125
Back	71.8	127

At the turn of the century, the far reaches of New Jersey were summer resort territory for men of means. So it was in Denville, situated in the foothills of the Poconos, in a picturesque valley through which the Rockaway River flowed.

Among the summer residents of Denville in 1915 was J. Henry Bacheller, a prominent banker and member of Baltusrol. But the long drive between Denville and Springfield was difficult and time-consuming, and so was planted the seed that flowered as the Rockaway River Country Club in 1915.

The original nine-hole course opened in 1916 on the west bank of the river, laid out by Tom Gourlay, a Scotsman who served as the Club's first professional. The present 10th, 11th, and 12th survive from that course, and its last two holes were later combined to create the 18th.

Plans to expand began unfolding in the early 1920s when the Club purchased land east of the river, including a small private cemetery, located to the left of the present first fairway and behind the eighth green. (The cemetery, once located next to a Methodist church that has since moved, is the final resting place for a number of Civil War veterans. The church retains the right to cross club property to decorate the tombstones each Memorial Day.)

Devereux Emmet built the new nine (the present front nine) and revamped the old. The finished 18 opened in 1923 and included the 660-yard 15th hole, perhaps the longest hole in the country at the time.

Today, Rockaway River features narrow, gently-rolling, tree-lined fairways and small greens. But it is water that makes the course, river and marshland that come into play on 12 holes.

The 12th hole packs enough danger into its 259 yards to have ruined many a promising round. The tee shot is played over a small pond, then up through a tight corridor of trees to a narrow fairway, with a potentially disastrous fall-off down a cliff to the right. The fairway ends 50 yards from the green, which is protected by seven bunkers.

Rockaway River parallels the left side of the home hole through the drive zone, then angles across the fairway. The final approach plays moderately uphill to a sloping green bunkered left, right, and behind.

For 30 years (1964-1994), the Club hosted the Dodge Open Charity Classic, which has a roster of winners that reads like a Who's Who of local golf professionals. The record score was Bruce Zabriski's 273 in 1990, when he became the only repeat winner. Other highlights include a four-way deadlock in 1985, won in a playoff by Jack Kiefer, and Billy Ziobro's 31-foot downhill putt on the 18th green to force a playoff (that he won) in 1971.

Rockaway River also has been the most frequent site of the MGA Junior over the years, hosting the nation's oldest junior championship seven times since 1974.

A name to know at the Club is Dante. Jim Dante served as Club professional for one year, 1920, the year his son Joseph was born. Jim was one of the founders of the NJPGA, while both father and son were excellent teachers, authoring best-selling instruction books. Joe Dante served as Rockaway River's professional for 36 years.

Among the members, Arthur Lynch, longtime MGA tournament official, received the MGA's Distinguished Service Award in 1988. ❍

The fairway bunkering on the long 15th hole.

ROCKLAND COUNTRY CLUB

"Country Roads"

**ROCKLAND
COUNTRY CLUB**
Sparkill, NY

YEAR FOUNDED: 1906

ARCHITECT:
Robert White
Alfred Tull

COURSE OPENED: 1930

TEES	PAR	YARDAGE
Forward	73	5663
Middle	71	6368
Back	71	6538

TEES	COURSE RATING	SLOPE
Forward	73.0	125
Middle	71.0	125
Back	71.8	127

Back in the days when Route 9W was just a dirt road and the only means of crossing the Hudson River above the city was a ferry, Rockland Country Club was a trailblazer. In the autumn of 1906, a group of 11 men, most of them New York City residents, gathered to discuss the possibility of establishing a club way out in the country where they might spend weekends hunting, fishing, and playing golf.

The Club was incorporated in November, 1906. The founders bought the Blauvelt Farm, which extended from the Hudson River to the land now occupied by the front nine. Henry Stark, greenkeeper at Englewood, the premier private golf club in the region at the time, was hired to build a nine-hole course that was ready, along with four tennis courts, by July of 1907.

Although additional land was purchased as early as 1910, it was almost two decades before the Club decided to expand the course to 18 holes. Robert White laid out what proved to be an entirely new golf course, which was ready for play in 1930. Perhaps only the present third green, which was approached originally from the direction of the 16th fairway, remains from Stark's original nine-holer.

Befitting a course on the western ledge of the Palisades, the land tumbles and falls. From its high point along a ridge that runs north to south, golfers can see for miles into Rockland County. But they'll rarely see a level lie, playing up, down, and along the ridge for most of the round.

The ninth is a short par four calling for a carry of 150 yards across a lake to a rising fairway that alternately falls off to both sides. Mounds just in front of the green leave a narrow alley in and often hide the flag. Shots too long can find the highway.

Number 12 is a long, treacherous par four, starting from an elevated tee, dropping into a valley, then climbing to a slick, two-tiered green. Thick trees line the right side out-of-bounds, with more trees on the left trimming the margin of error perceptibly.

A major change was made to the course in 1963 for reasons of safety. Until then, the eighth and ninth holes had been on the east side of the highway, playing to and from the river, with the ninth tee on a bluff, just 20 feet from the water's edge. But crossing the busy highway became increasingly dangerous, so the Club sold all but its present practice area east of the road to the Palisades Parkway Commission, and purchased acreage to the south on which the present 12th and 13th holes were built by architect Alfred Tull. Two difficult greens, the 15th and 17th, were rebuilt by Stephen Kay in 1995 as part of a master plan expected to carry the Club into the 21st century.

The most prominent and long-serving of Rockland's professionals was Ray Jamieson (1960-1985), whose driver may be worthy of a place in the Hall of Fame. Jamieson was an assistant to George Jacobus at Ridgewood in 1935, as was Byron Nelson, who later hired Jamieson as his own assistant at Inverness in Toledo, Ohio. One day, Nelson asked to borrow Jamieson's brand-new driver. That was the club Nelson used to forge his record-setting streak of 11 consecutive wins in 1945. Jamieson never did get it back.   ○

The 10th hole.

SHACKAMAXON GOLF & COUNTRY CLUB

"Back From The Depths"

It has fallen from the heights, then risen from the depths. Once in the forefront of Jersey clubs, Shackamaxon became an unwanted, bedraggled daily fee course. Then it rose to its former glory once again.

Robert W. Nelson wanted to build a private club on his family's farm in Westfield in 1915. He turned to A.W. Tillinghast, who designed a course known for velvet fairways, greens, and tees. Shackamaxon is Tillie's oldest enduring course in the Met Area.

At the center of the course and the Club's activities is a natural lake that was used for canoeing, fishing, and ice skating, and now encircles the tennis and swimming facilities. The lake also feeds the nine water crossings on the course.

The ninth hole is something special, a dogleg-left par four with two water carries. The drive must carry the lake before finding a rising fairway. The approach shot is blind, going back downhill to an island green, one of the first in this country.

The par-three 17th also plays over the lake, which cuts across on a right-to-left angle and passes the left side of the green.

Nelson built the three-story clapboard clubhouse specifically for the Club. Of its original 30 rooms, 15 were for the use of members who lived in New York City and spent weekends at the Club.

SHACKAMAXON GOLF & COUNTRY CLUB
Westfield, NJ

YEAR FOUNDED: 1915

ARCHITECT:
A.W. Tillinghast

COURSE OPENED: 1916

TEES	PAR	YARDAGE
Forward	73	5735
Middle	72	6386
Back	72	6592

TEES	COURSE RATING	SLOPE
Forward	74.4	131
Middle	70.5	124
Back	71.4	126

The 1928 Met Open was held at Shackamaxon. Tommy Armour, the previous year's U.S. Open champion, led all the way, but had to hold off a late charge by that year's Open champion, Johnny Farrell.

Shackamaxon fell victim to the Depression and was sold in 1941. After the clubhouse was destroyed by fire in 1942, the course opened to the public, then was leased to a number of private memberships and featured a new clubhouse and the state's largest club-operated swimming pool.

Bobby Cruickshank, Shackamaxon professional in the 1920's.

The resurgence began in 1953 with the inaugural edition of the LPGA's Triangle Round Robin, a 90-hole competition scored by points rather than strokes and restricted to a select field of 16. Jackie Pung came out on top despite shooting the fourth-best overall score.

In 1955 came the Cavalcade of Golf, the first PGA Tour event in New Jersey. The $50,000 purse attracted the game's biggest names. Reigning Masters champion Cary Middlecoff edged Sam Snead by one stroke, starting and ending his final round with eagle threes (on the resequenced course).

The local amateur circuit concludes each season at Shackamaxon with the Gregory Boff Invitational, honoring a prominent young local player (and Shackamaxon member) who died in a 1989 automobile accident.

What proved to be Shackamaxon's ultimate salvation was intended to be its demise. Philip Levin, a well-known lawyer, president of Madison Square Garden, and developer of shopping malls, purchased the Club in 1963, planning to trade it to the Suburban Golf Club in exchange for their property, where he hoped to build a shopping center. When Suburban turned him down, Levin accepted the challenge of restoring Shackamaxon to its former glory. ○

The island-green 9th as it appeared during the 1928 Met Open.

Spook Rock Golf Course

"Indian Vengeance"

TOWN OF RAMAPO
Department of Parks & Recreation

SPOOK ROCK GOLF COURSE
Suffern, NY
YEAR FOUNDED: 1967
ARCHITECT:
Frank Duane
COURSE OPENED: 1969

TEES	PAR	YARDAGE
Forward	72	4855
Middle	72	6366
Back	72	6894

TEES	COURSE RATING	SLOPE
Forward	73.4	128
Middle	70.3	125
Back	72.7	127

According to Indian legend, the "Spook Rock" marks the grave of an Indian princess who was murdered by white settlers. Every full moon, it is said, the ghost of the princess rises from her grave and haunts the descendants of her slayers. There really is a "Spook Rock," but it is located near the intersection of Airmont Road and Spook Rock Road, in the Village of Suffern, a half mile from the golf course that shares its name.

The course was the brainchild of Ramapo Director of Parks and Recreation Angelo Palermo in the mid 1960s, and approved by the Town Board in 1967. Three tracts of land were obtained and Frank Duane engaged to do the design. The first nine opened in the fall of 1969, with the full 18 ready by early 1970. Other facilities include an illuminated practice range and a practice putting green and bunker. Spook Rock is always finely manicured, making it worthy of its ranking among the nation's best public courses.

The course is located in a picturesque setting in the foothills of the Ramapo Mountains. Duane used the moderately hilly terrain well.

Marty Bohen, the 1976 and 1977 Met Open champion.

On several of the more scenic holes, the green cannot be seen from the tee. Unlike most other public layouts, the fairways are contoured, while most of the greens slope back to front and are bunkered at the front corners.

The par-five 11th is unforgettable. The elevated tee offers a beautiful vista of the mountains, with the angled fairway hidden in the valley below; after hitting their second shots towards a green protected by a pond at the left-front corner, golfers ring a bell to signal those at the tee that the fairway is clear.

Since 1984, the professional has been Marty Bohen, whose credits include back-to-back Met Open titles in 1976 and 1977. In the former, Bohen topped Jimmy Wright and Lloyd Monroe with a 35-foot birdie putt from the back fringe on Upper Montclair's famous 3 South, the final hole of a three-hole-aggregate playoff.

Spook Rock has hosted the MGA Public Links Championship three times—1987, 1990, and 1994—for the safety of the players, never coinciding with a full moon.

Above: The real "Spook Rock".

Left: The rock in the left side of the sixth fairway.

SPRING BROOK COUNTRY CLUB

"Triple Dip"

The tenth, middle hole of Spring Brook's unique threesome.

As the Roaring '20s started, the Morris County Golf Club was a thriving institution, with a new clubhouse, golf course, and a long waiting list. A group of locals decided it was time to build a second golf club in Morristown, so they leased part of the estate of banker Robert D. Foote, who took great interest in the Club and did much to insure its success prior to his death in 1924.

The new Club chose Robert Hucknell to design their course, and he responded with a challenging, albeit short, layout that opened in 1923 and has changed little over the years. The name honors the brook that meanders across the property, feeding a large pond that provides the backdrop for three consecutive outstanding par-threes—holes 9 through 11—all over water. In 1924, *Metropolitan Golfer* called the 10th the "finest water hole in the Met district."

Playing into the prevailing breeze, 10 is all carry from an waterside tee to a bowl-shaped green perched at water's edge with no bailout area for the weak-hearted. The green, wider than it is deep, also is hemmed in by five bunkers, one in front, one at each side, and two behind.

Of the longer holes, the most notable is the 13th, a long uphill par four with a lateral hazard along the left side that eventually crosses the fairway beyond the drive zone. The undulating, crowned green is the largest and most interesting putting surface on the course.

Over the years, Spring Brook has hosted five state championships-the New Jersey Open four times, and the NJPGA Championship once. The winners, respectively, were Stan Mosel, Al Mengert, Babe Lichardus, Art Silvestrone, and Emery Thomas, all top players.

The clubhouse was built in 1923 on the highest point of the property. A swimming pool was added in 1954, tennis and paddle courts in 1974. On January 6, 1996, the roof of the formal dining room collapsed under the weight of a blizzard's snow, and the Club decided at that point to demolish the old building and construct a new home overlooking the pond and Spring Brook's unique threesome. ○

SPRING BROOK COUNTRY CLUB
Morristown, NJ

YEAR FOUNDED: 1921

ARCHITECT:
Robert Hucknell

COURSE OPENED: 1922

TEES	PAR	YARDAGE
Forward	72	5398
Middle	70	6252
Back	70	6504

TEES	COURSE RATING	SLOPE
Forward	72.5	126
Middle	71.4	128
Back	72.6	130

SPRING LAKE GOLF CLUB

"Appellation Spring"

The short tenth.

In the last quarter of the 19th century, Spring Lake and neighboring Spring Lake Heights became fashionable summering grounds for New York industrialists who built palatial summer homes there. The New York & Long Branch Railroad reached the area in 1873, encouraging these same men to establish the Spring Lake Beach Improvement Company to promote the new seaside resort. They built a luxurious hotel—the Monmouth House—on the oceanfront, and in 1898 they laid out nine golf holes, which they named "Anticipation," "Desperation," "Trepidation," "Botheration," "Prostration," "Exasperation," "Darnation," "Aspiration," and "Culmination."

Spring Lake grew in popularity in the new century, and housing began to crowd the golf course. In 1909, the club purchased a 118-acre farm in Spring Lake Heights, and engaged George Thomas to design what would be his only Met Area course. Thomas, whose work included Riviera, Los Angeles, and Bel-Air, all in southern California, finished the course in 1911.

Spring Lake is marked by a stream flowing through a barranca that cuts across six holes, including four on an otherwise gently-rolling back nine. The front side is more rugged. Thomas' signature is the greenside bunkering; these hazards are shaped like a bathtub, sunken in the middle and raised on all sides.

The third is a long par five with out-of-bounds on the right. A steep rise crosses the fairway, giving the player the option of laying up short to a bowl-like landing area bunkered short-right and long-left, or attempting to clear the rise for a much shorter and visible third shot. A gully guards the plateau green, which is bunkered on the right.

The 12th is a par five that tempts long hitters to go for the green in two, but requires a heroic second over a pond. A big drive will ride a crest in the fairway, adding considerable yardage. The conservative player can lay up over a second crest, leaving an approach of perhaps 150 yards over water. The large elevated green tilts back to front.

The 17th is a strong dogleg-left that plays over water and a cross bunker to a fairway that bends around a 150-yard-long waste bunker on the left side.

The course gained instant recognition in 1912 when the summer White House was located at the nearby Sea Girt National Guard Encampment. President Woodrow Wilson was a frequent visitor to the Club that summer.

Byron Nelson also figures in Club history, winning the Spring Lake Calcutta in 1945. Thought to be the largest Calcutta in the country, it was held from 1939 through 1945, by which time the betting pool amounted to $73,000. Nelson shot 69-71=140 to edge Sam Snead and Herman Barron by one stroke. That year was the last of Nelson's brilliant career: He won 18 of the 30 tournaments he entered, including a record 11 in a row. Spring Lake actually was his 12th straight victory, but it wasn't considered official. In 1981, Spring Lake hosted the U.S. Women's Senior Amateur, won by Dot Porter of Cinnaminson, New Jersey. ○

**SPRING LAKE
GOLF CLUB**
Spring Lake Heights, NJ

YEAR FOUNDED: 1898

ARCHITECT:
George Thomas

COURSE OPENED: 1911

TEES	PAR	YARDAGE
Forward	72	5544
Middle	72	6178
Back	72	6364

TEES	COURSE RATING	SLOPE
Forward	72.3	123
Middle	70.1	120
Back	71.0	122

Byron Nelson

SPRINGDALE GOLF CLUB

"Academic Excellence"

**SPRINGDALE
GOLF CLUB**
Princeton, NJ

YEAR FOUNDED: 1895

ARCHITECTS:
Willie Dunn
Howard Toomey &
William Flynn

COURSE OPENED: 1902

TEES	PAR	YARDAGE
Forward	72	5655
Middle	71	6017
Back	71	6380

TEES	COURSE RATING	SLOPE
Forward	73.1	126
Middle	69.2	125
Back	70.8	128

No school has won the MGA Intercollegiate team title more often than Princeton University (15 times), and for good reason. Excepting Rutgers and West Point, no other Met Area college has a golf course on campus. Springdale Golf Club is on the grounds of Princeton, but it actually is a private club. Its $1-per-year lease from the University stipulates that students and faculty may play on weekdays on a daily-fee basis.

Its grounds are truly historic. The final stages of the Battle of Princeton took place in front of the present clubhouse in 1777. That skirmish and the Battle of Trenton that preceded it were turning points in strategy and morale in the war for independence, allowing the Americans to escape to the safety of Morristown for the winter.

The battle-site course is the second in Princeton history. The Club was originally organized as the Princeton Golf Club in 1895 by a group of young professors, with a nine-hole course about a mile from the present site. It was little more than a glorified pasture, complete with grazing cattle. In 1899, a group of alumni purchased the present property and engaged Willie Dunn to design an 18-hole golf course. Nine holes were ready for the 1902 season. The Club's name was changed to Springdale circa 1913.

The present clubhouse, formerly the tenant farmer's home, was a gift from the Class of 1886. Previously situated behind the sixth green, it was moved about 1913 so as not to interfere with the aesthetics of Cleveland Tower at the Graduate College.

The second nine was built in 1914, according to Dunn's plans, by Club professional Peter Eagen. The course was totally revised before 1928 by Howard Toomey and William Flynn, who had assisted Hugh Wilson in the construction of Merion in 1925 and were about to begin work on the present course at Shinnecock Hills (1929-1931).

Springdale is short by modern standards. But its greens are small and narrow—and tightly bunkered. The 12th hole, one of the many good par fours, turns right and rolls downhill, toward a brook crossing well short of the green. A tall tree overhanging the right side can force the golfer who hasn't hit the perfect left-of-center drive to lay up short of the water.

Equally challenging is the 17th. From an elevated tee, it curves and slopes to the right, while flirting with a brook that continues up the right amongst the willows.

Among the alumni of Princeton's golf team is Eugene Homans, runner-up to Bobby Jones in the 1930 U.S. Amateur, last leg of Jones' Grand Slam; George Dunlap, winner of the 1933 U.S. Amateur; and Bill Campbell, the 1964 U.S. Amateur champ who was president of the USGA (1982-1983) and is one of just a few Americans elected Captain of the Royal & Ancient Golf Club at St. Andrews, Scotland. All benefitted from an outstanding academic and athletic program at Princeton.

The 6th green, with the Cleveland Tower in background.

SUBURBAN GOLF CLUB
"They Shoot Turkeys, Don't They?"

Many of America's older golf clubs evolved from organizations founded for other purposes. The Suburban Club of Elizabeth was organized in 1896 as a gun club, although it did have two tennis courts and five golf holes. But its main activity was trapshooting, with the members often using live targets, primarily turkeys.

Suburban's original location was at the intersection of Morris and Colonial Avenues. This was historic territory, once the playground of the local tribe of the Leni Lenape nation. In fact, the eighth green was once used as a lookout, and the sixth green covered an old Indian burial ground.

There also was Revolutionary history. British soldiers marched up Colonial Avenue in 1777 as they pursued Washington and his army from New York to Trenton, hoping to trap the Americans at the Delaware River and squelch the uprising.

A century later, in 1896, the Suburban Club was founded on farmland three miles from the Elizabeth railroad station, accessible by a special stage coach. A roadhouse known as Park Villa was used as a clubhouse, but burned down in 1900. At that time, additional acreage was leased and the course expanded from five to nine holes despite the owner's demand that golf not be played on the property on Sundays. A farmhouse on the property became the clubhouse.

As the years passed, the Club acquired additional land and eventually hired A.W. Tillinghast, who responded with a relatively short 18-hole course that opened in 1922.

Suburban flourished. The Club had its own station on the Morris County Traction Line, a trolley that ran along Morris Avenue. The land across Colonial Avenue was acquired in 1924, and Tillinghast built three new holes there that opened the next year. The present name was adopted in 1927, by which time the golf course had assumed its present configuration. (The pond on the fifth hole was the inspiration of Hal Purdy in the 1980s.)

Suburban is a hidden gem, a challenging, but lovely, parkland course that rolls through significant undulations along fairways lined by beautiful mature trees.

The fifth is a picturesque, short par five offering the challenge of going for the green in two over water. The hole turns right, with a tall tree at the corner. A lake flanks the left side of the hole from 150 yards in and extends in front of the green. The elevated two-tiered putting surface is set above three bunkers.

The seventh is a short par four that calls for precision to avoid being blocked by trees on the approach. The tee is elevated, with trees overhanging the right side preventing a draw, so the tee shot is usually played with an iron to a two-tiered landing area. A slight incline at the front of the green prevents a roll-on approach.

Suburban concludes with an outstanding par four. The fairway rises gradually to a crest 190 yards from home, then cascades down three tiers to the green. The solid tee shot drive will find the first tier; long hitters may reach the second. Glance back up the fairway after putting out, and the Tillinghast artistry is ever present. ❍

SUBURBAN GOLF CLUB
Union, NJ

YEAR FOUNDED: 1896

ARCHITECT:
A.W. Tillinghast

COURSE OPENED: 1922

TEES	PAR	YARDAGE
Forward	72	5701
Middle	71	6123
Back	71	6426

TEES	COURSE RATING	SLOPE
Forward	73.6	125
Middle	69.8	127
Back	71.2	129

Suburban's picturesque finishing hole.

TWIN BROOKS COUNTRY CLUB

"Twin Towers"

View from behind the 18th green.

Today's Twin Brooks is a fourth-generation descendant of the Park Golf Club of Plainfield, which came to be in 1898. That Club had a nine-hole, Tom Bendelow-designed course located at the foot of the Watchung Mountains. The Club's golfers eventually broke away and formed a new club called Hydewood while continuing to play on the original course.

In 1926, Hydewood purchased a 178-acre dairy farm, built a new 18-hole course (architect unknown), and changed its name to Watchung Valley. The course was set in a rolling valley at the foot of the mountains, near the new highway (Route 22) built to connect the area with the Holland Tunnel. Three years later, Clifford C. Wendehack was hired to transform the clubhouse—a small, converted stable with a silo—into a sparkling example of French Medieval architecture, with twin towers. The project received lots of attention, but the Depression intervened and the Club's fortunes took a turn for the worse.

David Cronheim, a local realtor and avid golfer, bought the Club in a foreclosure sale in 1945 and renamed it Twin Brooks in recognition of two streams on the property. When Cronheim died in 1959, his son and daughter took over the operation. It remains a family-run private club: the members have no equity nor say in establishing fees and dues, but they do elect the board and run the golf and social programs.

The course plays over rolling terrain at the foot of the mountains, with several holes playing directly into or away from the mountainside.

The par-four eight hole requires a good poke to reach the two bunkers in the elbow of the left-bending dogleg. From there, golfers have a look at the green set below on a peninsula, surrounded on all but the right side by water.

The tee shot on the dogleg-right, par-four 12th must carry wetlands before finding a rolling fairway. One of the course's two brooks crosses halfway to the green, and a tall willow on the right side forces play to the left side. The elevated green is rimmed by seven bunkers.

The home hole, a long par five, is the Club's best known. Shots must flirt with wetlands just off the tee and a pond well down in the fairway; long hitters will have to deal with the pond on their second shots, average golfers on the third. The final 150 yards play uphill to a back-to-front-sloping green.

In the late 1980s, Twin Brooks added a ballroom that allows for hosting outside functions as well as satisfying the members' social needs. ◔

TWIN BROOKS COUNTRY CLUB
Watchung, NJ

YEAR FOUNDED: 1898

ARCHITECT:
Unknown

COURSE OPENED: 1926

TEES	PAR	YARDAGE
Forward	73	6132
Middle	71	6612
Back	71	6672

TEES	COURSE RATING	SLOPE
Forward	73.5	130
Middle	71.0	123
Back	72.4	126

WHITE BEECHES GOLF & COUNTRY CLUB

"From One Mayor To Another"

The seed that flowered as White Beeches was planted before the turn of the century, when the Country & Polo Club of Haworth built the first golf holes in the area. The Club was reorganized in 1902 as the Haworth Club by William McCulloch, the town's first mayor. The nine-hole course, designed by Val Flood, a Van Cortlandt Park player, featured a par three with an island green located near the present 17th green.

The Club dreamed of adding nine holes for a number of years, all the while coveting the nine-hole course across the street on the grounds of the summer home of former New York City mayor Hugh Grant. After Grant's death in 1910, the club attempted to lease that course; the merged course formally opened in 1915.

The original Haworth course encircled the clubhouse and numerous residences. The Grant course ran from near the present 10th green and 11th tee (where the Grant mansion once stood) to the top of Snake Hill, site of the present 7th and 14th greens. In 1915, two new holes were built joining the two nines, both of which were revised to form an 18-hole course. Over the next few years, additional changes were made under the supervision of Walter Travis.

The Club was reorganized for the 1919 season, when the name White Beeches was adopted in recognition of the many trees on the property. The 15th, 16th, and 17th holes were designed by Alfred Tull in 1950, bringing the course to its present configuration.

White Beeches is a beautiful, yet challenging, parkland course. No hole typifies this better than the fourth, a dogleg-left par four that requires strategic play around four trees. The first pair stands on the left side of the fairway, dictating a drive right of center—but not too far right, or else a third tree at the right-front of the green will block the approach. A fourth tree overhangs the left side of the sloping green.

Maureen Orcutt

A brook crosses the fairway on the par-five 11th hole 130 yards from home, then winds along the right side. The average player faces a difficult decision on his second shot, whether to lay up short of the water or attempt to carry it onto the left branch of the fairway.

The 18th is a long par three demanding a 150-yard carry over a pond. The long, narrow green rises to a plateau at the back and is flanked by two bunkers left and a complex of bunkers right, including two pots.

White Beeches is best known as the home club of Maureen Orcutt, 10-time winner of the WMGA Match-Play Championship and winner of everything in women's golf except the national championship, in which she was runner-up in 1927 and 1936. Orcutt also finished second in the White Beeches men's club championship at age 17. Once a golf writer for *The New York Times*, Orcutt's playing days lasted more than 40 years, during which time she won three Pinehurst's North & South, two Canadian Amateurs, and the prestigious Doherty Cup. Her career culminated with a victory in the 1966 U.S. Women's Senior Amateur. ❍

WHITE BEECHES GOLF & COUNTRY CLUB
Haworth, NJ

YEAR FOUNDED: 1902

ARCHITECTS:
Val Flood
Walter Travis
Alfred Tull

COURSE OPENED: 1915

TEES	PAR	YARDAGE
Forward	74	5756
Middle	72	6265
Back	72	6583

TEES	COURSE RATING	SLOPE
Forward	73.0	129
Middle	70.0	126
Back	71.5	129

The watery 18th.

APPLE RIDGE COUNTRY CLUB
Mahwah, NJ

YEAR FOUNDED: 1966

ARCHITECT:
Hal Purdy

COURSE OPENED: 1966

Built within the pleasant, rolling acreage of a working apple orchard, a number of trees are still pruned and harvested, providing players with delicious, seasonal snacks. Memorable holes here include the 2nd, a par four with a tall, oft-struck hardwood in the landing area, and the 13th, a tough par four.

TEES	PAR	YARDAGE
Forward	73	5734
Middle	71	6244
Back	71	6624

TEES	COURSE RATING	SLOPE
Forward	72.0	123
Middle	70.4	121
Back	72.2	124

BEAVER BROOK COUNTRY CLUB
Clinton, NJ

YEAR FOUNDED: 1965

ARCHITECT:
Alec Ternyei

COURSE OPENED: 1965

Beaver Brook features narrow fairways on hilly, rolling terrain. The fine condition of the greens may be a carryover from its days as a private layout. It's a strong test from the long tees.

TEES	PAR	YARDAGE
Forward	72	5283
Middle	71	6149
Back	71	6523

TEES	COURSE RATING	SLOPE
Forward	70.4	116
Middle	69.8	118
Back	71.6	122

BAMM HOLLOW COUNTRY CLUB
Lincroft, NJ

YEAR FOUNDED: 1959

ARCHITECT:
Hal Purdy

COURSE OPENED: 1961

Each of the three nines provides a uniform challenge with the White nine being a little stronger. Large greens, plentiful trees, rolling hills, a handful of water holes and a meandering creek combine to make this a very scenic place. Announcer Jim Nantz honed his game here as a youth.

RED-WHITE COURSE

TEES	PAR	YARDAGE
Forward	72	5857
Middle	72	6529
Back	72	6969

TEES	COURSE RATING	SLOPE
Forward	74.7	130
Middle	70.7	123
Back	72.7	127

WHITE-BLUE COURSE

TEES	PAR	YARDAGE
Forward	74	5833
Middle	72	6533
Back	72	6907

TEES	COURSE RATING	SLOPE
Forward	74.6	130
Middle	70.8	123
Back	72.5	127

BLUE-RED COURSE

TEES	PAR	YARDAGE
Forward	74	5768
Middle	72	6354
Back	72	6702

TEES	COURSE RATING	SLOPE
Forward	74.5	129
Middle	69.7	118
Back	71.2	121

BATTLEGROUND COUNTRY CLUB
Tennent, NJ

YEAR FOUNDED: 1967

ARCHITECT:
Hal Purdy

COURSE OPENED: 1967

The course is near Battleground State Park, which commemorates the Battle of Monmouth in the Revolution. This long, mature, tree-lined, central New Jersey layout occupies a former apple orchard, many trees of which still adorn the landscape. The rolling countryside also challenges with water on eight holes.

TEES	PAR	YARDAGE
Forward	72	5578
Middle	72	6749
Back	72	7117

TEES	COURSE RATING	SLOPE
Forward	72.3	122
Middle	72.1	123
Back	73.4	126

THE BEDENS BROOK CLUB
Skillman, NJ

YEAR FOUNDED: 1963

ARCHITECT:
Dick Wilson

COURSE OPENED: 1964

Architect Dick Wilson's only New Jersey course was one of his last. The two nines have contrasting styles with the front open and the back cut through forest. The large greens are cunningly bunkered with narrow openings. Bedens Brook itself crosses the signature 3rd hole twice.

TEES	PAR	YARDAGE
Forward	73	5571
Middle	72	6484
Back	72	6780

TEES	COURSE RATING	SLOPE
Forward	72.6	128
Middle	71.9	131
Back	73.2	134

BEACON HILL COUNTRY CLUB
Atlantic Highlands, NJ

YEAR FOUNDED: 1899

ARCHITECT:
Seymour Dunn

COURSE OPENED: 1899

The club started as The Highland Club of Atlantic Highlands, a social club, which added a nine-hole course in 1899 and changed its name to Highland Golf Club. Incorporated as Monmouth County Country Club in 1915, it adopted the Beacon Hill name in 1919, and expanded to 18 holes in 1962. Views of lower Manhattan, Brooklyn and Raritan Bay are among the sights.

TEES	PAR	YARDAGE
Forward	71	5454
Middle	71	5847
Back	71	6189

TEES	COURSE RATING	SLOPE
Forward	72.3	128
Middle	69.1	123
Back	70.2	124

BOWLING GREEN GOLF & TENNIS CLUB
Milton, NJ

YEAR FOUNDED: 1966

ARCHITECT:
Geoffrey Cornish

COURSE OPENED: 1966

Bowling Green's demanding public access course has hosted numerous MGA and NJSGA events. Its rolling fairways are framed by towering red pines. It features large undulating greens and water comes into play on six holes.

TEES	PAR	YARDAGE
Forward	72	4875
Middle	72	6224
Back	72	6689

TEES	COURSE RATING	SLOPE
Forward	69.4	122
Middle	70.3	126
Back	72.4	131

BROADACRES
GOLF CLUB
Orangeburg, NY

YEAR FOUNDED: 1962

ARCHITECTS:
H. Blaisdell & V. Margiotta

COURSE OPENED: 1962

*The name Broadacres for this nine
holer at Rockland Psychiatric
Center is misleading. Its fairways
are among the tightest in Rockland
County. It features one of
Rockland's most difficult holes—
the third plays 223 yards,
uphill to a small green.
Since 1993 it has operated as a
semi-private course.*

TEES	PAR	YARDAGE
Forward	35	2624
Middle	35	3047
Back	35	3138

TEES	COURSE RATING	SLOPE
Forward	70.4	121
Middle	69.6	124
Back	70.4	126

CEDAR HILL GOLF
& COUNTRY CLUB
Livingston, NJ

YEAR FOUNDED: 1921

ARCHITECT:
Nicholas Psiahas

COURSE OPENED: 1921

*Cedar Hill is the successor of Cedar
Ridge (1932-42), which closed its
doors for two years during WWII.
It reopened as Cedar Hill in 1945.
The picturesque course features
"twin" par 3s—the 10th, playing
straight downhill and the 16th,
recapturing the clubhouse level.*

TEES	PAR	YARDAGE
Forward	73	5508
Middle	71	6092
Back	71	6403

TEES	COURSE RATING	SLOPE
Forward	72.7	126
Middle	69.9	124
Back	71.4	126

CENTRAL VALLEY
GOLF CLUB
Central Valley, NY

YEAR FOUNDED: 1968

ARCHITECT:
Hal Purdy

COURSE OPENED: 1968

*Hal Purdy added nine holes to the
existing course in 1969. The new
holes uncovered decidedly more
dramatic terrain than that of the
older nine with several fairways
running straight up and down steep
hills. The sixth hole, a long,
flat dogleg left with out-of-bounds
left and a tiny green is the most
difficult hole.*

TEES	PAR	YARDAGE
Forward	73	5317
Middle	71	5644

TEES	COURSE RATING	SLOPE
Forward	70.9	120
Middle	67.7	116

CHERRY VALLEY
COUNTRY CLUB
Skillman, NJ

YEAR FOUNDED: 1989

ARCHITECT:
Rees Jones

COURSE OPENED: 1991

*Large farms formerly occupied the
land to this residential golfing
development. George Washington led
his Continental Army along the property's northern boundary, marching
from Valley Forge to Monmouth
Courthouse. Rees Jones framed holes
with mounds and moguls, enriching
the feeling of separation from others.
Water may affect play on eleven holes.*

TEES	PAR	YARDAGE
Forward	72	5614
Middle	72	6486
Back	72	6894

TEES	COURSE RATING	SLOPE
Forward	72.0	126
Middle	71.9	128
Back	73.6	131

COLONIA COUNTRY CLUB
Colonia, NJ

YEAR FOUNDED: 1898

ARCHITECTS:
Tom Bendelow,
Robert White
H. Purdy, F. Duane

COURSE OPENED: 1899

*Colonia has benefitted from arch-
itectural fine tunings by Hal Purdy
and Frank Duane over the years from
its Tom Bendelow and Robert White
beginnings. Colonia is a generally level
course, but with captivatingly undulating greens and a few blind shots. This
old, quiet, low-key club often plays
host to MGA and NJSGA events.*

TEES	PAR	YARDAGE
Forward	73	5330
Middle	72	6132
Back	72	6402

TEES	COURSE RATING	SLOPE
Forward	72.2	129
Middle	69.6	118
Back	70.4	120

COPPER HILL
COUNTRY CLUB
Flemington, NJ

YEAR FOUNDED: 1928

ARCHITECTS:
Members
Michael Hurdzan

COURSE OPENED: 1928

*Copper Hill underwent a makeover in
1991 by architect Mike Hurdzan. The
course features sloping terrain and a
meandering stream which affects play on
seven holes. Its generous length on modest
acreage means tight fairways and small
greens. A new clubhouse was added in
1994 and will serve the annual
Cortland Member-Guest comfortably.*

TEES	PAR	YARDAGE
Forward	73	5196
Middle	72	6204
Back	72	6517

TEES	COURSE RATING	SLOPE
Forward	70.1	119
Middle	70.1	125
Back	71.5	128

CREAM RIDGE
GOLF CLUB
Cream Ridge, NJ

YEAR FOUNDED: 1958

ARCHITECT:
Frank Miscoski

COURSE OPENED: 1958

*This popular semi-private club in
central New Jersey is well decorated with evergreens and with water
on at least nine holes—including
the demanding par-five 18th.
A new clubhouse has been added
recently. This medium-sized layout
offers more challenge than the
yardage would indicate.*

TEES	PAR	YARDAGE
Forward	70	5150
Middle	71	6081
Back	71	6491

TEES	COURSE RATING	SLOPE
Forward	69.6	119
Middle	69.5	121
Back	71.8	124

DARLINGTON
GOLF COURSE
Mahwah, NJ

YEAR FOUNDED: 1975

ARCHITECT:
Nicholas Psiahas

COURSE OPENED: 1979

*Fairways are individually carved from
what had been rocky, heavily forested
land. Nevertheless, this Bergen County
municipal remains quite walkable.
The greens and tees are huge. A few of
the par fives are reachable in two by
big hitters. The hills, doglegs, water
and trees will test skills of all levels
and delight with pleasing views.*

TEES	PAR	YARDAGE
Forward	72	5300
Middle	71	6049
Back	71	6484

TEES	COURSE RATING	SLOPE
Forward	69.9	117
Middle	68.8	118
Back	70.6	122

EAST ORANGE GOLF COURSE
Short Hills, NJ

YEAR FOUNDED: 1925

ARCHITECT:
Tom Bendelow

COURSE OPENED: 1926

East Orange is in a transition process from recent face-lifting. Over 150 trees were added in 1995-96, and further efforts have been made to add to its natural attractiveness and playability by adding mounding, reworking greens and bunkers, and generally upgrading the level layout.

TEES	PAR	YARDAGE
Forward	73	5640
Middle	72	6099

TEES	COURSE RATING	SLOPE
Forward	72.6	122
Middle	79.7	117

FOX HOLLOW GOLF CLUB
Somerville, NJ

YEAR FOUNDED: 1962

ARCHITECT:
Hal Purdy

COURSE OPENED: 1962

Fox Hollow is set among the scenic, rolling hills of Somerset County. Its fairways, with numerous elevation changes are lined with deciduous trees and are medium to tight in width. Players experience a clear view of tee shots, but may encounter water on a dozen holes.

TEES	PAR	YARDAGE
Forward	72	5329
Middle	70	6109
Back	70	6326

TEES	COURSE RATING	SLOPE
Forward	71.2	122
Middle	69.5	118
Back	70.5	120

EMERSON GOLF CLUB
Emerson, NJ

YEAR FOUNDED: 1968

ARCHITECT:
Alec Ternyei

COURSE OPENED: 1968

The scorecard does not tell the full story of Emerson, with the front nine playing much longer than listed. The back demands more accuracy. This relatively level, semi-private layout recently installed new irrigation and has applied an overall facelift to greens, tees, fairways and cart paths.

TEES	PAR	YARDAGE
Forward	71	5625
Middle	71	6420
Back	71	6702

TEES	COURSE RATING	SLOPE
Forward	70.8	117
Middle	70.6	112
Back	71.8	115

GALLOPING HILL GOLF COURSE
Union, NJ

YEAR FOUNDED: 1927

ARCHITECTS:
Willard Wilkinson
Stephen Kay

COURSE OPENED: 1927

A stream which meanders about the course affects play on a third of the holes. The course is both hilly and undulating and is a most popular and active facility for the Union County Park Commission. The par five 18th, then a par four, was voted among the Met Area's most difficult in the mid 1950s.

TEES	PAR	YARDAGE
Forward	73	5514
Middle	72	6373
Back	72	6690

TEES	COURSE RATING	SLOPE
Forward	71.2	120
Middle	70.5	120
Back	71.3	122

FARMSTEAD GOLF & COUNTRY CLUB
Lafayette, NJ

YEAR FOUNDED: 1960

ARCHITECT:
Bryam Thoebus

COURSE OPENED: 1960

This country setting on what had been a 275-acre farm is one of New Jersey's most popular outing destinations. A large, 200-year-old barn houses the pro shop, restaurant and bar; perfect for the occasional golf-motif wedding. With 10 water holes among the 27, the most memorable seem the closers at Lakeview and Clubview; short par threes surrounded by water and sand.

LAKEVIEW/CLUBVIEW

TEES	PAR	YARDAGE
Forward	70	4910
Middle	71	6033
Back	71	6680

TEES	COURSE RATING	SLOPE
Forward	67.0	112
Middle	68.4	112
Back	71.3	118

CLUBVIEW/VALLEYVIEW

TEES	PAR	YARDAGE
Forward	70	4822
Middle	69	5749
Back	69	6221

TEES	COURSE RATING	SLOPE
Forward	67.3	115
Middle	67.1	113
Back	69.3	117

LAKEVIEW/VALLEYVIEW

TEES	PAR	YARDAGE
Forward	70	4636
Middle	68	5464
Back	68	6161

TEES	COURSE RATING	SLOPE
Forward	65.6	111
Middle	65.8	110
Back	68.9	116

FLANDERS VALLEY GOLF COURSES
Flanders, NJ

YEAR FOUNDED: 1963

The present White and Red and subsequent Blue nines were the work of Hal Purdy. The White/Blue layout, which is among Golf Digest's best 75 Public Courses, hosted the USGA's 1973 Public Links and 1985 Women's Public Links Championships. Rees Jones later built ten holes which were distributed among the four nines.

RED-GOLD COURSE

ARCHITECT:
Hal Purdy

COURSE OPENED: 1963

TEES	PAR	YARDAGE
Forward	73	5540
Middle	72	6429
Back	72	6770

TEES	COURSE RATING	SLOPE
Forward	72.0	121
Middle	70.8	123
Back	72.4	126

WHITE-BLUE COURSE

ARCHITECTS:
Hal Purdy,
Rees Jones

COURSE OPENED: 1963; 1982

TEES	PAR	YARDAGE
Forward	72	4434
Middle	72	6417
Back	72	6765

TEES	COURSE RATING	SLOPE
Forward	72.6	122
Middle	71.1	122
Back	72.7	126

GREENACRES
COUNTRY CLUB
Lawrenceville, NJ

YEAR FOUNDED: 1938

ARCHITECTS:
Devereux Emmet & Alfred Tull
George Fazio

COURSE OPENED: 1932

George Fazio applied a major reconstruction of 14 holes here to satisfy the demands of I-295 in 1970-72, and Stephen Kay touched up the private beauty in recent years. Originally farm acreage, the fairways are typically tight, flat, doglegged, and separated by trees. The layout calls for careful shot selection and execution.

TEES	PAR	YARDAGE
Forward	74	5389
Middle	71	6111
Back	71	6647

TEES	COURSE RATING	SLOPE
Forward	71.6	122
Middle	70.1	122
Back	71.7	126

HARBOR PINES
GOLF CLUB
Egg Harbor Township, NJ

YEAR FOUNDED: 1995

ARCHITECT:
Stephen Kay

COURSE OPENED: 1996

This is a beautiful new parkland course which complements an upscale housing development. It features a complete practice facility, individually sculpted holes on generous bentgrass fairways and huge, undulating greens. Though the complex boasts 18 acres of water, there are only two forced carries.

TEES	PAR	YARDAGE
Forward	72	5099
Middle	72	6119
Back	72	6478

TEES	COURSE RATING	SLOPE
Forward	68.8	118
Middle	69.1	122
Back	70.7	125

HARKERS HOLLOW
GOLF CLUB
Phillipsburg, NJ

YEAR FOUNDED: 1929

ARCHITECT:
Robert White

COURSE OPENED: 1929

Harker's Hollow is a special place for those who dislike fairway bunkers—there are none. It is a hilly layout with small, fast greens. In addition to hosting a number of NJSGA events, The Francis Tarz Ford Memorial, a charity event of long standing, is played here.

TEES	PAR	YARDAGE
Forward	72	5681
Middle	70	6361
Back	70	6551

TEES	COURSE RATING	SLOPE
Forward	72.7	124
Middle	70.8	124
Back	71.7	126

HAWORTH
COUNTRY CLUB
Haworth, NJ

YEAR FOUNDED: 1966

ARCHITECT:
Albert Zikorus

COURSE OPENED: 1967

Haworth has hosted a number of professional and amateur events over the years. Its lasting impression is of old weeping willows lining fairways and obstructing approaches when tee shots are not properly placed. Three long par threes stand out—especially the long 11th with water lurking on the right.

TEES	PAR	YARDAGE
Forward	72	5781
Middle	72	6367
Back	72	6824

TEES	COURSE RATING	SLOPE
Forward	72.8	122
Middle	70.3	120
Back	72.4	124

The third hole at Bedens Brook.

ORANGE

HICKORY HILL GOLF COURSE
Warwick, NY

YEAR FOUNDED: 1992

ARCHITECT:
Hal Purdy

COURSE OPENED: 1992

In 1990 Hal Purdy began to wrestle some challenging property with steep hills, rocks and a deep ravine into a golf course for the Orange County Park System. It opened in 1992. Sharp doglegs, severe elevation changes, lay-up par fours, small greens, blind approaches and narrow fairways are complemented by grand vistas.

TEES	PAR	YARDAGE
Forward	72	5898
Middle	72	6374
Back	72	6797

TEES	COURSE RATING	SLOPE
Forward	74.2	125
Middle	70.9	119
Back	72.8	123

NEW JERSEY

HIGH MOUNTAIN GOLF CLUB
Franklin Lakes, NJ

YEAR FOUNDED: 1967

ARCHITECT:
Alec Ternyei

COURSE OPENED: 1968

This course has a proven record as a popular semi-private retreat for area players. The course is a challenging test, especially on the back nine, where water awaits errant shots on seven holes. A large pond fronts the 18th green.

TEES	PAR	YARDAGE
Forward	71	5426
Middle	71	6101
Back	71	6347

TEES	COURSE RATING	SLOPE
Forward	70.7	121
Middle	68.9	120
Back	70.0	123

NEW JERSEY

HOWELL PARK GOLF COURSE
Farmingdale, NJ

YEAR FOUNDED: 1972

ARCHITECT:
Frank Duane

COURSE OPENED: 1972

Monmouth County's early plan to introduce residents to the "game of a lifetime" included clinics and programs on all aspects of golf. Frank Duane's large, undulating greens, tree-lined fairways and doglegs protected by bunkers, leave a lasting impression.

TEES	PAR	YARDAGE
Forward	72	5693
Middle	72	6276
Back	72	6885

TEES	COURSE RATING	SLOPE
Forward	72.6	123
Middle	70.2	120
Back	73.0	126

NEW JERSEY

LAKE MOHAWK GOLF CLUB
Sparta, NJ

YEAR FOUNDED: 1928

ARCHITECT:
Duer Irving Sewall

COURSE OPENED: 1929

Bordered by the second largest inland body of water in New Jersey and Sparta Mountain on the other, this old, rolling layout was among the first to make property ownership a condition of membership. In promoting the club, its nearness to New York (42 miles) and "the new Hudson River Bridge when complete, two years hence," were highlighted.

TEES	PAR	YARDAGE
Forward	74	5505
Middle	70	6012
Back	70	6270

TEES	COURSE RATING	SLOPE
Forward	72.9	127
Middle	69.9	124
Back	71.1	126

NEW JERSEY

MADISON GOLF CLUB
Madison, NJ

YEAR FOUNDED: 1896

ARCHITECTS:
Members

COURSE OPENED: 1896

This hilly course with tiny well-bunkered greens began its life in 1896 as a four-hole layout. Its configuration later changed and grew to its present nine holes with dual tees. It features tight, tree-lined fairways and a clubhouse of original vintage.

TEES	PAR	YARDAGE
Forward	68	4102
Middle	62	4406

TEES	COURSE RATING	SLOPE
Forward	64.5	111
Middle	61.8	109

NEW JERSEY

MENDHAM GOLF & TENNIS CLUB
Mendham, NJ

YEAR FOUNDED: 1958

ARCHITECT:
Alfred Tull

COURSE OPENED: 1961

Founded as a tennis club in 1958, Mendham opened nine holes in 1961 and added nine in 1968—both Alfred Tull designs. Founded to protect the area from overdevelopment, the course is heavily wooded with 11 water holes. The 381-yard 18th is an exceptional challenge with a pond fronting a double-level, elevated green.

TEES	PAR	YARDAGE
Forward	72	5587
Middle	72	6475
Back	72	6683

TEES	COURSE RATING	SLOPE
Forward	72.2	127
Middle	70.6	125
Back	71.6	127

ORANGE

MONROE COUNTRY CLUB
Monroe, NY

YEAR FOUNDED: 1924

ARCHITECT:
unknown

COURSE OPENED: 1924

Monroe is a semi-private nine-hole course of modest length. Four fairways are bisected by a stream. Double tees allow for variety on the second trip. Sidehill lies are common and several greens are devilish to putt. Some short holes can tempt the brute in those wishing to improve on regulation figures.

TEES	PAR	YARDAGE
Forward	72	5428
Middle	70	5428

TEES	COURSE RATING	SLOPE
Forward	70.3	121
Middle	65.5	114

ROCKLAND

NEW YORK COUNTRY CLUB
New Hempstead, NY

YEAR FOUNDED: 1995

ARCHITECT:
Stephen Kay

COURSE OPENED: 1997

Rockland County's newest private club was built on land which, since the 50's, answered to the names Empire State, Spring Rock, Camelot, and Chateau D'Avie. The original Orrin Smith layout enjoyed spotty success for about 20 years, but it was ill-fated from the start by severe terrain. Stephen Kay tamed the expanded plot and added six water holes in his plan.

TEES	PAR	YARDAGE
Forward	72	5184
Middle	72	6155
Back	72	6570

Course will open and be rated in 1997.

NEWTON COUNTRY CLUB
Newton, NJ

YEAR FOUNDED: 1916

ARCHITECT:
Members

COURSE OPENED: 1916

The older front nine at this quiet, secluded layout is more forgiving than the newer, tighter back nine with undulating greens. Playing host to the Pro-Member, an annual event dating to the early 1970s, is the rare combination of husband/wife professionals Robin and Mary Beth Kohberger.

TEES	PAR	YARDAGE
Forward	71	5181
Middle	70	6043
Back	70	6295

TEES	COURSE RATING	SLOPE
Forward	70.8	123
Middle	69.2	123
Back	70.3	125

OAK HILL GOLF CLUB
Milford, NJ

YEAR FOUNDED: 1963

ARCHITECT:
William Gordon

COURSE OPENED: 1963

This hilly layout features fast, undulating greens. A number of up and down holes make club selection a constant challenge, and the large undulating greens make three putting commonplace. It has hosted a number of MGA and NJSGA events over the years.

TEES	PAR	YARDAGE
Forward	72	5732
Middle	72	6409
Back	72	6668

TEES	COURSE RATING	SLOPE
Forward	73.0	120
Middle	70.0	120
Back	71.2	122

OAK RIDGE GOLF COURSE
Clark, NJ

YEAR FOUNDED: 1928

ARCHITECT:
Willard Wilkinson

COURSE OPENED: 1928

Oak Ridge provides a straightforward golfing experience to Union County residents, its primary users. Its narrow fairways and small, flat greens host over 50,000 rounds in a typical year.

TEES	PAR	YARDAGE
Forward	74	5261
Middle	70	6001
Back	70	6388

TEES	COURSE RATING	SLOPE
Forward	69.7	106
Middle	68.0	107
Back	70.0	110

OLD TAPPAN GOLF CLUB
Old Tappan, NJ

YEAR FOUNDED: 1969

ARCHITECT:
Hal Purdy

COURSE OPENED: 1969

This private nine-holer, hard by the Hackensack Reservoir, lies on rolling countryside which had been the DeWolf farm since 1604. The narrow, uphill 8th is its feature hole.

TEES	PAR	YARDAGE
Forward	74	5508
Middle	70	6037

TEES	COURSE RATING	SLOPE
Forward	71.3	118
Middle	69.0	115

OSIRIS GOLF & COUNTRY CLUB
Walden, NY

YEAR FOUNDED: 1920's

ARCHITECTS:
Members
Frank Duane

COURSE OPENED: 1920's

Frank Duane added a spacious rolling back nine with large, well bunkered greens to this parkland club in the mid 1960s. The original nine holes, thought to be laid out by the membership in the 1920s, were more consolidated with small greens. Three of these were redesigned by Steve Esposito and opened in 1996. A new award winning clubhouse opened in 1994.

TEES	PAR	YARDAGE
Forward	72	5463
Middle	72	6019
Back	72	6317

TEES	COURSE RATING	SLOPE
Forward	71.8	121
Middle	68.2	121
Back	69.2	123

OTTERKILL COUNTRY CLUB
Campbell Hall, NY

YEAR FOUNDED: 1957

ARCHITECT:
William Mitchell

COURSE OPENED: 1957

Otterkill has benefitted from improvements fostered by an ownership change in the late 1980s. The Otterkill appears at six holes of this interesting and demanding course on what had been gently rolling farmland. Otterkill is a popular site for MGA and Westchester GA events.

TEES	PAR	YARDAGE
Forward	72	5551
Middle	72	6510
Back	72	6761

TEES	COURSE RATING	SLOPE
Forward	72.2	124
Middle	71.8	126
Back	72.9	129

PANTHER VALLEY GOLF & COUNTRY CLUB
Allamuchy, NJ

YEAR FOUNDED: 1977

ARCHITECTS:
Robert Trent Jones & Rees Jones

COURSE OPENED: 1969

A dramatic par-five opening hole spirals sharply downhill on a dogleg left adventure toward a green fronted by a pond. As the front nine levels out in the valley, water or wetland awaits on five other holes. Both the 12th and the 14th are sharply rising par fours. The water-protected 18th green presents a full view of the grand, newly rebuilt clubhouse.

TEES	PAR	YARDAGE
Forward	72	5469
Middle	71	6365
Back	71	6850

TEES	COURSE RATING	SLOPE
Forward	72.4	127
Middle	69.9	129
Back	73.7	137

PASCACK BROOK GOLF & COUNTRY CLUB
River Vale, NJ

YEAR FOUNDED: 1962

ARCHITECT:
John Handwerg Jr.

COURSE OPENED: 1962

Originally known as Parkvale, Pascack has long been a favorite haunt of New Jersey's daily-fee denizens. Most challenging are the tiny first green, the 443-yard par-4 second, and the 13th, most of which lies on an island in Pascack Brook. Pascack also features a complete catering service.

TEES	PAR	YARDAGE
Forward	71	5067
Middle	71	5991
Back	71	6287

TEES	COURSE RATING	SLOPE
Forward	69.3	117
Middle	69.0	119
Back	70.3	122

PASSAIC COUNTY GOLF COURSES
Wayne, NJ

YEAR FOUNDED: 1927

ARCHITECT:
Martin O'Loughlin

COURSE OPENED: 1927

This 36-hole complex plays host to 130,000 rounds annually, primarily by county residents. The Blue course features more hilly terrain than the Red, which is more heavily treed.

BLUE COURSE

TEES	PAR	YARDAGE
Forward	73	5720
Middle	70	6080

TEES	COURSE RATING	SLOPE
Forward	70.8	115
Middle	68.6	117

RED COURSE

TEES	PAR	YARDAGE
Forward	75	6097
Middle	69	6457

TEES	COURSE RATING	SLOPE
Forward	72.7	120
Middle	70.3	117

RIVER VALE COUNTRY CLUB
River Vale, NJ

YEAR FOUNDED: 1928

ARCHITECT:
Orrin Smith

COURSE OPENED: 1931

RiverVale makes stringent demands for accuracy on both tee shots and approaches with its small greens guarded by deep bunkers. When winter approaches, four cups are cut in each green. The flagstick goes in one and the others are plastic capped for alternate use. On premises is an authentic Japanese restaurant.

TEES	PAR	YARDAGE
Forward	74	5293
Middle	72	6196
Back	72	6470

TEES	COURSE RATING	SLOPE
Forward	70.7	123
Middle	70.2	125
Back	71.4	128

PLAINFIELD COUNTRY CLUB WEST
Edison, NJ

YEAR FOUNDED: 1932

ARCHITECT:
Tom Bendelow

COURSE OPENED: 1898

The nine-hole public course, once part of Plainfield Country Club, features roomy fairways on rolling terrain with small greens. The 308-yard 9th ends in an upside-down saucer shaped green on which four putts are not unusual. The course is home to Jeff Thomas, three-time MGA Player of the Year and 1993 U.S. Mid-Amateur Champion.

TEES	PAR	YARDAGE
Forward	35	2493
Middle	33	2493

TEES	COURSE RATING	SLOPE
Forward	67.0	102
Middle	63.0	97

PORT JERVIS COUNTRY CLUB
Port Jervis, NY

YEAR FOUNDED: 1921

ARCHITECTS:
A.W. Tillinghast
Harry Spears/Fred Conrad

COURSE OPENED: 1921

This is thought to be A.W. Tillinghast's only imprint in Orange County. In the late 1950's Harry "Chet" Spears and Fred Conrad interwove nine new holes with Tillie's existing ones, making a full 18 holes. Chet's son, Rick, won the 1964 MGA Junior Championship and the 1971 MGA Amateur at Winged Foot.

TEES	PAR	YARDAGE
Forward	70	4988
Middle	70	6093

TEES	COURSE RATING	SLOPE
Forward	68.6	116
Middle	69.3	121

RAMSEY GOLF & COUNTRY CLUB
Ramsey, NJ

YEAR FOUNDED: 1965

ARCHITECT:
Hal Purdy

COURSE OPENED: 1965

This former 220-acre estate featured elaborate landscaping and three lakes. The Norman clubhouse, destroyed by fire in 1986 and subsequently restored, was modelled after the famous Ramsey Abbey in England. Honored as the most beautiful estate in America in 1935, it was sold in 1940 for residential and golf club use. Hal Purdy designed the original nine-hole course as well as the 1995 expansion to 18 holes.

TEES	PAR	YARDAGE
Forward	69	4866
Middle	69	5335
Back	69	5540

TEES	COURSE RATING	SLOPE
Forward	68.7	114
Middle	66.5	113
Back	67.4	115

The par five 11th at Panther Valley.

ROCKLAND LAKE STATE PARK GOLF COURSE
Congers, NY

YEAR FOUNDED: 1969

ARCHITECT:
David Gordon

COURSE OPENED: 1969

Several spectacular holes on this generous Palisades Interstate Park layout—a public access facility-offer panoramic countryside views. Many elevated greens require high, well-struck approach shots—no mean task from fairways which are rarely level. An 18-hole par-3 course operates at the south end of the park.

TEES	PAR	YARDAGE
Forward	72	5735
Middle	72	6347
Back	72	6864

TEES	COURSE RATING	SLOPE
Forward	66.4	108
Middle	69.7	116
Back	72.0	121

ROCKLEIGH COUNTY GOLF COURSE
Rockleigh, NJ

YEAR FOUNDED: 1958

ARCHITECT:
Alfred Tull

COURSE OPENED: 1958

The Red nine at this popular Bergen County daily fee layout is the toughest test. The three nines, situated on rolling terrain are heavy on doglegs. The Blue Course offers numerous chances to visit water. County residents figure strongly among the users.

TEES	PAR	YARDAGE
Forward	72	6179
Middle	72	6312

TEES	COURSE RATING	SLOPE
Forward	71.6	118
Middle	69.1	115

Above is an average of three nines.

ROLLING GREENS GOLF CLUB
Newport, NJ

YEAR FOUNDED: 1954

ARCHITECT:
Nicholas Psiahas

COURSE OPENED: 1954

Nicholas Psiahas added nine holes to this public access course in 1968. The result is a demanding, well bunkered layout with seven par threes, each over 200 yards, on the back nine. All facets of one's game will find a test on this modest 65-acre plot.

TEES	PAR	YARDAGE
Forward	67	3988
Middle	65	4679
Back	65	5189

TEES	COURSE RATING	SLOPE
Forward	62.1	98
Middle	62.1	101
Back	64.8	110

ROSELLE GOLF CLUB
Roselle, NJ

YEAR FOUNDED: 1917

ARCHITECT:
Seth Raynor

COURSE OPENED: 1917

Roselle is a nine-hole, dual-tee layout with fast, sloping greens. The course is generally flat with hardwood-lined fairways. Morses' Creek provides Roselle with watery challenge on four holes. Pat Hatfield, an educator and the daughter of former pro/superintendent Jim Grady, is the club's celebrity. At this writing she has won 39 club championships and 23 in succession—both are national records.

TEES	PAR	YARDAGE
Forward	75	5370
Middle	72	6151

TEES	COURSE RATING	SLOPE
Forward	70.8	114
Middle	70.4	121

PHILIP J. ROTELLA GOLF COURSE
Thiells, NY

YEAR FOUNDED: 1983

ARCHITECT:
Hal Purdy

COURSE OPENED: 1984

This municipal features six of each— par threes, fours and fives. Enjoying steadily growing popularity since opening, the layout, named for the Haverstraw Town Supervisor, offers at least six chances to find a pond or the Minisceongo Creek as it meanders through.

TEES	PAR	YARDAGE
Forward	72	5507
Middle	72	6068
Back	72	6502

TEES	COURSE RATING	SLOPE
Forward	71.7	123
Middle	69.4	122
Back	71.4	126

SCOTTS CORNERS GOLF COURSE
Montgomery, NY

YEAR FOUNDED:
unknown

ARCHITECT:
unknown

COURSE OPENED:
unknown

This daily-fee nine-hole, dual-tee layout provides adequate challenge for most golfers. Essentially a level layout with gently sloping greens, its most difficult hole is the dogleg 419-yard 4th.

TEES	PAR	YARDAGE
Forward	73	5835
Middle	72	6079

TEES	COURSE RATING	SLOPE
Forward	71.3	115
Middle	67.4	107

SHORE OAKS GOLF CLUB
Farmingdale, NJ

YEAR FOUNDED: 1990

ARCHITECT:
Johnny Miller & Golden Bear Associates

COURSE OPENED: 1990

Built on former corn and soy bean farmland, a residential development was included in the plan. This Johnny Miller design was built by Golfforce, a Nicklaus group. It bears the Nicklaus look of the time with moundings along fairways and at greenside. Three par threes feature water from tee to green.

TEES	PAR	YARDAGE
Forward	71	5452
Middle	70	6505
Back	70	6919

TEES	COURSE RATING	SLOPE
Forward	71.2	121
Middle	71.6	128
Back	73.5	132

STANTON RIDGE GOLF & COUNTRY CLUB
Stanton, NJ

YEAR FOUNDED: 1993

ARCHITECT:
Stephen Kay

COURSE OPENED: 1993

Seeming older than its tender years, Stanton Ridge lies within a development of 150 tastefully tucked upscale homesites. Among many noteworthy holes are the 6th, a reachable par five with water left and bunkers long and the 12th, a 190-yard par three across a deep ravine.

TEES	PAR	YARDAGE
Forward	71	5084
Middle	71	6112
Back	71	6505

TEES	COURSE RATING	SLOPE
Forward	69.4	125
Middle	69.7	128
Back	71.5	132

STONY FORD GOLF COURSE

Montgomery, NY

YEAR FOUNDED: 1962

ARCHITECT:
Hal Purdy

COURSE OPENED: 1962

Orange County Park System's flagship layout doubles as a win-tertime playground with a ski slope operating on the driving range. The well balanced Hal Purdy course bordering the Wallkill River offers lovely views from its rolling and often hilly terrain. An occasional hang-glider reaches the property from the distant, but clearly visible, Shawangunks.

TEES	PAR	YARDAGE
Forward	73	5856
Middle	72	6182
Back	72	6651

TEES	COURSE RATING	SLOPE
Forward	74.0	128
Middle	70.3	124
Back	72.4	128

STORM KING GOLF CLUB

Cornwall, NY

YEAR FOUNDED: 1890

ARCHITECT:
unknown

COURSE OPENED: 1896

On the west bank of the Hudson, a few miles beyond West Point, lies one of the oldest clubs in the country. It started as a social club in 1890, and a nine-hole course was built in 1896. The purchase of additional land allowed later exten-sion of the seventh and creation of the present eighth.

TEES	PAR	YARDAGE
Forward	75	5703
Middle	71	6209

TEES	COURSE RATING	SLOPE
Forward	73.0	126
Middle	70.4	124

SUNEAGLES GOLF CLUB AT FORT MONMOUTH

Eatontown, NJ

YEAR FOUNDED: 1926

ARCHITECT:
A.W. Tillinghast

COURSE OPENED: 1926

Taken over by the county after bankruptcy in 1936, it operated as Monmouth County Golf Club until the Army purchased it in 1942. The deep bunkers guarding undulating greens are typical of Tillinghast's touch. Byron Nelson recorded his first professional victory here in the 1935 NJPGA Championship.

TEES	PAR	YARDAGE
Forward	73	5380
Middle	72	6021
Back	72	6357

TEES	COURSE RATING	SLOPE
Forward	71.2	117
Middle	69.1	117
Back	70.1	119

TOWN OF WALLKILL GOLF CLUB

Middletown, NY

YEAR FOUNDED: 1991

ARCHITECT:
Steve Esposito

COURSE OPENED: 1992

Carved from rocky, hilly, heavily wooded terrain, Wallkill offers a dozen chances for the golfer to find a water hazard. This demand-ing target course with fast greens is a must play when the leaves turn.

TEES	PAR	YARDAGE
Forward	72	5171
Middle	72	6104
Back	72	6437

TEES	COURSE RATING	SLOPE
Forward	66.3	111
Middle	69.7	119
Back	71.2	122

WARWICK VALLEY COUNTRY CLUB

Warwick, NY

YEAR FOUNDED:
unknown

ARCHITECT:
unknown

COURSE OPENED:
unknown

This dual-tee nine-holer offers multiple chances to add penalty strokes with a hungry ditch on five holes and water hazards fronting three others. Add to this a new watering system, postage stamp greens and three killer par threes of 200+ yards, and you have plenty of challenge.

TEES	PAR	YARDAGE
Forward	73	4932
Middle	71	5843

TEES	COURSE RATING	SLOPE
Forward	68.6	118
Middle	68.5	122

WEEQUAHIC GOLF COURSE

Newark, NJ

YEAR FOUNDED: 1915

ARCHITECTS:
George Low Sr.
Hal Purdy

COURSE OPENED: 1915

Weequahic dates to 1915 when a nine-hole George Low design was applied to reclaimed swampland. In 1969 an additional nine was added by Hal Purdy. The fair-ways and greens of this daily fee Essex County course, New Jersey's first county-operated public facility, occupy rolling terrain next to Weequahic Park.

TEES	PAR	YARDAGE
Forward	70	4922
Middle	70	5609

TEES	COURSE RATING	SLOPE
Forward	67.9	113
Middle	66.3	108

WEST POINT GOLF CLUB

West Point, NY

YEAR FOUNDED: 1946

ARCHITECTS:
Robert Trent Jones,
Lindsay Ervin

COURSE OPENED: 1946

West Point is among the first men-tioned by Robert Trent Jones as he reminisces of his projects. The lay-out is emerging from major surgery involving new holes, a bridge over Route 9W, new tees and additional water hazards. It may be the area's first to have sprinkler heads measured with pin-point accuracy by the Global Positioning system.

TEES	PAR	YARDAGE
Forward	72	4967
Middle	70	5710
Back	70	6007

TEES	COURSE RATING	SLOPE
Forward	68.1	120
Middle	67.2	124
Back	68.6	126

WOODLAKE GOLF & COUNTRY CLUB

Lakewood, NJ

YEAR FOUNDED: 1972

ARCHITECT:
Edward L. Packard

COURSE OPENED: 1972

Those counting strokes on the 5th green, a long par 5, may wonder if they've enough ammo to finish the round. With water threatening all around the green, it seems a different hole than the inviting one just viewed from the tee. Several more brushes with water are likely on the back nine of this tight, wooded layout.

TEES	PAR	YARDAGE
Forward	74	5557
Middle	72	6438
Back	72	6766

TEES	COURSE RATING	SLOPE
Forward	72.2	120
Middle	70.9	121
Back	72.5	124

The clubhouse at Winged Foot Golf Club, Mamaroneck, New York.

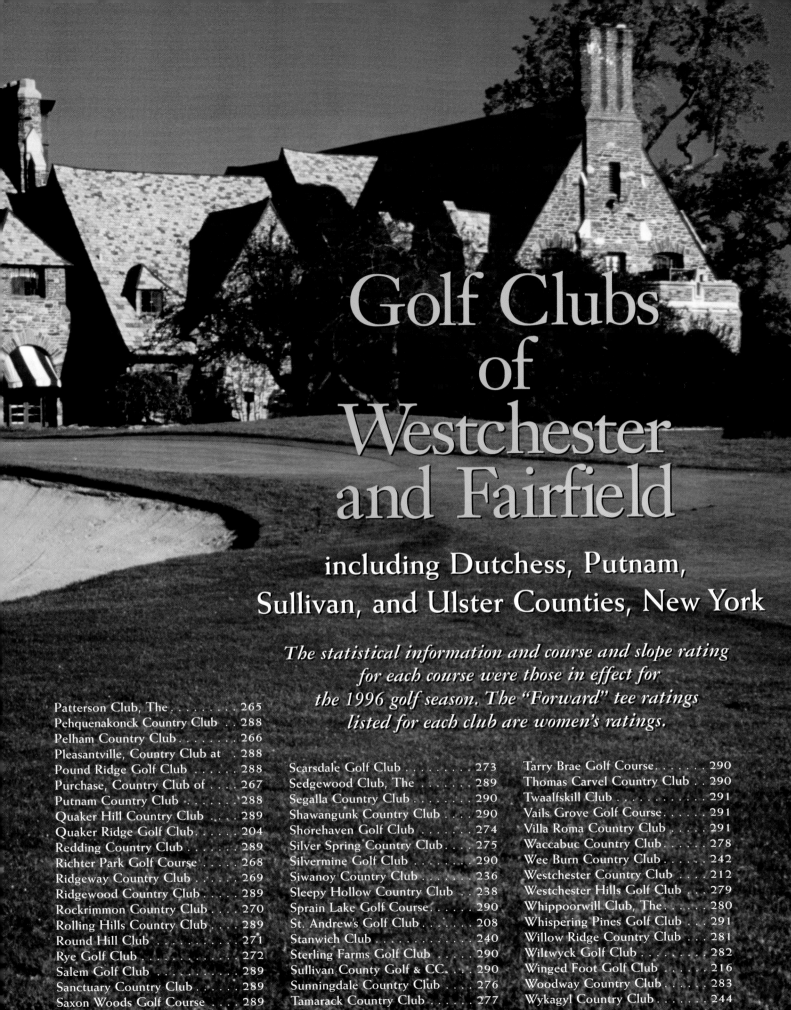

Golf Clubs of Westchester and Fairfield

including Dutchess, Putnam, Sullivan, and Ulster Counties, New York

The statistical information and course and slope rating for each course were those in effect for the 1996 golf season. The "Forward" tee ratings listed for each club are women's ratings.

QUAKER RIDGE GOLF CLUB

"The Course Down The Street"

At the conclusion of the 1974 U.S. Open, Jack Nicklaus was asked if he thought Winged Foot was the best golf course in the world. He replied, "It may be, but let me tell you, there is quite a golf course down the street."

Nicklaus acknowledged what Met Area players have known for years, that Quaker Ridge, like Winged Foot, was a "man-sized" golf course, and one of A.W. Tillinghast's finest creations. Unlike Winged Foot, though, Quaker Ridge has chosen to avoid the national spotlight. Of the clubs ranked by *GOLF Magazine* as the country's best, Quaker Ridge is one of very few never to have never hosted a national championship. That cloak of anonymity will be lifted slightly in 1997 when the Club welcomes the Walker Cup matches.

In 1774, Quakers owned the land and convened frequently at a meeting house at the intersection of Griffen Avenue and Weaver Street. So the name "Quaker Ridge" was given to the surrounding region. During the Revolutionary War, both sides passed through the area en route to the Battle of White Plains. British General Howe marched his troops up Weaver Street and encamped nearby. Washington and his army supposedly spent an evening on Club grounds; the general is said to have slept under the Quaker Ridge Oak, located to the right of the 10th hole adjacent to the lower parking lot.

Early in 1914, the new "Metropolitan Golf Links" purchased 112 acres on Quaker Ridge, then leased the land for 10 years to the Quaker Ridge Field & Country Club. In 1915, John Duncan Dunn was hired to lay out a nine-hole golf course. A rambling white clapboard house on

QUAKER RIDGE GOLF CLUB
Scarsdale, NY

YEAR FOUNDED: 1916

ARCHITECTS:
John Duncan Dunn
A.W. Tillinghast

COURSE OPENED: 1915

TEES	PAR	YARDAGE
Forward	73	5815
Middle	70	6405
Back	70	6810

TEES	COURSE RATING	SLOPE
Forward	75.0	137
Middle	72.3	138
Back	74.1	142

The approach shot on the fourth hole.

View from behind 5th green looking towards 4th hole.

the grounds became the clubhouse.

When the Metropolitan Golf Links faced money problems, a small group of members organized Quaker Ridge Golf Club in 1916. They purchased the land and engaged A.W. Tillinghast to expand the existing golf course to 18 holes. Tillinghast built 11 new holes and radically revised seven old ones. The new 18-hole course opened for play in 1918, and is now regarded as a Tillinghast original.

The present Tudor-style clubhouse, designed by Buchman & Kahn, opened on August 18, 1923, with a testimonial dinner for William Rice Hochster, the Club's first president (1916-1928) and Green Chairman from 1916 until his death—on the course—in 1933. Hochster was a stern ruler who ran the Club with an iron hand and the course with a green thumb. He lived in a house just to the right of the first green, from which he was known to emerge and give unsuspecting golfers lessons in golf etiquette, including raking bunkers and replacing divots. When a major course revision was arranged for 1924, Hochster was there to carry out Tillinghast's plans.

Byron Nelson

Other notable members have been Ira Mendell, past president of the MGA (1978-1979), for years a dedicated volunteer who was honored with the MGA's Distinguished Service Award in 1992, and Udo Reinach, who, together with his close friend Willie Turnesa, founded the Westchester Caddie Scholarship Fund in 1956.

Quaker Ridge's pro shop has been well-tended over the years. The Club hired the Farrell brothers, Jimmy and Johnny, in 1920. Johnny won seven tournaments on the Tour in 1927, including the Met Open, then a major. In 1928, he won the U.S. Open, beating Bobby Jones by one stroke in a playoff. The Club celebrated his return with a parade of 150 caddies and a gala party. Farrell remained at Quaker Ridge through 1933, when he moved to Baltusrol.

Victor Oberhammer served as a professional for over forty years before retiring in 1974. Jim McLean, one of the country's finest teaching professionals served Quaker Ridge (1983-1987). Among his pupils were David Glenz and George Zahringer, perhaps the area's leading professional and amateur, respectively, during that period.

Quaker Ridge has hosted three Met Opens and two Met Amateurs. The '36 Met Open was a landmark event. A great field, including Gene Sarazen, Paul Runyan, Johnny Farrell, and Tommy Armour, competed in what was then one of the "big four" events on the national Tour. All had won, or would soon win, a major title. But 24-year-old Byron Nelson, an assistant at Ridgewood, topped them all. This was Nelson's first important title, which he regarded as his stepping stone to later success. He earned $300 from the total purse of $1,750.

The Club's annual Hochster Memorial is one of the most prestigious amateur competitions in the Met Area. Begun in 1934, the 36-hole stroke-play event is limited by invitation to 60 players. It has been won by George Zahringer III (the only five-time winner); four-time winners Willie Turnesa, Frank Strafaci, and Dick Siderowf; as well as Jess Sweetser, Tommy Goodwin, Charley Whitehead, Bob Gardner, and Jerry Courville Sr. Only on rare occasions has the par been eclipsed over the two rounds.

Jack Nicklaus is not the only notable to have praised Quaker Ridge. Paul Runyan called it "the greatest golf course in the world." *The Met Golfer* ranked Quaker Ridge number one in the Met Area. The reason for the praise is evident: Few courses have as many great holes. At least seven holes have appeared on national and regional "best holes" lists over the years, including numbers 4, 6, 7, and 11—all par fours—and the short par-three water hole, number 5.

With nearly every hole lined by trees, and the greens lightning fast and cleverly bunkered in the Tillinghast style, Quaker Ridge is a course that places extreme demands on the positioning of every shot. For example, a large mound, built on rock, rises out of the center of the fourth fairway, forcing the player to choose either a high road to the left or a low road right. The former is narrowed by a tall oak to the left of the fairway, while the latter is lined with willows and falls to the right toward the trees. The green is bunkered in front on both sides.

The fifth is a strikingly beautiful par three over a pond shored up with a fieldstone retaining wall across the front of the green.

The extremely difficult sixth plays from a tee elevated

Former MGA president Ira Mendell.

well above a fairway that narrows to a slim waist in the landing area. A creek runs through the willows lining the left side of the fairway, and a tall oak stands guard at the corner of the dogleg-right.

Only slightly less confounding than the sixth, the seventh doglegs 60 degrees to the right, forcing most long hitters to lay up off the tee to avoid driving through the fairway. A creek crosses the hole within 130 yards of the tee, then ducks into the trees at the corner before reappearing to cross the fairway once again, effectively taking away the option of cutting the corner. The fairway is bunkered twice just beyond the second creek crossing, and the elevated putting surface is protected by two bunkers left and one right, and at the rear by a collecting bunker. Griffen Avenue behind the green is out-of-bounds.

The WMGA once called the 11th the most difficult hole in the region. It doglegs left to a green set behind a creek. The dominant feature on the approach is a tall oak on the left side no more than 50 yards ahead of the green, effectively blocking out most shots from that side of the fairway. The creek emerges from the trees along the left side, circles in front of the oak, then curls back before crossing in front of the green, where it is shored up by a fieldstone retaining wall. The putting surface, which falls sharply toward the creek, is bunkered left and behind.

That stretch of holes, from the 4th through the 11th, is one of the very best in both challenge and beauty in American parkland golf.   ○

Looking at 11th green from the left side of fairway.

ST. ANDREW'S GOLF CLUB
"The Apple Tree Gang"

The story has been told many times before, but bears repeating. It is the history of the St. Andrew's Golf Club, the oldest enduring golf club in the United States.

St. Andrew's traces its roots to Dunfermline, Scotland, and two former schoolmates named John Reid and Robert Lockhart. Reid became an executive in the iron industry and Lockhart a linen merchant, both in New York. During the summer of 1887, Reid suggested that Lockhart acquire some golf equipment while visiting Scotland. Lockhart stopped by the shop of Old Tom Morris at St. Andrews, and sent home a package that included six hand-made clubs and two dozen gutta-percha balls. That fall, on a field near the Hudson River at 72nd Street, Lockhart, his two sons, and a New York City mounted policeman tested the clubs, to the satisfaction of all. He gave the clubs to Reid soon thereafter, and the stage was set.

Washington's Birthday, 1888, was relatively mild and became the occasion for the first "rounds" of golf played in this part of the country. Reid gathered five acquaintances, John Upham, Henry Tallmadge, Harry Holbrook, Kingman Putnam, and Alexander Kinnan. In a hilly pasture across Lake Avenue from Reid's home, just east of Palisade Avenue in Yonkers, the six men built a triangle of three holes, each about 100 yards long. Since they possessed only one set of clubs, Reid and Upham played while the others made up American golf's first gallery. Holbrook's two sons were the first American caddies. Before the "sixsome" could enjoy another game, the infamous "Blizzard of '88" intervened.

After the April thaw, the pioneers sought more suitable land for their game. They found it around the corner, 30 rolling acres of pastureland and good turf owned by John Shotts, the neighborhood butcher. The golfers moved in without permission, but Shotts did not object since they were among his best customers.

Reid and friends built a six-hole course on Shotts' meadow, and played there throughout the rest of 1888. On November 14, Reid invited his gang to dinner at his home. After the meal, he announced the real reason for the gathering—to form a club that would preserve and foster their common interest in golf. While being serenaded with Scottish ballads, St. Andrew's Golf Club entered the world.

The Club flourished, expanding to 13 members. Their "nefarious rites of pasture" continued, despite criticism from local churchgoers who objected to their Sunday play. St. Andrew's first clubhouse was a table, later a tent.

The city announced plans to extend Palisade Avenue north through the heart of the golf course in 1892. So that April, the men of St. Andrew's moved to a 34-acre apple orchard four blocks north of Shotts' meadow on Palisade Avenue, situated on top of a hill overlooking the Hudson River. Again they built a six-hole course, this one steeply-banked and lush with apple trees. One tree served the dual function of locker room and 19th hole. The members hung their jackets, picnic baskets, and wicker decanters from its branches, some of which are now on display in the clubhouses of both St. Andrew's (New York) and St. Andrews (Scotland).

Life was splendid at the Apple Orchard, and soon the 20 members were known as the "Apple Tree Gang." However, a progressive-thinking faction within the ranks, led by Henry Tallmadge, the youngest of the original group, wanted to upgrade the facilities and bring St. Andrew's up to par with the other leading clubs of the time. Certainly, nine holes and a real clubhouse were reasonable requests, so Reid and company were on the move again, in May, 1894, to the Odell Farm off Saw Mill River Road in Grey Oaks, three miles northeast of the orchard. With Tallmadge in the lead, the members built a nine-hole course on abruptly rising terrain between Snake Hill and the road. For a clubhouse, they inherited one of the oldest farmhouses in Westchester County. Built in 1790 by Jacob Odell, an American patriot who fought in the War of 1812, it was said to be haunted, although the ghosts departed once the golfers arrived.

It was during the three years at Grey Oaks that St. Andrew's played its most significant role in the development of golf in this country. A field of 28—including eight from the host club—competed in an unofficial Amateur Championship at St. Andrew's in 1894. In the finals, Laurence Stoddart became the first, and to date only, St. Andrew's golfer to win a national title, defeating C. B. Macdonald in the finals, which required 19 holes. Macdonald, who was suffering the effects of a gala dinner party given by Stanford White the night before, hooked his

**ST. ANDREW'S
GOLF CLUB**
Hastings-on-Hudson, NY

YEAR FOUNDED: 1888

ARCHITECTS:
William Tucker Sr.
Harry Talmadge
Morris Poucher
James Braid
John Stutt
Jack Nicklaus

COURSE OPENED: 1897

TEES	PAR	YARDAGE
Forward	71	5134
Middle	71	6163
Back	71	6616

TEES	COURSE RATING	SLOPE
Forward	70.3	125
Middle	70.6	132
Back	72.6	136

Right: John Reid and son Archie, USGA president 1938 to 1939.

View from behind the 6th green.

shot into a corn field on the 19th hole and failed to recover.

As a sideshow, on the final day St. Andrew's staged a "U.S. Open," with four professionals competing at match play. In the first round, Willie Dunn of Shinnecock Hills defeated Willie Davis of Newport, and Willie Campbell of Brookline eliminated Samuel Tucker, St. Andrew's first professional. Dunn defeated Campbell to win the title, $100 first prize, and a gold medal.

As he had done after an earlier medal-play championship at Newport, Macdonald raised a considerable ruckus over the outcome of the St. Andrew's Amateur, complaining, among other things, that a single club could not conduct a national championship. It was apparent that an organization was needed to govern golf in the United States and conduct the national championships. A meeting was held in New York City on December 22, 1894, with representatives from five clubs—St. Andrew's, Shinnecock Hills, Newport, The Country Club, and Macdonald's Chicago Golf Club. The St. Andrew's delegation was Reid and Tallmadge. The meeting had been Tallmadge's idea, and he was elected the first secretary of the Amateur Golf Association of the United States, which later changed its name to the United States Golf Association.

The original Apple Tree, one of its branches now hangs in the John Reid room at St. Andrew's.

By 1897, discontent was growing again as a faction within the Club complained that St. Andrew's had fallen behind the times. So they moved in August, 1897, to a densely wooded parcel of 160 acres in Mount Hope, at the top of a long, steep hill about five miles north of Yonkers. A Dutch Colonial clubhouse was built overlooking the nine-hole golf course in the valley below.

Among the most enthusiastic of the early members was steel baron Andrew Carnegie, who joined in 1894 and built a summer cottage on the back of the hill behind the clubhouse. Carnegie, who like Reid and Lockhart hailed from Dunfermline, is credited with the observation that "golf is an indispensable adjunct to higher civilization." His love for the game was never more apparent than on the day in 1901 when he sold Carnegie Steel to U.S. Steel for $250,000,000, yet he was more excited about having parred the fifth hole for the first time!

Many have portrayed the men of St. Andrew's as golf's first missionaries, but John Reid actually wanted nothing more than a private retreat where he and his friends could enjoy a peaceful round, and that well describes St. Andrew's for the first 75 years of this century. But as times changed, and the family-oriented facilities of country club life grew in popularity, the Club suffered. In the mid-1970s, radical changes were necessary. Jack Nicklaus' organization was called in, and proposed a golfing community bordering a restored St. Andrew's course.

Work began late in 1981. New holes (10, 11, and 12) were built on newly purchased land, and much of the rest of the course was rerouted or rebuilt, although the basic flow was retained. The revision was ready on July 1, 1985.

The course is picturesque and challenging, contoured fairways rolling through tree-lined passages. Pot bunkers faced with thick fescue grass and greens with swales call to mind the old course at St. Andrews.

The clubhouse.

The fourth is an heirloom, a dogleg-left par four that begins on a tee 150 feet above the fairway. The drive must be long and away from the left corner, which is guarded by tall trees, to leave a clear shot at an elevated green 50 yards beyond a creek. (Nicklaus moved the green back 100 yards and to the left. The original was protected back and front by branches of the creek.)

The eighth is a big par four with a creek crossing the fairway some 75 yards from the green, a potentially difficult carry for the average member. The putting surface is angled to the approach, boasts a phalanx of four bunkers across its right side, and is divided into three sectors, with a "Valley Of Sin" running through the middle sector.

The 14th hole crosses a creek before rising to a punchbowl green hidden behind a 25-yard patch of rough. Two high-lipped bunkers are set into the rise leading up to the green.

One of the postcard holes at St. Andrew's is the 15th, which plays from an elevated tee over a pond that turns into a stream running up the left side before widening into a second pond in front of the green. Trees at the corner of the dogleg-right can block the approach. The green is shaped like a boomerang, wrapping around a rear bunker, and has a deep swale at the right-front.

Nicklaus considers the 16th one of his better par threes. The green is framed by trees in a cathedral-like setting. A creek passes the left side of the green, then empties into a pond right of the tee. The two-tiered putting surface is split by a ridge that starts at the right front and curves to the left.

From Reid to Nicklaus, St. Andrew's has remained in the mainstream of American golf for more than a century. ౦

The rustic par-three 16th hole.

WESTCHESTER COUNTRY CLUB

"The Mean 18"

Of the many fine golf courses in the Met Area, perhaps the one most familiar to the American golfer and golf fan is the West Course at the Westchester Country Club. Site of the Westchester Classic, the area's only regular PGA Tour stop, the West Course is visited annually by nearly 25,000 spectators each day of the tournament, and millions of television viewers.

The tournament's early June dates bring the promise of lush fairways and high rough. The combination of narrow target areas and slick greens make Westchester play very much like a U.S. Open course. Indeed, it is considered ideal preparation for the Open, which usually follows a week or two later.

Tour statistics substantiate its toughness. Four holes from the West course (2, 3, 6, and 17) are rated among the most difficult on Tour, giving Westchester stronger representation on the "Mean 18" than any other Tour course.

The Walter Travis-designed West Course is hilly and heavily wooded, rolling through thick stands of pine, oak, and maple. The terrain is dotted with rocky outcroppings, some of which create blind shots.

The second tee sits well above a fairway flanked by bunkers about 200 yards out. The hole bends slightly left beyond the drive zone, crosses a creek, then rises gently to a two-tiered green angled left to right. Trees to the left in the landing area and a large oak to the right 50 yards from the green complement one another and share the duties of blocking approach shots.

The third fairway is camelbacked, falling off to both sides and forward, and is hemmed in by bunkers along the landing area. A big drive leaves a long iron or fairway wood from a hanging lie to a green much higher than the fairway. The average player must worry about a water hazard at the foot of the hill and a steep fall-off to the right greenside.

The sixth is a big par four calling for a long drive to clear a large oak at the corner of the dogleg-right, 220 yards from the tee. Unless the drive is exceptionally long, the second shot will be blind as the hole crests before rolling downhill to the green.

The 13th may not make the Tour's "tough list," but it is potentially more dangerous than any of the "Mean 18" holes. The drive must be long and accurate to carry a high, rough-covered ridge and find a fairway that kicks right while bending left. Even a big drive leaves a long iron to a small green that features a small burial mound dead-center.

The 17th is another big par four, this one making a hairpin turn to the left just short of a large pond that cuts into the fairway and passes within 50 yards of the green. The drive must be long and into the left side of the fairway if the average player wants any chance of carrying the water on the second shot.

Travis' sportier, less demanding South Course was designed to accommodate women, seniors, and those learning the game. But it is no pushover, featuring small, loosely bunkered greens that can be quite challenging. Its terrain is undulating, although not quite so dramatic as its big brother.

The 13th on the South Course may be the most dangerous short (288 yards) par four in captivity. A lake flanks the left side of the fairway, which narrows as it approaches the green. It takes a drive of 200 yards to set up a clear approach to a sloping green bordered by water to the left and encircled right and rear by two bunkers.

Called "Crow's Nest" after a small, eagle-like rock formation to the right of the green, the par-three 14th plays straight uphill to the green. Toughening the route are rough to the left, a high mound greenside, and a bunker at the base of the hill.

Before the Westchester Classic became a Tour institution, the Apawamis Pro-Am was held at that Club annually from 1952 through 1962, when the Thunderbird Classic took its place, originally at Upper Montclair. That event moved to Westchester in 1963—Arnold Palmer and Jack Nicklaus won two of the first three—and within a few years was replaced by the Classic.

WESTCHESTER COUNTRY CLUB

Harrison, NY

YEAR FOUNDED: 1919

ARCHITECT:
Walter Travis

COURSES OPENED: 1922

WEST COURSE

TEES	PAR	YARDAGE
Forward	75	6134
Middle	72	6342
Back	72	6625

TEES	COURSE RATING	SLOPE
Forward	77.5	145
Middle	71.6	134
Back	73.2	136

SOUTH COURSE

TEES	PAR	YARDAGE
Forward	72	5540
Middle	70	5865
Back	70	6027

TEES	COURSE RATING	SLOPE
Forward	71.8	122
Middle	68.5	119
Back	69.4	121

The clubhouse—formerly the Westchester Biltmore Hotel.

The 9th hole of the West course.

Nicklaus won the first Westchester Classic in 1967 on a Wednesday afternoon! Rain postponed three days of play, and saved eventual runner-up Dan Sikes twice by washing out rounds that, had they counted, would have sent him packing. Sikes eventually established the course record at 62, which was matched by local Club professional Jimmy Wright in 1976 and by Peter Jacobsen in 1982.

Ben Hogan played his final competitive round on July 30, 1970, in the Classic. The 58 year-old Hogan, playing on aching legs in extreme heat, carded a 78.

In 1982, Bob Gilder concluded his third round by holing a 251- yard, 3-wood shot for a double eagle-2 that propelled him to a tournament record 19-under 261. The next year, Seve Ballesteros came to the home hole in a three-way tie for the lead. He rifled a 3-iron 225 yards to within 6 feet of the cup, then sank his putt for a winning eagle. In deference to Westchester's narrow drive zones, Ballesteros used a one-iron off the tee 23 times that week.

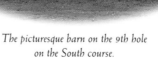

The picturesque barn on the 9th hole on the South course.

Today, it is easy to say that Westchester Country Club was destined to host a major Tour event. But that is not what the founder had in mind. John McEntee Bowman, a former stable boy who rose to become president of Bowman-Biltmore Hotels, one of the largest hotel chains in the world, envisioned a community for millionaire sportsmen, a residential development built around a golf course and an eight-story hotel with apartments for fulltime residents and luxurious rooms for well-heeled travelers. Private homes on the grounds would be serviced by the hotel with meals, maid service, and landscaping. Bowman estimated his project would cost $2,000,000, a figure that, along with his plans, astounded the golf world.

Bowman set to the task in 1919 by purchasing 583 acres from the Hobart J. Park estate. Work on the hotel began late that summer and lasted five years. The Westchester Biltmore Country Club was unveiled sooner, on May 15, 1922. The total cost had exceeded $6,000,000, but the facilities were without equal. In addition to golf and a beach club on nearby Manursing Island (in Long Island Sound), there was a brokerage office in the clubhouse, three polo fields (now the golf practice area), a bridle path, a horse track, and 20 tennis courts. Walter Hagen and Jim Barnes inaugurated the

West Course by losing to home professional Cuthbert Butchart and then-amateur Tommy Armour.

The Club was an immediate success. The initiation fee was $25, and 1,500 members signed up by opening day. The West course was advertised as being "reversible" for winter play; the holes could be played backwards, with the ample tees functioning as greens.

On October 7, 1922, the Club "arrived" by hosting the concluding half of the "Golf Championship of the World," a 72-hole contest pitting Gene Sarazen, winner of the 1922 U.S. Open and PGA, against Walter Hagen, 1922 British Open champion. The first 36 holes were played at Oakmont, where Sarazen came from 4-down to finish 2-down. He rallied in his backyard to win 3&2 and earn a check for $2,000 in a year the Open paid only $500.

The following summer, at the U.S. Women's Amateur, Edith Cummings upset the favored Alexa Stirling 3&2.

Despite the artistic success, the Club had financial problems. In realizing his dream, Bowman destroyed his empire.

Westchester Classic Chairman Bill Jennings congratulates Jack Nicklaus in 1972.

By 1929, 81 homes had been built on the grounds; the owners and other Club members had reason for concern. They were forced to protect their interests and insure the Club's future, so they purchased the facility from Bowman and renamed it the Westchester Country Club.

The membership long has had a strong contingent of top-flight players. The man many regard as the finest amateur developed at Westchester was Tommy Goodwin. During the 1940s and '50s, Goodwin captured numerous prestigious regional events such as the Met Amateur, Met Junior, Ike, and many others.

More recently, Peter V. Bisconti Jr. has won the Club championship 15 times, and son Greg won the 1988 MGA Boys. The Bisconti family was named the Met Golf Writers Association Family of the Year in 1990.

The most significant local tournament to come to Westchester was the 1990 Met Open. Larry Rentz' total of 68-64-72=204 broke the 54-hole record by three strokes and tamed the "Mean 18"— at least for a week.   ❍

The approach on the 17th hole on West.

WINGED FOOT GOLF CLUB

"A Sturdy Breed"

WINGED FOOT GOLF CLUB
Mamaroneck, NY
YEAR FOUNDED: 1921

EAST COURSE

ARCHITECT:
A.W. Tillinghast

COURSE OPENED: 1923

TEES	PAR	YARDAGE
Forward	73	5927
Middle	72	6390
Back	72	6664

TEES	COURSE RATING	SLOPE
Forward	75.7	138
Middle	72.2	135
Back	73.4	137

WEST COURSE

ARCHITECT:
A.W. Tillinghast

COURSE OPENED: 1923

TEES	PAR	YARDAGE
Forward	73	5988
Middle	72	6560
Back	72	6956

TEES	COURSE RATING	SLOPE
Forward	75.9	134
Middle	73.2	138
Back	75.2	140

Winged Foot did not come by its rugged reputation accidentally. The mandate given to architect A.W. Tillinghast was simple, yet firm: "Give us a man-sized course," the Club's founders demanded. "Tillie" responded with two magnificent tests of golf, the West Course and the lesser known but only slightly less difficult East course. (Actually, the two are entwined, with the "back eight" of the East running between the West's nines.)

A group of members within the New York Athletic Club wanted a golf course of their own, but their ideas were voted down in 1921. Undaunted, they incorporated the Winged Foot Golf Club on August 5, 1921, adopting as their name the NYAC's symbol, and as their logo a replica of the sculpture displayed in the lobby of the club building on Manhattan's Central Park South. Much of the early membership can be traced to the NYAC's roster.

In May, 1922, the Club took possession of 280 historic acres in Mamaroneck. The land had once been home to the Mohican Indians and camping ground for two armies during the Revolutionary War. The property also adjoined the home of James Fenimore Cooper, whose novels *The Spy* and *The Last Of The Mohicans* were set in the area.

Both courses were ready for play in June, 1923. Construction proved a monumental task. It is said that Tillinghast cut down 7,800 trees and moved 7,200 tons of rock in preparing the site. The rock was used to build the English Scholastic clubhouse, designed by Clifford C. Wendehack, that opened in 1924. Tillinghast's words describing the final product are considered classics:

"As the various holes came to life they were of a sturdy breed. The contouring of the greens places a premium on the placement of the drives, but never is there the necessity of facing a prodigious carry of the sink or swim sort. It is only the knowledge that the next shot must be played with rifle accuracy that brings the realization that the drive must be placed. The holes are like men, all rather similar from foot to neck, but with the greens showing the same varying characters as human faces."

Some consider Winged Foot the greatest example of strategic design in the United States, with each hole's challenge clearly visible from the tee and each hole's play reflecting Tillinghast's belief that "a controlled shot to a closely guarded green is the surest test of a man's golf."

The fairway bunkering defines the correct side from which to approach the greens, which are relatively small and pear-shaped, somewhat wider at the rear, and may drop as much as seven feet from back to front. They also are tightly bunkered. An off-line approach is almost certain to find a deep bunker or, worse, finish behind one.

Both Winged Foot courses are perennially ranked among the top 30 in America, the West regularly in the top 10.

Many consider the 10th hole on the West course the finest par three in the country; Tillinghast considered it the finest he ever built. The tee overlooks a sloping green with bunkers at the front corners, the one on the right extending into the entrance, another left of center well ahead of the green.

The West finishes with five picturesque holes, all of them long, difficult par fours for

Top: Jones and Espinosa. Above: A gallery at the ninth green during the 1929 U.S. Open.

One of America's great par threes, the tenth hole on the West course.

the pros. The 15th plays downhill through the landing area toward a creek that crosses about 300 yards out from the back markers. The ideal line is left of center, with a fairway bunker on the right in play for the average hitter. From the creek, the hole rises to a pear-shaped green set off slightly to the right.

The 16th is a members' par five that plays as a long par four in tournaments. The drive is the key shot. It must have the length to clear the corner of the dogleg-left, and the accuracy to thread its way through a chute of trees.

The finishing hole bends left, demanding a drive to the right center—the fairway bunker farthest out on that side gives the line. From the drive zone, the hole climbs slightly to a severely contoured green protected by a high-lipped bunker front left.

Greg Norman waves the white flag in surrender to Fuzzy Zoeller during the playoff in the 1984 U.S. Open.

The East has similarly memorable holes. The fourth is a par five requiring two solid shots to set up the final approach to the green, which is off to the right at nearly a right angle. The tee shot must carry a pond to a rising fairway, while a second pond lurks to the right behind the trees at the corner of the dogleg.

Number 13 is a lovely little par three with a severely sloping green guarded by a huge bunker in front that reaches to the dance floor with four sandy fingers. The 17th is a large par three that plays slightly downhill from tee to green. Both sides of the green are protected by steep drops into difficult rough. There are no bunkers on the hole today, although there once were three—one at either side and one dead center ahead of the green. They were taken out half a century ago, the only significant alteration to the original Tillinghast design of the 36 holes. The left greenside bunker was said to have been the largest on the course but preferable to the rough that replaced it!

Winged Foot's first time in the national spotlight was the 1929 U.S. Open. In the final round, Bobby Jones squandered a six-stroke lead with a pair of triple bogies. After a good drive on 18, he pulled his approach, barely clearing the bunker that guards the left side of the green. From deep rough, Jones pitched 12 feet short of the pin and faced a downhill putt with a sharp left-

View from behind the 12th green on the West course.

to-right break. He watched it hesitate on the lip of the cup, then fall into the hole on its last rotation. It gained him a playoff with Al Espinosa, whom he beat by 23 strokes.

Billy Casper put on a sand and putting clinic at the 1959 Open; his record total of 114 putts included 31 one-putt greens. During one stretch, Casper had nine consecutive one-putt greens. His 282 gave him a one shot victory ahead of Bob Rosburg.

The long, par-three third hole played a significant role during the '59 Open, forcing more bogeys than any hole on the course and stopping final-round bids by Ben Hogan and Sam Snead. Casper took no chances with the severe bunkers protecting the third green, playing short of them each day, then pitching on and sinking his putt for par.

Massacre At Winged Foot was the appropriate title of a book by Dick Schaap about the 1974 Open. The West course was considered the sternest Open test since Oakland Hills—"The Monster"—in 1951. The rough was penal, thick, and tangled, and the greens were lightning fast. Tom Watson, making his first serious bid for a major title, led going into the final round, but faltered with a 79. Hale Irwin won with a four-round total of 287, seven over par.

Sometime during that tournament, Jack Nicklaus was asked his opinion of Winged Foot's finishing holes. His

Claude Harmon

answer: "The last 18 are very difficult."

The most recent U.S. Open was in 1984. Only the embattled leaders managed to break par over the 72-hole route. Greg Norman, playing like Houdini down the stretch, drew into a tie with Fuzzy Zoeller after 17 holes. On Winged Foot's great finishing hole Norman pushed his second shot into the grandstand area. After taking line-of-sight relief, he pitched back all the way across the green, finishing 40 feet from the cup, and somehow managed to sink that putt. Zoeller, who was standing in the fairway, assumed it had been for birdie, so he took a white towel from his bag and waved it in mock surrender. After learning the truth, Zoeller parred 18 as well, forcing a playoff in which he overpowered Norman, 67 to 75.

Winged Foot has generously hosted numerous other events of significance. The 1940 U.S. Amateur was held on the West Course and won by the Club's own Dick Chapman. The local boy was the gallery favorite, after Bing Crosby failed to qualify for match play. The 1949 Walker Cup matches also were contested over the West, with the United States prevailing 10-2.

Two U.S. Women's Opens have been played on the East Course. In 1957, Jackie Pung apparently won the tournament, only to be disqualified for signing a scorecard with an incorrect score. Winged Foot members quickly raised more than $3,000, an amount larger than the prize awarded to winner Betsy Rawls, and gave it to the unfortunate Miss Pung. In 1972, Susie Maxwell Berning birdied the long par-three 17th to win by one shot. In 1980, the inaugural U.S. Senior Open was held on the East course, with Roberto DeVicenzo returning a 4-stroke victor.

Locally, Winged Foot has hosted five Met Opens, three Met Amateurs, and three Ike Championships. Amateurs Chet Sanok, Jerry Courville Sr., and Jim McGovern won three of the Opens.

Several notable professionals have run Winged Foot's shop. Craig Wood took over in 1939 and represented the Club during the war years, while winning both the U.S. Open and Masters in 1941. The previous year, he established the scoring record for the Met Open, carding rounds of 64-66-68-66=264 at the Forest Hill Field Club to finish 11 strokes ahead of runner-up Ben Hogan.

Looking at 10-East circa 1920s.

Claude Harmon, winner of the 1948 Masters, served Winged Foot from 1945 to 1978, earning a reputation as one of the game's finest teachers. He taught four U.S. presidents, and helped develop outstanding touring professionals like Mike Souchak, Jack Burke Jr., Dave Marr, and Dick Mayer.

Tom Nieporte, winner of the 1967 Bob Hope Desert Classic, came to Winged Foot upon Harmon's retirement in 1978, and has carried on the teaching tradition. His most successful pupils to date have included recent Met Open

winners Bobby Heins, David Glenz, Darrell Kestner, and Bruce Zabriski.

A number of notable golfers have come from the Club's membership. John G. Anderson twice won the French Amateur and was twice runner-up in the U.S. Amateur. Dick Chapman, who captured the 1940 U.S. Amateur, added the British Amateur 11 years later. The honorable Joseph Gagliardi, Justice of the Supreme Court of New York, won the Met Amateur in 1951 and was runner-up in the U.S. Amateur that year. George Voigt had Bobby Jones two down with five to play in the semifinals of the 1930 British Amateur, the first leg of Jones' Grand Slam. Mark Stuart Sr. was the 1933 Met Amateur champion and son Mark Stuart Jr. captured the same title in 1965.

Anderson was one of the Club's founders and five-time Club champion. His name was given to the Anderson Memorial, the finest four-ball invitational tournament in the country. It was established in 1933, two years before his death.

Another former member was Hall Of Famer Fred Corcoran, who was once director of the PGA Tour, as well as the first manager of professional athletes (including Sam Snead).

The two courses Tilinghast created have proven sturdy, indeed, challenging the greatest players in the world and providing the training grounds for a number of outstanding amateurs and professionals.   ○

The clubhouse as seen from 10-East today.

THE APAWAMIS CLUB

"Champagne Off The Rocks"

It may have been the most controversial shot played in an American championship. Eyewitnesses disagreed about what actually had transpired. Did the ball take a lucky careen off a rock and rebound conveniently onto the green? Or had it been a well-conceived shot that landed just inside the rocks and followed the contour of the land toward the green? We will never know for certain.

The shot in question was played by Harold Hilton on the 37th hole in the finals of the 1911 U.S. Amateur Championship, held at The Apawamis Club. It decided the championship, and was witnessed by what was the largest gallery at a golf event in the United States.

Hilton, who already had won two British Opens and three British Amateurs, was known for his ability to work the ball. But even he admitted that the spoon (3-wood) he hit to the 37th green that day was not a good stroke, despite finishing just 20 feet from the cup.

Hilton's arrival in this country in quest of our national title created quite a stir and drew a very competitive field to Apawamis. Hilton won the qualifying medal, then marched easily to the finals. Long-hitting Fred Herreshoff defeated Chick Evans in the semifinals to earn the right to meet Hilton.

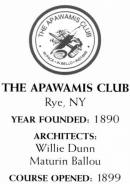

THE APAWAMIS CLUB
Rye, NY

YEAR FOUNDED: 1890

ARCHITECTS:
Willie Dunn
Maturin Ballou

COURSE OPENED: 1899

TEES	PAR	YARDAGE
Forward	73	5759
Middle	72	6115
Back	72	6471

TEES	COURSE RATING	SLOPE
Forward	74.2	133
Middle	70.5	128
Back	72.1	131

The Englishman took a 6-up lead after 23 holes, but Herreshoff charged back, spurred on by a boisterous pro-American gallery. He evened the match with a par three at the 16th, setting the stage for Hilton's shot, which so unnerved Herreshoff that he topped his 2-iron, making it nearly impossible to pitch close. Hilton won with a par four, and the rock—a tall slab now hidden under branches to the right of the green, well out of the line of play—has been "Hilton's Rock" ever since.

By this time, Apawamis was in its third decade, having been formed in 1890, to "further the intercourse of its members, and promote the welfare of the neighborhood." It was the first men's social club chartered by the state of New York, offering family activities during the day and an occasional "literary meeting" in the evening. The name came from the Indian term "Appoqua Mis," meaning "the covering tree."

The Club moved to a new home in 1896 and paid a man $10 to "stake out" a nine-hole course in an apple orchard. The club leased still another home in 1897, and built another nine-hole course, one that featured such unusual hazards as a swamp, trolley tracks, and a railroad signal tower.

As membership increased, so did the need for 18 holes. In 1898, the Club purchased 120 acres and built an 18-hole course designed by Green Chairman Maturin Ballou after consultation with Willie Dunn. Over the next few years, alterations were made by resident professionals Willie Davis and Herbert Strong, both among America's early golf architects. Another prominent Apawamis professional was Willie Anderson, a Scot from North Berwick who won the U.S. Open each of the three years (1903-1905) he represented the Club.

The course they molded plays over typically rugged Westchester terrain, and demands accuracy off the tee. But the real challenge lies in the small greens, which are fast and slick, demanding defensive approach shots to specific target areas below the cup. Ben Hogan once called Apawamis "the toughest short golf course I have ever played."

The most memorable hole is the fourth, called "Eleanor's Teeth" (for former first lady Eleanor Roosevelt) for the 12 bunkers that protect the elevated green—nine in front, on two levels, and four on the right side. The two-tiered green, which tilts severely back to front, is

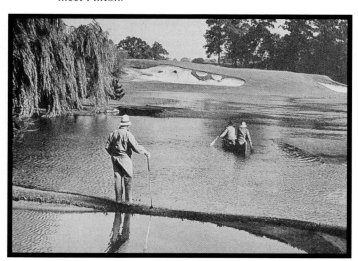

The aftermath of the hurricane of 1938.

"Eleanor's Teeth," the bunkering at the fourth hole.

regarded as one of the game's toughest. Hilton called the 11th "the best two-shot hole in the United States," despite driving out-of-bounds twice during the U.S. Amateur finals in 1911. The hole features a semi-blind drive to a slanting fairway, and a brook crossing in front of the green.

Apawamis has hosted the Met Amateur four times. The 1915 edition was a special occasion, marking Walter Travis' final tournament appearance. Fittingly, he ousted archrival Jerry Travers in the second round.

The PGA Tour's Westchester Classic had its genesis at Apawamis as a one-day pro-amateur for the benefit of United Hospital in Port Chester. It was first held in 1952, as a four-ball match among professionals and amateurs and soon offered the richest purse in the country for a one-day event. The standard pro-am format was adopted in 1954, and lasted through 1962. It became the Thunderbird Classic, and later the Westchester Classic, played at the Westchester Country Club.

In 1978, the Curtis Cup matches were played in the Met Area for the first time at Apawamis. The United States team, led by future LPGA star Beth Daniel, winner of the 1975 and 1977 Women's Amateur, easily defeated their British counterparts, 12-6. Helping organize the contests were two former Curtis Cup captains and Apawamis members, Allison "Sis" Choate and Jean Ashley Crawford.

No event, however, is more closely woven into the Apawamis fabric than the United States Seniors Golf Association's annual tournament. It was the brainchild of member Horace Hotchkiss, who in 1905 invited a group of friends and acquaintances, all at least 55 years of age, for a one-day, 36-hole stoke play competition. Some 50 players gathered on October 12 for the world's first-ever "seniors" tournament.

For years, it was played in the fall, but the date was changed after the surprise hurricane of 1938, which arrived mid-tournament and flooded the course. Today, the Seniors is held on the first Tuesday and Wednesday in June, with some 500 players competing over 36 holes, at Apawamis and nearby Round Hill and Blind Brook. ○

Horace Hotchkiss

ARDSLEY COUNTRY CLUB

"Midas Plaisance"

It was conceived on a grand scale, designed to take its place alongside Newport and nearby Tuxedo as a summer playground for the fabulously wealthy. Opened in 1896, it was the Ardsley Casino, known to many as "The Millionaires Club." The *New York Herald* dubbed it "Midas Plaisance."

The casino as it appeared from the river.

The objective was to create a parklike setting complete with an 18-hole golf course. No expense was spared. The total cost for the land, buildings, and golf course came to approximately $1 million—more than 100 years ago!

The clubhouse/casino was located on a craggy bluff overlooking the Hudson River. At its feet were the Club's yacht basin and private railroad depot. The three-story building included 60 bedrooms for members not spending the evening on their yachts.

The course was the work of Willie Dunn, who considered it his crowning achievement in this country. He needed 200 men and 50 teams of horses to clear the virgin forest. The first four holes played south from the clubhouse along the cliffs, which were cut by ravines at irregular intervals. The fourth, known as the "Chasm hole," required a 150-yard carry over a 100-foot-deep ravine that the players crossed via a rustle bridge.

In 1898, Ardsley hosted the third USGA Women's Amateur. Young Beatrix Hoyt of Shinnecock Hills won for the third consecutive year.

The original golf course straddled Broadway, nine holes on either side. Over the years, the course grew away from the river as additional land was obtained higher up the hills. The first change took place in 1900 when the four riverside holes were consolidated into two. Work in 1919 is attributed to Donald Ross, more in 1928 to Alister

Mackenzie, who left one of his trademarks—trees in the middle of a fairway. The fairway of the par-five fourth is divided beyond the landing area by a stand of trees, forcing the golfer to choose the high road to the right or the low road to the left.

The nature of the Club changed dramatically after 1927 when the stables on the hillside west of Broadway were converted into what would become the second clubhouse, replacing the Casino, which was razed in 1936 (The word casino had been dropped from the Club's name in 1897). These stables once housed as many as 100 horses, including the teams that pulled the Ardsley Tallyho, which commuted each weekday between the Club and the Hotel Brunswick on Fifth Avenue in Manhattan.

The Mackenzie course remained intact until 1966, when the Club moved to its present home, the former mansion of Frank Gould, situated high in the hills. From the terrace, members enjoy a panoramic view of the Hudson and the New Jersey Palisades beyond.

The course was revised by Robert Trent Jones, who eliminated the last two holes across Broadway and converted Mackenzie's 15th, an unusual par five crossing the crest of the hill, into today's first hole, a par four that drops 135 feet into a valley, with a pond at the right-front of the green nicely complemented by a stately willow standing brazenly in the left side of the fairway just short of the water. The hole calls for a carefully placed tee shot, most likely with an iron.

Architect Marvin Armstrong has redone the 8th and 17th greens and extended the 14th hole between 1993 and 1996.

The view of the river from the first tee has not changed, and has been enjoyed by Ardsley's members for more than a century. ○

**ARDSLEY
COUNTRY CLUB**
Ardsley-on-Hudson, NY

YEAR FOUNDED: 1895

ARCHITECTS:
Willie Dunn
Donald Ross
Alister Mackenzie
Robert Trent Jones
Marvin Armstrong

COURSE OPENED: 1896

TEES	PAR	YARDAGE
Forward	73	5673
Middle	72	6197
Back	72	6522

	COURSE	
TEES	RATING	SLOPE
Forward	73.6	128
Middle	70.8	128
Back	72.3	131

The breathtaking view from the first tee.

BROOKLAWN COUNTRY CLUB

"Of Human Kindness"

**BROOKLAWN
COUNTRY CLUB**
Fairfield, CT

YEAR FOUNDED: 1895

ARCHITECTS:
Members
A.W. Tillinghast

COURSE OPENED: 1895

TEES	PAR	YARDAGE
Forward	73	5536
Middle	71	6352
Back	71	6617

TEES	COURSE RATING	SLOPE
Forward	72.5	125
Middle	71.4	132
Back	72.5	135

When Gene Sarazen was a young man, he suffered a serious illness. His doctor prescribed a regimen of fresh air and sunshine, which played into Sarazen's career plans, converting his passion for golf into a vocation.

His first job in golf was as assistant to Al Ciuci at the (now defunct) Beardsley Park municipal course in Bridgeport, Connecticut. Ciuci quickly realized the exceptional talent of his protégé, and was determined to help him advance to a more suitable apprenticeship. After some difficulty, he arranged to introduce Sarazen to George Sparling, professional at the prestigious Brooklawn Country Club in Fairfield. After watching Sarazen hit some balls, Sparling turned him away, unimpressed. However, Sarazen's "interview" had been observed by two influential members of the Club, Archie and Willie Wheeler, twin brothers who persuaded Sparling to take on the young man as shop assistant at $8 per week.

The opportunity to work at a major club and his relationship with Archie Wheeler were the catalysts for Sarazen's career. Although he worked at Brooklawn for

The Brooklawn clubhouse.

just two summers (1918-1919), Sarazen found in Wheeler a lifelong friend and benefactor.

Archie and Willie were heirs to the Singer Sewing Machine fortune. Extremely wealthy, Archie chose to use his riches to help the poor. The downtrodden would come to his door for their daily or weekly help. Others were sought out by Wheeler, who gave them regular contributions.

Archie was an excellent golfer. A charter member of Brooklawn, he was the first Club champion. In 1904 he played an exhibition at Brooklawn against Walter Travis—and won. Willie, also a Club champion, was ambidextrous: He was known to play 18 holes in the morning right-handed, then another 18 after lunch left-handed, with equal dexterity.

The Wheelers were among the prominent residents of Bridgeport who organized the Club in 1895. Its birth was hastened along by the promise that a trolley line would be extended from the railroad station 15 minutes away to the proposed site for the Club, a sixty-acre farm. The farmhouse, located by the brook near the present 16th tee, became the first clubhouse. A barn was converted into a casino, with dancing, a game room, and bowling alleys.

The original member-designed nine-hole golf course included holes with fanciful names such as "Altar," "Ararat," "Slaughter," and "Toilsome." In 1910, the Club purchased a farm across Cornell Road from the original property, where an additional nine holes were built, and the original nine revised, most likely by the members themselves.

In 1929, the Club had the option of exchanging their property for the nearby site that now includes the 36-hole Fairchild–Wheeler public facility, but chose to remain where they were, and still are. A.W. Tillinghast was engaged to rebuild the course. He created three new holes, revised a few others, and built 18 new greens.

The baffling contours of Tillinghast's greens are Brooklawn's trademark. Also notable is another Tillinghast signature—deep bunkers that flank most of the greens. The course rolls up and down the steep hills, and across the Rooster River, which crosses six holes.

Anchoring the course is the seventh hole, a scenic par five of more than 600 yards that sweeps downhill and to the right to a tightly bunkered green beyond the river. Number

The picturesque 9th hole.

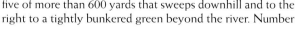

Gene Sarazen is reunited with his early sponsor, Archie Wheeler, at the Club's 50th anniversary in 1945.

eight is a very short par five that plays back across the river, through a narrow corridor of trees, then steadily uphill. The small bunker across the front of the green adds to the hole's character.

The hole people remember is the 15th, a short par three over a pond to an elevated green set above deep side bunkers. The tee shot must find its way between two tall trees well short of the green.

Brooklawn has hosted three USGA events during the last 23 years. The Junior Boys came in 1974 the winner being David Nevatt. In 1979, the Women's Open was won by Jerilyn Britz. The USGA recommended a new tee be built on the seventh hole, between the men's tee and the usual ladies' tee. It cost Nancy Lopez the championship, enticing her to go for the green on her second shot from a distance beyond 200 yards. The result was a pair of costly double bogies—Lopez finished six strokes behind Britz.

In 1987, Brooklawn was the stage for a virtuoso performance by Gary Player in the U.S. Senior Open. He became the first player in Senior Open history to score in the 60s all four rounds. His 69-68-67-66=270 (14 under par) beat the tournament record by nine strokes. Incredibly, Player never once three-putted on Brooklawn's baffling greens.

In 1997, Brooklawn will host the MGA Junior Championship, in the MGA's Centennial year.

From Gene Sarazen to Gary Player, Brooklawn has embraced the very best, a legacy traced to the Wheeler brothers.   ○

Gary Player won the 1987 U.S. Senior Open at Brooklawn.

*Ben
Hogan*

CENTURY
COUNTRY CLUB

"A Nice Appearance"

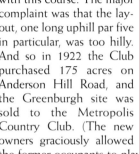

**CENTURY
COUNTRY CLUB**
Purchase, NY

YEAR FOUNDED: 1898

ARCHITECTS:
H.S. Colt &
Charles Alison

COURSE OPENED: 1924

TEES	PAR	YARDAGE
Forward	71	6078
Middle	71	6522
Back	71	6807

TEES	COURSE RATING	SLOPE
Forward	75.4	134
Middle	71.6	127
Back	73.0	130

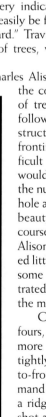

Century was founded in 1898 as the summer playground for a group of Wall Street bankers immortalized in Stephen Birmingham's book, *Our Crowd*. The Club's founding fathers leased a site along Long Island Sound in the Throgs Neck section of the Bronx, just north of the present-day toll plaza for the Throgs Neck Bridge. Tom Bendelow designed a nine-hole course that played alongside the water.

The Club's name probably came from the fact that it was established so near the turn of the century. Another theory is that the name refers to an intent of the founders to limit membership to an exclusive 100.

The members quickly grew restless at their leased home, wishing to own their property and expand their course to a more fashionable 18 holes. In 1904, they purchased a 100-acre site along Landers Road in Greenburgh, where they built an 18-hole course designed by Herbert Strong, several tennis courts, a toboggan slide, and riding stables.

By the end of World War I, many members found fault with this course. The major complaint was that the layout, one long uphill par five in particular, was too hilly. And so in 1922 the Club purchased 175 acres on Anderson Hill Road, and the Greenburgh site was sold to the Metropolis Country Club. (The new owners graciously allowed the former occupants to play their old golf course until the new facility was ready in 1924.)

Prior to the move, the famed amateur champion and architect Walter Travis was hired to evaluate the new property. He found the land first-rate, noting, "There is a brook fed by what bears every indication of being a perpetual spring. This may very easily be formed into a pond, making a splendid water hazard." Travis also commented on the comparative absence of trees, which he believed had no place on a golf course.

H.S. Colt and Charles Alison, who actually designed the course, were big proponents of trees. While the club wisely followed Travis' advice and constructed the beautiful pond fronting the 13th green, it is difficult to imagine what Century would look like today without the numerous trees that give each hole an identity and add so much beauty and character to the course. It is a testament to Colt & Alison that the course has changed little over the years, aside from some rebunkering work orchestrated by Robert Trent Jones in the mid-1960s.

Century's strengths are its par fours, several of which stretch more than 400 yards, and its tightly-bunkered and slick back-to-front greens. Several holes demand the drive carry the crest of a ridge to leave an open, visible shot at the green. At the sixth, a

The beautiful par-three 13th hole.

The approach to the 15th hole.

long par four considered among the most challenging holes on the course, the ridge sits about 200 yards off the tee. Just over it is a sharply sloping right-to-left fairway, while a severe bunker protects the left-front of the green.

Century's lone water hazard can come into play on two of its most picturesque holes. The short par-four 12th is closely guarded right-front by a huge willow and left-front by a large white pine, with the water off to the right. The par-three 13th requires a pitch across the pond to a small green fronted by a pair of flash bunkers and backed up by three larger bunkers.

The present clubhouse was designed by members Joseph Friedlander and Harry Allen Jacobs, and was completed early in 1924. It features a two-storied men's locker room, one of the few of its kind in America.

Ben Hogan joined the Century family as assistant professional in 1938 and remained

Dick Siderowf

for three seasons. His letter of recommendation, penned by a Century member, stated simply that "he made a nice appearance"—certainly one of the great understatements in golf history. After World War II, Century dodged two bullets fired by the State Highways Department, as the routings for both Interstates 287 and 684 skirted Club property.

Century's most prominent golfing member has been Dick Siderowf, the 1973 and 1976 British Amateur champion and member of three Walker Cup teams. Siderowf also won five Met Amateurs and was the first recipient of the MGA's Player Of The Year Award in 1976 and the Met Golf Writers Gold Tee Award in 1979.

Century's appearance has changed over the years, but the Club and course have retained their reputation as one of the Met Area's finest.   ❍

GREENWICH COUNTRY CLUB

"Curtiss' Folly"

The Greenwich clubhouse.

I n the spring of 1892, Julian Curtiss made a business trip to London representing A.G. Spalding & Brothers, America's foremost dealer in sporting goods. While there, he was introduced to golf and placed an order for $400 worth of clubs and balls on the company account. His employers failed to see the wisdom of his purchase, there being no evidence of golf in the United States at the time. Curtiss promised to promote the sport and help unload the equipment. That did not prove very difficult once the early players at St. Andrew's, Tuxedo, and Shinnecock Hills learned of Spalding's stash. (Curtiss later became president of Spalding and was responsible for bringing Harry Vardon over to tour this country in 1900.)

As well as promoting golf, Curtiss took it up himself. Upon his return from England, he and two other men laid out a five-hole course across the street from their homes in the Greenwich neighborhood of Belle Haven. Their little course attracted others, so they moved out into the hills west of town. By the spring of 1895, the Fairfield County Golf Club was organized, and in 1909 it changed its name to Greenwich Country Club when they decided to include a full range of activities.

The grounds were located on Electric Hill, named for a home there that was among the first elec-

Julian Curtiss

trified by Thomas Edison. The first clubhouse stood about 50 yards in front of the present 16th tee; it burned down in 1910, by which time the Club had already decided to build a much larger structure at the highest point on the property. That building eventually was destroyed by a spectacular fire on Labor Day, 1960. The present clubhouse was unveiled in 1963.

The first course was a nine-hole affair that rolled up and down hills and across brooks and stone walls. In 1906, the Club acquired additional property to the north and engaged Lawrence Van Etten to lay out a full 18-hole course, which opened in 1908. The present configuration came to be in 1946, when Donald Ross was called in for a redesign. Lost was the famous par-three 10th, which played from a tee on a cliff behind the present pro shop down to the current ninth green, an island surrounded by sand and mounds: Vardon had called it the most beautiful par three he had seen in America.

The present course rolls and tumbles over dramatic terrain. Blind shots abound and water is in play on five holes, most notably the eighth and ninth, which conclude a five-hole stretch that determines the outcome of many matches. For the average player, the eighth hole calls for a do-or-die carry over a creek that crosses the fairway 40 yards from the green. The ninth plays from an elevated tee to a fairway that curves to the right around a pond that parallels the right side. The last five holes are behind the clubhouse. For the long hitters, the second shot on the par-five 14th calls for a decision, since a creek crosses the fairway just short of the green; average players must keep their second shot close to the edge of the bluff overlooking the green.

Among the Club's charter members is an Englishman named F.E. Vivian Bond. Upon returning to England in 1897, he sent the Club a trophy, which he asked be played for on a date as close as possible to Queen Victoria's birthday (May 24). Since 1897 marked the Diamond Jubilee of Victoria's coronation, the trophy was called the Queen Victoria Diamond Jubilee Cup (or Bond Cup). It is one of the oldest club trophies in American golf, having been contested nearly every year since 1897 as an individual

**GREENWICH
COUNTRY CLUB**
Greenwich, CT

YEAR FOUNDED: 1892

ARCHITECTS:
Lawrence Van Etten
Seth Raynor
Donald Ross

COURSE OPENED: 1908

TEES	PAR	YARDAGE
Forward	74	5884
Middle	71	6385
Back	71	6706

TEES	COURSE RATING	SLOPE
Forward	74.7	130
Middle	71.2	128
Back	72.6	130

The approach to #8.

handicap competition among the members.

The Greenwich membership has included a number of superb players over the years, none more enduring than Sam Graham, who won the Bond Cup four times, the first in 1903 at age 15, the last in 1956 when he was legally blind due to cataracts. On that occasion, he had his caddie hold the flag over the cup on the 18th green, then chipped in from 60 feet to win. Graham also won the MGA Senior Championship three times.

The first name on the Club championship board was Findlay Douglas, winner of the U.S. Amateur in 1898 and runner-up the following two seasons. Also listed are Dick Chapman, the 1940 U.S. and 1957 British Amateur

"The picturesque old 10th", a hole much admired by Harry Vardon and for many years the signature hole of the course.

champion, and Jonas Saxton, the MGA's Player of the Year in 1983 and 1984, and winner of the Ike on three occasions.

The 1920 Met Open was contested at Greenwich, and after 72 holes Walter Hagen and Jim Barnes, the premier players of the day, were deadlocked at 292. Barnes' opening day 69 established a new record for the course, but then his putter deserted him until the closing holes. Hagen caught and passed Barnes with a third-round 69, but Barnes evened the score with a 30-foot birdie putt on the home green. Hagen missed from three feet for the par that would have given him victory without a playoff. Instead, he won the playoff the next day, shooting a 70 to Barnes' 74.

In 1958 Greenwich hosted the USGA Junior Girls Championship. Judy Eller successfully defended her title, and was presented the trophy by six-time Women's Amateur champion Glenna Collett Vare, once an honorary member of the Club, who refereed the final match. With the likes of Hagen and Vare part of its rich history, Greenwich can hardly be considered any man's folly. ❍

KNOLLWOOD COUNTRY CLUB

"The 19th Hole"

**KNOLLWOOD
COUNTRY CLUB**
Elmsford, NY

YEAR FOUNDED: 1894

ARCHITECTS:
Lawrence Van Etten
A.W. Tillinghast
Seth Raynor
Charles Banks

COURSE OPENED: 1927

TEES	PAR	YARDAGE
Forward	73	5714
Middle	71	6410
Back	71	6516

TEES	COURSE RATING	SLOPE
Forward	74.9	133
Middle	71.2	131
Back	71.7	132

At most clubs, the 19th hole is the bar. At Knollwood, it's a short par three over a pond and three bunkers. It was designed by Seth Raynor, who, while revising Knollwood's course in the mid-1920s, found himself with an outstanding 18th hole, which finished about 200 yards from the clubhouse. Rather than change the home hole, he designed an extra one as a way to bring the players back to the clubhouse and provide an exciting vehicle for settling the day's wagers.

Knollwood Country Club was a child of the 1890s, the planned centerpiece of an exclusive, Tuxedo-like colony in the Westchester hills between White Plains and Tarrytown. The idea was to offer such sports as horseback riding, shooting, and automobile driving, but by the time it was formally organized in 1894, the main interest of the members was golf.

One of the charter members was Lawrence Van Etten, who later would gain a limited amount of recognition as a course architect. His maiden design was the first Knollwood course, opened in 1895, a short layout with very small greens. That course eventually matured into a par-69 test of 5,305 yards that proved lay of the land was every bit as important as length for toughening a course. At that time, the 11th and 12th holes, both par threes, crossed each other and the pond that bisects the present 18th fairway.

Van Etten's short course proved immensely popular, and for years Knollwood resisted changing it to keep pace with advances in equipment. But the chance to expand could not be ignored when two adjacent plots of land became available. A.W. Tillinghast submitted a plan for a revised course and work began. But Tillinghast dropped out and Raynor was retained as his replacement. Raynor did little more than lay out plans for a new course when he died unexpectedly in January, 1926. With minor modifications, Charles Banks finished building the course, which opened in 1927.

The signatures of Tillinghast and Raynor are evident on the course today. The terrain is very hilly in spots, which no doubt delighted Raynor, giving him the green settings and fairway undulations he relished. Although water is a factor on just three holes, it is a major consideration twice on the 18th, perhaps the premier par four in the Met Area.

Played from an elevated tee over a pond to a fairway that slopes left to right, the drive at 18 must be long and accurate to leave a level lie and an open shot at the green. The pond empties into a brook that runs along the right side of the hole before widening again as it crosses the fairway a second time about 150 yards from the green. There is a bunker in the hillside left of the green and a steep fall-off down to the creek below.

The uphill par-three eighth hole plays from a slightly elevated tee over a brook to a Redan-style green set on an angle and falling away sharply to the right rear. Three bunkers wait below and ahead of the right front of the green.

Clifford Roberts, who with Bobby Jones created Augusta National Golf Club and The Masters tournament, was a Knollwood member. Early discussions that eventually led to the inception of The Masters are said to have taken place at Knollwood's "20th hole".

Another member was Al Maginnes, one of America's first professional football players. He arranged to house the West Point football team in the Knollwood clubhouse and allow them use of the fifth fairway as a practice field in preparation for their annual game in New York against Notre Dame.

But the most notable golfing member over the years has been Willie Turnesa, who joined in 1939. The youngest—and only non-professional—among seven golfing brothers, Willie first attained national prominence with his victory in the 1939 U.S. Amateur at Oakmont. Superb wedge play was the difference, earning him the nickname "Willie The Wedge". In the final match, he got down in two each of the 13 times his approach found a bunker. In 1947 Turnesa was unbeatable in Walker Cup competition at St. Andrews, which he followed by capturing the British

The arch at the club entrance.

Amateur title at Carnoustie. The next year, he regained the U.S. Amateur trophy. He also played on the 1949 Walker Cup team and captained the 1951 team. Locally, Willie won the 1937 Met Amateur, and twice took individual honors in the Ike Championship, three times leading Knollwood to team victory. With Udo Reinach of Quaker Ridge, Willie created the Westchester Caddie Scholarship Fund in 1956.

In 1943, Willie was joined by older brother Mike, who became head professional, a job he held until his retirement in 1987, when he was named director of golf. Mike played the Tour for 18 years before settling down at Knollwood. He is best known for finishing second to Ben Hogan in both the 1948 PGA Championship and the 1942 Hale America Tournament, the war-time substitute for the U.S. Open; to Sam Snead in the 1942 PGA Championship, as well as for a second-round loss to Byron Nelson in the 1945 PGA.

The national spotlight shone on Knollwood in 1985 when the Club co-hosted the LPGA's MasterCard International with Westchester Hills. Muffin Spencer-Devlin came from six shots back with a final round 64, scoring eight birdies on the last 10 holes and a back-nine 28 for her first victory. The following year, Ridgeway was added as a third host club, and Cindy Mackey won her first LPGA event.

Knollwood has always had a strong sense of its history.

When the course was redesigned in the '20s, the lake at the 19th hole was drained, revealing a large cache of gutta percha balls and setting the stage for the Club's first gutta percha tournament. The Club's best players reportedly averaged just 150 yards off the tee with the old-fashioned balls.

As part of the 60th Anniversary celebration in 1954, a second gutta percha tournament was held, this one featuring Mike and Willie Turnesa, Gene Sarazen, Johnny Farrell, Willie Klein, and Al Brosch, who dressed in 1890s garb and played with clubs from that era.

That was hardly the first great match among the old-timers. Van Etten's original course hosted an exhibition renewing the greatest rivalry of that time—Jerry Travers versus Walter Travis. Travers came to the final hole 1-up, but hooked his approach onto the roof of the clubhouse porch. Needing a par to win the match, Travers calmly waved the gallery aside, chipped from the roof to the green, and holed his putt for the winning par, avoiding a playoff at the 19th hole

Wille and Mike Turnesa at Jennings Cup, 1982.

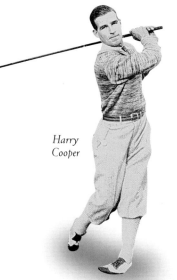

Harry Cooper

METROPOLIS COUNTRY CLUB
"Reading Time"

The Metroplis Country Club began life as the "country adjunct" of the Metropolis City Club, a dining and social organization on West 57th Street in Manhattan. The city club was organized in 1879 to "promote social intercourse among its members, and to encourage musical, literary, dramatic, and other exercises, and to establish a library."

Sporting activities included swimming, billiards, bowling, gymnastics, and cards. The Club also was known for its fine restaurant and men's grill, and boasted a membership roster of more than 700.

In 1922, the country club was incorporated, and purchased the former site of the Century Country Club, including a clubhouse and an 18-hole course. The original clubhouse, with white columns and a marble terrace, had once been a farmhouse. From its broad verandahs, the members enjoyed serene views of the Westchester countryside, and danced the night away on the two-level patio. That building burned to the ground in 1969 and was replaced by a more modern structure, which opened in 1972.

The Club survived the Depression thanks in large part to Edmund Waterman, a strict disciplinarian who ran a tight ship as longtime Club president. (One example of his legacy: Topless men's bathing suits were not allowed until well into the 1950s.) Another prominent member was Herman Freydberg, a former MGA president who was instrumental in the development of the modern handicap system.

The golf course that Metropolis inherited from Century was built by Herbert Strong in 1904. Members of

Jack Burke Jr.

both clubs used it during the years 1923 to 1924 while the new Century course was under construction. Toward the end of the decade, Metropolis purchased additional land and engaged A.W. Tillinghast to revise the course. He added the 7th and 12th through 14th holes. In the early '70s, Joe Finger built the par-three 15th hole.

Metropolis features rolling, tree-lined fairways and greens with tricky contours and multiple tiers. Not especially long and playing to par 70, the course also is known for its numerous tight doglegs that demand position off the tee, often combined with sufficient length to clear the corner.

The second is the water hole, a par four that plays along a lake extending from the left side of the fairway to the front of the green, leaving only a small way in on the right. The two-tiered putting surface is bunkered back-left, behind the lake, and front right, further narrowing the entrance. A huge tree once stood in the middle of the fairway about 100 yards from the tee, forcing the golfer to play a draw or fade to find the fairway.

The sixth, Metropolis' showpiece and one of the great holes in the Met Area, is a very tight, tumbling par four of moderate length that is the number-one handicap hole. The landing area for the average player is bunkered on both sides and falls to the left while rolling downhill toward the green. Many professionals lay up off the tee to avoid more trees on the left that tighten the hole. One bunker protects the front of the two-tiered green.

The 11th is a massive par five that rises to a crest in the drive zone, which is flanked by a pair of bunkers on each side. The fairway twice drops

METROPOLIS COUNTRY CLUB

White Plains, NY

YEAR FOUNDED: 1922

ARCHITECTS:
Herbert Strong
A.W. Tillinghast
Joe Finger

COURSE OPENED: 1904

TEES	PAR	YARDAGE
Forward	73	5763
Middle	70	6387
Back	70	6628

TEES	COURSE RATING	SLOPE
Forward	74.6	134
Middle	71.2	131
Back	72.2	134

Paul Runyan

The sixth, one of Westchester's finest.

sharply the last 200 yards into the green. A spine runs from front to back through the center of the putting surface.

A number of outstanding professionals served Metropolis over the years. The first of note was Paul Runyan, "Little Poison," who worked at the Club from 1931 to 1943. Runyan was that unique combination of teaching professional and top Tour player. While representing Metropolis, he won the 1934 and 1938 PGA Championships, the 1934 Met Open, and the 1931, 1935, and 1936 Met PGA titles.

Jack Burke Jr., who later would win both the Masters and PGA Championship, served briefly (1948-1950) as Club professional before joining the Tour full time. A few years later, "Lighthorse" Harry Cooper, one of the best shotmakers on Tour during the 1930s began his tenure, serving from 1953 until his retirement in 1978. Cooper still lives half a mile from the Club and gives lessons at the Westchester Country Club.

Metropolis' current professional is Gene Borek, a Yonkers native who arrived in 1981 with outstanding credentials, having won three Met PGA championships. In

Gene Borek

recent years, Borek has played an occasional event of the PGA Senior Tour.

Metropolis has been a favorite venue for local events, hosting four Met Opens and three Met Amateurs. The 1939 Met Open resulted in a three-way tie among PGA champion Henry Picard, Paul Runyan, and Vic Ghezzi, who eventually had to play two extra rounds to decide the issue in Picard's favor.

In the 1949 Met Open, Jack Burke Jr. was an easy six-shot victor over Gene Sarazen, posting a 274 total, including a final-round 64, which was matched by 1958 winner Bob Watson. The 1975 winner, Carlton "Slugger" White, is now a Rules official on the PGA Tour.

In 1937 Willie Turnesa captured his only Met Amateur trophy. In 1968, Dick Siderowf of Century won his first of five Met Amateur titles; his fifth victory came in 1990 at Metropolis at age 52, when he edged George Zahringer III on the 37th hole.

A book about "golf at Metropolis" would surely be a fascinating addition to any club's library.   ❍

OLD OAKS COUNTRY CLUB

"An Oak By Any Other Name"

During the Roaring 20s, golf became a craze that swept up almost everyone, whether he or she knew the first thing about the game. For example, Manhattan's Progress City Club, a light-exercise group, decided in 1924 to become golfers. So they bought 205 acres in Purchase, adjacent to the Century Country Club. The land, part of the estate of William A. Reed, a founder of the investment banking firm of Dillon, Reed & Company, once had been owned by a silk merchant named Trainer Park, who named it Hillcrest. His British manor house, which was completed in 1890, featured 19th-century woodworking, elaborate staircases, long hallways, massive rooms, and formal gardens.

Progress Country Club was organized in 1925. In the early years, a large portion of the membership hailed from the theatrical and motion picture world. Needless to say, lively entertainment was the rule of the day and night! Ethel Merman made her first public appearance at the Club in 1928.

The Reed mansion became the Progress clubhouse. The swimming pool was added in 1930, replacing a beautiful, rolling 18-hole putting green. The pool was rebuilt in the mid 1970s, and in 1976 was featured in the movie *Goodbye Columbus.*

Charles Alison is generally regarded as the course architect, but although he built the course, the plans were drawn up by A.W. Tillinghast in 1925. Tillinghast designed 27 holes, the main course and the West nine. But he and the Club failed to see eye to eye and parted ways. Alison completed the courses in 1926—beginning with the nineholer, built in a horseshoe around the clubhouse—but the holes bore Tillinghast's imprint, particularly on the greens, which tilted from back to front and were tightly bunkered at the front corners.

Most of the fairways today are tree-lined and bend slightly from tee to green. The greens are usually invisible from the tee but clearly in view from the landing area. And there is the seemingly ever-present fieldstone-bordered brook that meanders through the grounds. Tillie's greens present small targets whose difficulty is accentuated by their speed and firmness.

The 8th and 17th holes rank among the toughest par fours in the Met Area. Eight climbs to a difficult two-tiered green: Getting down in two from above the hole is possibly the most difficult assignment on the property. The long 17th (462 yards) comes out of a chute and rises, bending left in the drive zone, then slightly back to the right to a green perched on a knoll behind a pair of bunkers.

One of the early recorded instances of marathon golf took place at Progress. In 1928, member Leo DeKorn performed a feat worthy of *Ripley's Believe It Or Not,* playing 11 rounds in one day. When his record was broken elsewhere, DeKorn tried again, this time starting at dusk. Aided by automobile lights, DeKorn was able to play 19 rounds in 24 hours, reclaiming the record (which has since been eclipsed).

The Depression was truly depressing for Progress. First came several name changes—to Purchase, then Pine Ridge, and back to Progress. In 1935 it was agreed that the only way to save the Club was to merge with nearby Oak Ridge. The Purchase site, by far the more attractive, then became the home of the Old Oaks Country Club. The new name is said to have been chosen "in deference to Oak Ridge's chinaware."

Oak Ridge, established in 1916, was located on the Tuckahoe-Eastchester border. Eventually it became landlocked in the middle of residential and commercial developments. Its colonial clubhouse is now Eastchester Town Hall.

Oak Ridge professional Willie MacFarlane, who came to the Club in 1921, won the 1925 U.S. Open, beating Bobby Jones in a playoff. He remained with the Club through the merger, and became Old Oaks' first head professional.

In 1963, New York State condemned 13 acres of Club property for Interstate 684. This destroyed the West nine and effectively separated the first four holes from the last two, which were located on opposite sides of the clubhouse.

**OLD OAKS
COUNTRY CLUB**

Purchase, NY

YEAR FOUNDED: 1925

ARCHITECTS:
A.W. Tillinghast
Charles Alison

COURSE OPENED: 1926

TEES	PAR	YARDAGE
Forward	70	5652
Middle	70	6249
Back	70	6503

TEES	COURSE RATING	SLOPE
Forward	73.9	132
Middle	71.1	135
Back	72.3	139

The magnificent clubhouse.

The 16th green.

For a while the Club attempted to maintain a six-hole course, but by the mid 1970s this operarion ceased, leaving the Club with 18 holes.

Running the pro shop in recent years has been Bobby Heins, whose local victories include the 1988 and 1989 Met Opens. In 1984, the Club hosted the Met Open, won by Jim Albus' final round 69, which earned him a two-stroke victory and a second Met Open title.

In preparation for the 1989 Met PGA Championship, Old Oaks retained architect David Postlewait to restore the club's 57 bunkers to their original contouring. Postlewait, a native of Oklahoma, had done similar work preparing courses for the national PGA Championship.

At the same time, the Club took down the two rows of maples that lined the entrance road and replaced them with 32 young red oaks which someday will grow into beautiful old oaks.

SIWANOY COUNTRY CLUB
"Round Trip"

Siwanoy's nomadic wanderings in the early part of the century had the cumulative effect of crossing the street.

Back in the late 1890s, a harness track occupied a corner of the present Club property, attracting real-estate developers Augustus and Middleton Rose, who bought land adjacent to the track where they laid out a nine-hole course called Fairview Park.

Among those playing Fairview was a group of 18 men from Mt. Vernon. For them a day of golf included a half-hour ride on the Hokey Pokey Trolley up White Plains Road, their rounds, then—after a long wait—the return trip. Not surprisingly, they discussed establishing a club closer to home, a dream that became reality when they leased land along White Plains Road and built a nine-hole course in 1901. The club took its name from a Mohican tribe that lived in the area.

When they learned their lease would not be renewed after the 1903 season, the Club moved north to where White Plains Road now intersects the Cross County Parkway. A new nine-hole course, designed by Willie Dunn, opened in 1904. Siwanoy remained at this site through 1913, when it became obvious that nine holes couldn't satisfy the growing membership.

The choice was to purchase adjacent land and enlarge the existing course, or purchase a larger tract in Bronxville to the north and start over again. Donald Ross saw greater potential in Bronxville, so the Club purchased 110 acres of Paulding Manor, which had been given to Revolutionary War hero John Paulding by the Continental Congress for his role in the capture of the Major John Andre, co-conspirator with Benedict Arnold. Ironically, the Club's new home was across the

The meandering stream on the 15th hole.

street from the original Fairview course.

Siwanoy today is known for numerous elevated tees that offer lovely panoramic vistas, as well as brooks that cross several fairways near the greens, and small, severely bunkered, and fiendishly contoured greens.

After a blind tee shot, the 12th rolls downhill through the drive zone, leaving a delicate pitch over a brook that widens into a pond in the left center of the fairway.

The 15th is the number-one handicap hole, beginning

**SIWANOY
COUNTRY CLUB**
Bronxville, NY

YEAR FOUNDED: 1901

ARCHITECT:
Donald Ross

COURSE OPENED: 1913

TEES	PAR	YARDAGE
Forward	71	5009
Middle	71	6132
Back	71	6359

TEES	COURSE RATING	SLOPE
Forward	73.2	126
Middle	70.4	134
Back	71.4	136

JESS SWEETSER

Siwanoy member Jess Sweetser was arguably the best American amateur golfer of the early 1920s, rivaled only by Bobby Jones. In 1926, the broad-shouldered, powerful Sweetser became the first American-born golfer to win the British Amateur. But a serious illness contracted on the boat ride over sidelined Sweetser for nearly a year, and he never regained his peak form.

The ultimate tragedy of Sweetser's demise was that it prevented him from settling accounts with Jones, who was the same age. Through 1926, their records compared favorably. In their only prior head-to-head confrontation in a major, Sweetser had demolished Jones 8&7 in the 1922 U.S. Amateur at Brookline; Jones later termed this the "tidiest licking" he ever suffered in major amateur competition, calling Sweetser's play "the most devastating golf ever seen in our national amateur." In succession, Sweetser decisively defeated four of the tournament favorites, British Amateur champ Willie Hunter, defending champion Jesse Guilford, Jones, and Chick Evans in the finals.

Locally, Sweetser played in his first Met Amateur in 1919 at age 17, then won the event in 1922 and 1925. He remained at Siwanoy until 1940, serving golf as an official and the MGA as president in 1936. In 1940, business interests forced a move to the nation's capital, where he lived until his death in 1989.

with a drive played from an elevated tee to a rising fairway. Two high-lipped bunkers on the left and a copper beech on the right restrict the landing zone to a mere 18 yards. The approach must be played over a brook that starts along the left side of the hole before crossing in front of the green.

The par-five home hole bends slightly to the right along a tree-lined, undulating fairway that falls off dangerously on the right. The green is set among trees 20 yards beyond a brook.

In the fall of 1914, a young man named Tom Kerrigan came to Siwanoy as golf professional, a position he would hold for 50 years. A Massachusetts native, Kerrigan was an accomplished player who led the 1921 British Open by two strokes with just two holes to play before falling victim to a surging and unruly gallery.

Several outstanding young professionals developed under Kerrigan's tutelage, among them Johnny Farrell, Art Wall, and Tom Nieporte. Kerrigan also was instrumental in Jess Sweetser's success in amateur competition, helping him hone his game by arranging matches against the finest players in the area, including Farrell and Gene Sarazen.

Kerrigan was a driving force behind the creation of the PGA and the staging of its first championship, which was held in at Siwanoy in October, 1916. After qualifying rounds held across the country, the final field was 32. "Long Jim" Barnes won the last two holes to edge Jock Hutchison 1-up after a seesaw battle in their 36-hole final. In the afternoon round, Hutchison played what he later called the shot of his career, a 100-yard pitch from an embedded lie in the bank of the brook on the fifth hole to within 20 feet of the flagstick.

No story about Siwanoy would be complete without mention of the club's nationally famous "Sno-birds." Founded during the winter of 1907-08, this club within the Club became a national model for winter golf, at one time boasting 100 members. Today's headcount is closer to 40.

They play in all kinds of weather, using red balls and dressed in full winter paraphernalia. They have their own nine-hole course—a shortened version of the front nine—which they play whenever conditions prevent use of the Club's regular layout. The course has sand greens and brooms instead of flagsticks, which also lets players clear their line to the cup. Sno-birds are allowed to "tee up" anywhere on the course, can move the snow as they wish through the green, and suffer no penalty for a ball lost in the snow. The first rule is that "no competition will be postponed or canceled on account of the weather." ❍

Siwanoy Sno-birds in 1932.

SLEEPY HOLLOW COUNTRY CLUB

"The Legends Remembered"

SLEEPY HOLLOW COUNTRY CLUB
Scarborough, NY

YEAR FOUNDED: 1911

ARCHITECTS:
Charles Blair Macdonald
A.W. Tillinghast

COURSE OPENED: 1911

TEES	PAR	YARDAGE
Forward	74	5802
Middle	70	6348
Back	70	6547

TEES	COURSE RATING	SLOPE
Forward	74.6	134
Middle	70.7	130
Back	71.7	133

Washington Irving once wrote of it:

"There is a little valley, or rather lap of land, among high hills, which is one of the quietest places in the whole world. A small brook glides through it, with just murmur enough to lull one to repose; and the occasional whistle of a quail, or tapping of a woodpecker, is almost the only sound that ever breaks in upon the uniform tranquility. A drowsy, dreamy influence seems to hang over the land, and to pervade the very atmosphere."

That valley has long been known by the name "Sleepy Hollow." Part of it is now occupied by the grounds and tumbling fairways of the Sleepy Hollow Country Club, and the members will tell you that once they cross over the ridge to the fourth hole, they lose all contact with the reality surrounding them and the affairs of New York City just 30 miles away.

The inhabitants of Sleepy Hollow were, for many years, descendants of the original Dutch settlers. To quote Irving again:

The Headless Horseman

"They are given to all kinds of marvelous beliefs; are subject to trances and visions; and frequently see strange sights, and hear music and voices in the air. The whole neighborhood abounds with local tales, haunted spots, and twilight superstitions."

The legends of Sleepy Hollow are many, the most famous the story of the "headless horseman," supposedly the ghost of a Hessian soldier beheaded by a cannon ball during the Revolutionary War, and the local schoolteacher, Ichabod Crane. The Horseman supposedly threw his head at Crane at the foot of the "haunted bridge" that now connects tee to green on Sleepy Hollow's third hole.

The Club was formed in 1911 by a group of men of legendary wealth who purchased the grounds. Among the founders were William Rockefeller and his son Percy, Cornelius Vanderbilt, John Jacob Astor, Franklin Vanderlip, Oliver Harriman, and V. Everit Macy.

The present clubhouse was once the estate of Colonel Elliott Fitch Shepard, a lawyer who founded the New York State Bar Association in 1876, and his wife Margaret, a granddaughter of Cornelius Vanderbilt. The Shepards engaged Stanford White to design their manor house, a 75-room limestone and tan brick Victorian structure typical of the Italian Villa architecture popular for English Manor Houses of the 18th century. It featured high patterned ceilings, elaborate cornice work, hand-carved mahogany paneling, a ballroom, a huge library, and a graceful, winding stairway near the front entrance. Outside, an elaborate terrace offered a panoramic view of the Hudson River, and overlooked sunken, formal gardens. The property and building was sold to the Club in 1911.

Charles Blair Macdonald, the favored architect of the rich and famous, was brought in to design the golf course. Macdonald and his engineer, Seth Raynor, built the course during the summer of 1911. In the late 1920s, A.W. Tillinghast gave the course a major facelift, expanding it to 27 holes. Tillinghast's revision included seven new holes, the present first and 18th among them; he also designed the current 8th through 12th holes, which were cut through virgin forest. The course has seen little change over the years, until the early 1990s, when Rees Jones was engaged to restore the greenside bunkering.

Although not meant to be a severe course, Sleepy Hollow has matured into one of the Met Area's finest tests. The fairways tumble and roll, rarely leaving a level lie. Many of the greens are large, placing a premium on lag putting. Most of them are open in front, and the five designed by Tillinghast have a modified bowl-shape, raised at the sides and back.

The first of Tillie's five holes, and generally regarded as the course's best, number eight is a long par four that nar-

The scenic 16th, overlooking the Hudson River.

rows dramatically as it approaches the green, with tree limbs overhanging the fairway just ahead of the putting surface. The drive must contend with a huge mound down the center of the fairway in the landing area: Only a shot to the left of the mound leaves an open approach to the green, but the target area on that side is a mere 25 yards wide for the longer hitters.

There are two picture-postcard par threes. The 10th plays from an elevated tee over a pond that extends along the right side of the hole and across the front of the green. The 16th also plays from an elevated tee, over a gully and several bunkers to a table-top green flanked by more bunkers with a dangerous fall-off behind. All this, with the Hudson River in the distance!

Sleepy Hollow's facilities also have undergone some changes, most notably the consolidation into a single clubhouse. The Golf House served as a clubhouse, while the converted Shepard mansion was used primarily for Saturday night dances, the occasional costume ball, and "guests in residence." In 1960, the Club voted to add a new wing to the northern end of the mansion, with a men's locker room, grill room, and pro shop, and do away with the Golf House.

If the legends of Sleepy Hollow from a few centuries ago seem far-fetched and outdated, their recent counterparts were quite real indeed. For eight years, between 1986 and 1993, the Senior Tour staged its Commemorative Tournament at Sleepy Hollow, and the scores carded by golf's elder statesmen often belied their age. A three-round total of under 200 strokes often was necessary to carry the

day; the low score was Bob Charles' 193 in 1989.

Another legend is Jim Hand, whose service to golf spans half a century, including a term as president of the USGA from 1984 to 1985. Hand received the MGA's Distinguished Service Award in 1986.   ○

The winding staircase (left) in the clubhouse (above).

THE STANWICH CLUB

"The $485,000 Answer"

There was a time not long ago when the cities of Greenwich and Stamford were quiet villages. But the population explosion of the 1950s changed that emphatically. Sparked by the exodus of business and industry from New York City, the coastal towns of Connecticut grew at a rate faster than they could handle. Among the areas affected was recreation: The need for new private clubs was severe.

The Round Hill Club in Greenwich was crowded, with a five-year waiting list. Consequently, a group of members began investigating the possibility of a new club in the "Back Country" beyond the Merritt Parkway. In 1960, one of the most spectacular and devastating fires in Greenwich history claimed the Greenwich Country Club clubhouse. While that Club considered rebuilding on its existing site, a group of members joined those from Round Hill looking to move to a new location farther from the town.

One piece of property interested both groups, the Hekma Estate, also known as Semloh Farm, bordered by North Street and Stanwich Road west of the Merritt. Purchased in 1909 by Edwin T. Holmes, Semloh ("Holmes" spelled backwards) became a magnificent estate and farm. The property featured several lakes, a greenhouse, and 15 fountains in the extensive gardens. Today's fairways were pastures used for grazing cattle.

After Holmes' death, the property was purchased in 1930 by Jacob Hekma. When Hekma's business associate Wendell Willkie ran as the Republican candidate for president in 1940 against Franklin Roosevelt, numerous strategy meetings were held at the farm. (It was rumored that had Willkie won that election, Hekma would have been named Secretary of the Treasury.) Hekma put a lot of money into Semloh, which was a model farm in every respect. His widow continued to live on the estate after his death in 1949, and the farm and its pastures were kept in good condition. When she died in 1960, Semloh was 330 acres. But the

The 17th hole.

estate was tied up in litigation at the time Greenwich CC was contemplating a new home, and since no other suitable site was available, that Club stayed put.

The Round Hill and Greenwich groups joined to form the Northwich Development Company in 1962. Their intent was to purchase and develop Semloh Farm with a country club and golf course. Golf architect William Gordon was summoned to inspect the site and make recommendations. He told the group, "if you let this property get away from you, you're crazy."

Gordon gave the group three alternatives. For $300,000, they could have an "adequate, but not outstanding" course. For $375,000, an "interesting and challenging" one. Or, should they wish to go all out, for $485,000 a "superb and aesthetic" course would be theirs. The response, given by Jim Linen, was simple yet defined the Club's high goals and quest for quality. "Let's see how the $485,000 version would look," he said.

On October 16, 1962, Northwich purchased 270 acres of the Hekma estate, then sold 186 acres, including the main house and four other buildings, to The Stanwich Club, which had been organized that summer. The name of the Club had been part of the local lexicon for nearly 250 years, ever since a 1732 settlement of that name in the vicinity of the Mianus Gorge. The Holmes manor house was converted into the Stanwich clubhouse, formally opening in June of 1964.

William Gordon and his son, David, designed the course. Prior to joining the Toomey & Flynn organization in 1923, Gordon had built courses for Donald Ross, Devereux Emmet, and Willie Park Jr. However, the Stanwich people may have been more impressed by Gordon's central role in the revisions at both Shinnecock Hills and The Country Club carried out by Toomey & Flynn.

Construction began in September of 1963, with five holes built from reclaimed swampland. The course opened for play on July 11, 1964.

Long, tight, and relatively flat, with trees lining all 18 fairways, Stanwich is an

THE STANWICH CLUB

Greenwich, CT

YEAR FOUNDED: 1963

ARCHITECT:
William Gordon

COURSE OPENED: 1964

TEES	PAR	YARDAGE
Forward	74	5908
Middle	72	6588
Back	72	7133

TEES	COURSE RATING	SLOPE
Forward	76.2	139
Middle	73.1	139
Back	76.0	144

imposing test of golf. Perhaps its most memorable features are the Tillinghast-style greens, among the fastest in the Met Area, which are canted severely from back to front and bunkered tenaciously at their front corners. Lakes and streams come into play on eight holes.

The ninth is a long par five with a fairway divided beyond the drive zone by a stretch of rough infested with five bunkers.

The 13th is the postcard hole. From the back tees, it plays over a creek, then a lake, to a slightly-elevated L-shaped green built around a deep bunker at the left front. The putting surface is built up from the front, then falls away.

The 14th is an S-shaped par five requiring a conservative tee shot with a club other than the driver to avoid water straight ahead. The second shot must be played short or left of a second

Side view of the 16th hole.

lake on the right. The brave might consider trying to carry a stand of willows left off the tee, a feat that will be rewarded with the chance to go for the green—and carry the lake—with the second shot.

The 17th is a pretty par five. A brook parallels the left side behind a row of trees, eventually expanding into a lake

that must be carried on the shot onto the green.

Stanwich hired Billy Farrell in 1964 as its professional, a position he still holds. Farrell's father, Johnny, won the 1928 U.S. Open in a playoff against Bobby Jones.

The roster of Club champions includes George Zahringer III, five-time Met Amateur champion and the only player to capture the Met Open and Met Amateur titles the same year (1985); and Tom Yellin, a television producer who advanced to the quarterfinals of the 1988 U.S. Amateur.

Zahringer won his first Ike Championship at Stanwich in 1989; his second round 68 was the only subpar round of the tournament, and established a new amateur record for the course. Zahringer and Yellin won the team trophy.

Stanwich hosted the Met Open for the second time in 1996 with Bruce Zabriski putting on an overpowering display of talent with rounds of 68-70-70. He was the first player in history to finish under par at Stanwich in a multi-round event and his 12-stroke victory equalled a 36-year-old Met Open record.

Zabriski had all the right answers in 1996 but the members at Stanwich have had the right answer all along.   ○

WEE BURN COUNTRY CLUB

"A Brook With A Memory"

Many of our venerable clubs resulted from the indomitable spirit of a few men combining with the convenience of a nearby cow pasture. The story of the Wee Burn Country Club adds a slightly different twist. The man generally considered the Club's founder, John Crimmins, was not part of the pioneering group. One day in 1893, he and his son were out for a drive when they came upon two men playing golf in a field in Noroton, Connecticut. One had received golf clubs as a gift from a friend in Scotland; the other had learned the rudiments of the game from friends among the Apple Tree Gang of St. Andrew's. The two apparently had been playing for some time and had staked out two holes.

Crimmins was not an immediate convert. A national depression intervened, and he did not try the game until the fall of 1895. Even then, he never played the game seriously, but thought it would be beneficial to his children. Shortly thereafter, a Scot named George Strath (from the famous clan of St. Andrews, Scotland) entered the picture, and in April 1896, the group officially organized as the Wee Burn Golf Club with Strath serving as golf professional, architect, and greenkeeper.

Early in 1897, following the election of William McKinley to the presidency, the Club sensed better times ahead and expanded to a six-hole course designed and built by Strath. The landlord added the unusual stipulation that his cattle not be disturbed, so the fourth hole was encircled by a stone fence. An additional three holes were built during the winter of 1897 to 1898, and a small farmhouse next

**WEE BURN
COUNTRY CLUB**
Darien, CT

YEAR FOUNDED: 1896

ARCHITECT:
Devereux Emmet

COURSE OPENED: 1925

TEES	PAR	YARDAGE
Forward	72	5762
Middle	72	6569
Back	72	6809

TEES	COURSE RATING	SLOPE
Forward	74.5	135
Middle	72.7	137
Back	73.8	139

A turn of the century tee box.

to the Post Road was converted into the first clubhouse.

Even the name Wee Burn has an unusual story. According to Club legend, Crimmins invited his friend Andrew Carnegie to the Club in 1896, and asked the Scot to suggest a name. When Carnegie mentioned that the small brook crossing the course would be called a "wee burn" in Scotland, the deed was done. That burn, known as Stony Brook, plays a significant role in the play of the course today, which is at a different, albeit nearby, location.

During its early years, Wee Burn's fairways were graced by two outstanding golfers. Genevieve Hecker, the U.S. Women's Amateur champion of 1901 and 1902, was the first woman to write about golf, penning a series of articles for *Harper's* in 1902, then a book entitled *Golf For Women* that was the handbook of the day. Charles Seely was the class among the men. He won the Met Amateur in 1905 and again in 1908, beating Jerry Travers in a classic final match that required 38 holes. Seely lived across the Post Road from the golf course, and his family's home was used as a makeshift clubhouse after a fire destroyed the original building in 1900.

Wee Burn remained at Noroton, with its 9-hole golf

course, until 1923, when the decision was made to move to a larger tract and build an 18-hole course. The present site in the hills of Darien was purchased and Devereux Emmet commissioned to build a championship layout that was ready in 1925. The course today remains faithful to Emmet's original design, thanks in part to a restoration by Geoffrey Cornish in 1974.

True to its name, Wee Burn derives its character from the two "burns" that affect play on eight holes. Emmet also has left his signature small greens, set amidst mounds, many with sharp fall-offs behind.

Wee Burn offers a wonderful mix of holes, both long and short, requiring every club in the bag. The fifth is possibly the toughest sandless par four in the Met Area, with trees lining both sides of the fairway from tee to green. The uphill green is set in a horseshoe of mounds and split by a "valley of sin," a deep swale that separates front from back.

The sixth plays from a hillside tee down to a fairway crossed by a stream, beyond which are four grassy mounds, all of which must be carried on the second shot. The target for that shot is a fairway that angles sharply left from the original line.

Although relatively short, the 16th has often proved the pivotal hole. The drive is played over the corner of a pond to a fairly wide and level fairway. The approach is a simple pitch shot—to a small island green completely encircled by the burn.

World War II proved difficult for Wee Burn. A dilapidated school bus was purchased to transport a number of members to and from the Club when wartime gas rationing made non-essential travel impossible. The U.S. Navy commandeered the clubhouse in 1943 for use as a school for officers. The members used a gardener's cottage as their wartime clubhouse, a garage as their locker room, and a Howard Johnson's restaurant on the Boston Post Road as their dining room.

Wee Burn has hosted the U.S. Women's Amateur three times. Betty Jameson won the first in 1939. In 1958, Anne Quast, a three-time champion, came from three-down in each of her last three matches to win the title. In 1970, Martha Wilkinson won the championship match 3&2 over Cynthia Hill. The deciding stroke came when Hill put her approach to the 16th in the water.

The pro shop has a storied tradition of its own. "Lighthorse" Harry Cooper, Jimmy Demaret, and Bob Goalby all served as assistant professionals. Current professional Roy Pace has been with the Club since 1976, and his pair of Connecticut Open victories are just two of eight captured by Wee Burn professionals dating back to Johnny Golden in 1932.

The rest of the facilities, including a Beach Club in nearby Rowayton, are truly exceptional—a far cry from that pasture off the Post Road that was the center of activity a century ago.   ○

The island green at the 16th hole.

WYKAGYL COUNTRY CLUB
"The Cradle Of The PGA"

When golf first came to this country, it was accompanied by a steady flow of British professionals who nurtured the game through its early years in the New World. And while the game quickly gained acceptance at the highest levels of American society, the professionals did not. They were treated like servants, and for many years denied access to the clubhouse. Even the first U.S. Opens were mere side-shows to the far more significant Amateur Championships.

The professionals needed to organize, but it wasn't until 1916, almost 30 years after the game came to the U.S., that the national PGA organization was formed. The catalyst was Rodman Wanamaker, who may have had no greater notion than helping his father's sporting-goods business. He convened a meeting of leading professionals and prominent amateurs such as Francis Ouimet, A.W. Tillinghast, and John G. Anderson on January 16, 1916. At that meeting, he proposed putting up the prize money for the first PGA Championship. He also donated the Wanamaker Trophy, which is still awarded to the winner of that major championship.

From the first meeting, one man emerged as the new group's leader. Robert White had come to this country from St. Andrews, Scotland, in 1894, and from Chicago east in 1914 to be professional at Wykagyl Country Club in New Rochelle. He was a man of varied skills, golf's first entrepreneur. While at Wykagyl, he ran a string of golf shops, was titular greenkeeper at several local clubs, and imported, trained, and placed a number of young British professionals throughout the area. He also was an architect, with a dozen courses to his credit in the Met Area alone.

White also became the PGA's first president (1916-20), and because of his dedication and involvement, Wykagyl has been called the "cradle of the PGA."

Wykagyl was founded in 1898 as the Pelham Country Club with a nine-hole golf course on Prospect Hill, west of the Boston Post Road in Pelham Manor. When the Club lost its lease and was forced to move in 1904, it purchased the present site in New Rochelle, buying a bit of American history as well. Peter Faneuil, builder of Faneuil Hall, the "cradle of liberty" in Boston, was born on the property in 1700. *Common Sense* author Thomas Paine lived down the road. During the Revolutionary War, General Howe encamped his British troops at Wykagyl for 10 days while heading to the Battle of White Plains. Since British soldiers are known to have played golf in New York City at that time, it is possible they may have been Wykagyl's first golfers.

When the next group of golfers settled in New Rochelle, a new name was needed. William K. Gillett was elected a committee of one to choose something better than "New Rochelle Country Club." There remains some debate whether he was honoring the Wykagyl Indians, who once inhabited the region, or simply strung together the first letters of his own names.

Wykagyl's golf course has gone through three stages of development over the years. The original course, built in 1905, was designed by Club member Lawrence Van Etten. His course was described as "mountainous." The original 18th hole, known as "Cardiac Hill," was a 530-yard par five that played sharply uphill to a hidden green next to North Avenue. No less an authority than Harry Vardon called it

**WYKAGYL
COUNTRY CLUB**
New Rochelle, NY

YEAR FOUNDED: 1898

ARCHITECTS:
Lawrence Van Etten
Donald Ross
A.W. Tillinghast

COURSE OPENED: 1905

TEES	PAR	YARDAGE
Forward	73	5813
Middle	72	6053
Back	72	6460

TEES	COURSE RATING	SLOPE
Forward	75.0	138
Middle	71.5	135
Back	72.6	137

The approach to the 8th, around Wykagyl's famous oak tree.

From behind the 1st green.

"one of the greatest golf holes I have ever tackled." But the course also included three consecutive par threes—an architectural black eye.

There was talk of change for several years, but no action taken until after World War I, when Donald Ross revised the front nine. On the eighth hole, Ross built a new tee, created the sharp dogleg, and brought the famous old oak tree into the line of fire. The revised course opened for play in 1920.

When the Wykagyl Gardens apartments were built in the late 1920s, A.W. Tillinghast was hired for a redesign that debuted on Labor Day, 1931. He reversed the direction of the dogleg on the 17th and shortened the famous 18th.

The word that best describes Wykagyl today is "variety." As the course winds its way through trees and rolls over hilly terrain, the golfer finds no parallel fairways. No two holes are similar in concept, although many play from elevated tees to relatively small greens. And the course is unusual in that it has five par threes and five par fives—so just eight par fours.

The eighth is the showpiece, a challenging, 440-yard par four defined by the ancient oak—which also graces the Club's seal—hanging over the left side of the fairway about 100 yards from the green. The hole begins on an elevated tee set back in a chute, and plays to a fairway that falls left to right in the landing area before bending sharply left. Unless the drive is exceptionally long, the approach must be played over or around the oak.

The 17th turns left through a narrow, tree-lined fairway, then runs downhill to a typical pear-shaped Til-linghast green. Trees left off the tee and right near the green place a premium on accuracy. (The original 17th played from the same tee, but bent right over the hill and ran downhill to a blind plateau green preceded by six small bunkers.)

Many great golfers have played Wykagyl, but the greatest may have been a member, Val Bermingham. Between 1905 and 1933, Bermingham won the club championship at least 20 times. Amazingly, he was a weekend golfer with little time to practice. He ventured into big-time competition only once, losing 2&1 in the first round of the 1905 Met Amateur to Walter Travis, but led the country's most respected amateur after 10 holes. Bermingham did defeat the top local amateurs on numerous informal occasions and was considered the "greatest unknown golfer in the history of the game."

Betsy King

More recently, the professionals of the LPGA have come to Wykagyl for a few different events. The Girl Talk Tournaments in 1976 and 1977 were won by Pat Bradley and JoAnne Carner. Nancy Lopez won two of the three Golden Lights held at Wykagyl from 1978 to 1980. The Club also hosted the 1982 Chrysler-Plymouth Classic and 1984 Master-Card International, and since 1990 has been the host of the JAL Big Apple Classic.

The tournament, which was conceived by the late Peter Bonanni, former publisher of *GOLF Magazine*, attracts a strong international field, as shown in 1993 when Japan's Hiromi Kobayashi won, much to the sponsor's delight. Betsy King, winner of the first two stagings of the JAL, calls Wykagyl her favorite course, not surprising because it is one of the strongest layouts on the LPGA Tour.

BEDFORD GOLF & TENNIS CLUB

"A Young Man's Fancy"

The old clubhouse.

BEDFORD GOLF & TENNIS CLUB

Bedford Village, NY

YEAR FOUNDED: 1891

ARCHITECTS:
Members
Devereux Emmet

COURSE OPENED: 1896

TEES	PAR	YARDAGE
Forward	73	5683
Middle	71	6213
Back	71	6360

TEES	COURSE RATING	SLOPE
Forward	74.1	130
Middle	70.8	133
Back	71.4	134

Alongside the 10th hole of the Bedford Golf & Tennis Club, overlooking a pond, stands one of golfdom's relics—a dilapidated building that might be the oldest extant former clubhouse in American golf, predating the one at Shinnecock Hills, which opened in June of 1892.

Bedford's origins are traced back to the spring of 1890, when a group of young men became infatuated with tennis and decided to form a club. The grand opening of the Bedford Lawn Tennis Club—three courts, croquet grounds, and the clubhouse—took place in June of 1891. The house was located across Route 22, opposite the present third green. The clubhouse was moved in 1914 to its present site alongside number 10 when the present (and larger) building was constructed.

A nine-hole course was designed in 1896 by members A.W. Partridge and Colonel Thatcher T.P. Luquer. Though golf proved popular, expansion was delayed until 1927 while the club looked to purchase adjacent land. Then, Devereux Emmet built an entirely new 18-hole course that bore little resemblance to the original layout. He was capably assisted by member Beatrice Renwick, a player of national repute.

The most striking feature of the new (and present) course is the abrupt elevation changes that give so many holes their character. Water comes into play on six of the first 11 holes, and on five holes, the approach must carry a bunker fronting the green.

The picturesque fifth through eighth holes are the backbone of the course. Five is a relatively short par three played over a gully and guarding bunker to a plateau green.

The par-four sixth calls for a long carry over that same gully to reach an elevated fairway that bends sharply left, then rolls downhill to the green. The seventh is a strong par four that climbs a steep hill, while eight rolls back down the hill to a green with a pond at the right front.

Through the years Bedford, unlike many other golf and country clubs, has remained a family sports club, and nothing more. The members enjoy nine tennis and three paddle tennis courts, a swimming pool, and their golf course in the simple, spartan style of a century ago. ○

The par-three 10th hole.

BLIND BROOK CLUB

"Ike's Favorite"

The approach to the 18th green

During the summer of 1915, William Hamlin Childs, a New York restaurateur, visited the Old Elm Club near Chicago, an exclusive retreat known for restfulness and tranquility, and no wait at the first tee. The concept appealed to Childs, who wanted to recreate it in Westchester County.

Upon returning to New York, Childs quickly enlisted the aid of Edmund Converse of Greenwich and Frederick Wheeler of Apawamis. Within two weeks, the trio had put together both the membership and financing. By late fall of the same year, the Blind Brook Club was born, its name taken from the stream that forms the club's western border.

The course design, awarded to Charles B. Macdonald, came with an unusual request. The members were not interested in a championship course of staggering length. Rather, they wanted a course they could enjoy, a challenging layout of moderate length and tempered hazards, an easy-walking course for older men.

Macdonald withdrew before construction began to concentrate on Lido, but not before making design suggestions, turning the project over to his associate, Seth Raynor. The resulting design bears some trademarks of the typical Macdonald-Raynor course—notably copies of famous foreign holes and large, undulating, multi-tiered greens—although it is not as rugged as most of their work. The course opened on June 15, 1917.

Wide fairways give the average player ample room for error. The greenside bunkers are set back away from many of the greens. Several of the putting surfaces feature small ridges across the front that call for a deft chipping touch. And the gently-contoured fairways requested are often quite dramatic.

One of the most intriguing holes is the fifth, a very short dogleg-left par four that is long on problems. The drive is played from an elevated tee over a pond to a willow-lined tumbling fairway that falls to the left. The green is set on an angle to the fairway, with an upper tier at the right rear and a raised left front.

Most interesting of the holes modelled after others are the imposing "Short" (15), with a tabletop green set some 30 feet above the base of a swale in front, and the 17th, similar in concept to number eight at National, with a brook angling across the fairway from left to right dividing the drive zone; the longer carry to the left provides the better angle into the green.

Childs' dream came true. As proof, consider that former President Eisenhower, who was a dues-paying member (before becoming an honorary member), is said to have considered Augusta National and Blind Brook his two favorite courses. And late in life, 1898 U.S. Amateur champion Findlay Douglas considered Blind Brook his favorite retreat: Using hickory-shafted clubs, he would play nine holes daily, but no more than nine, since his longtime playing companions could go no farther.

The outside events held at Blind Brook reflect the club's close ties with the United States Seniors Golf Association, particularly the USSGA Championships for "Super Seniors," aged 75 years or more. These older players, some 70-90 strong, began playing at Blind Brook in 1973 to ease the burden on longtime hosts Apawamis and Round Hill.

Blind Brook has been rightfully called "a center for distinguished gentlemen who have mellowed in golf." ○

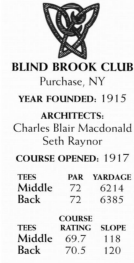

BLIND BROOK CLUB
Purchase, NY

YEAR FOUNDED: 1915

ARCHITECTS:
Charles Blair Macdonald
Seth Raynor

COURSE OPENED: 1917

TEES	PAR	YARDAGE
Middle	72	6214
Back	72	6385

TEES	COURSE RATING	SLOPE
Middle	69.7	118
Back	70.5	120

BONNIE BRIAR COUNTRY CLUB

"Rewrite The History Books"

There is a legend at the Bonnie Briar Country Club that golf was played on the grounds in the 1880s, over a six-hole course on land now occupied by the first and ninth holes. If true, golf's history books must be rewritten.

Bonnie Briar's golf history may, in fact, have begun during the American Revolution. There is no doubt that British troops under Sir Henry Clinton marched from New Rochelle up Quaker Ridge Road to Weaver Street en route to the Battle of White Plains. They are believed to have encamped where the Club now sits. The bunker 50 yards from the ninth tee may have been dug by these soldiers for protection against the winds. And since British soldiers are believed to have teed it up while stationed in New York, they may have been the first Bonnie Briar golfers!

Until history can officially be revised, Bonnie Briar dates back to 1921, when Edward Lyman Bill Jr., a 23-year-old World War I veteran, organized the Club and leased it some 140 acres, including his father's partially built mansion. The building became the clubhouse, a graystone-and-stucco structure that featured a large porch on the south side affording beautiful views of the countryside and Long Island Sound.

The new Club attracted the best families of New Rochelle, including Norman Rockwell, the world-famous illustrator. Indoors, Delmonico's of Fifth Avenue ran the kitchen. Outdoors, Devereux Emmet was engaged to lay out an 18-hole course, which opened on Decoration Day, 1923.

Bonnie Briar is a typical Westchester course—hilly, tree-lined, with rock outcroppings everywhere. Two branches of the Sheldrake River flow through the course, affecting play on seven holes. Front and cross bunkers add aesthetics and challenge.

Among the more challenging holes are number two, a short par four with a two-level fairway divided by a sharp drop-off. A brook crosses the hole on a left-to-right angle and curves around the right side of the green. The brook runs along the left side of the sixth fairway, eventually crossing well beyond the drive zone, where the hole turns sharply to the left. At the tightly wooded 13th, the stream crosses 50 yards short of the green.

The eighth is Bonnie Briar's landmark, a moderate-length par four played from an elevated tee to a tumbling fairway punctuated by three major-league mounds. The first precedes the normal landing area; the other two stand side-by-side as the terrain rises to another strip of fairway within reach of long hitters.

Doug Ford, who won the 1955 PGA and 1957 Masters, was a member during the late 1940s when he won the Westchester Amateur and finished second in the Met Amateur (1946). And you can look that up in the history books!

**BONNIE BRIAR
COUNTRY CLUB**
Larchmont, NY

YEAR FOUNDED: 1921

ARCHITECT:
Devereux Emmet

COURSE OPENED: 1923

TEES	PAR	YARDAGE
Forward	74	5714
Middle	71	6004
Back	71	6171

TEES	COURSE RATING	SLOPE
Forward	74.1	132
Middle	69.5	123
Back	70.3	124

Top: Bonnie Briar's clubhouse. Above: Approach to the 7th green.

BRAE BURN COUNTRY CLUB
"All In The Family"

Long before he built Atlantic out on Long Island, Lowell Schulman was an avid golfer and prominent builder of industrial parks. In the early 1960s, he planned to develop 600 acres in Purchase into a residential community with a golf course. Schulman contacted Frank Duane, long-time assistant to Robert Trent Jones, who was looking to begin his own business after making a reputation at Dorado Beach and Spyglass Hill.

Shortly after the course was in the works, Schulman was contacted by representatives of Fairview Country Club, who offered to exchange their property in Elmsford, a prime site for an industrial park, for the land in Purchase. Schulman declined. He then was approached by friends from Harrison Country Club, who wanted to form a membership-owned private club centered around the new course. They were joined by members of other non-equity Westchester clubs, so a meeting was held in 1964 and the Brae Burn Country Club was formally organized. It was the first new member-owned club in the county since the late 1920s.

Brae Burn was the name that won a contest among the members. (The original name, Purchase Hills, was abandoned because of its similarity to another club in the region.) The course was ready for play in June, 1965, and the clubhouse opened the following year.

The terrain is hilly and forested, with brooks and ponds in play on several holes. Ponds extend the length of two par threes, both of which finish with highly undulating greens.

Number three is a picturesque dogleg-right par four. A pond along the left side of the green convinces many average players to lay up on the approach.

The moderately long par-five 15th makes a steep drop in the drive zone: Out-of-bounds and a pond await on the left, a tall tree sits in front of the elevated tee on the right, and another pond fronts the left half of the green. For the

Ken and Marianne Springer

player willing to risk catching the downslope, the chance of reaching the green in two is very realistic.

The long, par-four 17th is the toughest hole. It curves gradually left, but the land angles severely left to right through the landing area, with a large tree on the left. The hole finishes by playing uphill passed a pond on the left to a two-tiered, hilltop green.

The first name in Brae Burn golf is Springer, for Ken, Marianne, and their sons Ron and Jerry. The parents won the MGA Mixed Pinehurst three times, Jerry won the MGA Boys (1983) and Junior (1985), and Ron has numerous high finishes in prestigious local events, including second in the 1987 Hochster and a tie for fifth in the 1992 Met Open.

Brae Burn today is among a family of outstanding courses in Purchase—and one of the Met Area's best kept secrets. ○

BRAE BURN COUNTRY CLUB
Purchase, NY

YEAR FOUNDED: 1964

ARCHITECT:
Frank Duane

COURSE OPENED: 1965

TEES	PAR	YARDAGE
Forward	74	6255
Middle	72	6518
Back	72	6825

TEES	COURSE RATING	SLOPE
Forward	74.6	134
Middle	72.2	130
Back	73.6	133

Looking up towards the 17th green.

BRIAR HALL COUNTRY CLUB

"A Sports Mecca"

In 1900, Walter W. Law built a nine-hole course on his estate in Briarcliff Manor. The Briarcliff Golf Club was open to guests of the adjacent Briarcliff Lodge. The first hole was a conversation piece, a 250-yard par four that began on the roof of the pro shop and ran down a toboggan-slide drop of 250 feet to a green nestled in the valley below. Arthur Lyons, the well-known one-armed professional who taught John D. Rockefeller the game, served the Club through 1921.

In 1922, a Devereux Emmet- designed course opened across the street. It was the brainchild of the lodge's new proprietor, Chauncey D. Steele, who wanted to make the Club, soon to be renamed Briar Hills, "one of the sports meccas of the East," with winter facilities rivaling those at Lake Placid.

Emmet's course was feared for its tall, punishing rough and greens surrounded by sand dunes punctuated with grass. There also was a choice of 14th holes— one a moderate par three of 155 yards, the other an uphill tester of 225 yards. Gene Sarazen served the Club in 1923-24, at a salary said to have been the highest ever paid to a club professional.

In 1948, the Club was sold by Theodore Law, son of the founder and an active MGA committeeman, to private interests, and the name changed again, this time to Briar Hall. The new owners tripled the size of the clubhouse and refashioned the golf course, building six new holes. This is the layout in play today, characterized by steeply sloping terrain. Position off the tee is crucial as several of the fairways are slanted and four turn quickly to the left. Many of the greens remain almost entirely encircled by sand.

The most memorable holes are a pair of tightly-bunkered par threes on the front: Six plays through an extremely narrow chute of willows, over a pond, and uphill to a green surrounded by five bunkers; eight crosses a brook that empties into a pond to the right of

The par-three 6th hole.

**BRIAR HALL
COUNTRY CLUB**
Briarcliff Manor, NY

YEAR FOUNDED: 1948

ARCHITECT:
Devereux Emmet

COURSE OPENED: 1922

TEES	PAR	YARDAGE
Forward	74	5538
Middle	71	6104
Back	71	6313

TEES	COURSE RATING	SLOPE
Forward	72.0	122
Middle	70.1	127
Back	71.0	129

the elevated green.

A number of big names won events played at Briar Hall. Ben Hogan was the medalist in U.S. Open qualifying here in the late 1930s, while three Met PGA Championships were won by Paul Runyan, Claude Harmon, and Doug Ford. In 1964, the Met Open was captured by Jack Patroni of Apawamis.

The Turnesa family was closely allied with Briar Hall. Willie won the 1938 U.S. Amateur while a Club member and his brother Jim won the 1952 PGA Championship while the Club professional.

The Turnesas helped to put Briar Hall in the limelight envisioned by Chauncey Steele. ○

BURNING TREE COUNTRY CLUB

"Leaving On A Jet Plane"

Half a century ago, many private golf clubs were primarily men's clubs, with little to offer the wife and children. Today, they provide a week-long second home for the family and a place where fathers gather with their families on weekends after being away on business during the week.

That was the rationale behind Burning Tree, which was conceived in 1962 by a group of young corporate executives as a family oriented country club that would provide a wide range of activities, including golf. The fledgling Club got its impetus from local real estate developers who envisioned it as part of a community being built on the Frye estate between North Street and Stanwich Road, just east of the Merritt Parkway. In 1962, the developers sold 196 acres to the newly formed Burning Tree Country Club.

In keeping with their avowed "family club" image, the members first built an Olympic-size swimming pool and a pool house/snack bar, the back of which became the Club's first dining room. Tennis courts also went in early on. A golf course and clubhouse proved a greater challenge.

The original clubhouse, which opened in 1966, was much smaller than the present building. It was designed,

with some modification, as a class project at Rice University. It was expanded and renovated to include a health club and spa in 1985, when new golf and tennis shops were built.

Hal Purdy had the unenviable job of laying out an 18-hole course. He decided to begin with the holes in the low-lying ground between the proposed clubhouse and the parkway, where he encountered wetlands and a stream that meandered through the property. Building these holes proved so difficult that the entire construction budget was spent on just the first half of the golf course. The stream was redirected and widened to form ponds that come into play on all but one hole on the outgoing nine. The back nine was carved through woods and rough terrain. The result was one of the area's most difficult tests of golf, with trouble lurking on virtually every shot.

Burning Tree's signature hole is the fourth, a long par five that has been called one of the toughest in Connecticut. It plays "single file," with the Merritt Parkway above the left tree line and a brook crossing the hole about 260 yards from the elevated green, which is partially hidden behind a hillock on the left, narrowing the angle of the approach.

A second unusual par five, the 15th, plays to what appears a wide, rising fairway. Beyond the crest, however, the hole turns slightly right, then left around a copse of tall pines that usually gets in the way of the approach shot.

During construction, the members needed temporary quarters until a clubhouse could be built, so they bought a tent that was used for lunch, dinners, and social functions, These "hard times" created a camaraderie among the early members not seen in many other clubs, and still exists today. ❍

**BURNING TREE
COUNTRY CLUB**
Greenwich, CT

YEAR FOUNDED: 1962

ARCHITECT:
Hal Purdy

COURSE OPENED: 1965

TEES	PAR	YARDAGE
Forward	73	5756
Middle	72	6482
Back	72	6902

TEES	COURSE RATING	SLOPE
Forward	74.1	134
Middle	72.2	134
Back	74.1	137

Trees (on right) deny a clear approach to the 15th green.

CONCORD GOLF RESORT

"Hang The Architect"

During a tournament for touring professionals held in 1965 over the Concord Hotel's new "Monster" course, architect Joe Finger asked Tommy Bolt what he thought of the twin pine in the middle of the 18th fairway. The tempestuous Bolt replied that it was a "perfect position to hang the golf course architect from!"

Comments like Bolt's from frustrated golfers have been echoed many times over the years, a fact that did not bother the late Ray Parker, owner of the hotel, in the least. Parker's charge to Finger had been to build "the greatest golf course in the world, one that Palmer and Nicklaus can't chop up."

The story starts with Parker's father-in-law, Arthur Winarick, a Russian immigrant who rose from barber to hotelier. He purchased the Kiamesha Ideal Hotel during the early 1930s, renamed it the Concord, and within a decade made it one of the largest in the Catskills, and eventually in the country, sprawling over 2,000 acres.

The name for the resort comes from the Indian "Kiamesha," which translates as "peaceful," a root meaning for the word "concord." But the waters of the Monster are anything but peaceful, coming into play on half the 18 holes.

The Concord's first golf course was a nine-holer, now called the Challenger, built in the mid 1940s. Next came the 18-hole International in 1951, designed by Alfred Tull and cut through the forests surrounding the hotel's ski trails. The Monster followed in 1964.

It was while the International was the Concord's centerpiece that the resort enjoyed its halcyon era. That was when big-name professionals Ed Furgol, Doug Ford, Cary Middlecoff, Miller Barber, and Orville Moody represented the hotel, and when Jimmy Demaret started his 25-year tenure as director of golf. The resort's playing professionals accounted for seven major titles while associated with the hotel, including an American "grand slam" in 1956 when Burke won The Masters and PGA and Middlecoff the U.S. Open.

Demaret also hosted several editions of the television series "All Star Golf" from the Concord, and later brought "Shell's Wonderful World Of Golf" for a visit to the Catskills.

The LPGA Tour visited in 1968 for the Concord Open, won by Shirley Engelhorn, then again in 1969 for Betsy Rawls' LPGA Championship.

Both tournaments were played on the Monster, whose reputation is based on its length—including six par fours more than 450 yards and intimidating water hazards on nine holes. Some of the more challenging water carries can be found on the par-five fourth hole which, according to *GOLF Magazine*, has never been "touched" in two, stretching to 632 yards from the "monster" tees; and on the 12th, a par five that twice bends to the right around a lake.

The Monster lies in a valley, while the shorter, sportier International plays over rolling mountainous terrain. Its most dramatic hole is the 11th, a long par four that drops 200 feet from a tee atop the mountain down to a three-tiered fairway in the valley below. The fourth green has a notorious reputation, its severe slope often enticing three or even four putts. Clearly, a good place to bury the architect!

Funny thing though, whether they want to bury the architect or hang him, golfers from the Met Area and around the United States keep returning to face the Concord's many challenges. ○

One of the Monster's monsters, the long 4th hole.

CONCORD GOLF RESORT
Kiamesha Lake, NY
YEAR FOUNDED: 1930s

INTERNATIONAL

ARCHITECT:
Alfred Tull

COURSE OPENED: 1957

TEES	PAR	YARDAGE
Forward	71	5194
Middle	71	5968
Back	71	6619

TEES	COURSE RATING	SLOPE
Forward	69.4	116
Middle	68.5	117
Back	71.4	123

MONSTER

ARCHITECT:
Joe Finger

COURSE OPENED: 1964

TEES	PAR	YARDAGE
Forward	72	5201
Middle	72	6989
Back	72	7471

TEES	COURSE RATING	SLOPE
Forward	70.7	112
Middle	72.2	122
Back	74.2	125

THE CONNECTICUT GOLF CLUB

"Rock Cornish Heaven"

Laurence Wien founded Connecticut Golf Club in 1966 as a businessman's golf club—not as a country club, not as a social club, but devoted to "the playing of golf." Membership was to be limited to 150, not including the fox, deer, geese, and ducks that also enjoy the land. Today, weekday play averages perhaps 30 golfers, double that on weekends.

Wien turned the property over to Geoffrey Cornish, the veteran designer and author of *The Golf Course*, the classic book on golf architecture. Cornish responded with a dramatic course that rises and falls through corridors of trees and granite and around several ponds, giving the golfer a taste of the great outdoors. The course, one of the few Cornish originals in the Met Area, was selected in 1984 by the American Golf Course Architects Association as one of the 150 best de-

THE CONNECTICUT GOLF CLUB
Easton, CT

YEAR FOUNDED: 1966

ARCHITECTS:
Geoffrey Cornish
William Robinson

COURSE OPENED: 1966

TEES	PAR	YARDAGE
Forward	71	5600
Middle	71	6467
Back	71	6824

TEES	COURSE RATING	SLOPE
Forward	72.9	130
Middle	71.9	133
Back	73.5	136

signed and most beautiful courses in America.

Among the memorable holes is the par-four third, where the sloping fairway is crossed by a trio of trees. The approach must be played with a feathery touch over or between the trees, then carry a front bunker to a fall-away green.

Two par fives are outstanding. Seven, the signature hole, features one lake in front of the tee and another along the right side that threatens the second shot. The final approach is uphill to a shallow, canted green with a nasty bunker lurking behind.

The 12th, shaped like an upside-down "L," calls for a blind second shot long enough to clear the dogleg but short enough to avoid the pond in front of the wide, yet shallow, green.

While the club has been the gracious host to the 1983 MGA Boys Championship and several USGA qualifying rounds, it has remained faithful to its character as a quiet retreat for Met Area businessmen. ❍

The watery conclusion to the 12th hole, with the 13th green in the background.

COUNTRY CLUB OF DARIEN

"Money Was No Object"

The 3rd green.

In the early 1900s, the land was a dairy farm that never made money. That didn't matter because it was owned by the wealthy and socially prominent Auchincloss family as their retreat from the stifling summer heat in New York City.

When the family patriarch died in the 1950s, one option was to sell the property for commercial development. Instead, son Edgar convinced his mother and sisters to let him turn it into a private golf club for local residents. So the Country Club of Darien, owned and operated with a firm yet benevolent hand by Edgar Auchincloss, was founded in 1957.

To design his course, the Scotsman Auchincloss chose an Englishman, Alfred Tull, who came to this country as a teenager in 1914 and eventually apprenticed under Walter Travis, A.W. Tillinghast, and Devereux Emmet. Tull had the course ready by 1958 after carving the back nine through wooded swampland and bringing water into play on eight holes.

The opener presents a stiff challenge—the fairway slopes 45 degrees from the left toward bunkers and out-of-

**COUNTRY CLUB
OF DARIEN**

Darien, CT

YEAR FOUNDED: 1957

ARCHITECT:
Alfred Tull

COURSE OPENED: 1958

TEES	PAR	YARDAGE
Forward	72	5780
Middle	72	6589
Back	72	6908

TEES	COURSE RATING	SLOPE
Forward	73.7	128
Middle	71.5	128
Back	73.1	132

bounds on the right. A drive down the middle will kick right, leaving a hanging lie for the approach to a two-tiered green with a bunker front-left and a major drop-off right.

The most memorable hole is the third, a sloping, dogleg-left par four that entices long hitters to try cutting the corner over trees. Average players will find that a straight drive to the top of the hill kicks left, gaining yardage and rolling onto a level lie for the approach to a bulkheaded, two-tiered green protected by a pond and two bunkers.

Beginning on a tee high above the fairway, the par-four 12th is the most scenic hole, with out-of-bounds left and a pond right. The fairway rises significantly about 140 yards from the inverted-bowl-shaped green.

Once again turning down a fistful of development dollars, Edgar Auchincloss sold the Club to the members in 1986.

The Club remains today an informal, family-oriented facility, with active tennis and pool programs, and three platform tennis courts that keep busy throughout the winter. ❍

DUTCHESS GOLF & COUNTRY CLUB

"Perfection"

Dutchess was one of several counties created by the British in the late 1600s as a way to claim land in upstate New York for the British, thereby thwarting the colonial expansion of the Dutch from New England. At the time, the only inhabitants of the region were the Wappinger Indians, who were oblivious to this cartographic chicanery. The British named the "countie" for Maria Beatrice D'Este, the Dutchess of York.

Dutchess County grew to become a focal point of state governance. At different times, both Fishkill and Poughkeepsie served as state capital. The U.S. Constitution was ratified by New York State in Poughkeepsie. Later, Franklin Delano Roosevelt, once the Governor of New York, made his home in the county, at Hyde Park, which served as an experimental lab for his New Deal ideas.

On April 10, 1897, a group of 18 gathered to usher Dutchess County into the modern era by establishing Dutchess County Golf Club of Poughkeepsie, which they soon adorned with a nine-hole course designed by Mungo Park. The eighth hole, which closely resembles today's 17th, possessed a beautiful view across the Hudson River, and was called, simply, "Perfection."

The members designed an almost all-new 18-hole

DUTCHESS GOLF & COUNTRY CLUB
Poughkeepsie, NY

YEAR FOUNDED: 1897

ARCHITECTS:
Mungo Park
Members

COURSE OPENED: 1897

TEES	PAR	YARDAGE
Forward	72	5740
Middle	70	6278
Back	70	6475

TEES	COURSE RATING	SLOPE
Forward	73.1	123
Middle	70.3	123
Back	71.2	125

course in 1925. By accident, they planned out only 17 holes, so it became necessary to squeeze in one more. That's how the present 92-yard 13th hole, the shortest par three on a regulation-size golf course in the Met Area, came into existence.

The terrain is similar to that in Westchester County. As a result, the fairways toss and tumble through tree-lined passages, and the small greens are tenaciously bunkered.

The sixth, regarded by many as the best par three in the county, plays from a raised tee to its plateau green. The shot off the tee is narrowed by trees, while the green is squeezed by six bunkers, including three across the front. The green is perched 25 feet above its surroundings, with the fall-off to the left known as "Hell's Kitchen." The putting surface features a "burial mound" right of center.

The eighth is a picturesque par three over a pond cutting across the hole from left to right, with a footbridge at the far right side.

The 14th is the most dramatic hole. It is dominated by a large pond that crosses the hole left to right, runs along the right side, then passes close to the green. The conservative tee shot to the left-center leaves the golfer a long, blind approach from a large bowl. The more daring drive—over the trees at the corner of the right dogleg—leaves a shorter, more visible approach from a level lie.

Roosevelt, who was an excellent golfer, joined the Club in 1919, but switched to a house membership in 1924 when his health began to deteriorate.

The greatest player to represent Dutchess was Ray Billows, winner of the Met Amateur at Winged Foot in 1948, the same year he finished runner-up to Willie Turnesa in the U.S. Amateur. Billows won the New York State Amateur a record seven times from 1935 to 1949.

Speaking of seven, Dutchess is the only club to have hosted all seven of the New York State Golf Association's championships—another way of defining perfection. ○

The picture-perfect modern 8th hole.

Joe Turnesa

ELMWOOD COUNTRY CLUB

"Pride Of The Yankees"

ELMWOOD COUNTRY CLUB
White Plains, NY

YEAR FOUNDED: 1925

ARCHITECTS:
A.W. Tillinghast
Alfred Tull

COURSE OPENED: 1925

TEES	PAR	YARDAGE
Forward	73	5770
Middle	71	6213
Back	71	6487

TEES	COURSE RATING	SLOPE
Forward	73.3	122
Middle	70.2	126
Back	71.5	129

The Pelhamhurst Golf Club was formed in 1922 with a nine-hole golf course. It survived until 1925, when the Elmsford Country Club was organized and took over the property. That spring, the original course was rebuilt, with credit for the design going to A.W. Tillinghast.

The membership came from New York City, and predominantly from the garment district. For a number of years, the king of the Club was Henry Bermant, a developer of chain stores and supermarkets. His word was law. Members still recall that when Bermant entered the lockerroom, the radio would be switched to the Yankee game, regardless of the number of Giant or Dodger fans on hand. Yankee great Lou Gehrig was a frequent guest.

Elmsford suffered through the Depression, went bankrupt, and was reorganized in 1943 as Elmwood. Bermant's generosity helped keep the Club afloat.

The present clubhouse was dedicated in 1930. One wing was called the "Hotel," a 43-room facility above the men's locker room, now used to house members and staff. It

Bridge and Japanese garden.

was so popular in the early years that a raffle determined who would occupy the rooms for a week or weekend.

After World War II, the membership began to age and complain about the hilly front nine. In 1954, additional land was purchased and Alfred Tull engaged to soften the hills. His alterations eliminated two imposing climbs, including two holes that ascended the present third fairway and another that played up the range.

But the land still tumbles between the tees and generally flat greens, making Elmwood both challenging and fun to play.

The first hole is one of the prettiest openers in the Met Area. The hole first climbs uphill, with a 240-yard drive necessary to bring the green into view. Then the fairway drops sharply downhill and to the left, to a green that falls away from the approach. To complicate matters, a giant elm hangs over the left half of the fairway about 75 yards from home, blocking any approach from that side.

The 14th is a tantalizing short par five that even the mid–handicapper can reach with two solid hits. It begins uphill to a wide landing area, then rolls downhill and turns to the right about 100 yards from the green. With good position, a strong fade might roll down the hill and around a huge mogul to a relatively small green.

The Turnesa family put its stamp on Elmwood over the years. Phil worked as teaching professional alongside brothers Joe (the titular head professional) and Mike, all of them starting in 1927. Phil stayed active through the mid-1960s, when he retired to become emeritus professional.

Between the eighth green and ninth tee is a lovely Japanese garden, crossed by a stone bridge. It was built in 1989 to honor the memory of Dr. E. Raymond Topol, green chairman for nearly half a century and the man who helped shape the landscape at Elmwood. ○

The tricky approach to the first hole.

COUNTRY CLUB OF FAIRFIELD

"Fewer Golfers"

Many Met Area clubs were formed because others proved too crowded. Members wanted peace and quiet, or unrestricted tee times, so founded clubs of their own. But all too often, the new clubs were as busy as the old ones. That definitely was not the case with the Country Club of Fairfield.

Oliver G. Jennings didn't like what was happening to Brooklawn Country Club, the only club in the area early in the century. "What Fairfield needs," Jennings mused, "is a golf club with fewer golfers." As the son of a founder of Standard Oil, he could afford to pursue his musings. On February 12, 1914, Jennings, his sister, and four others incorporated the Country Club of Fairfield, creating a simple family club with a converted farmhouse as clubhouse.

Jennings deserves credit for tremendous foresight in choosing the location. While it offered magnificent views of Long Island Sound, the land was nothing more than onion fields stretching along a malodorous tidal marsh adjacent to Southport Harbor at Sasco Hill, suitable for only sea birds, shell fish, and mosquitoes. He also obtained a salt meadow, some marshland, and some beachfront, although town residents retained beach rights.

Building a golf course on such land was no easy task, but Jennings chose the right man for the job—Seth Raynor, who had done marvelous work assisting C.B. Macdonald at The National and was in the process of molding Lido from an even more unlikely site. Construction began in 1916. Raynor obtained land fill from the bottom of Southport Harbor and transported topsoil from Long Island via barge. Progress was slow, due to drainage problems and World War I. Although four holes were ready for play in 1919, it took five years to complete the project. What resulted was a course better than the spectacular view.

A links-style course, Fairfield is sprinkled with wetlands, ponds, and seagrass. There are five par threes, three of which cross water hazards,

View from behind the 18th green.

while another (the ninth) is a sparkling Redan situated between the clubhouse and the beach. The most notable of the longer holes is the sixth, where a wide inlet from Southport Harbor (called the "lagoon") crosses in front of the tee and continues up the right side of the hole, sneaking into play a second time just short of the green. A lone tree on the right in the drive zone adds spice to the tee shot and gives the hole a Cape effect.

Starting in 1924, the Club attracted many of the big names in amateur golf, both male and female, to its annual Gold Ball tournament. It was two competitions, one between men's and women's teams, with each male giving his female opponent seven bisques (strokes to be used when desired) and the other, the Gold Ball, a better-ball competition at match play between teams of one man and one woman.

In 1927, the team of Jess Sweetser and Glenna Collett, both former national amateur champions, captured the Gold Ball. It was not until 1928 that a women's team, led by Collett and Maureen Orcutt, won the team competition. The tournament was held for the last time in 1929.

The present clubhouse was built in 1960 after a fire leveled the previous building. Club facilities also include a beach pavilion, complete with salt-water pool and nine tennis courts, located near the seventh tee, where Southport Harbor empties into the Sound.

The club has certainly made full and beautiful use of the land obtained by Oliver Jennings over 80 years ago.   ○

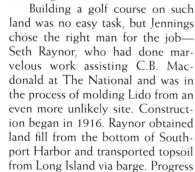

**COUNTRY CLUB
OF FAIRFIELD**
Fairfield, CT

YEAR FOUNDED: 1914

ARCHITECT:
Seth Raynor

COURSE OPENED: 1920

TEES	PAR	YARDAGE
Forward	71	5483
Middle	70	6160
Back	70	6358

TEES	COURSE RATING	SLOPE
Forward	71.8	126
Middle	70.7	131
Back	71.6	133

FAIRVIEW COUNTRY CLUB

"The Fountain Of Youth"

John Inglis came to Fairview in 1907 as golf professional/caddiemaster, and remained for 57 years before retiring in 1964. The list of caddies who apprenticed under Inglis is long and impressive. Prominent were the seven Turnesa brothers—Joe, Jim, Mike, Phil, Frank, Doug, and Willie. Their father, Vitale, came to the United States from Naples, and is said to have walked the 26 miles from Manhattan to Elmsford in 1908, where he saw construction of the new Fairview course underway. He got a job and remained with the Club for 54 years.

Fairview's caddie ranks also included the Farrell brothers, Johnny and Jimmy (the former won the 1928 U.S. Open); the Creavy brothers, Bill and Tom (the latter claimed the 1931 PGA); and Tony Manero, winner of the 1936 U.S. Open.

The Club was founded in 1904, on land leased from the Fairview Links in Bronxville, the nine-hole course that also spawned Siwanoy. The lease ended after the 1907 season, so the Club moved to a farm in Elmsford. Within a few years that land was needed by New York City for an aqueduct, so the Club moved 500 yards across the road. A huge English Tudor mansion with a great view across the Saw Mill River Valley became the clubhouse.

"If, as American universities are rated by their football teams, golf clubs were rated by the expert golfers produced by their caddiemasters, Fairview Country Club of Elmsford, New York, would occupy a position analogous to Notre Dame's. The Knute Rockne of Fairview is John Inglis, a fatherly little man with no children of his own."

– NOEL BUSH, *NEW YORKER* MAGAZINE, 1937

The new 18-hole golf course, designed by Donald Ross, opened in 1912. It served until 1968, when, as a result of the commercialization of the Elmsford area and the development of Interstate 287, the Club moved to its present site in Greenwich, where Robert Trent Jones designed a new course.

Fairview's two nines offer a marked contrast. To score well on the relatively short front nine, one must avoid water, which is very much in play on five of the first seven holes, then rely on length and accuracy on the longer back nine.

The second is a scenic par five cut through the woods. Two bunkers flank the fairway to the left at the top of a sharp fall-off into the woods. Few players go for the green in two because a large pond dominates the final 100 yards, with just a narrow landing area to the right. The green is elevated beyond the water, but falls off steeply toward a pond on the left.

The short par-five fifth features a divided fairway. A large pond on the left side of the fairway leaves a relatively narrow landing area to the right approaching the green.

Fairview hosted two major MGA championships, the 1930 Met Open and the 1959 Met Amateur. John Inglis' caddies handled the winners in both events. ○

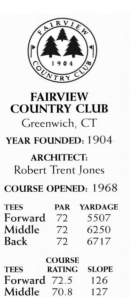

**FAIRVIEW
COUNTRY CLUB**

Greenwich, CT

YEAR FOUNDED: 1904

ARCHITECT:
Robert Trent Jones

COURSE OPENED: 1968

TEES	PAR	YARDAGE
Forward	72	5507
Middle	72	6250
Back	72	6717

TEES	COURSE RATING	SLOPE
Forward	72.5	126
Middle	70.8	127
Back	73.0	131

Alumni reunion of Fairview caddies.

FENWAY GOLF CLUB

"Where's The Wall?"

FENWAY GOLF CLUB
Scarsdale, NY

YEAR FOUNDED: 1921

ARCHITECTS:
Devereux Emmet
A.W. Tillinghast

COURSE OPENED: 1922

TEES	PAR	YARDAGE
Forward	73	5674
Middle	70	6248
Back	70	6494

TEES	COURSE RATING	SLOPE
Forward	74.3	130
Middle	70.9	125
Back	72.0	128

One day in 1920, Max Marx brought a handful of friends to the 40-acre Scarsdale estate of Eugene Reynal, which he thought would be an ideal spot for golf. The mansion, destined to become the clubhouse, was a wedding gift from Reynal to his bride.

By April of 1921, Marx and company had purchased additional land and organized their club. They named it Fenimore after James Fenimore Cooper, who lived on a farm in Scarsdale when he wrote *The Spy* in 1821. Scenes from this landmark story of the Revolutionary War period, the first American novel, supposedly were set on the land that 100 years later would be occupied by the Fenimore Golf Club.

Devereux Emmet designed Fenimore's first 18-hole course as well as a 9-hole "bijou" course (five par threes and four par fours) for women, both of which were ready for play by Decoration Day, 1922. The big course was replaced in 1924 by an A.W. Tillinghast layout, considered one of his finest.

Fenimore failed with the Depression, and was reorganized as Fenway in 1936. Its moment in the national spotlight came in 1938 when the Club hosted the "Westchester 108," offering a purse of $13,500, highest of the season, for a five-day, six-round extravaganza. Sam Snead snared the $5,000 first prize with an aggregate 430 despite hitting three balls out-of-bounds on the third hole, each time overhitting the green while attempting to get home in two (a loss-of-distance-only penalty in those days).

During the late 1920s, Fenway was one of the first clubs in the country to be represented by a playing professional in addition to the standard head professional who worked at the Club on a daily basis. The Club had an arrangement with two of the leading golfers of that era, Leo Diegel and "Wild Bill" Mehlhorn. Herman Barron came to Fenway in 1936 and stayed as head professional for nearly 40 years, winning four Tour events and playing on the 1947 Ryder Cup team. He was succeeded in 1976 by seven-time Met PGA Player of the Year Jimmy Wright, winner of four Met PGA's, one Met Open, and a fourth-place finish behind Raymond Floyd in the 1969 PGA Championship.

Fenway is best-known for its greens, many of which are pear-shaped and sloping, with deep bunkers protecting narrow entrances, similar to those at nearby Winged Foot. The par-five third hole is the Club's centerpiece. The drive must avoid three fairway bunkers, and the second shot a nest of four bunkers. The elevated green is two-tiered, the higher right side set behind a pair of huge bunkers.

The 15th is a devilish little par four with a small, tightly-trapped hourglass green that slopes severely back toward the fairway. The front of the green can't be more than 12 feet wide, making it an extremely difficult target to hit and hold, even with a perfect explosion from one of the greenside bunkers.

No doubt many a golfer has entered the grounds with the facetious thought "where's the wall?" in the back of his mind, the reference being to the "green monster" in left field at Fenway Park. After doing battle over 18 holes with Tilinghast's deep bunkers, most golfers have seen their share of "walls." ◯

The postcard 17th (above) and the imposing clubhouse.

HAMPSHIRE COUNTRY CLUB

"Letter Perfect"

The 13th hole as seen from the right rough.

**HAMPSHIRE
COUNTRY CLUB**
Mamaroneck, NY

YEAR FOUNDED: 1926

ARCHITECTS:
Devereux Emmet
Alfred Tull

COURSE OPENED: 1928

TEES	PAR	YARDAGE
Forward	72	5466
Middle	71	6248

TEES	COURSE RATING	SLOPE
Forward	73.9	132
Middle	70.1	128

In 1926, four millionaires, along with 75 fellow men of means, purchased a tract of swampy land near Long Island Sound, built dikes, and waited two years for their property to dry out. The members called their club Hommocks after the numerous natural mounds on the property, and engaged the team of Emmet & Tull to design an 18-hole course, which opened in 1928.

The clubhouse resembled an English Tudor mansion. It featured high ceilings, rafters supported by sculpted monks and two walk-in fireplaces with a knight's shield over each—one bearing crossed swords, the other crossed golf clubs, both of which appear on the Club's logo. The china and silverware were imported from England, bearing the letters "HCC" that would in later years dictate the Club's subsequent names.

The grounds were magnificent. Formal gardens encircled the southern half of the building, and at the back was a grove of trees adjacent to the entrance to the indoor pool, dominated by a stately Colorado Blue Spruce.

Despite its nearness to the water, the golf course was hilly, wooded, and rocky. At the 13th, the fairway bends right, with water extending from approximately 125 yards in front of the tee all the way up the right side before cross-ing in front of the green and wrapping around the left side.

The rugged second hole is an unusual little par three that plays across a large outcropping of rock that partially conceals the greenside setting, especially the chasmlike bunker guarding the right-front and side. The eighth is a short par four that angles 90 degrees to the right, then flies straight up to a hilltop green.

Hommocks had a short existence, crashing with the stock market in 1929. In 1934 it became the Harbor Country Club (keep the proper initials), which appeared positioned to flourish during a post-Depression boom until the surprise hurricane of 1938 inundated the golf course and destroyed the Club. The Town of Mamaroneck took over as landlord in 1940, and sold the property to the new Hampshire Country Club in '44.

Hampshire's heyday ran from 1950 to 1965, when the relatively small membership used the Club as an extension of their homes. Many spent the day there, from breakfast to midnight snack. Entertainers like Carol Burnett and Red Buttons, imported from the Catskills, performed every Wednesday night before they became famous. Today, Hampshire has just about everything to offer its members—golf, tennis, platform tennis, swimming, and fine dining.

HUDSON NATIONAL GOLF CLUB

"Twice Blessed"

**HUDSON
NATIONAL
GOLF CLUB**

Croton-on-Hudson, NY

YEAR FOUNDED: 1994

ARCHITECT:
Tom Fazio

COURSE OPENED: 1996

TEES	PAR	YARDAGE
Forward	72	5693
Middle	72	6276
Back	72	6885

TEES	COURSE RATING	SLOPE
Forward	72.6	123
Middle	70.2	120
Back	73.0	126

Hudson National, which celebrated its grand opening on June 1, 1996, has been twice blessed. Once with a spectacular setting, high on the cliffs overlooking the Hudson River. Twice with the inspired architect Tom Fazio, who has been honored by his peers each of the last three years (1993-1995) as the top course designer in the country. He said "the land built the course" at Hudson National. No matter where the credit is due, the result is one of the area's—and the country's—finest courses, 18 holes that highlight the natural beauty of the site.

It has been almost four centuries since Henry Hudson first sailed up the river that now bears his name, and two centuries since the American Colonists and their Hessian allies used the 260-acre site in Croton-On-Hudson, average elevation 450 feet above the river, as a strategic lookout for British warships during the Revolutionary War.

And it has been almost a century since the nine-hole Hessian Hills Country Club was founded on this site during the 1920s. A fire destroyed the clubhouse in 1932, at the depths of the Depression, when there was no funding to rebuild. (Clubhouse ruins were incorporated into the present fifth tee.) So the Club was disbanded and the course allowed to return to nature.

Hudson National was organized on January 31, 1994 by co-developers National Fairways, owned by Marc Bergschneider, and Tom Plant, and construction started the following October. The course was sodded by the fall of 1995, and scattered play began early in 1996. The clubhouse, a four-story stone manor house, is scheduled to be completed by early 1997.

The river is in view from no less than 12 holes, and there are many lovely inland vistas as well. When golfers finally stop gazing into the distance, they'll find four sets of tees, allowing them to choose their best level of challenge and distraction.

The course rises and falls, making masterful use of its mountain setting. The 12th hole is a sharp dogleg-left that can be played as a short par five or long par four, depending on the tee used. Both the landing area and green are nicely framed by bunkering.

The 14th is a long, gentle dogleg-right par five that drops significantly about halfway to the hole. A lake extends along the right side from greenside well back into the fairway, causing many players to lay up well to the left on their second shots.

The 16th is a long, downhill par three that seems to reach to the river. The kidney-shaped green is bunkered at both sides.

The home hole offers a magnificent view of the clubhouse. A long, narrow par four, bunkers to both sides further shrink the landing area. The green is elevated, with wetlands short on the right side.

In October of 1996, Hudson National received its competitive baptism as the site for the Hugh L. Carey Cup, a revival of the Irish-American Challenge. Teams representing the MGA and Golfing Union of Ireland competed over the lush fairways amidst a grand, New York autumnal setting, with the home team coming out on top.　❍

The approach on the dogleg-right 15th hole.

INNIS ARDEN GOLF CLUB

"Good Enough For God"

Asked why he spelled his last name with just one "d," Scottish millionaire banker J. Kennedy Tod replied, "What's good enough for God is good enough for me." God probably would have been quite comfortable at Tod's estate on Greenwich Point, and that takes us to the roots of Innis Arden.

In 1893, Tod purchased Greenwich Point, soon to be known as Tod's Point. He built a 37-room Victorian mansion, with a beach house, pond, and small zoo on the grounds. He called the estate Innis Arden, Scottish for "little peninsula."

Tod was among the pioneer golfers of Greenwich, and it was only a matter of time before he built a course on his estate, a nine-holer "just a biscuit's throw from the Sound, with the sound of waves and the smell of salt in the air." The best hole, known as "The Crescent," curved gracefully along Greenwich Cove, with the short route home calling for two heroic shots flirting with disaster.

His friends and neighbors were allowed to play his course. In fact, Tod went so far as to give his blessing to the

1899

INNIS ARDEN GOLF CLUB
Old Greenwich, CT

YEAR FOUNDED: 1899

ARCHITECT:
Members

COURSE OPENED: 1908

TEES	PAR	YARDAGE
Forward	73	5390
Middle	70	5863
Back	70	6155

TEES	COURSE RATING	SLOPE
Forward	72.6	134
Middle	69.1	125
Back	70.3	128

Club they formed in 1899, the original Innis Arden, and built a clubhouse for them just outside the estate gates. All went smoothly until a crystal-clear spring day in 1904 when Tod arrived only to find no caddies available. The public was expelled from Eden.

That afternoon, the town's golfers formed a new club, the Sound Beach Golf Club. (Tod joined and remained a member until his death in 1925.) They laid out a nine-hole course on farmland across Greenwich Cove, but it was not enough and soon they leased 53 acres straddling Tomac Avenue. An old homestead became the clubhouse and a course was constructed by the members in 1908; the holes quite similar to what exists today. The second nine holes opened in 1926 after the Club purchased additional land.

The Club's most prominent golfer was Dick Mayer, the 1957 PGA Golfer of the Year, with victories in the U.S. Open and Tam O'Shanter World Championship. Mayer began playing at Innis Arden in 1931—at age eight—but never won the Club championship. He lost in the finals twice—to his father.

Hilly and tree-lined, the real trouble at Innis Arden is wet: A variety of water hazards affect play on 13 holes. A creek flows across four holes on the front-nine, which also features two ponds. A large lake, built during the 1960s, figures on three back-nine holes.

The seventh is a unique par three, nothing more than a little pitch over a pond—and a tree dead-center halfway to the green! The putting surface is small and bunkered left, right, and across the front.

The 15th is Innis Arden's key hole, a long, uphill, par four around the lake (and its man-made swans). The drive is played from an elevated tee, with the lake encroaching from the left. The second shot must carry the corner of the water then climb to a hilltop green.

What was good enough for J. Kennedy Tod a century ago continues to give pleasure to hundreds of Innis Arden members. ○

The Innis Arden gates at the first tee, formerly at the entrance to J. Kennedy Tod's estate.

MOUNT KISCO COUNTRY CLUB

"Joy In Mudville"

The village of Mount Kisco, located at the eastern base of Kisco Mountain, traces its history back to the 17th century when Algonquin tribes led by chiefs Katonah and Wampus inhabited the area and harvested the beaver colony that thrived in the wet lowlands of the Harlem Valley. The Indian name for the region was "cisqua," which means "muddy place," and was later anglicized to "kisco."

The region was transformed in 1847 when the New York & Harlem Railroad extended its line north. A community named Mount Kisco was formed in 1848, and eventually grew from a farming community to a highly desirable locale for a summer retreat.

The first golf course was the Mount Kisco Golf Club, which opened in 1917 on property adjacent to the present course. It was followed by Lawrence Farms, established in the late 1920s, a 185-acre residential community anchored by the Lawrence Farms Country Club and also offering tennis, horseback riding, swimming, and skating. The Lawrence Farms course, set in a natural depression between low, wooded hills, was designed by Tom Winton, who had come to this country in 1916 to be the greenkeeper at Siwanoy, which he prepared for the inaugural PGA Championship that year. The original Mount Kisco Golf Club closed its doors during World War II, but its spirit was kept alive by the members who joined Lawrence Farms and convinced the newer Club to take the older one's name.

Mount Kisco's chief player over the years was Wilson Barnes, who won the 1953 Met Amateur. Recently his

MOUNT KISCO COUNTRY CLUB

Mount Kisco, NY

YEAR FOUNDED: 1928

ARCHITECT:
Tom Winton

COURSE OPENED: 1928

TEES	PAR	YARDAGE
Forward	73	5466
Middle	71	6216
Back	71	6458

TEES	COURSE RATING	SLOPE
Forward	72.4	129
Middle	70.0	126
Back	71.1	129

ranking has been challenged by professional Nick Manolios, who finished second in the 1978 Met Open, and by Joe Sommers with numerous top finishes in area amateur events.

The most notable feature of the course is a network of streams that crosses 13 holes, often presenting a major obstacle. The course also gains some of its resistance to scoring from small, fast greens, several of which are devilishly bunkered.

The fifth is the number-one handicap hole, a long, uphill par four that pitches to the right in the drive zone and again in front of the green. Both a modest swale and a bunker front the green, which slopes left to right while tilting back to front.

The 16th fairway rises gently to a crest in the landing area before sweeping down and to the left, leaving a downhill lie the reward for a long drive. The par-five 17th plays from an elevated tee to a level fairway, with out-of-bounds all the way along the right and a creek crossing just in front of the green.

Overall, Mount Kisco is a joy to play, providing a beautiful challenge for golfers of all skill levels. ❍

The 6th green, with Mount Kisco in background.

COUNTRY CLUB OF NEW CANAAN

"Tee And Tennis"

COUNTRY CLUB OF NEW CANAAN
New Canaan, CT

YEAR FOUNDED: 1893

ARCHITECTS:
Willie Park
Alfred Tull
Robert Trent Jones

COURSE OPENED: 1900

TEES	PAR	YARDAGE
Forward	74	5809
Middle	71	6268
Back	71	6442

TEES	COURSE RATING	SLOPE
Forward	74.1	131
Middle	70.6	129
Back	71.5	132

Back in the 1890s, bucolic New Canaan (population less than 3,000) was a popular summer community. The Oenoke Field Club opened in August, 1893, so the summer residents, most from Manhattan and Brooklyn, would have a place to get together. Original amenities included two lawn tennis courts and a pavilion for socializing, highlighted by Saturday afternoon tea.

A few original members also were interested in golf, and two or three holes were squeezed onto the property as early as 1893. By 1895, the game's popularity had grown, but there was no room for a real course on the site. A group of Oenoke members incorporated as the New Canaan Golf Club to lease (and later purchase) the 208-acre St. John farm. Dr. Edward Lambert, the Club's first president, put up the $5,000 that also got the members the dilapidated farmhouse that became their clubhouse.

Willie Park Jr. was engaged to design a nine-hole golf course, which he did one Sunday afternoon in 1895 during his first visit to this country. Following Park's plans, but without his speed, the members built the course themselves, digging the bunkers, removing trees, and clearing the underbrush. Four holes were ready for a grand opening on July 4, 1897; it was not until 1900 that all nine were ready. The course had two sets of tees, which allowed for

some variety: The "front nine" had one par three and one par five, while there were two of each on the "back." (This was the layout that remained until 1947.)

The course caused a rift between the golfers and the "tea and tennis" set that was not resolved until 1904, when the Club built two clay tennis courts and a croquet green, and remodeled the old farmhouse into a respectable clubhouse.

Again working on their own, the golfers attempted to expand the course to 18 holes in 1923, but the project failed and nearly put the Club into bankruptcy. A second nine finally was built in 1947, designed by Alfred Tull.

In the early '50s, Robert Trent Jones redid the first, 10th, and 18th holes.

The result was a course that bore little semblance to the original nine holes, even though the present back nine has an old fashioned flavor, pot bunkers, blind shots, and the like.

New Canaan is a thinking man's course, not long but demanding accurate placement of tee shots to approach the greens from the best angle. Local knowledge is a prerequisite, as a number of greenside bunkers are hidden from view, cleverly tucked into the rolling terrain.

Typical is the 17th, a short par four with tree limbs overhanging the left side of the fairway, and a slightly elevated, fall-away green protected by two pot bunkers at the front-left. Lee Trevino played the course in 1968, a week before winning his first U.S. Open, and said 17 was the kind of hole he would like in his backyard for practice.

New Canaan today is a family-oriented club with a relatively young membership. Facilities include a swimming pool; tennis, paddle tennis. and squash courts, and an outstanding junior golf program. Not to be left out, the "Senior Swingers" have been playing golf together since 1972, with the season's best player receiving the "Silver Pig" trophy.

So, after all these years, golf has found a way to coexist peacefully with tea and tennis. ❍

The tiny, tightly-bunkered 17th green.

THE PATTERSON CLUB

"Lights Out"

The Patterson Club was organized in 1929 as a dining and social club for General Electric employees, located in downtown Bridgeport. The name came from a GE vice-president, Charles E. Patterson. In 1946, the company purchased the rolling, 173-acre Carleton Palmer farm in the Greenfield Hill section of Fairfield. Palmer, Chairman of the Board of SQUIBB, used the farm for training horses; under GE, it was used for golf, tennis, and swimming.

That same year, the farmhouse was converted into a clubhouse, a barn became the lockerhouse/pro shop, and course construction began. The course was designed by Robert Trent Jones, who also gave the Club its first professional, Neil Martin. While serving with Patton's army in Europe following World War II, Martin was assigned to supervise construction of a Jones course being built in Belgium for American troops. Upon returning to the United States, he was offered a similar position with Jones at Patterson; once the course was finished, he stayed on as head professional.

Construction was budgeted to cost just $110,000, but was complicated by four miles of stone wall on the property and a horsetrack near the 11th green. Many of the boulders became foundation for tees, greens, and mounds.

The course opened on June 28, 1947. A gallery of 1,500 watched as Bobby Jones and Gene Sarazen joined a couple of GE executives in the ceremonial first foursome. Both legends carded 74 in a match that ended even when Sarazen holed out from the back bunker for a birdie on 18.

The second, a long par four, is rated the number-one handicap hole. The fairway slopes hard right to left in the landing area, demanding a drive to the right side. The approach plays considerably downhill, with a sharp fall-off behind the wave-like bunkers (a Patterson trademark) at the front corners of the green.

Among the prettiest holes is the par-three third, which has water in front of the tee that becomes a lateral hazard up the left side. The "three-club green" angles toward the left rear, bringing the water into play when the hole is middle to back. Balancing the water is a bunker to the right. Two other par threes (6 and 14) also play across water.

The approach to the right-dogleg par-four 15th gets the nod as Patterson's most heroic shot. It plays uphill to a rolling plateau green set above two huge beautifully-sculpted bunkers that leave but a narrow entrance.

In the late '40s, the Club was opened to non-GE employees. In 1968, the company sold the property to the Club, which became member-owned for the first time. Today, Patterson is a hidden gem deserving the spotlight. ○

The water carry on the par-three third.

THE PATTERSON CLUB

Fairfield, CT

YEAR FOUNDED: 1929

ARCHITECT:
Robert Trent Jones

COURSE OPENED: 1947

TEES	PAR	YARDAGE
Forward	73	5687
Middle	71	6429
Back	71	6795

TEES	COURSE RATING	SLOPE
Forward	73.0	122
Middle	71.3	130
Back	72.8	134

PELHAM COUNTRY CLUB

"Spaghetti And Golf Balls"

One of the most dramatic shots in American championship golf was struck by Gene Sarazen from deep rough off the second fairway at the Pelham Country Club. It proved to be the decisive blow in the 1923 PGA Championship, but if it were to be re-enacted today, it would be necessary to halt traffic on the New England Thruway, which was built through the course in the early 1950s, directly over the site of the old second green.

Sarazen's 36-hole final match against Walter Hagen ended all even, and the two matched birdies on the first extra hole. The second was a short par four with a 90-degree turn to the left at the end. The green was surrounded by sand and rough, but could be reached with a daring drive over trees flirting with an out-of-bounds line that bordered a small Italian neighborhood. Hagen, playing first, placed his drive just short of a greenside bunker. Sarazen, taking a gamble, went for the green. His shot caught the trees and came to rest in long, thickly matted rough. Sarazen lofted his ball to within two feet of the cup.

PELHAM COUNTRY CLUB
Pelham Manor, NY

YEAR FOUNDED: 1898

ARCHITECTS:
Devereux Emmet
Alfred Tull

COURSE OPENED: 1921

TEES	PAR	YARDAGE
Forward	72	5708
Middle	71	6032
Back	71	6318

TEES	COURSE RATING	SLOPE
Forward	73.5	132
Middle	69.4	125
Back	70.4	128

Unnerved, Hagen dumped his little pitch into the bunker in front of him. Sarazen won with a birdie.

Hagen jokingly claimed that Sarazen's ball had fallen out-of-bounds and was thrown back in by a sympathetic Italian fan. And that some red markings on Sarazen's ball were proof that it had landed in someone's spaghetti dinner.

Pelham Country Club evolved from a club of the same name that was founded in 1898 across the Boston Post Road from the present site. When that club was forced to move in 1904, it spawned both the Wykagyl Country Club in New Rochelle and the present Pelham Country Club, the latter composed of the many members who did not fancy the long trip up to New Rochelle.

The Club moved to its present site in 1908, but it was not until 1919 that golf again became a part of Club life. Devereux Emmet built an 18-hole course that was ready for play in 1921.

Shortly before the Club's opening, Jim Barnes was signed as professional and immediately won the U.S. Open. Warren G. Harding was on hand to present the winner's cup, the only known instance of an American president doing the honors.

The New England Thruway came in the early 1950s. Major renovations were needed, and Alfred Tull was given the assignment. He built five new holes (4 through 8) across Mount Tom Road. The holes on the east side of the Thruway and railroad are connected to the rest of the course by a tunnel.

The terrain is rugged. Many holes play from elevated, even hillsides, tees to narrow, tree-lined fairways, placing extreme demands on accuracy. A stream wanders through the course, crossing six holes.

The ninth fairway is divided by a rough-covered ridge, although the average player will need a career drive to reach the upper fairway. An outgrowth of rocks to the right will punish a slice or push. From the top of the hill, the hole rolls downhill to the green, with the entire left side falling away dangerously toward the woods.

The 14th is a moderate par five that demands a precise drive to open up the second shot. The wide green is set behind a fieldstone-bordered stream.

As for the new, par-three second, one of the strongest holes on the course, it is well clear of the highway—and anyone's pasta dinner. ○

The uphill climb to #4.

COUNTRY CLUB OF PURCHASE

"A Dream Come True"

The 17th, a babe in the wetlands.

I n the affluent community of Purchase, already blessed with three magnificent golf clubs (Brae Burn, Century, and Old Oaks), the creation of a new club of equal distinction would be a mammoth undertaking. But with a signature Jack Nicklaus golf course precariously winding its way between forest and wetlands, the Country Club of Purchase is well on its way to achieving its lofty goals.

The Country Club of Purchase was envisioned as a high-quality golf experience with the same tone and character as Augusta National or Muirfield Village, international in scope and reputation. It would be an open-membership club, easily-accessible and not far from New York City to foster national and international gatherings. Jack Nicklaus was chosen as architect because of his outstanding record in international competition which, it was felt, would enhance the Club's reputation. The course would be a showcase in the Met Area for Nicklaus' architectural talents.

On the property but separate from the golf facility, Purchase Estates will have one-acre lots for 73 homes ranging from $600,000 to $1 million. (Home ownership does not guarantee club membership.)

The Country Club of Purchase was the dream of Japanese businessman Tokio Kasuga and his son Masahiko. To realize his father's dream, Masahiko, a real estate developer, purchased more than 400 acres in Purchase in 1988, the core of which was the old Pforzheimer farm, bisected by Purchase Street and less than five minutes from Westchester County Airport.

COUNTRY CLUB OF PURCHASE
Purchase, NY

YEAR FOUNDED: 1996

ARCHITECT:
Jack Nicklaus

COURSE OPENED: 1996

TEES	PAR	YARDAGE
Forward	72	5267
Middle	72	6455
Back	72	6876

TEES	COURSE RATING	SLOPE
Forward	70.7	126
Middle	71.5	133
Back	73.5	136

Kasuga dedicated 192 acres to the course, which would share the land with 45 species of wildlife and a number of majestic stone outcroppings. The land already has been designated part of the Audubon Society.

Purchase opened for play in the fall of 1996, although Tokio had passed away years earlier after witnessing only the early stages of the development.

Most holes at Purchase are narrow avenues cut through the trees, many bordered by water or wetlands, which come into play on 13 holes. Among the strongest holes is the long par-four fourth, which requires a long carry over a ravine to reach the fairway, then a nerve-wracking long second shot to an island green set in the wetlands.

The par-five seventh is equally treacherous, with wetlands close off the tee and a pond in front of the green. The hole is a dogleg-left that entices the aggressive player to try getting home in two.

Purchase's final four are a strong and picturesque finish. Wetlands protect the green on the par-three 17th, then flank the right side of the right-dogleg 18th before crossing in front of the green. The 16th calls for an imposing water carry into the green. The 15th is a short par five that bends to the right before climbing to a hilltop green. A nasty pot bunker dead-center in front of the green is a threat to all.

Plans call for a 34,000-square-foot clubhouse to be ready for the 1998 season. Membership will be by invitation only and when the clubhouse is finished and the membership in place the Country Club of Purchase will truly be "a dream come true." ○

RICHTER PARK GOLF COURSE

"Water, Water, Everywhere"

**RICHTER PARK
GOLF COURSE**
Danbury, CT
YEAR FOUNDED: 1968
ARCHITECT:
Edward Ryder
COURSE OPENED: 1971

TEES	PAR	YARDAGE
Forward	72	5202
Middle	72	6325
Back	72	6740

TEES	COURSE RATING	SLOPE
Forward	71.6	128
Middle	71.1	126
Back	73.0	130

The Stanley L. Richter Memorial Park was established in 1968 when his widow donated 85 acres of land, the couple's summer estate, for recreational purposes, and the city of Danbury matched her gift. Today, the park features tennis courts, hiking trails, basketball courts, fishing, a fitness trail, and a variety of winter sports, and an 18-hole golf course consistently ranked among the country's best. A $1,000,000 Activity Center, with restaurant, pro shop, and locker room, was completed in 1988, replacing the old cottage—converted dog kennel—that had served golfers for years.

The course is set against a backdrop of rolling hills and scenic lakes and ponds, and is without doubt the most dramatic public course in the Met Area, if not the country. The course was designed by little-known local architect Edward Ryder, whose portfolio consists of perhaps five courses, all but one in the immediate vicinity, the most noteworthy the back nine at nearby Morefar. Richter's front nine opened for play in 1971, the back side two years later.

Richter Park is quite hilly, and features exceptionally large, undulating, often two-tiered greens. But its most striking characteristic is water—and more water! It lurks on 16 holes; serious water crossings are required on no fewer than eight holes, including long carries on two par

Sign on the 15th hole.

threes, the third and fifth.

Two corners of the course vie for the accolade "most picturesque." The seventh hole, a par five, demands a solid blow off the tee to carry a tentacle of a lake. The tee shot on the eighth is blind, often played with an iron. The approach to the green must clear the same lake that threatens the seventh-hole drive.

The second idyllic spot includes the 11th and 12th holes. Number 11 plays from an elevated tee well above the hidden fairway; the pitch to the green must carry a wide stream. The par-five 12th bends to the right off the tee, and the fairway beyond the turn also pitches right. The green is set at the tip of a small peninsula extending out into yet another lake, so any approach from the right side must carry water to reach the green.

Touring professional Ken Green, a native of Danbury, has played Richter Park in 65 strokes. He hosted the Deltron Richter Park Pro-Am for a number of years. Held the Monday after the Greater Hartford Open, it attracted a number of his fellow Tour professionals. Richter Park hosted that event for a number of years, and the MGA Public Links Championship in 1988, 1992, and 1995. thereby exposing one of the country's finest public facilities to a wider audience. ○

The peninsula green at the 12th hole.

RIDGEWAY COUNTRY CLUB
"Left Out"

A few of the bunkers leading to the 17th green.

In 1922, Westchester Hills Country Club was organized as a private club and used the layout of the Gedney Farm Hotel. Within a few months, the hotel built a new nine-hole course for its guests—located across Ridgeway Avenue from its predecessor. A complete 18-hole course was open by 1923, designed by Pete Clark, who had been responsible for the original layout.

On September 20, 1924, a fire destroyed the hotel, closing it forever. The course became a private club called Gedney Farm Country Club, which twice hosted the Met PGA Championship in the 1930s. But the Depression and World War II took their toll and the Club closed, its remaining membership crossing the street to Westchester Hills. The course operated on a semi-private basis until 1952, when it was sold to a group of local businessmen who formed the Ridgeway Country Club, named for the street between the two courses.

Ridgeway is known for small greens and numerous bunkers, but is feared for the constant threat of out-of-bounds on the left—a

RIDGEWAY COUNTRY CLUB
White Plains, NY

YEAR FOUNDED: 1952

ARCHITECT:
Pete Clark

COURSE OPENED: 1922

TEES	PAR	YARDAGE
Forward	72	5497
Middle	71	6192
Back	71	6377

TEES	COURSE RATING	SLOPE
Forward	73.0	126
Middle	70.6	126
Back	71.4	128

frightening reality on no less than 15 holes. The signature hole is the sixth, a 268-yard par four with a lake on the right side spilling into a brook that crosses in front of the green. Most players wisely lay up off the tee, but that means avoiding a bunker to the left and a large mound in the fairway 100 yards from the green. The approach must carry a bunker, which takes away any chance of running the ball onto the putting surface.

The par-five 17th hole begins resembling the Sahara 150 yards from home, where four bunkers cross the fairway. Just past them on the right is another bunker, with still more sand nearly circling a green that breaks from back to front.

Ridgeway enjoyed its moment in the tournament spotlight when it co-hosted the 1986 and 1987 MasterCard International Pro-Am on the LPGA Tour. It was won in 1986 by Cindy Mackay and the following year by Val Skinner.

Members today enjoy tennis, a swimming pool, and great food, on a smaller scale than the old Gedney Farm Hotel, but no less rewarding.

ROCKRIMMON COUNTRY CLUB

"Golfalator"

ROCKRIMMON COUNTRY CLUB
Stamford, CT

YEAR FOUNDED: 1949

ARCHITECT:
Robert Trent Jones

COURSE OPENED: 1949

TEES	PAR	YARDAGE
Forward	75	5778
Middle	72	6590
Back	72	6832

TEES	COURSE RATING	SLOPE
Forward	73.6	130
Middle	72.7	126
Back	73.8	128

While adding a back nine to the Rockrimmon Country Club, Robert Trent Jones recommended installing a "Golfalator" to carry golfers up the steep, 50-foot grade between the 9th green and 10th tee. So in went 330 feet of railroad tracks and ties—a gift from the New York, New Haven & Hartford Railroad—and the members purchased a fully-automated tram seating six to eight people. The tram, powered by a five-horsepower engine, moved at walking speed, slow enough that golfers could add their scores and rearrange their bets for the back nine.

The tram is used only occasionally today, another victim of the golf cart revolution.

Rockrimmon, located on the New York-Connecticut border, sits partly in Stamford, Connecticut, partly in Pound Ridge, New York. The clubhouse is in Connecticut while most of the golf course in New York, and the tram crosses the state line, making it the shortest interstate railroad in the nation.

The original Jones-designed nine holes opened in 1949, the second nine came along in 1953. Rockrimmon is surprisingly difficult and beautifully condi-

The tram.

tioned. The fairways are tree-lined avenues that offer glorious vistas, especially in the spring and fall. Much of the course's appeal comes from the variety of its par fours, including a number of holes that require irons or fairway woods off the tees.

The par-four sixth sweeps to the left, calling for a lay-up off the tee or a daring high drive over a lone tree at the corner. The hole then plays severely uphill to a two-tiered green.

The eighth is Rockrimmon's toughest par four, its fairway and greenside sloping severely left to right. The punchbowl green is difficult to master, as is any attempt at an up-and-down from the left side.

The 15th is a tight, short par five, cut by a creek 100 yards from the green. The creek flows into a pond that lurks along the left side just shy of the green. The par-three ninth is the postcard hole, demanding a long carry over water that is only half the battle. The elevated green is shallow and two-tiered, and positioned behind three monstrous bunkers. And then comes Rockrimmon's unique golfalator. ○

The narrow par-five 15th hole.

ROUND HILL CLUB

"Aged To Perfection"

Prescott Bush

Billie Burke

tumbles, creating abrupt and dramatic changes in elevation. Typical are a pair of outstanding par fives, 2 and 16. The landing area on the second is dominated by a huge, saddle-shaped mound, with the right side of the fairway sloping severely toward the rough. The fairway of the 16th slopes dramatically to the left through the drive zone. The second shot must be played to the left, near the tree line, and away from two large humps on the right side.

The 11th is a pretty par three over a lake that stretches from tee to green, and is framed by willows.

Billie Burke was the Round Hill golf professional for three years (1930–1932), during which he won the 1931 U.S. Open. He needed a 36-hole playoff against George Von Elm to do it.

No member has been more prominent than former U.S. Senator Prescott Bush. Son-in-law of George Walker, donor of the Walker Cup, "Pres" was the father of former U.S. President George Bush. He and fellow member Ward Foshay both served terms as president of the USGA.

Whether it be the USA, USGA or USSGA, such ties permeate the Round Hill fabric. ❍

ROUND HILL CLUB
Greenwich, CT
YEAR FOUNDED: 1922

ARCHITECTS:
Walter Travis
Robert Trent Jones

COURSE OPENED: 1924

TEES	PAR	YARDAGE
Forward	74	5721
Middle	71	6312
Back	71	6525

TEES	COURSE RATING	SLOPE
Forward	73.8	128
Middle	70.3	124
Back	71.3	127

Many Met Area golfers associate the Round Hill Club with the United States Seniors Golf Association, and for good reason. Since 1971, Round Hill has been a second home for the USSGA, its golf course and clubhouse used for two days each June for the association's championship.

But Round Hill existed long before that, having been formed in 1922 at the Greenwich Field Club. Prominent among the early members was H. Arnold Jackson, who oversaw the construction of the golf course. Jackson's wife was the former Kate Harley, two-time U.S. Women's Amateur champion.

The first act was to purchase property in the "Round Hill" section of Greenwich. "Round Hill" is located between the Club and the Merritt Parkway to the north. The interesting topography remains the most memorable feature of the course.

Walter Travis designed the course, but it was Emilio "Mollie" Strazza, the superintendent of grounds from 1922 until 1964, who gave it flair, using trees and mounds. He also designed and created the distinctive—some might say devilish—contours in the greens.

One major change came in 1965 when Robert Trent Jones built the present 11th hole and the ponds on 11 and 12. Jones' hole followed Travis' original blueprint.

Befitting a course on a hill, the terrain rolls and

From behind the 16th green.

RYE GOLF CLUB

"Caught In The Rye"

There was a time, a century ago, when the intiation fee for a fine golf club was just $25 or $50, and the annual dues about the same. Costs escalated quickly.

In 1920, a group from Rye, NY unable to afford the rising costs of joining a golf club, formed the Rye Country Club. They purchased Whitby Towers and adjoining land extending from the Boston Post Road to Long Island Sound, and planned to offer their members an 18-hole golf course, tennis courts, an outdoor saltwater pool, and 1,200 feet of beachfront, all for $50 a year plus per diem fees.

Whitby Towers, a Gothic Revival mansion destined to take its place in the National Register of Historic Landmarks, was built in 1854, modelled after Whitby Abbey in England. It was situated on a prominence overlooking the Sound, with lawns extending from the Post Road to water's edge, where there was a stone dock 175 feet in length. Whitby Tower's forty acres included landscaped gardens and a pond filled with fish, and the walls of the building were covered with English ivy and other vines.

The members chose Devereux Emmet to design their golf course, which opened for play in 1921. Recently fine-tuned by Rees Jones (1982) and Stephen Kay, it features some pretty rugged topography — and several holes by the water.

The strongest hole is the seventh, one of the toughest par fours in Westchester. Its undulating fairway rolls downhill through the drive zone, then bends left and rises to a crest 100 yards from the hidden green.

Rye's postcard hole is the 16th, where a prodigious drive will catch a downslope and leave a pitch of some 135 yards to the green. A tree set in a rock formation sits in the left side of the fairway at the top of the hill, where the golfer can look out upon a beautiful vista of the wetlands and inlet beyond.

The back nine features three rather unique par threes. The tenth plays uphill from a tee in the cattails to a green watched over by two mature trees on its left and guarded

RYE GOLF CLUB
Rye, NY

YEAR FOUNDED: 1920

ARCHITECT:
Devereux Emmet

COURSE OPENED: 1921

TEES	PAR	YARDAGE
Forward	73	5493
Middle	71	6046
Back	71	6295

TEES	COURSE RATING	SLOPE
Forward	71.7	124
Middle	69.1	120
Back	70.3	123

The 18th hole (above) and clubhouse.

by a long bunker right. The 14th plays over a massive rocky outcropping to a hidden hilltop green, with a precipitous dropoff to the left. And the 17th plays from an elevated tee down to a green set next to the marshland of the harbor.

The Club experienced difficult sailing during the Depression and war years, and folded shortly thereafter. The course became a public facility called Glen Castle, then was converted to a private club called Ryewood before the present club took over in 1965 when the city of Rye purchased the property and operated it exclusively for Rye residents. The membership today consists of 1,200 families, who enjoy the golf course and the olympic-size swimming pool—at a reasonable cost the Club's founders would have found appealing. ○

SCARSDALE GOLF CLUB

"Believe It"

Before establishing the Scarsdale Golf Club, the founders were more interested in shooting another type of birdie—clay pigeons. After forming the Scarsdale Gun Club, they discovered golf. One Saturday morning in 1896, they laid out a nine-hole course and played it that same afternoon, a feat recognized by *Ripley's Believe It Or Not.*

The golf club opened in 1898—absorbing the membership of the gun club—with a nine-hole golf course, designed by Willie Dunn, adjacent to the railroad station. The signature hole was a long par three over a lake to a green below the present first tee.

Carl Fox, the first professional, expanded the course to 18 holes in 1900. By the end of the decade, a clubhouse was built at the top of the hill overlooking the lake, but was twice destroyed by fire. The present building was christened in 1922.

The sloping approach to the 14th, one of the Met Area's most difficult par fours.

SCARSDALE GOLF CLUB

Hartsdale, NY

YEAR FOUNDED: 1898

ARCHITECTS:
Willie Dunn
C.A. Fox
A.W. Tillinghast
Geoffrey Cornish

COURSE OPENED: 1896

TEES	PAR	YARDAGE
Forward	74	5693
Middle	72	6093
Back	72	6322

TEES	COURSE RATING	SLOPE
Forward	73.6	128
Middle	70.1	128
Back	71.2	130

In the early 1920s, the Club purchased additional land and engaged A.W. Tillinghast to revise the course. His work was extensive, including 10 new holes. Most of the back nine was laid out over extremely wooded and rocky terrain, and proved a considerable undertaking, with immovable boulders often governing the routing of holes. The new course opened in 1923 and remained basically unchanged until 1962, when Geoffrey Cornish relocated the first two holes to accommodate a driving range, and discarded Dunn's par three, building the present ninth hole in its place.

The dogleg-left par-five sixth offers the golfer a choice of avenues to the green, one of them through a gap in the trees that flank the left side of the drive zone. The average golfer will utilize the fairway, laying up to the turn on his second shot. The longer hitter may attempt to place his drive so as to set up a "do or die" second shot through the gap, over deep rough, toward the green.

The ninth calls for a good poke over the lake to reach the fairway, which angles to the left. The water extends up the left side, and must be carried a second time to reach a left-side hole location.

The 14th is among the toughest holes in the Met Area. It is a long, narrow par four calling for an accurate drive left of center, then a precise second shot through a saddle of rocks and trees downhill to a landing area that funnels many shots back toward the target. But the tiny green falls away from the approach, with a steep drop-off behind.

At the heart of the Scarsdale golf calendar is the Wilson Cup, inaugurated in 1972. Each May 50 two-man teams of top amateurs are invited for a one-day, 36-hole, better-ball competition. The tournament honors the late Charles E. Wilson, a former member who served as director of the war production board, responsible for converting American industry to the manufacture of military supplies under Presidents Roosevelt and Truman.

The most significant tournament held at Scarsdale was the 1914 Met Open, won by Macdonald Smith with a score of 278. At the time, it was the lowest four-round score in a major American tournament nearly giving Scarsdale a second entry in *Ripley's Believe It Or Not.*

SHOREHAVEN GOLF CLUB

"Like Father..."

Shorehaven Golf Club is a child of the 1920s, conceived with grandiose plans for golf, tennis, a polo field, riding stables and bridle paths, a beach with salt water bathing, and a yacht club. While the Depression hindered the dream, the Club was born with sufficient vigor to weather the storm and sail securely into the modern era as a very successful golf club.

The Club is located between Norwalk and Westport, overlooking Long Island Sound and Shorehaven Island, on an exceptional natural setting, two-thirds of which is bordered by salt water. The course was designed by Willie Park Jr., one of his last in this country. Park sailed for England in 1924, critically ill, and died the following year.

The construction was done under the direction of Robert White. Stone walls were removed and the fairways were plowed by horse power. A group of boy scouts spent two weeks clearing rocks and stones from the fairways. Then the fairways were seeded in August, and the course opened for play in October.

Not especially long, the course plays tough thanks to tight, tree-lined fairways and small, back-to-front-sloping greens, many framed by mounds. A good score must be secured on the two extremely long par threes (#5 and #13),

The Courvilles

then protected over the marshland holes at the round's end.

The second is a short yet treacherous par three. The tiny back-to-front green sits atop a 25-foot rise, with steep fall-offs to either side. The 16th is a heroic par five, starting with a 160-yard carry over the marsh to a rising fairway. Unless the drive was perfect, the second shot is a lay-up, smartly positioned between the trees and marshland that narrow the fairway before the elevated green.

The home hole is exceptional. Marshes force a 150-yard carry off the tee and flank the entire left side of the hole. A tall maple stands in the right center of the fairway, out of reach but very much in play—it must be avoided to leave a clear shot to the green. Despite a large bunker, there is ample room to the left, although a mistake may flirt with sand or water. The final approach is uphill, with marshes close along the left, to a tiered green.

The Jerry Courvilles, father and son, are a central part of the Shorehaven story. Jerry Sr., who passed away in 1996, became a member in 1957 and won the Club championship 26 times, establishing a national record for one club. He came to prominence in the 1960s, when he won the Ike a record six times. His greatest achievement was the 1967 Met Open, a four-stroke tour de force at Winged Foot. The Met Amateur proved more elusive, but after three runner-up finishes, he broke through in 1973, beating future Tour pro George Burns in the finals. He won again six years later, beating a young George Zahringer III in the finals.

Jerry Jr. has followed in his father's footsteps, winning back-to-back editions of the Ike in 1990 and 1991, the latter with a final-nine 30 that tied Jeff Thomas, whom he beat in a three-hole playoff. He had a record-breaking season in 1995, when he won the Met Amateur, U.S. Mid–Amateur, a place on the U.S. Walker Cup team, and MGA Player of the Year honors.

SHOREHAVEN GOLF CLUB
East Norwalk, CT

YEAR FOUNDED: 1922

ARCHITECT:
Willie Park Jr.

COURSE OPENED: 1923

TEES	PAR	YARDAGE
Forward	74	5445
Middle	71	6260
Back	71	6599

TEES	COURSE RATING	SLOPE
Forward	72.9	132
Middle	71.0	131
Back	72.4	134

The links flavor of the 17th hole.

SILVER SPRING COUNTRY CLUB

"A Little Club In The Country"

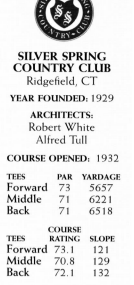

**SILVER SPRING
COUNTRY CLUB**
Ridgefield, CT

YEAR FOUNDED: 1929

ARCHITECTS:
Robert White
Alfred Tull

COURSE OPENED: 1932

TEES	PAR	YARDAGE
Forward	73	5657
Middle	71	6221
Back	71	6518

TEES	COURSE RATING	SLOPE
Forward	73.1	121
Middle	70.8	129
Back	72.1	132

Had Silver Spring not been founded as an unpretentious "little club in the country," it may not have survived its infancy. In 1929, when the economy was still booming, a group of golfers from Ridgefield and Wilton formed a corporation to purchase 265 acres of land and build a golf course. It was designed by Robert White (with suggestions from Charles Banks) and ready for play by May, 1932, during the depths of the Depression.

The Club managed to ride out the '30s, but due to its remote location, was forced to close in 1944, as World War II wound down. The clubhouse was boarded up for the duration, but member Dan McKeon made a 24-mile round-trip on a tractor several times to keep the grass mowed.

Things returned to normal after the war, and the course remained much as it has always been, except for a little work by Alfred Tull in 1954. He converted the 11th hole from a straight-away par four into a dogleg par five to make room for additional parking.

Silver Spring's two nines could hardly be more different. The front nine is heavily wooded, while the back plays over open meadow. The strength of the course is its par threes and its four long par fours (holes 6, 7, 12, and 16).

The third is an uphill "Redan-like" par three, although the green does not run away from the shot. The tenth is a beautiful par three that drops 50 feet from tee to pear-shaped green; one bunker narrows the right-front entrance, another waits along the left side.

The downhill landing area of the par-four seventh adds yardage to the tee shot, which assists the golfer since his approach must fly uphill to a raised, angled green above a deep left-side bunker. The par-four 12th features a huge crossbunker that proves an intimidating presence for the average golfer.

Silver Spring's original clubhouse was a small building designed by Roger Bullard, who also built the clubhouses at Maidstone and Plainfield. It has grown over the years, and recently underwent a major renovation/addition, completed in 1995. This work modernized the facilities without disturbing the "little club in the country" feeling. ○

Approaching the sixth green.

SUNNINGDALE COUNTRY CLUB

"London Bridge"

**SUNNINGDALE
COUNTRY CLUB**
Scarsdale, NY
YEAR FOUNDED: 1913

ARCHITECTS:
Walter Travis
A.W. Tillinghast

COURSE OPENED: 1918

TEES	PAR	YARDAGE
Forward	74	5856
Middle	71	6269
Back	71	6461

TEES	COURSE RATING	SLOPE
Forward	74.9	136
Middle	70.8	126
Back	71.6	128

For the American golfer traveling in England, the Sunningdale Golf Club on the outskirts of London, Britain's first acclaimed inland course, is perhaps the most reminiscent of home. It is not unlike Pine Valley, with rolling, tree-lined fairways interrupted by intrusions of sand. In fact, H.S. Colt, the world-famous golf architect who helped George Crump with the routing at Pine Valley, first took an interest in his future profession while club secretary at Sunningdale.

There must have been a golfer in New York during the early part of the century with a special affection for London's Sunningdale, and he was instrumental in having the club in Scarsdale take its name.

The Westchester club was established in 1913 by a group of 12 men, the majority of them in the clothing business. They leased a ready-made nine-hole Willie Dunn golf course in Mt. Vernon, which had been the second home of the Siwanoy Country Club. But like Siwanoy, Sunningdale soon felt the need for an 18-hole course, and in 1916 moved to the present 175-acre site on the western edge of Scarsdale, high above the Sprain Brook Parkway. The property was of some historical interest, having been an encampment site during the Revolutionary War for the French troops who had come over in 1781 to aid the American cause.

Sunningdale's first 18-hole golf course, opened in 1918, was the work of Walter Travis, and was then reworked slightly in the early 1930s by A.W. Tillinghast when a swimming pool was built encroaching on a few holes. Recently, local architect Stephen Kay rebuilt the bunkers, repositioning a few in the process.

The terrain is typically rolling Westchester, helping to make Sunningdale a precise driving course, with seven doglegs and six severely tilting fairways. Among the most picturesque holes are three par threes—one over a pond, another across a deep gully, and the third downhill and seemingly falling off the face of the earth.

The third hole is a long par three that rises 30 feet between tee and green and far more from the gully that crosses the hole midway and opens into a pond off to the left. Three bunkers protect the severely back-to-front green.

The par-four 10th narrows considerably from tee to green, with out-of-bounds along the tree line on the right. A large mound punctuates the prime landing area, kicking everything to the right. The final run rises slightly to a green that falls severely back to front.

The 11th is a short, devilish par four, the kind Tillinghast became famous for. Sloping downhill through the fairway, driver is too much weapon off the tee. The table-top, pear-shaped green is surrounded by bunkers on all sides.

The 17th is a par three with an elevated tee, a pond, and a slightly sloping green hemmed in by four sizable bunkers.

During the last 30 years, Sunningdale has assumed a prominent place on the local scene. The first major tournament was the 1962 Met Amateur, when Bob Gardner captured his third of five consecutive titles. Another prime-time player on the local stage, Dick Siderowf, walked off with the 1974 Met Amateur at Sunningdale.

Among the more notable members is Jim Stotter, 12-time Club champion between 1948 and '82, and president of the MGA from 1985 to 1986.

London's Sunningdale has too much of the Pine Valley flavor to be considered a parkland course. Westchester's Sunningdale however, is a true parkland delight. ○

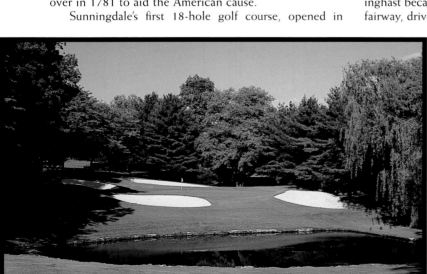

The picturesque 17th hole.

TAMARACK COUNTRY CLUB

"I Like Ike"

The clubhouse overlooking the 18th green.

**TAMARACK
COUNTRY CLUB**

Greenwich, CT

YEAR FOUNDED: 1909

ARCHITECT:
Charles Banks

COURSE OPENED: 1929

TEES	PAR	YARDAGE
Forward	74	5650
Middle	71	6567
Back	71	6834

TEES	COURSE RATING	SLOPE
Forward	72.2	125
Middle	71.7	124
Back	72.9	126

This story begins in 1909, across the Connecticut border in Port Chester, New York, where a group of local businessmen formed the Port Chester Country Club. They built a nine-hole golf course, with fairways maintained by a flock of sheep. In 1923, they expanded to 18 holes. Five years later, the town of Port Chester wanted the land as a site for a new high school, and the Club was told it would have to move.

With the proceeds from the sale of the land, the Club purchased the Griffen Farm on Locust Road in Greenwich. Charles Banks was engaged to build an 18-hole course of championship proportions, which was joined by a charming New England-style clubhouse that nestled perfectly into the setting. The facilities opened on July 4, 1929, and also featured a new name: The Club was called Tamarack, after a species of pine indigenous to the region.

The course is characterized by rugged terrain and elevated greens protected by deep, grass-faced bunkers and steep fall-offs. In typical Banks style, the course features a Redan, a "Short," and a "Biarritz" par three, and a "Punchbowl" green.

The 12th is a stunning Biarritz, a long par three with a swale in front of the green that once was part of the putting surface. Two bunkers, one on each side of the swale, flank the right side. To the left, the swale is sandwiched between a bunker and a steep fall-off.

The dogleg-right 17th is an extremely narrow hole, the fairway also falling sharply to the right in the landing area. The par five then turns right and rolls downhill before its final ascent to the green. Tamarack's most famous bunker, "Big Bertha," sits below the right side of the green.

Tamarack gained local fame as co-host of the Ike Tournament during its formative years, 1953 to 1962. Winners during that period include some of the big names in Met Area golf—Willie Turnesa, Bob Gardner, and Jerry Courville Sr. among them. The tournament was the idea of F.M. Flynn, publisher of the *Daily News*, who wanted to sponsor a golf tournament. He asked sportswriter Dana Mozley to arrange a meeting with a group of leading players. Their consensus was that a stroke-play tournament for amateurs was needed. After President Eisenhower gave permission to use his name, the Ike Tournament became a reality.

The tournament was held for the first time in 1953, with the public-course golfers playing players at Bethpage, the private club golfers at Tamarack. The groups competed together at Tamarack in 1954, when the first team competition was held. From 1955 through 1962, Tamarack and nearby Whippoorwill co-hosted the event. The lowest individual score during this time was the 280 established by Willie Turnesa in 1957 and equaled by Jerry Courville Sr. in 1961. ○

WACCABUC COUNTRY CLUB

"52 Miles Across Time"

The 18th hole, with twin ponds guarding the green.

A stone marker on the front lawn of the Waccabuc Country Club states that the distance to New York City is 52 miles. The marker dates back to the Colonial era, part of a system instituted by Ben Franklin when he was Postmaster General. The town of Waccabuc retains the charming, family-oriented country lifestyle of previous centuries; the hub still is nothing more than a small post office.

The name Waccabuc is believed to be an Anglicization of the Algonquin "wequa-paug" for "long pond," a reference to Lake Waccabuc at the northern edge of town.

The Waccabuc Country Club was formed in 1912 so that residents could continue enjoying the nine-hole golf course on the grounds of the Lake Waccabuc Inn, a country resort that attracted clientele from as far away as Boston. The Club and the Inn operated as a cooperative venture until 1927, when the Club took over 200 acres, including the inn and the course. The inn became its clubhouse.

The course was expanded to 18 holes in 1923 by a few members and Club professional Jack Gullen. It was given a significant facelift by Alfred Tull in 1962.

The two nines have two different looks. The front nine, behind the clubhouse, is hillier, and has several slanting fairways; the back nine, out front across Mead Road, is only moderately rolling. Front or back, the key to success is putting on greens that come in all manner of shapes and challenging undulations.

The most challenging hole is the par-four third. It plays uphill from tee to green, tilts sharply left to right, and has out-of-bounds short right and a tall ash tree reaching into the fairway from the left 220 yards from the tee. Bunkers sit both right and left ahead of the green.

Number six is a dramatic par five calling for a drive over a deep gully to a rising fairway that sweeps and slopes to the right, with a forest and out-of-bounds on that side. The ideal second shot finds a narrow landing area, beyond which the hole drops precipitously through rough. A spine angling across the green creates sharp slopes on both sides and a steep fall-off beckons from behind.

The challenging and dangerous par-four finishing hole plays into the prevailing wind. If the drive can pass a huge fairway bunker on the right, it may gain extra yards off a sharp downslope. The approach to the sloping green must clear ponds left and right and a bunker just right of center, yet avoid a pair of bunkers at the back.

And just across the road, the clubhouse, and Waccabuc's timeless marker.   ○

**WACCABUC
COUNTRY CLUB**
Waccabuc, NY

YEAR FOUNDED: 1912

ARCHITECTS:
Members
Alfred Tull

COURSE OPENED: 1912

TEES	PAR	YARDAGE
Forward	74	5648
Middle	70	6255
Back	70	6422

TEES	COURSE RATING	SLOPE
Forward	72.7	123
Middle	70.2	124
Back	70.9	127

The Waccabuc clubhouse.

WESTCHESTER HILLS GOLF CLUB

"Saratoga Style"

**WESTCHESTER HILLS
GOLF CLUB**
White Plains, NY

YEAR FOUNDED: 1922

ARCHITECT:
Pete Clark

COURSE OPENED: 1913

TEES	PAR	YARDAGE
Forward	74	5460
Middle	70	6026

TEES	COURSE RATING	SLOPE
Forward	72.8	125
Middle	70.2	127

They called it the "Saratoga of Westchester County," and for a few years after the turn of the century, it attracted the cream of New York society. It was the 300-room Gedney Farm Hotel in White Plains, which sat on 300 acres extending from Mamaroneck Avenue to North Street. Guests could partake of a beach club, tennis and squash courts, polo field, swimming pool, bowling alleys, trap shooting, tobogganing, riding horses, and the famous "Liberty Coach" for sightseeing. And, of course, an 18-hole golf course.

The hotel was named for the Gedney family. John Gedney purchased the site in 1740, and the property was run as a successful farm during the latter half of the 19th century by Bartholomew Gedney II, so successful that the Czar of Russia sent his Commissioner of Agriculture to study its operation.

After Bartholomew Gedney's death in 1897, millionaire horseman Howard Willets bought the property and used it to raise prize-winning cattle and thoroughbred steeplechasers. He also built a showplace mansion.

*Westchester Hills juniors
George Brush and R.A. Jones Jr..*

Following Willets' death in 1912, the huge barn west of Ridgeway Avenue was converted into a luxury hotel; the silos were adorned to create a French Chateau look. Two stables were converted into wings of guest rooms that resembled cabins on a luxury liner—low-ceilinged, cozy, and compact. The dining rooms also had a nautical theme; the ballroom glistened with immense crystal chandeliers; and the convention hall stage was graced by famous actors and musicians.

In 1913, a nine-hole course was built across the road; it was expanded to 18 holes in 1915. The architect was the first professional, Pete Clark, likely advised by Donald Ross. Clark was one of the first Scots to come to this country and one of the first golf professionals to gain admittance to the locker room.

The golf course was available to guests of the hotel but was used primarily by golfers operating under the name Gedney Farm Country Club. The Club purchased the golf course property in 1922, at which time it was reorganized under the name Westchester Hills.

The course is known for tight fairways and extremely fast greens, many of them pitched or crowned to heighten the challenge. In true Ross style, there are numerous crossbunkers and fairway bunkers well ahead of the greens.

The sixth hole calls for a precise drive over a pond to an abruptly rising fairway. A knob dead-center at the crest deflects off-line shots. The fairway beyond rolls downhill through two levels en route to a green fronted by a pond.

A rocky ridge divides the 13th fairway. Most long hitters will lay up short and to the left of center to avoid trees on the right. The small green is unbunkered.

Pete Clark helped make Westchester Hills a leading nursery of junior golfers during the 1920s, developing a number of outstanding youngsters. Among his pupils was Richard A. Jones Jr., winner of the 1923 and 1924 Met Juniors and semifinalist in the 1925 U.S. Amateur.

The current professional, Kevin Morris, was named Met PGA Player of the Year in 1984 and 1985. He captured the 1984 Met PGA at Bethpage Black.

Westchester Hills had a moment in the tournament spotlight as co-host of the LPGA Tour's MasterCard International Pro-Am between 1985 and 1987. Muffin Spencer-Devlin won in 1985, Cindy Mackay in 1986, and Val Skinner in 1987.

The only thing missing was first-class accomodations nearby at the Gedney Farm Hotel. ○

From behind the second green.

THE WHIPPOORWILL CLUB

"My Green Heaven"

According to local legend, Charles Banks lost one of his steamshovels in quicksand under what is now the lake fronting the seventh tee at Whippoorwill. If so, this is an extreme example of a golf architect stamping his signature on one of his courses!

Banks was not the first choice for Whippoorwill. In fact, Donald Ross built a course in 1927. The members quickly decided they needed a professional to handle the development of the course and adjoining property. Fred Ruth was hired in 1928 and promptly advised abandoning the Ross course and building a distinctive 27-hole layout designed by Banks, with whom Ruth had worked at Fishers Island. He also envisioned that the course would be surrounded by magnificent summer homes, but his plans ran headlong into the Depression.

Only 18 holes were constructed, and the Club never materialized. The proposed clubhouse was never built, and starting in 1932, Whippoorwill operated as a semiprivate club. Course maintenance was nothing more than cutting the fairways until gas rationing put an end to golf entirely, and the course grew hip-high in weeds.

Louis Calder purchased the property and paid off the Club's debt in 1942, a speculative move that began to pay dividends when the war ended and the present Club was incorporated. Course restoration began in 1946, and golfers returned the next spring.

The course rises and falls over typically rugged Westchester terrain. The greens are imposing—boldly contoured and set above deep, grass-faced bunkers—with steep drop-offs to the sides and back.

The par-four fifth is the number-one handicap hole. From an elevated tee, it plays to a rising fairway with a pronounced kick to the right. Beyond the crest, the hole tumbles downhill before its final ascent into the green, which is guarded by a huge bunker across the left front.

The par-four ninth climbs "Cardiac Hill" from tee to green, which, at 740 feet in elevation, is the highest point in Westchester County. On a clear day, golfers can see all the way to Manhattan.

The 14th is a long, uphill par four that offers the choice of an easily accessible fairway low and to the left, or the challenge of carrying a pair of bunkers dead ahead to gain added yardage from the downhill kick beyond.

Within the first decade of its return, Whippoorwill assumed a prominent position on the Metropolitan tournament calendar by co-hosting eight Ike Tournaments with nearby Tamarack from 1955 to 1962. A two-time winner of the individual competition during those years was Willie Turnesa. He avoided three-putting the treacherous greens by aiming directly at the flagstick, reasoning that he had a better chance to recover close to the pin with his wedge than by attempting a long putt.

THE WHIPPOORWILL CLUB
Armonk, NY

YEAR FOUNDED: 1946

ARCHITECTS:
Donald Ross
Charles Banks

COURSE OPENED: 1927

TEES	PAR	YARDAGE
Forward	73	5888
Middle	71	6372
Back	71	6697

TEES	COURSE RATING	SLOPE
Forward	74.1	136
Middle	71.2	132
Back	72.7	134

The par-three 11th- a "Redan".

WILLOW RIDGE COUNTRY CLUB

"The Name Game"

Over the years, Willow Ridge has done business under six different names, more than any other club in the Met Area. Being located between two of the area's better-known clubs, Westchester and Apawamis, plus the many name changes have made Willow Ridge among the best-kept secrets in Westchester County—despite a spectacular clubhouse setting high atop a knoll overlooking six exceptionally scenic and challenging holes.

In 1917, a group of men fed up with crowded conditions at Apawamis established Green Meadow Country Club. The new Club leased, and later purchased, a 121-acre site including what was once the New York State Home for the Insane. Maurice McCarthy, a golf professional, was hired to design and build an 18-hole course.

Green Meadow suffered severe problems during the Depression and eventually was dissolved. It was succeeded in 1941 by

**WILLOW RIDGE
COUNTRY CLUB**
Harrison, NY

YEAR FOUNDED: 1917

ARCHITECT:
Maurice McCarthy

COURSE OPENED: 1917

TEES	PAR	YARDAGE
Forward	73	5510
Middle	71	6086
Back	71	6280

TEES	COURSE RATING	SLOPE
Forward	72.6	125
Middle	70.0	128
Back	70.9	129

the Green Valley Country Club, a public course that was forced to close during the war. Next came a private club called Hasty Brook in 1946, followed in close order by two other private ventures, Willows Country Club in 1950 and Harrison Country Club in 1953.

In 1965, a small group of dedicated golfers, all members of the Harrison Country Club, organized Willow Ridge Country Club. Within a year, the town of Harrison attempted to condemn Club property and take it over for municipal recreation facilities, but the attempted coup was thwarted. The new Club has prospered ever since.

Willow Ridge is blessed with dramatic, tumbling terrain, beginning with the opening hole. The dramatic dogleg-right par four rises and falls several times on its rollercoaster journey from tee to green.

From the tee of the par-four fifth, the golfer faces a pair of large boulders, which seem along the tree line in the left rough, yet are marked with a bulls-eye. Locals know a drive over the rocks will catch a downhill slope and kick forward and sharply to the right. A drive which starts down the middle usually finds the right rough and will have the approach complicated by a large tree overhanging the right entrance.

The sixth is a medium-sized par four with a right-to-left-sloping fairway. The hole has long been known as "double dam" because from 110 yards in, a pair of ponds connected by a waterfall splits the fairway, posing a serious threat to the average player.

The 9th and 18th are beautiful, challenging, short par fives leading back up the hill to the clubhouse. Both fairways rise and bend slightly to the left, reaching their crests about 100 yards from home.

All in all, Willow Ridge is a demanding course that is clearly establishing a name for itself. ❍

Around the bend at the first hole.

WILTWYCK GOLF CLUB

"Far North"

In the unlikely year of 1933, a group of local working men culminated two years of discussion by forming a golf club. They named it "Wiltwyck," Dutch for "wild refuge," the name given to the area by Dutch Governor Peter Stuyvesant nearly 300 years earlier. Wiltwyck is now the northernmost member club of the MGA.

The new Club purchased an estate on the western outskirts of Kingston. Construction of a nine-hole course began late in 1933, and the course opened in 1934. It was a tough track, with out-of-bounds on both sides of each hole and the rough cut just twice a year with a sickle.

In the early 1950s, the New York State Thruway was routed through the heart of the course. So the move was made to a 140-acre farm half a mile south of the original site, with Robert Trent Jones hired to mold it into a championship 18-hole course, which was ready in 1956. It has matured over the years under the watchful eye of Kingston native Hal Purdy.

Architect Geoffrey Cornish has been retained as a consultant since 1977. Besides recommending contour mowing of the fairways, Cornish built the new 7th and 15th greens in 1990, and produced a long-range plan in 1993. Before that, the only significant change took place in 1959 when construction of the swimming pool meant cutting 100 yards off the 600-yard 17th hole, a change orchestrated by the membership.

Wiltwyck is a parkland course, albeit one with numerous severe elevation changes and water in play on four holes. The greens are typically small and well bunkered.

The seventh is a long par five with a humpbacked fairway that kicks off-line first

From behind the 9th green.

WILTWYCK GOLF CLUB
Kingston, NY

YEAR FOUNDED: 1933

ARCHITECTS:
Robert Trent Jones
Geoffrey Cornish

COURSE OPENED: 1956

TEES	PAR	YARDAGE
Forward	74	5711
Middle	72	6575
Back	72	6858

TEES	COURSE RATING	SLOPE
Forward	72.7	126
Middle	71.5	123
Back	72.8	126

and second shots farther right or left. A pair of mature trees stand like pillars guarding the entrance to the drive zone. The green is framed by high mounding.

The par-four ninth is a dogleg-right with a lake in play across the right side of the hole immediately in front of the green. The drive on the par-four 15th plays downhill from a narrow chute to a landing area bordered on the right by a lake about 160 yards from the green.

Wiltwyck hosts the premier invitational tournament in the Hudson Valley, the Wiltwyck Invitation. The first edition in 1958 came down to a final match between the two greatest players in the Club's history: Harvey Bostic, now the Club professional, prevailed over Leon Randall, both "household names" in the far north. ○

WOODWAY COUNTRY CLUB

"A Natural Beauty"

Many American clubs, and particularly those in the Met Area, began life with a nine-hole golf course, then found it necessary to look elsewhere when it came time to expand to 18 holes.

There are several instances when the need to expand and relocate split a club. That is exactly what happened when the Wee Burn Golf Club thought about expanding to 18 holes from its land-locked nine on the Post Road. When a majority of the membership rejected a proposal to move, a small group proceeded nonetheless and founded Woodway in 1916. Incredibly, the motion to build a new club came from Wee Burn's second and third presidents rather than from the grass roots.

Woodway took its name from the dairy farm that owned the lion's share of the Club's property. It took its course design from Willie Park Jr., but not before having Walter Travis appraise the property. He was enthusiastic about the site:

"If ever nature intended a plot for a first-class course, it is here. I will go so far as to say that I have never seen anything, anywhere, so suitable in all respects for the creation of a magnificent course."

Park was a "naturalist" who believed that golf holes were not made, but found. He had the Woodway course ready for play by June 30, 1918, the Club's official opening. It was the longest course in Connecticut at the time, giving the Club the championship layout it desired.

The key to success at Woodway is staying dry: 17 water hazards affect play on 15 holes. The course plays over rolling terrain, with a number of greens sitting atop natural plateaus. Most are tightly bunkered and sharply contoured.

The picturesque par-four fifth calls for an accurate drive past trees on the right side, across a gully to the top of a ridge where the fairway begins. The fairway tumbles downhill beyond the crest and is crossed by the Noroton River well short of the green.

Revised by Geoffrey Cornish in 1986, the par-four eighth is Woodway's most controversial hole. A sharp dogleg-right, a 200-yard tee shot is necessary to cross the Noroton River, a rough-filled gully, and clear the tree line on the right. The shot to the double-decked, plateau green must carry a pond and a sinewy bunker.

The par-five 12th starts behind a pond and finishes 50 yards beyond another stream crossing, with a typical dose of trees and undulations in between.

The 13th is Woodway's toughest hole, a long par four that sweeps up and to the left, with one fairway bunker at the turn and another off to the right. The fairway rises in the landing area, then drops into a deep gully before climbing through rough to the green.

Clearly, the architect has taken full advantage of the natural beauty of the setting, making Woodway one of the Met Area's most delightful courses. ❍

WOODWAY COUNTRY CLUB
Darien, CT

YEAR FOUNDED: 1916

ARCHITECT:
Willie Park Jr.

COURSE OPENED: 1918

TEES	PAR	YARDAGE
Forward	74	5829
Middle	71	6425
Back	71	6716

TEES	COURSE RATING	SLOPE
Forward	74.1	131
Middle	71.5	136
Back	72.8	139

From behind the green at the 11th hole.

APPLE GREENS GOLF COURSE
Highland, NY

YEAR FOUNDED: 1995

ARCHITECT:
John Magaletta

COURSE OPENED: 1995

Nine new holes were added to this rolling, apple-tree lined layout in 1996. The course rewards players with lovely views of the Shawangunk Mountains. Water comes into play on eight holes. Every club in the bag is needed here, perhaps on just one hole— the 610-yard 4th.

TEES	PAR	YARDAGE
Forward	71	4959
Middle	71	6049
Back	71	6510

TEES	COURSE RATING	SLOPE
Forward	67.6	122
Middle	68.4	120
Back	70.4	124

ASPETUCK VALLEY COUNTRY CLUB
Weston, CT

YEAR FOUNDED: 1966

ARCHITECT:
Hal Purdy

COURSE OPENED: 1966

Aspetuck Valley may be of average length, but tree-lined tightness, hills, doglegs, six water holes and large, undulating greens provide plenty of challenge. Aspetuck Valley is growing in popularity as a site for MGA and CSGA events.

TEES	PAR	YARDAGE
Forward	72	5762
Middle	71	6198
Back	71	6594

TEES	COURSE RATING	SLOPE
Forward	73.7	126
Middle	71.8	126
Back	73.7	129

JAMES BAIRD STATE PARK
Pleasant Valley, NY

YEAR FOUNDED: 1939

ARCHITECT:
Robert Trent Jones

COURSE OPENED: 1939

Baird is a well-maintained course with small greens on gently rolling terrain. It was built by the Civilian Conservation Corps on property donated to the state by James Baird, a contractor who built the Lincoln Memorial.

TEES	PAR	YARDAGE
Forward	74	5436
Middle	71	6201
Back	71	6616

TEES	COURSE RATING	SLOPE
Forward	70.9	122
Middle	69.5	120
Back	71.3	124

BEEKMAN COUNTRY CLUB
Hopewell Junction, NY

YEAR FOUNDED: 1964

ARCHITECT:
Phillip Shatz

COURSES OPENED: 1964

The Taconic nine is the toughest of the three nines. The Highland and Valley courses are more forgiving, but present a suitable challenge for a range of abilities. Outings are expertly handled. A nicely maintained driving range encourages practice.

TACONIC-VALLEY COURSE

TEES	PAR	YARDAGE
Forward	73	5407
Middle	71	6010

TEES	COURSE RATING	SLOPE
Forward	70.7	120
Middle	68.6	118

HIGHLAND-TACONIC COURSE

TEES	PAR	YARDAGE
Forward	73	5529
Middle	71	6151

TEES	COURSE RATING	SLOPE
Forward	71.4	125
Middle	69.3	123

VALLEY-HIGHLAND COURSE

TEES	PAR	YARDAGE
Forward	72	5266
Middle	70	5967

TEES	COURSE RATING	SLOPE
Forward	69.7	120
Middle	68.3	121

BIRCHWOOD COUNTRY CLUB
Westport, CT

YEAR FOUNDED: 1946

ARCHITECT:
Orrin Smith

COURSE OPENED: 1946

Birchwood is a challenging nine-hole, dual tee layout. A creek may catch errant shots on three holes. Fairways and greens are well bunkered. Oaks and pines, as well as birches, line the rolling fairways.

TEES	PAR	YARDAGE
Forward	74	5786
Middle	72	6310

TEES	COURSE RATING	SLOPE
Forward	73.7	124
Middle	70.0	118

E. GAYNOR BRENNAN GOLF COURSE
Stamford, CT

YEAR FOUNDED: 1925

ARCHITECT:
Maurice McCarthy Sr.

COURSE OPENED: 1925

Formerly known as Hubbard Heights, gently rolling terrain with small, fast greens, several blind shots and eight water holes mark this busy (52,000 rounds) public-access course. Operated by the Stamford Parks System since 1949, Brennan co-hosts with Sterling Farms the annual Stamford City Championship.

TEES	PAR	YARDAGE
Forward	73	5591
Middle	71	5868

TEES	COURSE RATING	SLOPE
Forward	72.3	124
Middle	67.8	122

BRUCE MEMORIAL GOLF COURSE
Greenwich, CT

YEAR FOUNDED: 1965

ARCHITECT:
Robert Trent Jones

COURSE OPENED: 1965

Hills on the back and hardwoods all over make Bruce a visual treat. It hosts the Greenwich Men's Town Championship, an event of World War II vintage, and the Women's Town Championship as well.

TEES	PAR	YARDAGE
Forward	73	5710
Middle	71	6093
Back	71	6492

TEES	COURSE RATING	SLOPE
Forward	73.6	128
Middle	69.3	120
Back	71.1	124

CANYON CLUB
Armonk, NY

YEAR FOUNDED: 1963

ARCHITECT:
Albert Zikorus

COURSE OPENED: 1963

Once named Bel Air Country Club, the Canyon Club features severe elevation changes on both nines with water present on four holes. Adding to these challenges are the long par threes and gently sloping greens.

TEES	PAR	YARDAGE
Forward	70	4942
Middle	70	5829
Back	70	6356

TEES	COURSE RATING	SLOPE
Forward	69.7	122
Middle	69.4	126
Back	71.8	131

DOGWOOD KNOLLS GOLF CLUB
Hopewell Junction, NY

YEAR FOUNDED:
unknown

ARCHITECT:
unknown

COURSE OPENED:
unknown

This nine-holer climbs upward through four holes and then back down toward the clubhouse. This is a busy place on weekends and popular with evening leagues on most weekdays.

TEES	PAR	YARDAGE
Forward	73	6041
Middle	72	6371

TEES	COURSE RATING	SLOPE
Forward	72.7	112
Middle	68.9	103

DORAL ARROWWOOD GOLF CLUB
Rye Brook, NY

YEAR FOUNDED: 1992

ARCHITECT:
Robert Von Hagge

COURSE OPENED: 1992

This nine-hole course complements the Doral-Arrowwood Conference Center. It lies on the former site of the Arrowwood Golf Course, itself a successor to both the Purchase Country Club and Green Valley Golf Course. The new course features dramatic mounding alongside the tight fairways. Water is in play on seven holes.

TEES	PAR	YARDAGE
Forward	70	5552
Middle	70	5552
Back	70	6032

TEES	COURSE RATING	SLOPE
Forward	72.6	131
Middle	68.0	127
Back	71.6	132

DUNWOODIE GOLF COURSE
Yonkers, NY

YEAR FOUNDED: 1905

ARCHITECT:
unknown

COURSE OPENED: 1905

A private club before the Depression, Dunwoodie is widely considered a fine Westchester County public layout. Tight, hilly and somewhat unforgiving of stray shots on the front nine, the back levels out in parkland fashion.

TEES	PAR	YARDAGE
Forward	72	4511
Middle	70	5815

TEES	COURSE RATING	SLOPE
Forward	67.8	117
Middle	68.3	117

DUTCHER GOLF COURSE
Pawling, NY

YEAR FOUNDED: 1890

ARCHITECT:
James Dutcher

COURSE OPENED: 1890

Once a campground for Washington's troops during the Revolution, Dutcher is one of the nation's oldest. Originally a three-hole course laid out in 1890 by James Dutcher, a New York Central Railroad executive, it has since grown to nine holes with dual tees.

TEES	PAR	YARDAGE
Forward	68	4050
Middle	68	4471

TEES	COURSE RATING	SLOPE
Forward	65.6	101
Middle	61.7	95

GARRISON GOLF CLUB
Garrison, NY

YEAR FOUNDED: 1963

ARCHITECT:
Dick Wilson

COURSE OPENED: 1963

Garrison occupies an enviable plot of land overlooking West Point. Originally North Redoubt, the site, with some relics still present, was first used as a post for pickets watching the river for the approach of the British during the Revolution. The bold front nine descends dramatically through rugged, rocky woodlands, then rises to make the turn. The older back nine is more consisely ensconced on the higher ground.

TEES	PAR	YARDAGE
Forward	70	5041
Middle	72	6139
Back	72	6412

TEES	COURSE RATING	SLOPE
Forward	69.3	122
Middle	70.0	128
Back	71.3	130

GRANIT HOTEL & COUNTRY CLUB
Kerhonkson, NY

YEAR FOUNDED: 1958

ARCHITECTS:
Leslie Aaron &
Artie Horowitz
Lou Block &
Ron Pritchard

COURSE OPENED: 1958

This lovely Catskill Mountain design features many elevation changes on rolling terrain. The fairways are separated by tall hardwoods. The Granit is a favorite destination of those seeking relief from summer's heat and crowds.

TEES	PAR	YARDAGE
Forward	71	5180
Middle	70	5888
Back	70	6310

TEES	COURSE RATING	SLOPE
Forward	68.8	115
Middle	67.6	115
Back	69.6	119

HARLEM VALLEY GOLF CLUB
Wingdale, NY

YEAR FOUNDED:
unkown

ARCHITECT:
unkown

COURSE OPENED:
unkown

This nine-hole double tee course is a challenging public-access facility. The 587-yard 17th is a most challenging hole where placement of the second shot is critical. Water is a factor on the last few holes on the front.

TEES	PAR	YARDAGE
Forward	73	4977
Middle	70	6073
Back	70	6434

TEES	COURSE RATING	SLOPE
Forward	68.6	114
Middle	69.3	119
Back	71.0	122

GROSSINGER RESORT
Liberty, NY

YEAR FOUNDED: 1928

The Valley and Lake nines stand out among Catskill Mountain courses. The Etess family, long-time supporters of golf, was instrumental in attracting the New York State Open, and keeping it there for a number of years. Noteworthy is the par-five 4th on Lakeside featuring an island green. The Vista nine offers a pleasant alternative to the demanding "Big G" nines.

VALLEY-LAKE COURSE

ARCHITECTS:
Andrew Salerno
W. Mitchell
Joe Finger

COURSE OPENED: 1970

TEES	PAR	YARDAGE
Forward	75	5879
Middle	71	6456
Back	71	6846

TEES	COURSE RATING	SLOPE
Forward	74.3	129
Middle	71.7	129
Back	73.5	133

VISTA COURSE

ARCHITECT:
Andrew Salerno

COURSE OPENED: 1928

TEES	PAR	YARDAGE
Forward	37	3024
Middle	36	3166
Back	36	3268

TEES	COURSE RATING	SLOPE
Forward	37.0	125
Middle	35.1	122
Back	35.6	124

HERITAGE HILLS COUNTRY CLUB
Somers, NY

YEAR FOUNDED: 1975

ARCHITECTS:
Geoffrey Cornish
William Robinson

COURSE OPENED: 1975

The Heritage Hills courses, the West Hill 18 and the East Hill nine, operate within an upscale residential community. Though separate in geography and membership, they are both hilly, tight, and tree-lined with numerous water holes and several blind shots to test one's skills. The West's 563-yard par five dogleg fifth presents a real problem for the fader, with water lurking along the right and fronting the green.

EAST HILL COURSE

TEES	PAR	YARDAGE
Forward	35	2086
Middle	35	2720
Back	35	2889

TEES	COURSE RATING	SLOPE
Forward	68.8	119
Middle	68.0	126
Back	69.6	129

WEST HILL COURSE

TEES	PAR	YARDAGE
Forward	71	4972
Middle	72	6050
Back	72	6284

TEES	COURSE RATING	SLOPE
Forward	69.2	118
Middle	69.9	124
Back	71.0	126

HIGHLANDS COUNTRY CLUB
Garrison, NY

YEAR FOUNDED: 1898

ARCHITECT:
unkown

COURSE OPENED: 1898

The use of several double tees makes this nine-holer a popular and interesting course. The narrow tree-lined eighth at 467 yards is the brute of the layout. A view of the Hudson and West Point awaits at the seventh. The annual Shad Fest golf/cookout is well attended, even by a celebrity or two.

TEES	PAR	YARDAGE
Forward	68	4362
Middle	68	4538

TEES	COURSE RATING	SLOPE
Forward	63.5	105
Middle	61.6	105

LAKEOVER NATIONAL GOLF CLUB
Bedford Hills, NY

YEAR FOUNDED: 1965

ARCHITECTS:
Albert Zikorus
Gary Player

COURSE OPENED: 1966

The original design by Albert Zikorus was redone in 1990 by Gary Player. The course is located on the former Lakeover Estate with rolling terrain wherein the middle holes lie in a basin and the rest occupy the upper perimeter of the property. Elevated tees and greens bracket fairways graded to provide a natural look with gentle mounding. A seven acre lake gets much attention.

TEES	PAR	YARDAGE
Middle	72	5929
Back	72	6271

TEES	COURSE RATING	SLOPE
Middle	69.0	123
Back	70.7	126

KUTSHER'S COUNTRY CLUB & RESORT
Monticello, NY

YEAR FOUNDED: 1958

ARCHITECT:
William Mitchell

COURSE OPENED: 1958

This is a lovely Catskills course with the expected rolling terrain. A glorious test in its own right, its narrow, tree-lined fairways and rolling greens, originally clad with velvet bentgrass, are reminiscent of Tarry Brae, a similar vintage Mitchell design.

TEES	PAR	YARDAGE
Forward	71	5676
Middle	71	6510
Back	71	7001

TEES	COURSE RATING	SLOPE
Forward	73.3	124
Middle	72.0	122
Back	74.3	126

LAKE ISLE PARK
Eastchester, NY

YEAR FOUNDED: 1926

ARCHITECT:
Devereux Emmet

COURSE OPENED: 1926

This was originally Mount Vernon Country Club when it occupied the former nine-hole course that had nurtured both Siwanoy and Sunningdale. The club moved to its present site off the White Plains Post Road in 1926 with a picturesque new Devereux Emmet course. Known as Lakeview in 1940, Vernon Hills in 1941, Lake Isle Country Club in 1979, it is now Lake Isle Park.

TEES	PAR	YARDAGE
Forward	72	5429
Middle	70	5770
Back	70	6009

TEES	COURSE RATING	SLOPE
Forward	70.9	120
Middle	67.9	118
Back	69.0	120

LEEWOOD GOLF CLUB
Eastchester, NY
YEAR FOUNDED: 1922
ARCHITECT:
Devereux Emmet
COURSE OPENED: 1924

Movie producer D.W. Griffiths was among the founders; Henry Bacon, architect of the Lincoln Memorial, designed the clubhouse; South African pro Bobby Locke called it home; and Babe Ruth was a member. On less than 100 acres, with small greens and deep bunkers, it is, "...the toughest short course I ever played," said Met Open winner and former assistant professional Marty Bohen.

TEES	PAR	YARDAGE
Forward	72	5590
Middle	71	5966
Back	71	6175

TEES	COURSE RATING	SLOPE
Forward	73.7	134
Middle	69.2	125
Back	70.1	127

MAHOPAC GOLF CLUB
Lake Mahopac, NY
YEAR FOUNDED: 1898
ARCHITECT:
Tom Bendelow
COURSE OPENED: 1900

What began in 1897 as a three-holer and grew to nine by 1899 was unraveled by 1900. An unrenewed lease brought the Club to the north shore of Lake Mahopac, where a nine-hole Tom Bendelow course was built. A renovated clubhouse and 18 holes with small, well-bunkered greens now overlooks the sparkling waters.

TEES	PAR	YARDAGE
Forward	72	5296
Middle	70	6161
Back	70	6400

TEES	COURSE RATING	SLOPE
Forward	71.9	119
Middle	69.3	117
Back	70.4	120

MAPLE MOOR GOLF COURSE
White Plains, NY
YEAR FOUNDED: 1924
ARCHITECTS:
Archie Capper
Tom Winton
COURSE OPENED: 1924

This once private, and now busy (55,000 rounds) Westchester County course challenges a wide range of skills. Water appears on five holes on the front. Though rolling terrain is visible from the Hutchinson River Parkway, Maple Moor is generally more level and open on the back nine.

TEES	PAR	YARDAGE
Forward	74	5812
Middle	71	6226

TEES	COURSE RATING	SLOPE
Forward	71.9	116
Middle	68.8	110

McCANN MEMORIAL GOLF COURSE
Poughkeepsie, NY
YEAR FOUNDED: 1969
ARCHITECT:
William Mitchell
COURSE OPENED: 1971

The challenging Mitchell design was named for James McCann, a Poughkeepsie merchant who funded various sporting, educational and recreational endeavors through a foundation. It features large greens and narrow fairways.

TEES	PAR	YARDAGE
Forward	72	5359
Middle	72	6090
Back	72	6524

TEES	COURSE RATING	SLOPE
Forward	71.4	123
Middle	70.0	124
Back	72.0	128

MID-HUDSON VALLEY COUNTRY CLUB
Poughkeepsie, NY
YEAR FOUNDED: 1945
ARCHITECT:
Robert Trent Jones
COURSE OPENED: 1945

Water is a factor on nine holes at this semi-private layout. The course features a number of elevation changes. The greens are generally small and many are elevated. Conditions have not suffered in the transition from its private days as an IBM Country Club.

TEES	PAR	YARDAGE
Forward	72	4769
Middle	72	6153
Back	72	6659

TEES	COURSE RATING	SLOPE
Forward	72.3	124
Middle	69.9	125
Back	72.2	130

MILBROOK CLUB
Greenwich, CT
YEAR FOUNDED: 1923
ARCHITECT:
unkown
COURSE OPENED: 1923

Anyone favoring large, subtly undulating greens will like those at this nine-hole, dual tee layout. Though there are no water holes, the fairways are tight and the rough unforgiving. A newly added practice range will help to hone one's skills for this target course.

TEES	PAR	YARDAGE
Forward	73	5945
Middle	70	6264

TEES	COURSE RATING	SLOPE
Forward	74.4	130
Middle	70.3	120

MILLBROOK GOLF & TENNIS CLUB
Millbrook, NY
YEAR FOUNDED: 1963
ARCHITECT:
Geoffery Cornish
COURSE OPENED: 1963

Small, tricky undulating greens mark this nine-hole layout. With a few tempting, short par fours, generous stands of fescue grasses and five water holes keep long hitters honest.

TEES	PAR	YARDAGE
Forward	72	4779
Middle	72	5872

TEES	COURSE RATING	SLOPE
Forward	68.3	121
Middle	69.1	121

MILL RIVER COUNTRY CLUB
Stratford, CT
YEAR FOUNDED: 1930
ARCHITECT:
Tom Winton
COURSE OPENED: 1930

Once called Mill Hill and Weatogue, Mill River was designed by Siwanoy's superintendent, Scottish-born Tom Winton. In typical Donald Ross style, Mill River's bunkers are placed well ahead of greens to snare faulty approaches. Mill River itself cuts through six holes of the hilly course.

TEES	PAR	YARDAGE
Forward	72	5513
Middle	72	6194
Back	72	6595

TEES	COURSE RATING	SLOPE
Forward	70.5	115
Middle	68.8	123
Back	69.8	126

MOHANSIC GOLF COURSE

Yorktown Heights, NY

YEAR FOUNDED: 1925

ARCHITECT:
Tom Winton

COURSE OPENED: 1926

Mohansic is often described as the gem of the Westchester County courses. Wooded, with reasonably wide fairways and small targets for approaches are its earmarks. Mohansic's annual pro-am has grown so popular over the past 20 years that the challenge to get in is as tough as the course itself.

TEES	PAR	YARDAGE
Forward	75	5594
Middle	70	6376

TEES	COURSE RATING	SLOPE
Forward	71.6	119
Middle	69.9	120

MOHONK MOUNTAIN HOUSE GOLF COURSE

Lake Mohonk,
New Paltz, NY

YEAR FOUNDED: 1897

ARCHITECT:
unkown

COURSE OPENED: 1897

Also enjoying its centennial in 1997, Mohonk may boast of its clubhouse—built in 1903 —as one of America's oldest. Tree-lined, hilly fairways on this nine-holer provide a beautiful choice among the many other activities at the resort.

TEES	PAR	YARDAGE
Forward	37	2422
Middle	35	2569

TEES	COURSE RATING	SLOPE
Forward	66.7	109
Middle	64.6	106

NEW PALTZ GOLF COURSE

New Paltz, NY

YEAR FOUNDED: 1972

ARCHITECT:
Hal Purdy

COURSE OPENED: 1972

Located on historic Huguenot Street, one of America's earliest settlements dating back to the 1600s, this public-access course is known for its scenic Catskill mountain beauty. There are eight chances to find water or wetlands on this nine-hole layout.

TEES	PAR	YARDAGE
Forward	36	2658
Middle	36	3300
Back	36	3450

TEES	COURSE RATING	SLOPE
Forward	70.4	120
Middle	71.7	126
Back	73.0	129

OAK HILLS PARK GOLF COURSE

Norwalk, CT

YEAR FOUNDED: 1968

ARCHITECT:
Alfred Tull

COURSE OPENED: 1968

The wooded fairways give one a "vision far removed from urban life." This busy layout (50,000+ rounds annually) is tight and demanding, especially on the first seven holes. There is more room on the next eleven, but they present a challenge of increased length, with seven water holes among this mix.

TEES	PAR	YARDAGE
Forward	72	5221
Middle	71	5920
Back	71	6407

TEES	COURSE RATING	SLOPE
Forward	69.2	119
Middle	68.0	120
Back	70.5	125

PEHQUENAKONCK COUNTRY CLUB

North Salem, NY

YEAR FOUNDED: 1923

ARCHITECT:
Malcus Knapp

COURSE OPENED: 1923

This nine-hole, dual tee course dates to the 1920s. The narrow tree-lined fairways are cut through hilly, rocky terrain. Its 4th hole is a tight 115-yard straight uphiller known as "Mt. Kilimanjaro." Many members also enjoy activities at nearby Peach Lake.

TEES	PAR	YARDAGE
Forward	72	4241
Middle	66	4458

TEES	COURSE RATING	SLOPE
Forward	64.7	102
Middle	62.0	99

COUNTRY CLUB AT PLEASANTVILLE

Pleasantville, NY

YEAR FOUNDED: 1920

ARCHITECT:
unknown

COURSE OPENED: 1920

The name was changed from the original Nannahagan Golf Club in the 1950s. The fairways are narrow on rolling hills and the greens are tiny, elevated and undulating. The design was rumored to be that of A.W. Tillinghast, who was a family friend of the Manvilles—then owners of the property.

TEES	PAR	YARDAGE
Forward	64	4188
Middle	64	4188

TEES	COURSE RATING	SLOPE
Forward	64.7	111
Middle	61.2	109

POUND RIDGE GOLF CLUB

Pound Ridge, NY

YEAR FOUNDED: 1951

ARCHITECTS:
Albert Zikorus
Mike Di Buono

COURSE OPENED: 1951

Known as High Ridge and Twin Ridge from the 50s into the 70s, its Connecticut acreage was lost to housing in 1977. Mike DiBuono, the professional then as now, redesigned a few holes, maintaining the flavor of small, elevated greens. It continues as a popular nine holer.

TEES	PAR	YARDAGE
Forward	69	5178
Middle	69	5710
Back	69	5724

TEES	COURSE RATING	SLOPE
Forward	69.0	114
Middle	67.3	113
Back	68.3	115

PUTNAM COUNTRY CLUB

Mahopac, NY

YEAR FOUNDED: 1959

ARCHITECT:
William Mitchell

COURSE OPENED: 1959

Putnam offers a challenging test on rolling terrain with a few dramatic elevation changes. The greens and fairways are well-bunkered and have benefitted from recent improvements. The fairways often allow for minor deviations in direction.

TEES	PAR	YARDAGE
Forward	73	5799
Middle	71	6372
Back	71	6774

TEES	COURSE RATING	SLOPE
Forward	73.0	125
Middle	70.5	125
Back	72.4	129

DUTCHESS

QUAKER HILL COUNTRY CLUB
Pawling, NY

YEAR FOUNDED:
unknown

ARCHITECT:
Robert Trent Jones

COURSE OPENED: 1939

The clubhouse sits above the Harlem Valley, and the many side hill lies in the windswept valley prepare members well for tamer ventures away from home. The well-bunkered greens, more deep than wide, make accuracy in approaches a bigger factor than club selection. Commissioned by Lowell Thomas, the founder, Quaker Hill also counted Edward R. Murrow and Thomas E. Dewey among its members.

TEES	PAR	YARDAGE
Forward	74	5597
Middle	70	6067

TEES	COURSE RATING	SLOPE
Forward	72.2	122
Middle	69.4	123

FAIRFIELD

REDDING COUNTRY CLUB
West Redding, CT

YEAR FOUNDED: 1973

ARCHITECTS:
Ed Ryder
Rees Jones

COURSE OPENED: 1974

With narrow fairways, many elevation changes, eight blind tee shots, six blind approaches and water on 14 holes, members frequently invoke the Rules of golf. Redding uses the "Bob Tway Rule," which allows one qualified junior player into its club championship. Tway won it as a 13-year-old.

TEES	PAR	YARDAGE
Forward	72	4372
Middle	71	6027
Back	71	6317

TEES	COURSE RATING	SLOPE
Forward	69.5	124
Middle	70.4	129
Back	71.7	133

FAIRFIELD

RIDGEWOOD COUNTRY CLUB
Danbury, CT

YEAR FOUNDED: 1920

ARCHITECT:
Devereux Emmet

COURSE OPENED: 1920

Hilly and tree-lined, with small, firm, well-bunkered greens, Ridgewood is Ken Green's favorite tune-up location for such testing events as the U.S. Open. This picturesque, New England layout surrouned by green hills and church spires offers plenty of challenge, such as the par-four 16th, a 460-yard downhill dogleg right to a two-tiered green.

TEES	PAR	YARDAGE
Forward	72	5403
Middle	71	6254
Back	71	6570

TEES	COURSE RATING	SLOPE
Forward	71.9	120
Middle	70.9	135
Back	72.5	138

FAIRFIELD

ROLLING HILLS COUNTRY CLUB
Wilton, CT

YEAR FOUNDED: 1965

ARCHITECT:
Alfred Tull

COURSE OPENED: 1965

Occupying 120 acres that had been farmland of the Amber Estate, this tight, hilly, tree-lined layout features small elevated greens protected by the bulk of 85 bunkers. It features one of the Met Area's toughest pair of back-to-back par fours. The seventh is a 420-yard uphill dogleg right which is followed by a 439-yarder with a two-tiered fairway.

TEES	PAR	YARDAGE
Forward	73	5555
Middle	71	6304
Back	71	6692

TEES	COURSE RATING	SLOPE
Forward	72.2	122
Middle	71.0	130
Back	72.7	134

WESTCHESTER

SALEM GOLF CLUB
North Salem, NY

YEAR FOUNDED: 1966

ARCHITECTS:
Edward Ryder
Van Carlson

COURSE OPENED: 1966

Salem was organized in 1966 on what had been a dairy farm and a family home of 1902 vintage. On its hilly back nine, the 14th is most scenic—a dogleg left 591-yard par five where the shot to the green must carry stream and pond. If trees are not lining a fairway, water might be, as it is present on seven holes.

TEES	PAR	YARDAGE
Forward	74	5680
Middle	72	6446
Back	72	6734

TEES	COURSE RATING	SLOPE
Forward	73.1	128
Middle	71.9	130
Back	73.2	133

WESTCHESTER

SANCTUARY COUNTRY CLUB
Yorktown Heights, NY

YEAR FOUNDED: 1966

ARCHITECTS:
Nat Squire
Harry Lewis & Pete Donnelly

COURSE OPENED: 1966

Formerly known as Loch Ledge, much of the challenge here lies in the demand for accuracy both off the tee and on approaches to small greens. Length, too, is necessary on several holes, the par fives in particular. Rolling terrain makes for interesting tests.

TEES	PAR	YARDAGE
Forward	73	4997
Middle	72	5484

TEES	COURSE RATING	SLOPE
Forward	68.6	115
Middle	66.6	114

WESTCHESTER

SAXON WOODS GOLF COURSE
Scarsdale, NY

YEAR FOUNDED: 1931

ARCHITECT:
Tom Winton

COURSE OPENED: 1931

Saxon Woods has enjoyed a recent facelift and remains one of the busiest and most popular public access destinations in Westchester County. The rolling fairways are narrow and the greens are small.

TEES	PAR	YARDAGE
Forward	73	5465
Middle	71	6397
Back	71	6452

TEES	COURSE RATING	SLOPE
Forward	71.2	120
Middle	70.5	121
Back	70.8	122

PUTNAM

THE SEDGEWOOD CLUB
Carmel, NY

YEAR FOUNDED: 1928

ARCHITECT:
unknown

COURSE OPENED: 1928

This hilly nine-holer, originally called Carmel Country Club, got its new name in the late 1950s. It is tree-lined with small, well bunkered greens. The scenic 260-yard sixth features a 200-foot drop to what appears to be a dime-sized green—a vestige of an earlier function as a ski slope.

TEES	PAR	YARDAGE
Forward	75	5846
Middle	71	5846

TEES	COURSE RATING	SLOPE
Forward	71.0	116
Middle	66.2	108

SEGALLA COUNTRY CLUB
Amenia, NY

YEAR FOUNDED: 1992

ARCHITECT:
Albert Zikorus

COURSE OPENED: 1992

A parkland course awaits those surviving the elevation changes, granite, trees and water on the front nine. In only a few years of operation Segalla has come to enjoy a reputation for, fair prices, good pace of play, quality of layout, course conditioning, it's 19th hole and customer satisfaction.

TEES	PAR	YARDAGE
Forward	72	5601
Middle	72	6226
Back	72	6617

TEES	COURSE RATING	SLOPE
Forward	72.3	129
Middle	70.3	129
Back	72.0	133

SHAWANGUNK COUNTRY CLUB
Ellenville, NY

YEAR FOUNDED: 1927

ARCHITECT:
Otto Lang

COURSE OPENED: 1927

This nine-hole, dual-tee course was laid out on hilly farmland by Otto Lang, one of the Club's early professionals. Shawangunk (locally pronounced shongum) is the easterly mountain range—the Catskills border westerly.

TEES	PAR	YARDAGE
Forward	72	5003
Middle	68	5621

TEES	COURSE RATING	SLOPE
Forward	69.3	121
Middle	67.6	118

SILVERMINE GOLF CLUB
Norwalk, CT

YEAR FOUNDED: 1959

ARCHITECTS:
John E. Warner Jr.
Alfred Tull

COURSE OPENED: 1959

The course is hardwood lined on rolling terrain with water present on seven holes. The greens are small, fast and sloping. The 17th tee, on Norwalk's highest point, offers a view of Long Island. Proceeds from the Frostbite Open in March target the developmentally disabled.

TEES	PAR	YARDAGE
Forward	71	4771
Middle	70	5077
Back	70	6077

TEES	COURSE RATING	SLOPE
Forward	68.9	120
Middle	66.3	112
Back	65.0	107

SPRAIN LAKE GOLF COURSE
Yonkers, NY

YEAR FOUNDED:
unknown

ARCHITECT:
unknown

COURSE OPENED: 1928

Tucked neatly between the north and southbound lanes of the Sprain Brook Parkway lies one of the busiest courses in Westchester County. Sprain's fast greens and ten possible places to lose a ball in water keeps adrenaline flowing.

TEES	PAR	YARDAGE
Forward	76	5344
Middle	70	6008

TEES	COURSE RATING	SLOPE
Forward	70.2	115
Middle	68.6	114

STERLING FARMS GOLF CLUB
Stamford, CT

YEAR FOUNDED: 1971

ARCHITECTS:
Geoffrey Cornish &
William G. Robinson

COURSE OPENED: 1971

This moderately hilly public-access course has well-bunkered and subtly undulating greens. Its annual 55,000 rounds attests to its popularity. Views of Long Island Sound, New Canaan, Stamford, Darien, and Salem set Sterling Farms apart.

TEES	PAR	YARDAGE
Forward	73	5495
Middle	72	5922
Back	72	6308

TEES	COURSE RATING	SLOPE
Forward	72.8	125
Middle	69.3	115
Back	71.1	118

SULLIVAN COUNTY GOLF & COUNTRY CLUB
Liberty, NY

YEAR FOUNDED:
unknown

ARCHITECT:
unknown

COURSE OPENED:
unknown

Members enjoy many spectacular views from this 70-year-old country course. Sullivan is a hilly layout with small greens and a distinct links flavor. A pitch-and-run game will save many shots here.

TEES	PAR	YARDAGE
Forward	72	5862
Middle	72	6123

TEES	COURSE RATING	SLOPE
Forward	73.6	127
Middle	69.9	121

TARRY BRAE GOLF COURSE
South Fallsburg, NY

YEAR FOUNDED: 1958

ARCHITECT:
William Mitchell

COURSE OPENED: 1958

Mitchell made fine use of the rolling terrain in routing this interesting gem through forested property in 1958. Separated fairways, doglegs, tees to fit one's game, and gently undulating greens have made this Town of South Fallsburg course a popular destination since opening day. The appeal of cool summer days in the Catskills is another plus.

TEES	PAR	YARDAGE
Forward	76	5608
Middle	72	6270
Back	72	6888

TEES	COURSE RATING	SLOPE
Forward	72.2	126
Middle	70.3	126
Back	73.4	129

THOMAS CARVEL COUNTRY CLUB
Pine Plains, NY

YEAR FOUNDED: 1967

ARCHITECT:
William Mitchell

COURSE OPENED: 1967

Tom Carvel's "Giant Equalizer" is big, fair, enjoyable and challenging. An aura of spaciousness fills the eyes upon entering the gates. The unrivaled panoramic views may lull one into thinking the yardage is overstated. It isn't. Water awaits fades on five holes. Soft ice cream awaits at the 19th.

TEES	PAR	YARDAGE
Forward	75	5066
Middle	73	6600
Back	73	7100

TEES	COURSE RATING	SLOPE
Forward	69.0	115
Middle	71.6	123
Back	73.5	127

TWAALFSKILL CLUB

Kingston, NY

YEAR FOUNDED: 1898

ARCHITECT:
unknown

COURSE OPENED: 1898

Established as an elite,
all-male club, it was the only game
in Kingston from the turn
of the century through the 1920s.
It survives nicely as a
dual-tee, nine-holer with tiny,
sloping, undulating greens, leasing
land for some of its holes from
Montrepose Cemetery.

TEES	PAR	YARDAGE
Forward	71	4725
Middle	70	5676

TEES	COURSE RATING	SLOPE
Forward	72.8	121
Middle	67.9	115

VAILS GROVE GOLF COURSE

Brewster, NY

YEAR FOUNDED: 1929

ARCHITECT:
Marcus Knapp

COURSE OPENED: 1929

The fairways of this
semi-private nine-hole course
are lined with hardwoods.
Dual tees provide a different
look on the second pass.

TEES	PAR	YARDAGE
Forward	71	3920
Middle	66	4238
Back	66	4490

TEES	COURSE RATING	SLOPE
Forward	61.9	94
Middle	60.1	93
Back	61.3	95

VILLA ROMA COUNTRY CLUB

Callicoon, NY

YEAR FOUNDED: 1988

ARCHITECT:
David Postelwaite

COURSE OPENED: 1988

Some yardage was recently
added to this picturesque,
shotmaker's course. Much of
the challenge lies in handling
the large, lovely greens. The
conditioning and scenic beauty
are also noteworthy.

TEES	PAR	YARDAGE
Forward	72	4813
Middle	71	5420
Back	71	6237

TEES	COURSE RATING	SLOPE
Forward	68.3	117
Middle	66.9	118
Back	70.6	125

WHISPERING PINES GOLF CLUB

Poughkeepsie, NY

YEAR FOUNDED: 1938

ARCHITECT:
unknown

COURSE OPENED: 1938

Sidehill lies are common at this
state-owned course on the rolling
grounds of the Hudson Valley
Psychiatric Center. Now open to
the public, the par-33 layout offers
enjoyment and lovely views of
the Catskills.

TEES	PAR	YARDAGE
Forward	66	4490
Middle	66	4854

TEES	COURSE RATING	SLOPE
Forward	65.7	105
Middle	63.4	102

The 6th hole at Doral Arrowwood Golf Club, Rye Brook, New York.

THE CREATORS

COW PASTURE POOL," they called it. Two seemingly incongruous words described the new game in town before the turn of the century. Golf has come a long way from the cow pastures of the 1890s, thanks in large part to the professionals who created the pool table-like layouts we now take for granted.

With few exceptions, the early architects were outstanding golfers, either professionals from the British Isles or amateurs groomed on these shores. It was a simple application of Descartes' principle: I play, therefore I design. After all, who was better qualified? Willie Davis was the first of the Scottish professionals to set foot on this side of the Atlantic, coming to Montreal from Carnoustie in 1885. He took a brief leave of absence in 1891 to design the Shinnecock Hills course, then came to the United States for good in 1893, moving to Newport, Rhode Island, where he built that club's second course and served seven years as professional. He left Newport for Apawamis in 1900, but died in 1902 at age 39.

Walter Travis

Willie Dunn came from Musselburgh, Scotland, in 1893, and won the "unofficial" U.S. Open of 1894 at St. Andrew's. His first course here was the nine-holer for the Golf Club of Lakewood (New Jersey), which became America's first great winter resort course. Dunn considered his American masterpiece the course for the Ardsley Casino: He needed a crew of 200 to cut the virgin forest and build the course over extremely hilly terrain broken up by several deep ravines cutting into the bluffs overlooking the Hudson River.

The most accomplished golfer among the Willies was Willie Park, Jr., also from Musselburgh, two-time winner of the British Open (1887, 1889). Park first came here in 1895 to play in a series of high-stakes matches, and laid out a few courses on the side. After returning home in 1898, he came into his own as an architect: He was the pioneer of the "heathlands era," demonstrating that championship courses, such as England's Sunningdale, could be built inland, well away from the water. Ironically, Park's major accomplish-

ment in this country, built during his second visit (1916-1924), was the revised links course at Maidstone.

Another import, the English professional Herbert Strong, was right in the thick of things in the historic Ouimet-Vardon-Ray U.S. Open of 1913, finishing fifth. Strong's crowning achievement as an architect here was the Engineers course in Roslyn Harbor, Long Island, site of the 1919 PGA Championship and 1920 U.S. Amateur. He also built the original course for the Century Country Club, which was purchased by the Metropolis Country Club in 1922; several holes remain intact today.

The most significant and prolific of the early professionals was Donald Ross, who came to Boston in 1898 from Dornoch, Scotland, after gaining hands-on experience on

Charles Blair Macdonald

and around two of the world's greatest links courses, St. Andrews and Royal Dornoch. Working from his winter headquarters at Pinehurst, North Carolina, Ross is credited with as many as 600 courses. Ross was a naturalist, who once said that God built golf courses—he just found them. Crowned greens, perched atop natural elevations, typify his best work. Among his many Met Area designs were the original courses at Siwanoy, Knickerbocker, and Plainfield.

The early amateur golfers-turned-architects were a colorful lot too. Tom Bendelow, a Scot from Aberdeen, nearly gave golf architecture a black eye. A typesetter by trade, working for the New York Herald, Bendelow parlayed a Scottish burr, and little else, into a career as a roving course designer for the sporting-goods company A.G. Spalding & Bros. Known for his "18 stakes on a Sunday afternoon" approach, Bendelow would visit a prospective site, stake out locations for nine tees and greens, then be on his way—all for just $25! He wasn't all bad. A few of his courses in this area received critical acclaim—including Fox Hills and Dyker Meadow—and he both revised and added to Van Cortlandt Park, the first public course in America.

Left: A.W. Tillinghast.

Willie Park Jr.

Robert White and Herbert Strong

Devereux Emmet was a lifelong resident of Long Island, a socialite who married into the royal family of Garden City, the Stewarts. Emmet's avocation was hunting dogs, which he purchased in the south in the spring, trained on Long Island during the summer, then sold in Ireland in the fall, after which he would play the better courses of Britain. When the Garden City Company decided to build the Island Golf Links (forerunner of the Garden City Golf Club) in 1897, Emmet, the resident expert, was given the assignment. With this landmark course under his belt, Emmet's career was assured. Indeed, seven of his courses (Garden City Golf, Salisbury #4, Cherry Valley, Wee Burn, Pelham, Pomonok, and Congressional) have hosted national championships.

Walter Travis followed in Emmet's footprints at Garden City, his four national amateur championships (three American and one British) between 1900 and 1904 giving him carte blanche to alter the course as he saw fit. And he did, adding deep pot bunkers and severe green undulations, making the course one of the most feared in the country.

Travis was born in Australia, and came to America in 1885. He didn't take up golf until he was 35, but quickly mastered the new sport. An adherent of the penal school of architecture, his courses reflected his strengths—short but accurate, consistent, and with a deft touch on the greens. His legacy includes such courses as Westchester, and Round Hill.

Charles Blair Macdonald came to New York in 1900, from Canada via Chicago, with a four-year diversion at St. Andrews University for good measure. It was there he heard the call to spread the gospel of the Royal & Ancient game to the new world, a noble task complicated by his humorless, egotistical, overbearing personality. It was Macdonald's sour grapes complaints during the unofficial national championships of 1894 that led to the formation of the USGA that winter, and it was he who won the first "official" U.S. Amateur in 1895. That was the peak of his career as a golfer, and within a decade he had turned full-time—and full-bore—to architecture. His course at the National Golf Links of

America raised American architecture to a new plateau.

Albert Warren (A.W.) Tillinghast was perhaps the most colorful figure in the history of golf architecture. He set up shop in midtown Manhattan during the Roaring '20s, where both his business and his reputation thrived. He made a fortune and spent it just as rapidly, losing money backing Broadway musicals that went bust. A notorious drinker, he occasionally disappeared, often with his wife's jewelry and furs, for weeks at a time. Tillinghast was fond of the "liquid lunch," sitting in the shade of the majestic trees that frame his greens, watching a worker sculpt one of the undulating back-to-front horrors for which he became famous.

Tillinghast, whose talents also included writing and sketching, was one of the leading golfers in the Philadelphia district at the turn of the century, and played in several U.S. Amateurs. He turned to course design at Shawnee in 1906, and migrated to New York circa 1917. His local portfolio is impressive, featuring such championship layouts as Winged Foot (West and East), Baltusrol (Lower and Upper), Quaker Ridge, Ridgewood, Somerset Hills, and the original Fresh Meadow. His last hurrah was Bethpage Black, where he was allowed to let his creative juices run wild one last time, with the result a publinx version of Pine Valley, with which Tillinghast was intimately familiar.

The Oxford & Cambridge Society golf team that toured this country in 1903 included just one undergraduate, Charles H. Alison. A few years later, he met the great British architect H.S. Colt, and the partnership they formed after World War I (which at one time employed Alister Mackenzie) populated the globe with outstanding courses. Alison was responsible primarily for this country and Japan: Called the father of Japanese golf course architecture, the deep-faced bunkers he built into the faces of greens became known as "arisons." His flagship courses in the Met Area include the modern Century, Canoe Brook (South), and once ultra-exclusive Timber Point.

Not every architect was an outstanding player. Among the high handicappers was Seth Raynor. As a 12-year-old, he held the stakes for his father, who was the surveyor for the original

Seth Raynor

Devereux Emmet

course at Shinnecock Hills. That was his only taste of golf until he surveyed for C.B. Macdonald at National. He stayed on as Macdonald's right-hand man, then began designing on his own—still in the Macdonald style—in 1915. His work includes such outstanding courses as Fishers Island, Fairfield, Westhampton, and Creek, all near the water. He was working on a never-to-be-used routing plan for Cypress Point when he died of pneumonia in January, 1926 at 47.

Charles Banks came out of Academia. The Yale graduate taught English at the Hotchkiss School in Connecticut, where he met Raynor, who was building a golf course for the school. When Raynor moved on, Banks went with him, and when Raynor died, Banks kept the business—and the Macdonald tradition—going. He became known as "Steamshovel" Banks for moving great amounts of earth to create huge elevated greens and the deep bunkers that protected them. The awesome bunkers of Forsgate, his last work, reaffirmed his reputation.

A number of leading architects graduated from the work crews to the designing of courses. Alfred Tull and Orrin Smith were both construction chiefs, who, like Raynor, went out on their own. William Mitchell, Tom Winton, and Dick Wilson started with the grounds crew. Wilson worked at Merion, where he apprenticed under William Flynn and later became a major contributor to Flynn's new Shinnecock Hills course in 1931. Wilson's headline courses in this area were Meadow Brook and Deepdale, both built in the mid 1950s.

Most modern architects came to their profession better trained, with degrees in allied fields such as agronomy or landscape architecture. Among these are Tom Fazio, who has confirmed his reputation here with Hudson National, and the Met Area's own Stephen Kay, whose recent works at Blue Heron Pines, Harbor Pines, and New York Country Club reveal a distinctive flair for the traditional.

Robert Trent Jones devised his own curriculum at Cornell and actually majored in golf course design. He started his long career in 1930 with Canadian Stanley Thompson, then began designing courses here in the late 1940s. An advocate of strategic design, Jones is known for plentiful water hazards and multiple teeing grounds that give his courses maximum flexibility. Many believe his best design here to have been one of his first, Tuxedo, and is his most recent, Metedeconk. Jones' son Rees unveiled his Met Area masterpiece in 1992, when the Atlantic Golf Club opened. Rees was voted "Architect of the Year" in 1995, and is highly regarded for his restoration of U.S. Open courses and was recently selected by the USGA to work on Bethpage Black for the 2002 Open.

Hal Purdy, who designed more courses in the Met Area than anyone else, was a golf professional for 10 years, before going to work as a supervisor for Robert Trent Jones at Wiltwyck in 1954. Within two years, he had his own firm. Among his top courses in the Met Area are LPGA Tour sites Navesink and Fairmount.

Talented men, all of them, blessed with some of the finest terrain in the world on which they have created the world's greatest collection of golf courses. ○

Willie Dunn

Land That Time Forgot

OVER THE YEARS, THE MET AREA HAS LOST A NUMBER of courses that once played a prominent role on the local, even national, scene. The Depression and World War II forced many clubs to close their doors, a sad reality played out across the country. In the New York area, however, and especially on Long Island, there was another contributing factor. As the masses began their move to the suburbs, the "green areas" of nearby counties became the targets of real estate developers. Few clubs were able to refuse when large sums of money were offered for their land. This is the story of our most significant lost courses.

The "Gibraltar" hole at Timber Point, 1931.

FLUSHING/POMONOK

The oldest club in Queens County began in 1886 as the Flushing Athletic Club in the "quaint and picturesque village of Flushing," just a short walk north of Northern Boulevard along Whitestone Avenue.

The Club had a short nine-hole golf course, built by Tom Bendelow in 1896. The feature hole was the par-five ninth, which "stretched out like the crack o'doom," according to the turn-of-the-century magazine *Golf*. Golf soon became the most popular activity at the club, and in 1902 the Flushing Country Club was formed. Walter Travis was an early member, as was Gardiner White, the 1921 Met Amateur champ.

With its lease scheduled to expire in 1919, the Club found itself at a crossroads. The majority of the membership favored finding a new site and building an 18-hole course. Others were sentimentally attached to the original site. And so the Club split, with the larger contingent moving on to form Pomonok Country Club in 1920.

Those who remained reorganized as The Old Country Club. In 1923, they engaged Devereux Emmet to build an additional nine holes, giving them a course with more sandy area than any on Long Island. The 13th was the "glory hole," a relatively short par four that finished with a small island green of 5,500 square feet completely surrounded by 15-foot-deep bunkers. The Old Country Club failed to survive the Depression, however, and was sold to developers in 1936.

Pomonok was named after a tribe of Indians that once inhabited the area. The Club leased land south of Flushing, near the intersection of Kissena and Horace Harding Boulevards, overlooking what is now the Long Island Expressway just east of Queens College. Its 18-hole course, also designed by Emmet, was regarded as one of the most interesting in the East. It rolled over hilly terrain and featured exceptionally large greens, several of which, including four of the final six, were almost completely encircled by sand.

Pomonok's claim to fame was the 1939 PGA Championship, held "in conjunction with" the nearby World's Fair. Henry Picard won by beating Byron Nelson on the 37th hole of the finals in a dramatic match with a bizarre touch. On the first extra hole, Picard pushed his drive into the rough near a newsreel truck, while Nelson split the fairway. Moving the truck, the driver accidentally drove over Picard's ball, embedding it in the soft ground. After a free drop, Picard approached to within 10 feet. Nelson's pitch finished just six feet away, but it was Picard who holed out to win.

After the war, Pomonok found itself surrounded by housing developments. In 1949, the Club closed and the property sold to developers.

OAKLAND

The second oldest golf club in Queens was located in Bayside, a few miles east of Pomonok, on what once was an estate known as "The Oaks." On the estate was a mansion high in the hills overlooking Little Neck Bay, and a horticultural business known throughout the country for roses and orchids.

Early in 1896, John H. Taylor incorporated the Oakland Golf Club and leased 111 acres from The Oaks. Most of the original members knew little about the game. Among them was Walter Travis, who played his first round ever there in 1896, at age 35, and used it as his home course until 1900. Travis attributed his later success to the diversity of Oakland's holes.

Oakland started with a nine-hole Bendelow course in 1896. It was best known for a hole called "Heavenly Twins" that played across two valleys—one on the tee shot, the other on the approach. Another nine holes were added in 1906. Seth Raynor later did a renovation that rolled over and across the tremendous hills and valleys. The course was admired for the variety of its holes—and condemned for its preponderance of blind shots.

Helping golfers find their way were some excellent

The second green at Richmond Hill Golf Club.

female caddies. The following is the chorus from an "Oak-land Ditty," published in a 1910 issue of *The American Golfer:*

I have a caddie, a perfect
lady caddie,
If you knew her you would
like her just as well:
When you drive into the spinach
You can always see the finish,
She finds it? - she does like ——.

In time, the membership boasted a "Who's Who of New York Society," including, among others, H.P. Whitney, W.K. Vanderbilt, Bernard Baruch, and Governor Alfred E. Smith.

The original clubhouse was destroyed by fire as the 1915 club championship was being played. The replacement, known affectionately as "Golfer's Paradise," would later become the administration building for Queensboro Community College, which now occupies a portion of the club's property.

In 1952, construction on the Long Island Expressway cost Oakland its private status. It remained open as a public facility until 1960, when construction of the Clearview Expressway forced it to close permanently.

ST. ALBANS

Perhaps the most exclusive club in Queens was the St. Albans Golf Club, which was populated primarily by wealthy conservative politicians, bankers, and lawyers. But St. Albans also was reputed to have been Babe Ruth's favorite course, a fact that could not have pleased the members, who wanted their club kept out of the limelight.

In 1915, Willie Park Jr., was commissioned to build an 18-hole course on what had been a vegetable farm bounded by Baisley and Linden Boulevards, Merrick Road, and the elevated tracks of the Long Island Railroad. A.W. Tillinghast was called in for a renovation in 1923, and in 1930 St. Albans hosted the Met Amateur.

The Club expired after World War II. Its land was acquired to house a large Navy hospital, which was decommissioned in 1974. Half the land was deeded to the state and became Roy Wilkins Park.

RICHMOND HILL

Richmond Hill Golf Club existed for no more than a decade. Organized in 1896, a nine-hole course was quickly laid out on hilly farmland leased from the village of Richmond Hill. The clubhouse was perched above the course, which was set along the edge of "seven miles of forest" (today's Forest Park).

In 1906, a large pond at the foot of the hill was filled in to make way for an LIRR station in Kew Gardens. The construction destroyed the course.

LIDO

Back in the 1920s, the crown jewel of Met Area golf was the links course at Lido Beach, an engineering marvel sculpted by Charles B. Macdonald on land

The 17th and 18th at Pomonok, 1939.

reclaimed from the sea. It was possibly the most daring experiment in golf course architecture ever conceived.

Henry Winthrop, then president of Piping Rock, gave Macdonald the idea of building a course on the marshland on Long Beach Island between Reynolds Channel and the ocean. At first, Macdonald thought the idea utter folly. But Winthrop struck a nerve by promising complete design freedom. "To me, it seemed a dream," Macdonald would recall. "It really made me feel like a creator."

Work began in 1914, but the course wasn't playable until 1917, about the time the United States entered World War I, so the official opening wasn't until after the war. Total cost was nearly $800,000, a staggering sum in those days.

Macdonald incorporated several ideas from foreign courses, as well as versions of holes he first designed at the National Golf Links in Southampton. He also enlisted the aid of British journalist Bernard Darwin, who sponsored a contest in *Country Life* magazine asking readers to design a par-four hole of 360 to 460 yards. Judging was done by Darwin, golfer/writer Horace Hutchinson, and architect Herbert Fowler. The winner was a little-known architect, Dr. Alister Mackenzie, whose design was implemented as Lido's 18th hole. The hole was the ultimate in strategic design, including three separate "tongues of fairway," landing areas that required carrying some rough country, with the more daring drives rewarded with simpler second shots.

Lido was built by Seth Raynor, who is said to have pumped 2,000,000 cubic yards of sand from the channel floor to shape Macdonald's contours. A lagoon was built to form the famous fourth, the "Channel Hole," which Macdonald considered the best two-shotter in the world. (In fact, it could be played either as a par four of 466 yards or a par five of 510 yards "around the horn." Its C-shaped, island fairway was bordered on the left by the lagoon,

Looking at Lido's Channel Hole from the third green.

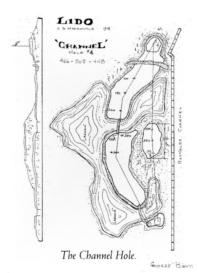

Lido today.

which had to be carried from the tee and again on the approach. The tee shot offered the intriguing alternative (to the conservative play to the left) of a long and risky carry of 210 yards over water to a separate fairway to the right, 100 yards long and 30 yards wide guarded by sand and rushes. Carried successfully, the player was left with a grand second over the lagoon; short or off-line and the following shot was a difficult recovery from knee-deep "eel grass." Darwin called the fourth "the most majestic two-shot hole I have ever seen, truly awe-inspiring."

Another hole that generated considerable comment was the sixth, a 90-degree-right dogleg that called for a long, blind second shot over sand hills and a forest of giant sea rushes; known as "Raynor's Prize Dogleg," the concept for this hole had won second prize in the *Country Life* contest. Also noteworthy was the "Ocean Hole," the 160-yard par-three eighth, with the beach to the right: When the prevailing breeze blew, the shot had to begin out over the sand.

The course received high praise. During the late 1920s, *Metropolitan Golfer* magazine conducted a survey of 50 prominent professionals, asking each to list his top American courses. Their consensus placed Pine Valley first and Lido second, ahead of such highly-regarded local courses as the National and Garden City.

In 1922, Darwin was asked to compare Lido, Pine Valley, and the National: "I should say that Lido was the finest course in the world, Pine Valley the hardest course in the world, and that I would rather play on the National than either of them."

Lido was very difficult for the average player. No fewer than seven holes demanded tee shots that carried a huge trap or series of bunkers guarding the entrance to

The Channel Hole.

the fairway. The sand-based, bentgrass rough was so thick it usually was difficult to find one's ball, then impossible to do anything with it but play a niblick recovery back to the fairway.

During its heyday, Lido was a force in Metropolitan golf, regularly hosting major regional events, including two Met Amateurs and three Met Opens. The scores in the 1922 Met Open attested to the difficulty of Macdonald's original design: Marty O'Loughlin won with a four-round total of 309, three strokes ahead of runner-up Johnny Farrell. Among the also-rans in '22 was Gene Sarazen, his score of 322 under very windy conditions, 34 strokes higher than his winning score that year in the U.S. Open at Skokie.

Despite its acclaim, Lido never hosted a major national event. The closest it came was sectional qualifying for the 1925 U.S. Open. Playing what he called "some of his greatest golf," Bobby Jones qualified with rounds of 72-71, his first round played in a steady downpour. Macdonald Smith's duplicate 70s led the qualifying, and were considered at the time one of the greatest displays of shot-making ever seen.

In 1928, Lido unveiled a new Spanish Mission-style clubhouse. Known as "The Lido Club," it was as large and lavishly appointed as the most palatial American hotels, and included 400 guest rooms. The 1,500 members enjoyed a dining room noted for its cuisine and broad windows overlooking the ocean, outdoor dancing to live orchestras on the broad verandahs, an umbrella-studded promenade along the ocean's edge, and a casino with adjoining grandstand overlooking tennis courts.

But the glory that was Lido's was short-lived. The

course was neglected during the Depression, eventually falling into the hands of developers. Rumors persisted that the ocean-front holes would be abandoned and that valuable land developed as residential plots. But during World War II, the Navy took over much of Long Beach Island. The Club ceased operations after the 1942 season, then reopened in 1949 with a new Robert Trent Jones course located entirely on the Channel side of Lido Boulevard. That private club lasted until financial difficulties won out in 1977. Since 1978, Lido has been a public facility.

The original Channel Hole didn't survive, although the present 16th is similar in concept. What was the Channel Hole likely played from a tee alongside the present 12th green, in the opposite direction up the 14th fairway, then across the lagoon to the second part of the present 16th fairway (the present 16th green might be the original). The separate alternate fairway was located somewhere on the present 13th hole near the green.

SALISBURY

Nassau County's Salisbury Country Club was called the "Sports Center Of America" because, among its other amenities were five golf courses. Salisbury opened in 1917 at the foot of Stewart Avenue, just east of Garden City, to replace the Salisbury Links, which had become the private Cherry Valley Club. The new club was the vision of J.J. Lannin, proprietor of the Garden City Hotel, who wanted courses that would cater to his hotel guests and unaffiliated golfers from New York City and Brooklyn.

The first course (1917) became the highly-acclaimed site of the 1925 U.S. Public Links Championship. During the golf boom of the 1920s, it was joined in rapid succession by #2 (1922), #3 (1923), #4 (1924), and #5 (1925), all designed, as the first had been, by Devereux Emmet. Courses 3 and 4 were operated as a private club, with number 4 the showcase, even though it featured just two par threes and two fives. The fourth hole on #4 was a 433-yard par four with a 90-degree dogleg to the left and a long, narrow bunker 50 yards in front of the green in the right rough. Both par threes—5 and 16—were relatively short, but fiercely bunkered.

In 1926, three major championships were contested over #4. In July, a memorable Met Open resulted in a 54-hole playoff between Macdonald Smith and Gene Sarazen, who tied at 286 after 72 holes, then tied again after two playoff rounds. Smith finally won the third extra round, 66 to 70, earning $250 for his efforts. The 126 holes were believed to have been a world's record for a major championship, which the Met Open was considered at the time.

The PGA Championship came to Salisbury in September and Walter Hagen putted his way to a third straight PGA title. Hagen was virtually unbeatable, his closest match ending 3&2.

In mid-October, the Met PGA held its inaugural championship at Salisbury, won by Joe Turnesa. The prize money was donated by Lannin, who also provided the champion's silver trophy, still known today as the Lannin Trophy.

Salisbury did not survive the Depression, was taken over by Nassau County in 1940, and turned into a park in 1944. Courses #1 and #4 remained open to the public; the other three were closed after years of neglect.

Number 4, renamed the Red, remains a reasonable facsimile of the course that saw the Club through its glory years. The first and 18th holes are entirely new, having been built in 1946 in anticipation of a new clubhouse, which opened in 1950.

In 1950-51, the new White and Blue courses, designed by Robert Trent Jones, opened. They were unique in that both had 22 holes, with duplicate versions of the par threes side by side to allow faster golfers to play through. At the same time, #1 was turned into picnic grounds, athletic fields, and a man-made lake. In 1969, the entire facility was renamed in honor of former president, and avid golfer, Dwight Eisenhower.

TIMBER POINT

The seed that eventually flowered as Timber Point was planted in the early 1900s, when a group of millionaires, led by Horace Havemeyer, the "Sultan of Sugar," built their mansions on a series of promontories below East Islip on the south shore of Long Island. When one died in 1922, the others bought his 231-acre estate and converted it into a private club with membership restricted to a select 100.

After organizing in July of 1923, the founders hired Colt & Alison to design an 18-hole course. It was nearly two years before the project was completed, because it took a year to dredge up enough sand to fill in the marshland and reclaim 100 acres from Great South Bay. The result was a magnificent test of golf among the sand dunes. It quickly took its place among the country's finest courses, while handling only a smattering of play on any given day. The members further surrounded themselves with an exquisite clubhouse, outstanding chefs, and a large boat basin.

Timber Point's members were obsessed with privacy. When the Suffolk County Mosquito Commission asked for contributions to aid their work controlling what had become a severe problem, the members refused, preferring to contend with the insects than with the masses who subsequently would find the area more attractive. And when a 1,500-acre estate adjacent to their course went up for sale, they quickly purchased it for use as a private hunting preserve. (This led to a confrontation with New York Parks Commissioner Robert Moses, who wanted the property converted into a public park. He eventually seized the land, and created Heckscher State Park.)

The first nine at Timber Point played through forests of pines, with several holes reminiscent of Pine Valley. With the 10th hole, the course "emerged to the glistening sands and the water, with its inevitable tang of the sea." All the notable holes were on the back nine. The 11th, a 460-yard par four known as the "Three-Island" hole, was similar to 18 at Lido, offering the player three fairways from the tee, with the ideal line demanding a carry of 200 yards over sand and rough. The 12th ("Harbor") was a 140-yard par three offering a magnificent view of the bay. Played over water from an elevated tee to an elevated green, it demanded deadly accuracy; the water of the yacht basin extended from tee to green on the left, while a vast wasteland of sand

The lineup of players at one of the annual Scotch vs. Irish (Thistles vs. Shamrocks) matches at the Sound View Golf Club.

engulfed the green.

The most memorable hole may have been 15, known as "Gibraltar." A 200-yard, uphill par three, its green was perched atop a bluff overlooking the bay. Vast expanses of sand on either side would catch the off-line shots of players straining to reach the green into the prevailing southwesterly wind.

Both 16 and 17 played with the bay down their left sides. When the wind blew, the drive had to start over the water to avoid the rough on the right.

The original owners sold out in the 1940s. With subsequent ownership changes often came name changes, with the club alternately known as Timber Point and Great River. Suffolk County purchased the club in 1971 and began operating it as a public facility. In 1972, William Mitchell designed a third nine that necessitated destroying six of the original holes. Three Island no longer exists, but Harbor and Gibraltar are part of the Blue nine.

SOUND VIEW

The theatrical and literary set favored two clubs in the Great Neck area. One, Lakeville, ultimately became the second home for Fresh Meadow. The other, Sound View, was located in the southwestern corner of the Great Neck peninsula, in what is now Great Neck Estates, overlooking Little Neck Bay. Organized as the Great Neck Golf Club during the winter of 1911-1912, the name changed to the Great Neck Field & Marine Club in 1915, to the Golf & Country Club, Inc., in 1916, and finally to Sound View in 1920. In 1914, the original nine-hole golf course was expanded to 18 holes.

Sound View's members were great fans of the game, and in 1921 entered golf history by staging the first "World Series Of Golf" between the year's American and British Open champions, Jim Barnes and Jock Hutchison. Barnes narrowly won that first match, and the series continued for several years, although at different clubs and with different formats.

In its heyday, Sound View was a fun place. One of their intraclub matches was the annual "Shamrocks vs. Thistles," which pitted Irish members against Scottish, each clad in the traditional garb. A group of Sound View members tried to organize a national society of club throwers in the mid 1920s. And there was a parrot behind the ninth green whose vocabulary was limited to one word—"fore!"

The best remembered hole was the 10th, a picturesque par three of 120 yards across a pond. The 17th also was a short pitch over water, while the drive on the home hole crossed the same hazard.

The Depression hurt Sound View. Its name was changed to Sound Shore in 1931, then back to Sound View again in 1933. The Club operated as a semi-private facility for a few years after World War II, but the end came after the 1947 season, when the property was sold to developers.

WESTBROOK

Westbrook Golf Club in East Islip, organized in 1894, was very exclusive, with a membership list that never exceeded 100. Its most prominent golfer was Fred Herreshoff, winner of the 1910 Met Amateur and runner-up in the 1911 U.S. Amateur. H.B. Hollins, first president of the MGA, was a central figure in the club's affairs. He also was the father of the 1923 Women's Amateur champion, Marion Hollins.

Westbrook's nine-hole golf course was built by Willie Dunn in 1895, and was one of the best conditioned in the country, despite staying open for winter play. The course featured two unusual hazards, railroad tracks that crossed the second hole and a horsetrack—the private training track of Pierre Lorillard—that encircled the 135-yard fourth hole.

Westbrook expanded to 18 holes just after the turn of the century, but by 1915 nine of the holes had been abandoned. The Club disbanded in the late 1930s.

BROOKLYN

Brooklyn once was dotted with golf courses, the most prominent a triumvirate that overlooked the Narrows, Staten Island, and the Atlantic Ocean. Dyker Meadow and Marine & Field were neighbors, situated within the confines of what is now Dyker Beach Park. The third, Crescent Athletic, eventually moved to Huntington as the Huntington Crescent Club.

The earliest was Dyker Meadow Golf Club, which was organized in 1895 and located in Fort Hamilton, off 7th Avenue and 92nd Street, at the southwest corner of the park. A turn-of-the-century *Harper's Golf Guide* called the 3,003-yard Tom Bendelow layout the "best (and longest)

9-hole course in the United States." It rolled through a series of natural undulations and around two ponds as it gradually approached the beach at Gravesend Bay.

The Marine & Field Club sat at the northern boundary of today's park, with its clubhouse at 13th Avenue and 86th Street. It was organized in 1885, but as the name implies, with other sports in mind. Golf came in 1896 in the form of a five-hole course that Bendelow expanded to a short but sporty nine-holer the following year.

In 1909, the two clubs consolidated their courses: The Marine & Field course became the front nine, Dyker Meadow the back.

Late in 1915, Marine & Field lost six of its holes to the construction of new buildings; the following season, Dyker Meadow was sold to Brooklyn Polytechnic Institute. The city subsequently created Dyker Beach Park, and allowed Marine & Field's 200 members to build a new 18-hole course that was operated on a semi-public basis.

In 1926, the Marine & Field course was condemned and plowed under. The city combined that land with 81 acres adjoining Dyker Beach Park, and in 1928 the new Dyker Beach public course (also known as Shore View) opened. A par 68 of just 4,815 yards, the new course was the training ground for the Strafaci brothers, Frank Tom, and Doug, the first two eventual winners of the Met Amateur. Dyker Beach today is par 71 and 6,260 yards.

FOX HILLS

Fox Hills Golf Club, near the north shore of Staten Island at Stapleton, overlooking the Narrows, was considered by many among the best in the Met region. The property was said to command magnificent views of hills, lakes, forest, and the ocean.

Golf was first played in the Fox Hills area of the island in 1894 over a rudimentary course (without greens) that produced two competitors in that year's unofficial amateur championship at St. Andrew's. In 1898, the nearby Staten Island Cricket and Baseball Club leased some local property and hired Tom Bendelow to design an 18-hole course. Construction began the following spring, but the club had financial difficulties and folded before the course was finished.

In 1900, a group of 10 Staten Island golfers leased the property and incorporated the Fox Hills Golf Club. The Bendelow course was ready for play by Memorial Day 1901. Its most notable feature was "Hell's Kitchen," a huge chasm that cut across the property, and was the principle hazard on the 12th through 15th holes, each requiring a carry of some 140 yards.

It was barren, windswept terrain, with not a tree, artificial bunker, nor man-made pond in sight. The course had abrupt, often imposing undulations, seldom providing a level stance. The greens were large—the home green alone occupied an acre and a half. Walter Travis called Fox Hills "the most natural and varied course in the country." Harry Vardon also praised it, predicting that "Fox Hills will become the classic course in the United States."

In 1905, Fox Hills hosted the inaugural Met Open and the seventh Met Amateur. The first Met Open champion was Alex Smith, who defeated four-time U.S. Open winner Willie Anderson.

Smith played a legendary match against Fox Hills' professional Isaac Mackie in 1909. Mackie had been unbeatable at his home course, so one of the members offered to bet any amount of money that Mackie could beat any professional over 36 holes at Fox Hills. One clever fellow mentioned a young man who once had caddied for him in Scotland, and the betting started. When the former caddie proved to be Smith, the Fox Hills' faithful were somewhat shaken, but the match proved to be a good one. Smith took a 1-up lead in the morning round, despite some uninspired golf. In the afternoon both players fired course record-tying 66s, and Smith still had his one-hole advantage at the end.

Fox Hills' fortunes failed with the Depression and the grounds were covered by military barracks during World War II. Hell's Kitchen has since been filled in, with the land now under apartment buildings and homes.

GRASSY SPRAIN

Grassy Sprain Golf Club in Yonkers opened in 1921 on a site straddling Central Avenue, a busy thoroughfare even in those days, just south of Tuckahoe Road. Throughout its short existence, Grassy Sprain catered to a middle-class audience.

The golf course was quite hilly and picturesque. The "postcard" hole was the 245-yard, par-three eighth, called "Robbers Roost." Possibly the most difficult par three in Westchester, its tee was perched high on a rock (the roost) well above the fairway. Two large elms about 60 yards ahead of the green protected the left side, while Sprain Brook paralleled the hole along the right.

The quality of the course attracted several prominent players as members, most notably U.S. and British Amateur champion Jess Sweetser and two–time French Amateur champion John G. Anderson. The notorious gambler Titanic Thompson played there frequently, once losing $2,500 to George McLean, Grassy Sprain's only professional, another time winning $13,000 from the pro by hitting his approach to the final green within two feet of the cup. Grassy Sprain was the site of the 1925 Met Open, won by Gene Sarazen with a hot putter.

By 1938, the loss of members to higher-class clubs and the ensuing financial difficulties proved fatal. Located at the intersection of two major roads, Grassy Sprain's property was too valuable not to sell.

ROCKWOOD HALL

According to a 1927 issue of *The American Golfer*, Rockwood Hall Country Club "for calculated beauty transcends all other golfing territory in this part of the country." The land, just north of Tarrytown and west of the Albany Post Road, was part of a former country estate of William Rockefeller. He had spared no expense on the landscaping, which was modeled after parks around the world, particularly England. Trees were

Fox Hills' splendid 15th hole (1924).

imported from distant parts of the globe, with the result a woodland paradise.

The Club was organized in 1925 and took its name from the Rockefeller mansion that became its clubhouse. A Tudor graystone castle featuring beautiful woodwork and stonework, it included a glassed-in dining room with a wide view of the Hudson and the shining waters of the Tappan Zee.

The golf course was designed by Devereux Emmet, who had all 18 holes ready by mid 1926. Among the featured holes was the 11th, a 140-yard par three over a lake whose waters lapped the edge of a well-bunkered green. The spectacular view from the elevated 15th tee made the 527-yard hole look like a mere drive and pitch. .

Rockwood Hall's life was short, another victim of the Depression. Before closing in 1939, it operated for two years under the name Washington Irving Country Club.

SAEGKILL/HUDSON RIVER

During the 1890s the unwritten policy at St. Andrew's regarding lady golfers was simple: "To the ladies, God bless them, always welcome but never invited." And so in 1895 a group of St. Andrew's women, among them Mrs. John Reid, organized the Saegkill Golf Club. They leased land and a cottage off North Broadway, in north Yonkers. By the spring of 1896, the Club numbered nearly 100 members, the majority women, and had a six-hole golf course designed by two members of the "Apple Tree Gang."

The Saegkill experiment—a majority of membership and executive committee being women—ended in 1915 when the men took over. They changed the Club's name to Hudson River, and engaged Donald Ross to modernize the golf course, which by then was located off Odell

Avenue in Greystone. The facilities were considered among the most luxurious in Westchester, and hosted the second edition of the MGA Senior Championship in 1929.

Hudson River ultimately lived out its existence under private ownership. The Club closed its doors late in 1966 when the members were unable to match industrial offers for the land following the owner's death. The land is now occupied by the Lower Westchester Industrial Park.

LAKEWOOD

Lakewood, New Jersey, was golf's first popular off-season gathering place. Before the turn of the century, visitors to Lakewood had their choice of several excellent hotels and two outstanding resort courses whose season lasted from October through May. The semi-annual tournaments held there, in late April and Thanksgiving, were the oldest on the local calendar, attracting fields second only to the U.S. Amateur.

The first of the area's courses belonged to the Golf Club of Lakewood, which was organized in 1894. It was designed by Willie Dunn, who had a memorable first visit to the site: Clad in a scarlet golf jacket, Dunn had an encounter with a bull in the nearby fields, from which Dunn, but not his cloak, escaped unscathed.

The biannual tournaments began at the Golf Club in 1895, and were dominated over the years by U.S. Amateur champions Walter Travis and Findlay Douglas.

In the spring of 1898, the Golf Club moved to a new home, a converted farmhouse that featured a magnificent cafe with a large fireplace and floor-to-ceiling windows overlooking the golf course. The Club's new 18 holes, designed by Tom Bendelow, were surrounded by forest, although there were but a few trees on the course itself. Laid out over flat terrain, many of the holes ran parallel, and there were no water hazards. Nevertheless, the course was considered a good test of golf, due primarily to the clever arrangement of bunkers.

The Ocean County Hunt and Country Club was established in 1895 and soon sported a nine-hole course. Its Dutch Colonial clubhouse was supplemented by stables, kennels, and a pigeon house for hunting and trap shooting. Yet the name was changed in 1899 to the Country Club of Lakewood.

In the spring of 1902, the Golf Club learned that its lease, with one year left, would not be renewed. This set in motion a chain of events that led to the two clubs merging to form the Lakewood Country Club. On February 11, 1903, a three-story clubhouse and 18-hole golf course at a new site opened with a grand party. (The clubhouse burned to the ground on December 18, 1917, and was not rebuilt. The present clubhouse was a home, purchased in the early 1920s.)

The club reorganized in 1919, when the decision was made to open to the public and operate year-round.

The course was reworked by Travis during the summer of 1920, with special attention paid to the four-hole stretch from 12 to 15. Twelve became a short par four played over a wide brook 75 yards ahead of the tee, to a hilltop green protected by a huge bunker dead-center high on the slope. The tee shot on 14 had to carry a huge expanse of sand, called the "Sahara Desert," before reaching the safety of the fairway, which rolled downhill to a bottlenecked drive zone; Travis was not alone in his belief that 14 was the equal of any two-shotter in the country. The 15th played across a pond, then a brook, to a small green protected in front by a nest of shallow traps forming the letters "LCC."

The 1922 Met Amateur was contested over the new Lakewood, and 20-year-old Jess Sweetser whipped Eddie Hale 10&8 for the title. The match was closer than the score suggests until Sweetser fired a course-record 71 in the afternoon round.

Lakewood's glory faded with the Depression, which hit Ocean County especially hard. But just as fatal was the growth in popularity of southern resort areas such as Pinehurst, Sea Island, and the state of Florida. Each offered consistently better weather than Lakewood ever could.

Today, Lakewood is semiprivate, open to the public while catering to a small membership. The basic routing of the course remains faithful to Travis' 1920 redesign, although a good deal of the original bunkering was removed in the early 1970s.

YOUNTAKAH

The Yountakah Golf Club began as the nine-hole Nutley Golf Club in 1897, with a course laid out by Tom Bendelow on the side of a hill that sloped down to the banks of the Passaic River in Nutley, New Jersey. The region was steeped in the traditions of the Lenape Indians, who gathered there each fall for their annual harvest celebration. The festival, several days of dancing and feasting, was called Yantacaw, which meant "Meeting Place." Hence, the Club adopted the name in 1898.

Yountakah's golf facilities were expanded to 18 holes in 1899 by member Adrian H. Larkin, who designed the interior faces of his bunkers entirely of sand, totally without grass, thereby giving the amateur a better chance at getting out.

A charter member of the New Jersey State Golf Association, Yountakah hosted an historic edition of the New Jersey Open in 1942, when Charley Whitehead of Plainfield became the first amateur to capture that title. Yountakah also had hosted the 1939 New Jersey Open, won by "Long Jim" Barnes, then professional at Essex County. It was the last victory of Barnes' illustrious career.

Gene Sarazen and Tommy Kerrigan playing in the Met Open Championship at Grassy Sprain.

The old tenth hole at Lakewood.

It also was Yountakah's last hurrah. Declining membership, high maintenance costs, and the effects of World War II forced the Club to close. The property was sold to I.T.T. in 1943. Today, a 325-foot-tall radio tower stands near the Colonial-style clubhouse from an earlier era.

THE KNOLL

In 1928, 46 very wealthy men established The Knoll Golf Club in Parsippany-Troy Hills. They wanted an ultra-exclusive club, and spent more than $2 million on 392 acres of land, a golf course, and a Georgian brick clubhouse with a locker room upholstered in red leather. But by the time the Club opened on July 4, 1930, nearly half of the founders were paupers!

The Depression threw the men into a financial downspin from which most never recovered. They sold the club in 1946. This was the start of The Knoll's glory years, hosting numerous regional tournaments that placed it firmly in the public eye.

In the 1954 Met Open, Otto Greiner's 10-over-par 290 edged Tour star Jay Herbert by one stroke. The 1958 Met Amateur marked the beginning of the "Bob Gardner era," the first of six such titles won by the Montclair star in a seven-year span. In 1960, as site for the New Jersey Open, The Knoll hosted the first leg of Al Mengert's "Jersey Slam," the Met Open, New Jersey Open, and New Jersey PGA.

The glory was gone by the late '60s, and since 1976 The Knoll has been semi-private, catering to a regular membership and outings. In 1986, a fire destroyed the old clubhouse, sparing only the basement, which housed the locker rooms and pro shop.

The original course was built by Charlie Banks, with large undulating greens protected by deep bunkers, many of them 10 to 20 feet below the raised putting surfaces. The 13th hole is a memorable par three, of the Biarritz genre, a waterless adaptation of the "Valley Of Sin" hole (#9) at Yale, although the valley is part of the fairway, a landing area for those unable to negotiate the full 248 yards. The green is flanked by long bunkers, two on either side.

The strength of The Knoll is its par fours, six of which exceed 415 yards. The second demands a solid poke off the tee to carry a pond, and features a huge green set on a left-to-right angle to the fairway, with separate back tiers left and right. The fourth, also a right dogleg, demands a carry off the tee over a wide fairway bunker on the short side. The green is protected by a vast bunker at the front left, and features a ridge from front to back that creates some very touchy hole placements on the smaller left side.

Perhaps the best holes are the pair leading back to the clubhouse. The green on the tree-lined ninth sits well above the fairway and is protected by bunkers at the front corners 20 feet below its surface. The route along the long, uphill 18th is complicated by four fairway bunkers, while the elevated green is long and narrow, set on a right-to-left angle, and bunkered left, right, and rear.

ENGLEWOOD

In northern New Jersey, on the western slope of the Palisades, was one of the most talked-about clubs in the country. Organized in 1896, the Englewood Golf Club was a frequent host to tournaments of national and regional significance in its early years. But its true renown came in its later years, when the membership was an unlikely mix of comedians, big bettors, and mobsters. The unusual and the bizarre were commonplace—$20,000 Nassaus, automobiles in place of golf carts, and eightsomes (each player in his own cart and another for each caddie).

The old wooden clubhouse sat atop the hilly property amidst trees and mansions. At the foot of the hill, streams crisscrossed the course and affected play on several holes. "The brook at the second hole is not a mental hazard, but a foregone conclusion," a member once joked.

The first course was a nine-holer built in 1898, then expanded to 18 holes in 1900, when Englewood was recognized as one of the premier hillside courses in the country, with the tournaments to prove it. The Club hosted the 1906 U.S. Amateur, won by Eben Byers of Pittsburgh 2-up over George Lyon, the first great Canadian player. Three years later, it was the U.S. Open: Englishman George Sargent set a new record for the tournament (290) over a course labeled "moderately easy." Among the other firsts at that Open, Boston's Tom McNamara finished second, becoming the first American-bred player to do well in his national championship, while his second-round 69 and David Hunter's opening-round 68 were the first sub-70 scores in tournament history.

In 1911, the Met Open was won there by Gil Nichols, who beat the field by eight strokes with a four-round total of 70-74-71-66=281, establishing a new world's record for 72 holes that lasted until Harry Vardon broke it in Germany later that season. Jack Hobens, Englewood professional who represented the Club in 14 U.S. Opens, finished second.

The 1914 Met Amateur was captured by Englewood's own Oswald Kirkby, who defeated Walter Travis 4&2 in the finals. This was the first of three Met Amateur titles for Kirkby in six years (interrupted by World War I). The club's professional, Cyril Walker, won the 1924 U.S. Open at Oakland Hills, finishing three strokes ahead of runner-up Bobby Jones. Member Eugene Homans—a former Met Junior and Met Amateur champion—earned a spot in the history books as Jones' opponent in the finals of the 1930 U.S. Amateur, making

him the last man in the way of the Grand Slam. Of course, Homans lost. (His victim in the semifinals was Californian Charles Seaver, father of baseball's Tom Seaver.)

The Club's descent began with the opening of the George Washington Bridge in 1931. The highways and housing developments that followed changed the bucolic nature of the area forever. The golf course was neglected during World War II, then operated as a public course for six years before reverting to private-club status.

In 1960, Interstate 95 was routed through the heart of the course, destroying six holes. What was left was redesigned, but the comics left for Los Angeles, the mobsters disappeared, and the club's fortunes sagged. The name was changed to Rolling Hills in 1976, but a year later the Club was closed for failing to pay its taxes. That winter, the old clubhouse burned to the ground.

NEW BRUNSWICK

Founded in 1894, the New Brunswick Golf Club never amounted to more than nine holes. But it was one of New Jersey's first golf sites, its original course in what is now the center of New Brunswick. In 1897, the club moved north across the Raritan River to Piscataway Township. The new clubhouse was Ross Hall, a large brick mansion built in 1740: George Washington slept there for six days after the Battle of Monmouth in 1778.

Sometime between 1909 and 1915, the Club moved within Piscataway, off Hoes Lane, west of Rutgers Stadium. The clubhouse and tennis courts were just north of River Road, with the course spreading to the north and crossing a brook six times. The new course was possibly the longest of its era—3,410 yards. The first hole was a staggering 560 yards.

The club failed with the Depression, closing in the spring of 1933. The land was sold to Rutgers, and is now the site of the university's golf course, an 18-hole layout built by Hal Purdy in 1963. ❏

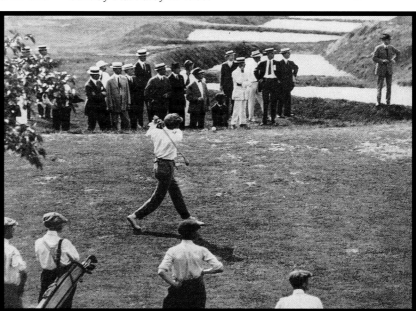

Oswald Kirby driving at Englewood.

RECORDS OF THE METROPOLITAN GOLF ASSOCIATION

MGA AMATEUR CHAMPIONSHIP

YEAR	CHAMPION	SITE
1899	H.M. Harriman	Garden City Golf
1900	W.J. Travis	Nassau
1901	F.S. Douglas	Apawamis
1902	W.J. Travis	Tuxedo
1903	F.S. Douglas	Deal
1904	H. Wilcox	Garden City Golf
1905	C.H. Seely	Fox Hills
1906	J.D. Travers	St. Andrew's
1907	J.D. Travers	Nassau
1908	C.H. Seely	Baltusrol
1909	W.J. Travis	Apawamis
1910	F. Herreshoff	Morris County
1911	J.D. Travers	Garden City Golf
1912	J.D. Travers	Baltusrol
1913	J.D. Travers	Fox Hills
1914	Oswald Kirkby	Englewood
1915	W.J. Travis	Apawamis
1916	Oswald Kirkby	Nassau
1917	*No Competition*	
1918	*No Competition*	
1919	Oswald Kirkby	Brooklawn
1920	D.E. Sawyer	Apawamis
1921	G.W. White	Garden City Golf
1922	Jess W. Sweetser	Lakewood
1923	F.W. Dyer	Siwanoy
1924	W.M. Reekie	Lido
1925	Jess W. Sweetser	Hollywood
1926	W.M. Reekie	Winged Foot
1927	E.H. Driggs Jr.	Nassau
1928	Eugene Homans	Fenimore
1929	M.J. McCarthy Jr.	Montclair
1930	M.J. McCarthy Jr.	St. Albans
1931	Leonard Martin	Quaker Ridge
1932	T.S. Tailer Jr.	Plainfield
1933	Mark J. Stuart	Pomonok
1934	T.S. Tailer Jr.	Wykagyl
1935	John Parker Jr.	Canoe Brook
1936	George Dunlap Jr.	Lido
1937	Willie P. Turnesa	Metropolis
1938	Frank Strafaci	Ridgewood
1939	Frank Strafaci	Nassau
1940	John P. Burke	Century
1941	Michael Cestone	Montclair
1942	*No Competition*	
1943	*No Competition*	
1944	E.H. Driggs Jr.	Sleepy Hollow
1945	Frank Strafaci	Garden City Golf
1946	Frank Strafaci	Essex County
1947	Frank Strafaci	Meadow Brook
1948	Ray Billows	Winged Foot
1949	Joseph McBride	Canoe Brook
1950	Frank Stafaci	Apawamis
1951	Joseph Gagliardi	Hempstead
1952	Joseph Marra	Ridgewood
1953	Wilson Barnes Jr.	Fenway
1954	Frank Strafaci	Garden City CC
1955	Robert W. Kuntz	Plainfield
1956	Thomas J. Goodwin	Century
1957	Paul Kelly	Nassau
1958	Robert W. Gardner	The Knoll
1959	Paul Kelly	Fairview
1960	Robert W. Gardner	Meadow Brook
1961	Robert W. Gardner	Canoe Brook
1962	Robert W. Gardner	Sunningdale
1963	Robert W. Gardner	Nassau
1964	Robert W. Gardner	Hackensack
1965	Mark J. Stuart Jr.	Sleepy Hollow
1966	James E. Fisher	Inwood
1967	John C. Baldwin	Plainfield
1968	Richard Siderowf	Metropolis
1969	Richard Siderowf	Garden City CC
1970	Richard Siderowf	Upper Montclair
1971	Richard Spears	Winged Foot
1972	George F. Burns III	Deepdale
1973	Jerry Courville Sr.	Canoe Brook
1974	Richard Siderowf	Sunningdale
1975	Bill Britton	Wheatley Hills
1976	Bill Britton	Plainfield
1977	Dave Farrell	Century
1978	Mike Burke Jr.	Garden City Golf
1979	Jerry Courville Sr.	Mountain Ridge
1980	Howard Pierson	Stanwich
1981	Peter Van Ingen	Cherry Valley
1982	George J. Zahringer III	Somerset Hills
1983	Mark Diamond	Sleepy Hollow
1984	George J. Zahringer III	Deepdale
1985	George J. Zahringer III	Ridgewood
1986	George J. Zahringer III	Quaker Ridge

T.S. Tailer Jr.

George Dunlap Jr.

1987	George J. Zahringer III	Meadow Brook
1988	Jim McGovern	Plainfield
1989	Richard Siderowf	Metropolis
1990	John C. Baldwin	Piping Rock
1991	Dennis Slezak	Mountain Ridge
1992	Mike Muehr	Wee Burn
1993	Jeff Putman	Sands Point
1994	Dennis Hillman	Hackensack
1995	Jerry Courville Jr.	Century
1996	Ken Bakst	Nassau

MGA OPEN CHAMPIONSHIP*

YEAR	CHAMPION	SITE
1905	Alex Smith	Fox Hills
1906	George Low	Hollywood
1907	*No Competition*	
1908	Jack Hobens	Baltusrol
1909	Alex Smith	Wykagyl
1910	Alex Smith	Deal
1911	Gil Nichols	Englewood
1912	Tom McNamara	Apawamis
1913	Alex Smith	Salisbury Links
1914	Macdonald Smith	Scarsdale
1915	Gil Nichols	Fox Hills
1916	Walter Hagen	Garden City Golf
1917	*No Competition*	
1918	*No Competition*	
1919	Walter Hagen	North Shore
1920	Walter Hagen	Greenwich
1921	Bob MacDonald	Siwanoy
1922	Marty O'Loughlin	Lido
1923	Bob MacDonald	Canoe Brook
1924	Mike Brady	Engineers
1925	Gene Sarazen	Grassy Sprain
1926	Macdonald Smith	Salisbury
1927	Johnny Farrell	Wykagyl
1928	Tommy Armour	Shackamaxon
1929	Bill Mehlhorn	Lido
1930	Willie MacFarlane	Fairview
1931	Macdonald Smith	Crestmont
1932	Olin Dutra	Lido
1933	Willie MacFarlane	Winged Foot
1934	Paul Runyan	Echo Lake
1935	Henry Picard	Lakeville
1936	Byron Nelson	Quaker Ridge
1937	Jimmy Hines	Forest Hill
1938	Jimmy Hines	Fresh Meadow
1939	Henry Picard	Metropolis
1940	Craig Wood	Forest Hill
1941-	*No Competition*	
1948	*No Competition*	
1949	Jackie Burke Jr.	Metropolis
1950	George Stuhler	Garden City CC
1951	Claude Harmon	Forest Hill
1952	Chet Sanok-*a*	Winged Foot
1953	Pete Cooper	Rockville Links
1954	Otto Greiner	The Knoll
1955	Art Doering	Fenway
1956	Doug Ford	Inwood

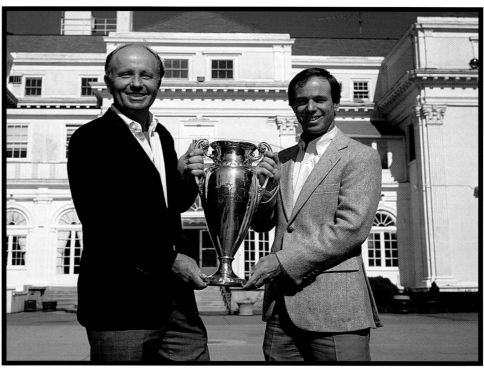

Bobby Heins and Bill Britton

1957	Wes Ellis	Plainfield
1958	Bob Watson	Metropolis
1959	Jim Turnesa	Woodmere
1960	Al Mengert	Ridgewood
1961	Wes Ellis	Winged Foot
1962	Miller Barber	Nassau
1963	Wes Ellis	Plainfield
1964	Jack Patroni	Briar Hall
1965	Jerry Pittman	Woodmere
1966	Tom Nieporte	Mountain Ridge
1967	Jerry Courville Sr.- *a*	Winged Foot
1968	Jerry Pittman	Inwood
1969	Jimmy Wright	Fenway
1970	James Albus	Ridgewood
1971	Ron Letellier	Fresh Meadow
1972	Don Massengale	Stanwich
1973	Peter Davison	Hackensack
1974	Bob Bruno	Middle Bay
1975	Carlton White	Metropolis
1976	Martin Bohen	Upper Montclair
1977	Martin Bohen	Meadow Brook
1978	David Glenz	Quaker Ridge
1979	Bill Britton	Plainfield
1980	George Bullock	Woodmere
1981	Kelley Moser	Knollwood
1982	Darrell Kestner	Montclair
1983	Darrell Kestner	Old Westbury
1984	James Albus	Old Oaks
1985	George J. Zahringer III-*a*	Mountain Ridge
1986	David Glenz	Nassau
1987	James McGovern-*a*	Winged Foot
1988	Bobby Heins	Baltusrol

1989	Bobby Heins	Bethpage Black
1990	Larry Rentz	Westchester
1991	Mike Diffley	Hollywood
1992	Mark Mielke	Nassau
1993	Bruce Zabriski	Quaker Ridge
1994	Charlie Cowell	Ridgewood
1995	Darrell Kestner	Atlantic
1996	Bruce Zabriski	Stanwich

a - amateur

MGA JUNIOR CHAMPIONSHIP*

YEAR	CHAMPION	SITE
1912	Stuart Connolly	Plainfield
1913	Philip V.G. Carter	Plainfield
1914	Philip V.G. Carter	Plainfield
1915	Philip V.G. Carter	Garden City Golf
1916	Vincent Helton	Englewood
1917	*No Competition*	
1918	*No Competition*	
1919	Peter Harmon	Siwanoy
1920	J.G. McMahon	Sleepy Hollow
1921	J.A. Fuller	Belleclair
1922	Charles L. Pierson	Ardsley
1923	R.A. Jones Jr.	Garden City Golf
1924	R.A. Jones Jr.	Westchester Hills
1925	Eugene Homans	Sleepy Hollow
1926	Eugene Homans	Cherry Valley
1927	Sidney W. Noyes Jr.	Sleepy Hollow
1928	Sidney W. Noyes Jr.	Wheatley Hills
1929	A.F. Kramer Jr.	Morris County
1930	R.A. Moffett	Ardsley

Arthur Weber with Jim and Howard McGovern

Tommy Armour

1931	T.S. Tailer Jr.	Lido
1932	Tommy Goodwin	Hackensack
1933	Ralph Strafaci	Sleepy Hollow
1934	August Boyajian	Nassau
1935	Frank Strafaci	Apawamis
1936	Robert J. Jacobson	Wheatley Hills
1937	Wilson H. Flohr	Englewood
1938	William Clark	Sunningdale
1939	John Humm	North Hempstead
1940	Robert W. Kuntz	Montclair
1941	Stanley Calder	Bonnie Briar
1942-	*No Competition*	
1945	*No Competition*	
1946	Edward P. Travis Jr.	Hempstead
1947	William Edwards	Essex Fells
1948	William Edwards	Briar Hills
1949	William Edwards	Hempstead
1950	William Edwards	Upper Montclair
1951	William Edwards	Siwanoy
1952	James DePiro	North Hills
1953	James DePiro	Forest Hill
1954	Charles Slicklen Jr.	Ardsley
1955	James E. Iverson	North Shore
1956	Alan Gilison	Morris County
1957	Rick Gleacher	Bonnie Briar
1958	Ralph W. Johnston	Brookville
1959	Ralph W. Johnston	Morris County
1960	Thomas Luddy	Sleepy Hollow
1961	Claude Harmon Jr.	Inwood
1962	Dennis Troy	Morris County
1963	Jim Conace	Waccabuc
1964	Richard Spears	North Hempstead
1965	Paul Samanchik	Morris County

1966	Billy Ziobro	Apawamis
1967	Richard Spain	Rockville Links
1968	Bill Harmon	Morris County
1969	Bill Furey	Knollwood
1970	Jim Ulozas	Nassau
1971	Art Silverstrone Jr.	Morris County
1972	Michael Occi	Apawamis
1973	Bruce Paolini	Inwood
1974	Robert Heidenberg	Rockaway River
1975	Bill Newman	Ardsley
1976	Tom Patri Jr.	Whippoorwill
1977	Jon Saxton	Rockaway River
1978	Martin Vybihal	Nissequogue
1979	Robert Mattiace	Knollwood
1980	Randolph Rogers	Rockaway River
1981	Michael Arasin	Inwood
1982	Mike Lopuszynski	Brooklawn
1983	Jeff Putman	Rockaway River
1984	Darrell Bock	St. George's
1985	Jerry Springer	Apawamis
1986	Adam Spring	Essex Fells
1987	Adam Spring	Plandome
1988	Robert Fisher Jr.	Ardsley
1989	Peter Dachisen Jr.	Rockaway River
1990	Gregory Bisconti	Wheatley Hills
1991	Michael Gazlay	Apawamis
1992	Rich Jeremiah	Rockaway River
1993	Bill Olin	Plandome
1994	Marc Turnesa	Mt. Kisco
1995	Ken Macdonald	Rockaway River
1996	Taylor Walsh	Hempstead

THE IKE – MGA STROKE PLAY CHAMPIONSHIP*

YEAR	CHAMPION	SITE
1953	George Berggren	Bethpage Black (Public Links)
	Bob Wilke	Tamarack (Private)
1954	Tommy Goodwin	Tamarack
1955	Bob Kuntz	Tamarack-Whippoorwill
1956	Tommy Goodwin	Tamarack-Whippoorwill
1957	Willie Turnesa	Tamarack-Whippoorwill
1958	Willie Turnesa	Tamarack-Whippoorwill
1959	Paul Kelly	Tamarack-Whippoorwill
1960	Bob Gardner	Tamarack-Whippoorwill
1961	Jerry Courville Sr.	Tamarack-Whippoorwill
1962	Bob Gardner	Tamarack-Whippoorwill
1963	Bob Gardner	Winged Foot
1964	Jerry Courville Sr.	Winged Foot
1965	Jerry Courville Sr.	Wykagyl
1966	Jimmy Fisher	Wykagyl
1967	Jerry Courville Sr.	Wykagyl
1968	Denny Lyons	Wykagyl
1969	Jerry Courville Sr.	Bonnie Briar
1970	Jerry Courville Sr.	Bonnie Briar
1971	Gene Francis	Wheatley Hills
1972	John Ruby	Forest Hill

1973	Mike Ford	Knollwood
1974	George Burns III	Wheatley Hills
1975	Chet Sanok	Upper Montclair
1976	Bob Housen	Wykagyl
1977	Mike Giacini	North Hills
1978	Jimmy Dee	Upper Montclair
1979	*No Competition*	
1980	*No Competition*	
1981	Jon Saxton	North Hills
1982	Mike Diffley	North Hills
1983	Jon Saxton	North Hills
1984	Jon Saxton	North Hills
1985	*No Competition*	
1986	John C. Baldwin	Tuxedo
1987	Mike Kavka	Essex County
1988	Robert Byrnes	Garden City Golf
1989	George J. Zahringer III	Stanwich
1990	Jerry Courville Jr.	Upper Montclair
1991	Jerry Courville Jr.	Old Westbury
1992	Mike Muehr	Shorehaven
1993	George J. Zahringer III	Preakness Hills
1994	Edward Gibstein	Bethpage Black
1995	Jeffrey Putman	Winged Foot (East)
1996	Jeff Thomas	Metedeconk Nat'l

THE IKE – MGA STROKE PLAY TEAM CHAMPIONSHIP*

YEAR	CHAMPIONS	CLUB
1954	Howard Miller / Walter Peek Jr.	Wykagyl
1955	Dave Lapkin / Joe Scarp	Pine Hollow
1956	Willie Turnesa / Frank Malara Jr.	Knollwood
1957	Willie Turnesa / Frank Malara Jr.	Knollwood
1958	Willie Turnesa / Fred Fiore	Knollwood
1959	Paul Kelly / Dave Mance	Sleepy Hollow
1960	Jerry Courville Sr. / Mike Vitti	Shorehaven
1961	Ben Costello / Al Compo	Mill River (CT)
1962	Bob Gardner / Ken Gordon	Montclair
1963	Bob Gardner / Ken Gordon	Montclair
1964	Walt Zembriski / Jeff Spangler	Rockleigh
1965	Ron Goldburg / Joe Spizzo	Twin Brooks
1966	Tom Berberian / Jerry Lepre	Forest Hill
1967	Rick Spears / Fred Woerner	Port Jervis
1968	Jim Maver / Billy Harmon	Winged Foot
1969	Chet Sanok / Vince Cassel	Upper Montclair
1970	Greg Powers / John Gentile Jr.	Sterling Farms
1971	Pete Bostwick Jr. / Jimmy Bostwick	Meadow Brook
1972	Dave Muraskin / Bruce Young	Rutgers
1973	Chet Sanok / Fred Massimi Jr.	Playboy
1974	Bill Britton / Bob Senese	Silver Lake
1975	Chet Sanok / Dave Sanok	Upper Montclair
1976	John Dreyfus / Jon Benson	Century
1977	Bill Messina Jr. / Jim Craffey	Pascack Valley
1978	Ken Green / John Parsons	Newtown
1979	*No Competition*	
1980	*No Competition*	
1981	Jerry Courville Sr. / Jerry Courville Jr.	Shorehaven
1982	Peter Van Ingen / John C. Baldwin	Meadow Brook
1983	Jerry Courville Sr. / Jerry Courville Jr.	Shorehaven
1984	Gene Holmes Sr. / Tom McQuilling	North Hills
1985	*No Competition*	
1986	Anders Johncke / Claes Johncke	Winged Foot
1987	Mike Kavka / Jeff Thomas	Plainfield West
1988	Mike Kavka / Jeff Thomas	Plainfield West
1989	George J. Zahringer III / Tom Yellin	Stanwich

George J. Zahringer III

Mike Muehr

Mike Diffley

1990 Jerry Courville Jr. Shorehaven
     Jack Curran
1991 Duke Delcher Plainfield West
     Jeff Thomas
1992 George J. Zahringer III Stanwich
     John Kiernan Jr.
1993 Jerry Courville Sr. Shorehaven
     Jerry Courville Jr.
1994 Sean Hartman Nassau Players
     Matt Esposito
1995 Ken Dardis Sterling Farms
     Joe Polizzano
1996 Jeff Thomas Plainfield West
     Robert Godfrey

MGA/METLIFE BOYS CHAMPIONSHIP*

YEAR	CHAMPION	SITE
1969	Jeff Hadley	Westchester
1970	Mike Occi	Deepdale
1971	Mark McAvoy	Bedens Brook
1972	Doug Thomas	Darien
1973	Richard Kerper	Powelton
1974	David Azen	Scarsdale
1975	Jon Saxton	Bedford
1976	Robert Mattiace	Ardsley
1977	Dan Dinan	Whippoorwill
1978	John Marino	Scarsdale
1979	Gregg Vincent	Waccabuc
1980	Don Edwards	Powelton
1981	Don Edwards	Essex Fells

Charlie Cowell

1982 Jeffrey Putman St. George's
1983 Jerry Springer Connecticut
1984 Steven Spencer Rumson
1985 Brian Soldon Gardiner's Bay
1986 Brian Soldon Garrison
1987 Mike Stamberger Rumson
1988 Gregory Bisconti Gardiner's Bay
1989 Rob Bradley Bedford
1990 Mike Ragone Rumson
1991 Frank Leo Gardiner's Bay
1992 Steve Oh Bedford
1993 Gary Blados Rumson
1994 Joseph Horowitz Gardiner's Bay
1995 Taylor Walsh Bedford
1996 Justin Van Hyning Rumson

MGA/METLIFE PUBLIC LINKS CHAMPIONSHIP*

YEAR	CHAMPION	SITE
1936	John Cunniff	Hendricks Field
1937	Michael Cestone	Bethpage Black
1938	Pat Mucci Sr.	Aviation
1939	Charles Amandoles	LaTourette
1940	George Davidson	Hendricks Field
1941	Dominic Strafaci	Bethpage Black
1942	No Competition	
1943	No Competition	
1944	Gilbert Smith	LaTourette
1945	Charles Amandoles	Hendricks Field
1946	Arnold Gray	Engineers
1947	Steve Maurath	Split Rock
1948	Ray Sullivan	Galloping Hill
1949	Charles Amandoles	Essex Cty West
1950	Frank Kaminski Jr.	Hendricks Field
1951	Al Bange	Salisbury
1952	George Baskiel	Island Hills
1953	Bernard Kane	Hubbard Heights
1954	Roy Faber	Ash Brook
1955	George Baskiel	Bethpage Black
1956	Jerry Buchetto	Hubbard Heights
1957	James Torre	River Vale
1958	Sam Petrone	Bethpage Black
1959	Sam Petrone	Mohansic
1960	James O'Neill	Rockleigh
1961	Sam Petrone	Orchard Hills
1962	Stan Lugovich Jr.	Fairchild Wheeler
1963	Sam Petrone	Spring Rock
1964	James Alverson	Timber Point
1965	Joseph Roccisano	Timber Point
1966	Leonard Dahl	Hubbard Heights
1967	Neil Donovan	Mill River
1968	Harry Kaufman	Richmond Cty
1969	Robert Issler	Ardsley
1970	James Stalarow	North Redoubt
1971	John Riccardo	Salem
1972	Robert Britton	Lakeover
1973	William Cariello	North Redoubt
1974-	No Competition	
1983	No Competition	
1984	Carl Campanelli	Bethpage Black
1985	Carl Campanelli	Blue Hill
1986	Charles Cowell	Hominy Hill
1987	Mark Mielke	Spook Rock
1988	Del Kinney Jr.	Richter Park
1989	Del Kinney Jr.	Spring Lake
1990	Alan Specht	Spook Rock
1991	Robert Fisher Jr.	Hominy Hill
1992	Jeff Thomas	Richter Park
1993	Lee Richardson	Oyster Bay
1994	Lee Richardson	Spook Rock
1995	Jerome Kim	Richter Park
1996	Paul Dickinson	Hominy Hill

MGA SENIOR CHAMPIONSHIP

YEAR	CHAMPION	SITE
1928	Frank H. Hoyt	Garden City Golf
1929	Hugh Halsell	Hudson River
1930	Charles Cooke	Arcola
1931	T. Henry Clarkson	Garden City Golf
1932	Enos S. Booth	Sleepy Hollow
1933	Alex P. Gray	Montclair
1934	Morton P. Downs	Rockaway Hunt.
1935	Rex Beach	St. Andrew's
1936	Dwight Rockwell	Englewood
1937	Bechtel Alcock	Garden City Golf
1938	Wilfred Garretson	Siwanoy
1939	August F. Kammer	Essex County
1940	Charles H. Jennings	Garden City Golf
1941	August F. Kammer	Siwanoy

1942	Charles P. Burgess	Baltusrol
1943	Samuel J. Graham	Garden City Golf
1944	Samuel J. Graham	Winged Foot
1945	Charles McMillen	Baltusrol
1946	Samuel J. Graham	Seawane Harbor
1947	Ellis Knowles	Winged Foot
1948	Ellis Knowles	Upper Montclair
1949	Thomas Robbins	Seawane Harbor
1950	Thomas Robbins	Siwanoy
1951	Jack Brittain Sr.	Upper Montclair
1952	Vincent Fitzgerald	Wheatley Hills
1953	Thomas Robbins	Winged Foot
1954	Carl W. Timpson	Ridgewood
1955	Thomas Robbins	Rockaway Hunt.
1956	Martin M. Issler	Hudson River
1957	Jack Dowling	Mountain Ridge
1958	Edward M. Smith	Upper Montclair
1959	Paul A. Dunkel	Rockaway Hunt.
1960	Mike Cestone	Sunningdale
1961	Martin M. Issler	Arcola
1962	Jack Mullen	Century
1963	John N. Ledbetter Jr.	Rockville Links
1964	Stephen Berrien	Knickerbocker
1965	Olin Cerrochi	Innis Arden
1966	Anthony J. Vileno	Garden City CC
1967	J. Wolcott Brown	Raritan Valley
1968	J. Wolcott Brown	Leewood
1969	J. Wolcott Brown	Glen Oaks
1970	William Y. Dear Jr.	Knickerbocker
1971	Seymour Holub	Apawamis
1972	Ed Majka	Rockville Links
1973	Arthur Lefelar	Mountain Ridge

1974	James F. Tingley	Mount Kisco
1975	John J. Humm	North Hempstead
1976	Gerold Lauck	Canoe Brook
1977	John Rogers	Old Oaks
1978	John Humm	Rockville Links
1979	Tony Macellaro	Sunningdale
1980	Norb Harrer	Edgewood
1981	Mike Mattwell	North Hempstead
1982	Joseph A. Donahue	Ridgeway
1983	Mike Mattwell	Dellwood
1984	Mal Galletta Sr.	Woodcrest
1985	Michael LoBosco	Glen Ridge
1986	Art Thomas	Wee Burn
1987	Mike Mattwell	Huntington
1988	John Farrell Jr.	Suburban
1989	Mike Mattwell	Elmwood
1990	Joe Davis	North Shore
1991	Don Edwards	Hackensack
1992	Jerry Courville Sr.	Westchester Hills
1993	Mario Posillico	Cherry Valley
1994	John French	Spring Brook
1995	William Sala	Sunningdale
1996	Richard Siderowf	Arcola

MGA SENIOR NET TOURNAMENT

YEAR	CHAMPION	SITE
1993	Alvin Ziegler	Cedar Brook
1994	Nelson Wolther	Brooklake
1995	Matt Juenger	Hampshire
1996	John Stewart	Engineers

MGA FATHER & SON CHAMPIONSHIP

YEAR	CHAMPION	SITE
1951	John & Stewart Ledbetter	St. Andrew's
1952	John & John J. Humm	Seawane Harbor
1953	Joseph & James E. Fisher	Forest Hill
1954	John & Stewart Ledbetter	Westchester Hills
1955	Louis & Harry Kaufman	Brookville
1956	Sid & Alan Gillison	Englewood
1957	Mark & Mark Jr. Stuart	Westchester Hills
1958	Mark & Mark Jr. Stuart	Seawane Harbor
1959	Mark & Mark Jr. Stuart	Essex Fells
1960	Cleeko & Dick Marchetti	Fenway
1961	Bob & Bob Jr. Tobin	Essex County
1962	Pat & Pat Jr. Mucci	Pelham
1963	Dr. John & John Jr. Shepard	Sands Point
1964	Joseph & Terry McBride	Montclair
1965	Joseph & Terry McBride	Tuxedo
1966	Joseph & Terry McBride	Richmond Cty
1967	Olin & Richard Boone	Colonia
1968	Pat & Pat Jr. Mucci	Hampshire
1969	William & Paul Samanchik	Montammy
1970	Joseph & Michael McBride	Piping Rock
1971	Pat & Pat Jr. Mucci	Woodway
1972	William & Paul Samanchik	Alpine
1973	Pat & Kerry Mucci	Scarsdale
1974	John & John Jr. Rogers	Tamarack
1975	Manny & Michael Doppelt	Knollwood
1976	Nicholas & Nick Jr. LeRose	Elmwood
1977	Alan & Jim Greene	Alpine
1978	Robert & David Gilmartin	Sunningdale
1979	Nicholas & Claude Colabella	Garden City CC

Jeff Thomas

Bob Housen

Bruce Zabriski

The final field for the 1988 MGA/MetLife Women's Net Team Championship.

1980	Fenn & Jeff Putman	Fox Run
1981	Daniel & Cary Geensburg	North Jersey
1982	Claes & Peter Johncke	Apawamis
1983	Ken & Jerry Springer	Fresh Meadow
1984	Gifford & Edward Weber	Canoe Brook
1985	Gifford & Edward Weber	Woodway
1986	Bob & Brian Soldon	Rockville Links
1987	John & Mark Loomis	Alpine
1988	Jules & Carl Alexander	Westchester Hills
1989	Alan & Jim Greene	Fresh Meadow
1990	Jules & Carl Alexander	Preakness Hills
1991	Peter & Peter Jr. Keller	Sunningdale
1992	Gil & Gil Jr. D'Andrea	Richmond Cnty.
1993	Peter & Gregory Bisconti	Crestmont
1994	Peter & Gregory Bisconti	Fairfield
1995	William & Joseph Madden	Apawamis
1996	Bob & Chris Housen	Garden City Golf

MGA FATHER & SON NET TOURNAMENT

YEAR	CHAMPIONS	SITE
1990	John & Chris Campbell	Knickerbocker
1991	Robert & Gary Templeton	Tamarack
1992	Thomas R.&Thomas Keenan	Indian Hills
1993	Robert E. & Robert H. Wood	White Beeches
1994	Joseph & Vincent D'Auria	Burning Tree
1995	Charles & Charles Mattina	Bonnie Briar
1996	James & Peter Mataglio	Tam O'Shanter

MGA MIXED PINEHURST CHAMPIONSHIP

YEAR	CHAMPIONS	SITE
1964	Kenneth T. Gordon, Mrs. Phillip Cudone	Rockville Links
1965	Austin Straub Gwen Pallante	Upper Montclair
1966	Tony Macellaro Martha Pesci	Century

1967	Eli Hochman Jean Cici	Brookville
1968	Al Orlian Judy Baris	Hackensack
1969	Peter Bisconti Jr., Charlotte DeCozen	Apawamis
1970	Mike Mattwell Carol Beinbrink	Elmwood
1971	Manny Doppelt Harriet Doppelt	North Shore
1972	Peter Bisconti Jr. Charlotte DeCozen	Upper Montclair
1973	Mike Mattwell Edith Larkin	Sleepy Hollow
1974	Paul Samanchik Agnes Guard	Plandome
1975	Manny Doppelt Harriet Doppelt	Alpine
1976	Greg Zorila Jane Schultz	Canyon

1977	Lawrence Israel Barbara Israel	North Shore
1978	Ken Springer Marianne Springer	Knickerbocker
1979	Dennis Slezak Bernice Stambaugh	Tamarack
1980	Brian Darby Bernice Cotter	Indian Hills
1981	Dennis Slezak Bernice Slezak	Tuxedo
1982	Jon Doppelt Allison Doppelt	Mountain Ridge
1983	Robert Bossone Valerie Faulkner	No. Hempstead
1984	Ken Springer Marianne Springer	Mountain Ridge
1985	Ken Springer Marianne Springer	Rock Spring
1986	Richard Remsen Penne Nieporte	Woodmere
1987	John Richart Helen Aitken	Sunningdale
1988	Michael LoBosco Jean Bartholomew	Tuxedo
1989	Peter E. Bisconti Margaret Platt	North Jersey
1990	Mal Galletta II Claire Galletta	Indian Hills
1991	Len Braccio Cathy Ronan	Elmwood
1992	Michael Brown Lisa Griffin	Metuchen
1993	John Lewis Jr. Gail Flanagan	North Shore
1994	Michael Brown Lisa Griffin	Ridgeway
1995	Adam Kugler Helen Bernstein	Alpine
1996	Adam Kugler Helen Bernstein	Mill River (L.I.)

The 1996 FRED's CUP Teams.

MGA INTERCOLLEGIATE CHAMPIONSHIP

YEAR	WINNER	INDIVIDUAL WINNER	SITE
1950	Columbia	Al Bange, Seton Hall	Nassau
1951	Princeton	William E. Ragland, Princeton	White Beeches
1952	Princeton	Frank Rhodes, Princeton	St. Andrew's
1953	Princeton	Ray Gebhardt, Fairleigh Dickinson	Glen Oaks
1954	Princeton	Paul Kelly, Rutgers	Rock Spring
1955	Princeton	Joseph A. Lucas, Rutgers	Winged Foot
1956	Fordham	Lawrence Whyte, Fordham	Seawane
1957	Rutgers	Charles Fatum, Rutgers	Hackensack
1958	Princeton	James Iverson, Columbia	Bonnie Briar
1959	Princeton	James Iverson, Columbia	Seawane
1960	Manhattan	Richard Granger, Wagner	Essex County
1961	Princeton	Lyn Adelman, Princeton	Pelham
1962	St. John's	Leonard Santoro, St. John's	Inwood
1963	Rutgers	John Rockefeller, Rutgers	Montclair
1964	Bloomfield	Richard Boschen Jr., Bloomfield	Rockland
1965	Princeton	Charles Iobst, Princeton	Huntington
1966	F. Dickinson	Russel Spahr, Fairleigh Dickinson	North Jersey
1967	Fairfield	David Muraskin, Rutgers	Mt. Kisco
1968	Princeton	Dom Ferrone, Brooklyn	Knoll
1969	Princeton	David Muraskin, Rutgers	Sands Point
1970	Rider	Dennis Swirsky, Adelphi	Willow Ridge
1971	Rutgers	Bob Marzoli, Rutgers	Englewood
1972	Princeton	Robert Fritz, Wagner	Richmond
1973	Rutgers	Greg Barkavskas, Princeton	Pelham
1974	Princeton	Greg Farrow, Glassboro	Bamm Hollow
1975	St. John's	Bill Haughton, NY Tech	Rockland
1976	St. John's	Kevin Nery, FDU/Teaneck	Woodrest
1977	Manhattan	Kerry Mattern, Glassboro	Rutgers
1978	St. John's	Andrew Anello, Queens	Rockland
1979	St. John's	Frank Darby, St. John's	Cold Spring
1980	Ramapo	Mike Diffley, St. John's	Rolling Hills
1981	St. John's	Vin Cirino, St. John's	Bamm Hollow
1982	Ramapo	Jeff Thomas, Ramapo	Richmond
1983	Ramapo	Mike Knight, Montclair	Rockland
1984	Ramapo	Tom Ansbro, Ramapo	Bethpage Black
1985	St. John's	Frank Esposito, Rutgers	Orange County
1986	Army	Rob Tozzoli, Columbia	Richmond
1987	Army	Carl Campanelli, Ramapo	Crestmont
1988	St. John's	Tim Ertmer, Army	Hempstead
1989	St. John's	Pat Mullin, Army	Tamarack
1990	Army	Joe Gullion, Army	Spring Brook
1991	St. John's	Mike Laudien, Trenton State	Cherry Valley
1992	Seton Hall	Jim Engler, Seton Hall	Rolling Hills
1993	St. John's	Mike Fleischer, Columbia	Montammy
1994	Princeton	Gregory Bisconti, St. John's	The Creek
1995	Princeton	Jerry Jeong, Princeton	North Jersey
1996	Seton Hall	Clark Topping, Seton Hall	Wykagyl

MGA/METLIFE NET TEAM CHAMPIONSHIP*

YEAR	CLUB	CHAMPIONS	SITE
1977	Bonnie Briar	Jim Livingston, Al Rutel	Westchester
1978	Stony Ford	Bob Seman, Steve Smith	Westchester
1979	Winged Foot	Win Stevens, Phil Hartnett	Westchester
1980	Haworth	Harvey Jaffe, Marc Meltzer	Westchester
1981	Knickerbocker	Dennis Visich, F. DeMartiniJr.	Century
1982	Clearview	George Latham, Wally Fuchs	Quaker Ridge
1983	Huntington Cres.	Arthur Roche, Joe Cameron	Plainfield
1984	Baltusrol	Steve Boyd, Bob Boyd	Metropolis
1985	Burning Tree	Jacques Isaacs, Carl Palermo	Sleepy Hollow
1986	Leewood	V. Mancuso, G. Stanzione	Glen Oaks
1987	Middle Bay	Philip Glantz, Leonard Wilner	Canoe Brook
1988	Rockland Valley	F. Ruggiero, S. Rosenzweig	Sunningdale
1989	Mahopac	Tom & Al Lotrecchiano	North Hills
1990	Loch Ledge	P. Douglas, R. Mauriello	Alpine
1991	Innisfail	Jim Scully, Matthew Slattery	Sleepy Hollow
1992	Wheatley Hills	B. Wiggington, F. Osanitch	Hempstead
1993	Silver Lake	Nils Lambert, Vic Stora	Forest Hill
1994	Mohansic	Peter Rubeo, John Stelluti	Siwanoy
1995	Mohansic	Peter Rubeo, John Stelluti	Engineers
1996	Mohansic	Peter Rubeo, John Stelluti	Suburban

MGA/METLIFE WOMEN'S NET TEAM CHAMPIONSHIP*

YEAR	CLUB	CHAMPIONS	SITE
1985	Innis Arden	Janet Peters, Nancy Allen	Sunningdale
1986	West. Hills	Mary Acerbo, Mary Marino	Shackamaxon
1987	Swan Lake	Chris Lovizio, Sally Robbins	N. Hempstead
1988	Twin Brooks	Lorrie Garfinkel, Isabell Heller	Westchester
1989	Swan Lake	C. Lovizio, C. Pellegrini	Edgewood
1990	Innis Arden	Helen Delago, Sally Malconian	Towers
1991	Indian Hills	P. Oglesby, E. Elkins	Ardsley
1992	Swan Lake	Chris Lovizio, Sally Robbins	Shackamaxon
1993	High Mountain	Anna Appel, Joyce Trabattoni	Huntington Cres.
1994	High Mountain	Anna Appel, Joyce Trabattoni	New Canaan
1995	Bamm Hollow	Debbie Hoermann, Peggy Ford	Morris County
1996	Bergen Point	Grace Johnson, Merry Masi	Seawane

CHALLENGE MATCH
(MGA VS. GOLFING UNION OF IRELAND)

YEAR	WINNER	SITE
1990	MGA	Metedeconk National
1992	GUI	Waterville, Ireland
1996	MGA	Hudson National

FRED's CUP
(MGA/WMGA VS. LIGUE DE PARIS)

YEAR	WINNER	SITE
1990	Ligue de Paris	Chantilly, France
1991	MGA	Baltusrol
1992	Ligue de Paris	St. Germain, France
1993	Ligue de Paris	Sleepy Hollow
1994	Ligue de Paris	St. Cloud, France
1995	Tie	The Creek Club
1996	Ligue de Paris	La Boulie, France

*Sponsored by MetLife

The FRED's CUP Trophy.

ACKNOWLEDGEMENTS

No book of this scope can be written in isolation. The author wishes to acknowledge the following for their valuable assistance: Fellow golf writer and good friend Howie Munck, for reading the manuscript and validating much of the statistical data; Sandra Tomassetti, the MGA's Assistant to the Executive Director, who oversaw the preparation and trafficking of the manuscript; MGA Executive Director Jay Mottola, Assistant Executive Director Gene Westmoreland, Senior Director of Communications Jeanne McCooey, Assistant Communications Manager Matt Huck, and Centennial Committee members C.A. "Tony" Wimpfheimer and Cornelius E. "Connie" DeLoca, all of whom read the manuscript and offered many helpful improvements. Just about every member of the MGA's dedicated staff has contributed in some form to this book, and I thank them all.

I would also like to acknowledge the talented staff at Golf Magazine Properties, especially Editors Jim Frank and Alena Bubniak and Production Coordinators Kit Taylor and Kelli Daley.

This book is more than just words, and for its stylish design we are deeply grateful to the talent and genius of our Art Director, Larry Hasak. The beautiful photographs that do so much to enhance our stories are the work of Dan McKeon, Jules Alexander, Jim Krajicek, Larry Lambrecht, John Varian, Fred Vuich, and several others.

I would like to convey special thanks to the wonderful staff at Golf House, especially Patti Moran, Nancy Stulack, and Andy Mutch, for their untiring aid in researching the extensive and invaluable library at the USGA museum. No request was ever too difficult, or failed to be met with an enthusiastic response.

Last, and certainly not least, we would like to express our gratitude to the many members at the various clubs profiled in this book who graciously took the time to provide a "guided tour" of their club's facilities and discuss their club's history.

— *Dr. Bill Quirin*

PHOTO CREDITS

Alexander, Jules: 17 (top right), 18 (top right), 46, 66 (bottom), 92, 211 (top), 211 (bottom), 212-213, 239 (bottom), 239 (inset), 274 (top), 309
American Golfer: endpapers, 9, 22 (bottom left), 26 (right), 27 (left), 38, 40, 44 (left), 66, 102, 177 (top), 219 (top), 232 (top), 237 (bottom), 250 (top), 258, 271 (top left), 271 (top right), 294 (right), 295 (left)
Apawamis Club, The: 220 (bottom)
Bahto, George: 298 (bottom)
Baltusrol Golf Club: 120 (bottom)
Beard, Ann: 158 (bottom)
Bedford Golf & Tennis Club: 246 (top)
Briar Hall Country Club: 250
Brooklawn Country Club: 225 (middle)
Crystal Springs Golf Club: 153 (top), 153 (bottom)
Darien, Country Club of: 254
Dunnam, Thomas: 114
Ferris, Louis: 30 (left), 30 (right)
Golden Bear International: 118 (left)
GOLF Magazine Properties: 6, 24, 27 (right), 29 (left), 61 (bottom), 99 (top), 206 (bottom), 217 (bottom), 218 (bottom), 226, 232 (middle), (top), 245 (bottom), 295 (left)
Golf Illustrated: 17 (left), 41 (bottom), 59 (top), 74 (top), 75 (top), 122 (top), 126, 209, 221 (bottom), 228 (bottom), 232 (bottom), 279 (top), 295 (right), 296-297, 298 (top), 300, 302, 303, 304, 305, 308 (left)
Golf: 8, 25 (bottom left), 166 (top), 296
Greenwich Country Club: 279 (bottom)
Hainline, Wallace: 263
Hampshire Country Club: 260
Innis Arden Golf Club: 262
Kirk, Russell: 31 (left), 250 (middle), 250 (bottom)
Klein, Bob: 67
Knollwood Country Club: 222, 230
Krajicek, Jim: 18 (bottom), 25 (top left), 31 (right), 58, 59, 59 (inset), 60, 61 (top), 68 (top), 72, 73, 74 (bottom), 77 (top), 77 (bottom), 80, 81, 83, 85 (top), 86, 87, 88, 93 (top), 93 (bottom), 97, 101, 104,105, 189, 261, 314 (bottom)
Labye, Jacques: 199
Lambrecht, Larry: 4, 5, 16 (top), 18 (top left), 19 (top left), 23 (bottom), 25 (middle), 42-43, 43 (right), 44-45, 311 (left), 313 (right)
Lawrence, George: 94, 103
Marx, Lawrence: 215 (inset)
Masloski, Richard: 238
Metropolitan Golf Association: 14 (top), 14 (bottom), 15 (left), 15 (right), 19 (middle right), 21 (top), 22 (bottom right), 20-21, 22 (top right), 25 (top middle), 29 (right), 71 (inset), 136 (left), 137 (top left), 138 (top right), 165 (bottom), 186 (top), 207 (bottom), 231 (bottom), 277 (bottom), 310, 312 (right), 313 (middle), 314 (top)
Metropolitan Golfer: 63, 128, 192 (top)
McKeon, Dan: 34-35, 36, 37, 41 (top), 48 (top), 49, 52 (left), 55 (top right), 56, 57 (top), 64, 64-65, 65 (bottom), 70-71, 76 (top), 76 (bot-

tom), 84, 89 (bottom), 99 (bottom), 116-117, 118 (bottom), 120 (top), 121 (top), 121 (bottom), 122 (bottom), 122-123, 124 (top), 125 (top), 125 (bottom), 126-127, 128, 129 (bottom), 131 (top), 131 (bottom), 132, 133, 149, 152, 153, 154, 155, 156, 158 (top), 159, 161, 162, 164, 165 (bottom), 166 (bottom), 167, 168, 169, 170, 171, 173, 174, 175 (bottom), 179 (top), 179 (bottom), 180, 181, 182, 183, 183 (inset), 187, 188 (top), 190, 191, 192 (bottom), 202-203, 204-205, 206 (top), 207 (bottom), 217 (top), 218 (top), 219 (bottom), 220-221, 224, 225 (top), 225 (top), 228 (top), 229 (top), 234, 235, 240-241, 241 (bottom), 243, 247, 248 (bottom), 248 (top), 249, 251, 253, 257, 259, 259 (inset), 265, 269, 270 (top), 270 (bottom), 271 (bottom), 272 (top), 272 (bottom), 275, 277, 278 (top), 278 (bottom), 279 (bottom), 281, 283
McLoughlin, James: 16 (bottom)
Middle Bay Country Club: 85 (bottom)
Munck, Howard: 150, 176, 177 (bottom), 196, 239 (top), 246 (bottom), 255, 264, 282
New Jersey Country Club: 175 (top)
New York Historical Society: 9
Pateman, Michael: 115
Pelham Country Club: 266
Petrillo, Larry: 75 (bottom), 136 (right), 226, 233 (bottom), 240
Petrillo, Larry/USGA: 225 (bottom)
PGA Magazine: 299
Purchase, Country Club of: 267
Sarazen World Open Championship: 7
Schiller, Evan: 67, 82, 210, 214 (top), 214 (bottom), 215 (bottom), 222-223, 235 (inset), 245, 276
Shackamaxon Golf & Country Club: 185
Shinnecock Hills Golf Club: 52 (middle)
Silverman, Les: 147, 157
Skyshots: 48 (bottom), 96
Southward Ho Country Club: 100 (bottom)
Spring Lake Golf Club: 188 (bottom)
St. Andrew's Golf Club: 210 (bottom)
USGA: 25 (top right), 26 (left), 28 (left), 28 (right), 45 (right), 50, 52-53, 57 (bottom), 79 (top), 89 (top), 100 (top), 122 (bottom), 128 (bottom), 151 (top), 216 (bottom), 216 (inset), 237 (top), 294 (top), 295 (top), 295 (bottom), 308 (right)
Varian, John: 19 (bottom), 39, 78, 78 (inset), 95, 98, 130, 134-135, 137 (bottom), 151, 160, 172 (left), 172 (right), 178, 184, 186 (bottom), 186 (inset), 226-227, 231 (top), 231 (inset), 244, 252, 273, 288 (top), 288 (bottom), 298 (inset), 311 (right), 312 (left), 315 (right)
Vuich, Fred: cover, 2-3, 32-33, 46-47, 50-51, 53 (top), 54-55, 62, 69 (bottom), 79 (bottom), 119, 233 (top), 236, 274 (bottom), 291
Walker, Robert: 313 (left)
Walker, Robert/USGA: 129 (top)
Wee Burn Country Club: 242
Whippoorwill Club, The: 280
Wolff, Brian: 13